PROFESSIONAL DIPLOMACY
IN THE UNITED STATES
1779-1939

PROFESSIONAL DIPLOMACY

IN THE UNITED STATES
1779-1939

A STUDY IN ADMINISTRATIVE HISTORY

WARREN FREDERICK ILCHMAN

THE UNIVERSITY OF CHICAGO PRESS

Library of Congress Catalog Number: 61-11991

The University of Chicago Press, Chicago, 37
The University of Toronto Press, Toronto 5, Canada

© 1961 by The University of Chicago. Published 1961
Composed and printed in the U.S.A.

PREFACE

THE following chapters are part of a larger study tracing the growth of professional diplomacy in the United States. Many of the larger study's facets, both comparative and analytic, have been subordinated in order that I might first document the evolution of a career service for foreign affairs. Nevertheless, several issues required to deal with the larger topic have been raised in this work, and the directions for their subsequent treatment have been indicated. Before the major study is completed, the American experience will be compared with Great Britain's in order that it may be seen alongside the developments occurring in a nation dependent for a longer period upon professional diplomacy. A more intensive analysis will be made of the continuous changes in the upper service (the ambassadorial and ministerial level) and their influence on decision-making at specific missions. Finally, the effect of professional diplomacy on American foreign policy will be considered.

A first book is a golden opportunity for a scholar to thank the many people who have helped him on his way. And my debt to persons in official and unofficial capacities is enormous. It is particularly great to several active and retired members of the Foreign Service and to employees of the Department of State. The Honorable James B. Stewart, former ambassador to Nicaragua, offered endless encouragement and suggestions and facilitated my meeting other members of the service. The Honorable Joseph Coy Green, former Chief Examiner, and the Honorable Robert P. Skinner, former ambassador to Saudi Arabia, assisted me by answering questions concerning their roles in the development of the career service. The Honorable Herbert S. Bursley, former chief of Career Development, the Honorable Robert Newbegin, former Deputy Undersecretary for Administration, the Honorable Cromwell Riches and the Honorable Herbert B. Fales, both Chief Examiners, and the Honorable Dr. Albert B. Franklin, III, formerly of the Foreign Service Institute, aided me in the study's early stages. Great appreciation is due Dr. E. Taylor Parks of the Advisory and Review Branch for his continuous assistance at every stage. I am also grateful to the members of Diplomatic and Consular Officers Retired (DACOR), particularly the Honorable George Gregg Fuller and the Honorable Richard F. Boyce, for their willingness to be interviewed on specific topics. And I wish to thank the Honorable Joseph C. Grew for his permission to quote from *Turbulent Era* (Boston: Houghton Mifflin Co., 1952).

Hosts of other people assisted me in the researching and writing of this book. Dr. Henry M. Wriston first interested me in the machinery of diplomacy and aided me in the work's initial stages. The staffs of the Foreign Affairs Section of the National Archives, the Record Center of the Department of State, the Library of Congress, the Harvard University Library, the John Hay Library of Brown University, the Williams College Library, the State Paper Room of the British Museum, the Library of the University of Cambridge, and the Foreign Office Library gave generously of their time. I am also grateful to Professors Elmer E. Cornwell and Lea E. Williams, Dr. Erwin L. Levine, and Mr. Frederic J. Fleron, all of Brown University, Professor Richard N. Rosecrance of the University of California at Los Angeles, the Marshall Aid Commemoration Commission, Dr. O. G. M. MacDonagh, Dr. W. R. Brock, and Mr. John E. Vaizey of the University of Cambridge, Professor Max Beloff of Oxford University, President James P. Baxter, III, Professor James MacGregor Burns, and Mr. John D. Leech of Williams College, and Miss Jeannette E. Hopkins for their aid and valuable criticism. Most particularly, I am grateful to Mr. F. H. Hinsley of St. John's College who supervised me at the University of Cambridge. My acknowledgments would be incomplete without thanking Mr. Herbert B. Kennison, Dr. Barnaby C. Keeney, and Dr. Robert L. Stearns for their many-faceted encouragement. And it would be impossible to enumerate the many ways in which my wife, Alice Stone Ilchman, has assisted me. This study is dedicated to my parents and to Him who has made all things possible.

WILLIAMS COLLEGE
March, 1961

CONTENTS

CHAPTER ONE

THE EARLY DIPLOMATIC SERVICE

1779–1888

THE distinguished international jurist, Henry Wheaton, wrote in 1836, "There is no circumstance which marks more distinctly the progress of modern civilization than the institution of permanent diplomatic missions between different states." [1] Particularly after the treaties of Westphalia and Ryswick, diplomatic representation in Europe was ceasing to be *ad hoc* and was becoming continuous. By 1800, it was highly extraordinary to send a temporary mission.[2] Along with this development came the movement to professionalize the ranks of diplomacy. In 1816, Great Britain was considering nominal payments as incentives for its attachés.[3] In 1856, Lord Clarendon instituted qualifying examinations for candidates.[4] France also had taken steps to perfect its diplomatic administration.[5] Only one Western nation in the nineteenth century steadily refused to consider its

[1] *Elements of International Law* (London, 1836), p. 257.

[2] See Harold Nicolson, *Diplomacy* (London, 1934), pp. 9–55; *idem, Evolution of Diplomatic Method* (London: Constable, 1954), pp. 24–71; Sir Ernest Satow, *Guide to Diplomatic Practice* (4th ed.; London: 1957), p. 116; Graham H. Stuart, *American Diplomatic and Consular Practice* (New York, 1936), pp. 3–22.

[3] See S. T. Bindoff, "The Unreformed Diplomatic Service — 1812–60," *Transactions of the Royal Historical Society*, 4th Series, XVIII (1935), 147–48.

[4] See Algernon Cecil, in *Cambridge History of British Foreign Policy*, eds. Sir A. W. Ward and G. P. Gooch (Cambridge, 1923), III, 592–600; Sir John Tilley and Stephen Gaslee, *The Foreign Office* (London, 1933), pp. 72–89; "Changes in the Organization of the Foreign Office and Diplomatic Service," *British Yearbook of International Law*, I (1920–22), 97–108.

[5] See Frederick L. Schuman, *War and Diplomacy in the French Republic* (New York, 1931), p. 41.

missions as permanent and their members as constituting a career service. It was the United States.

In 1939, the United States had permanent diplomatic missions throughout the world and a trained service of over eight hundred members to staff them.[6] These members, after having passed a competitive examination or its equivalent, entered the service at its lowest rank. They were promoted on the basis of merit and remained in the service until they reached a compulsory retiring age. Of all ministerial and ambassadorial positions, 54 percent were held by service professionals. By any standard, diplomacy in America had achieved a career status.

This remarkable development, which occurred largely after 1900, was one of the many repercussions attending the change in America's international position. As a result, the growth of the career service for foreign affairs can best be viewed from the vantage point of 1939.[7] Yet it is impossible to evaluate its growth without first considering the forces that influenced the service in the previous century and against which its later course was largely a reaction.

In seeking the origins of professional diplomacy in America, however, the obvious sources are misleading. They cannot be found in the course of legislation, in formal changes in the upper or ministerial level, or in developments of the consular service.

An analysis of nineteenth-century legislation dealing with the diplomatic service refutes the attempt to see the service as the conscious creation of laws. The first piece of legislation merely recognized the practice existing under the Articles of Confederation and in international usage. Subsequent laws, at best, only remedied faults or codified prevailing practice. When Senator Mason informed Congress in 1854 that a pending bill was the first attempt to obtain "systematized legislation upon the subject . . . of our diplomatic intercourse," [8] he exaggerated only in his description of the bill. Even the important developments in the first decade of the twentieth century were made exclusively through Executive Orders, not legislation. And it was not until after the service had been professionalized that legislation, both comprehensive in scope and beneficial in nature, was passed.

[6] *Biographical Register of the Department of State* (Washington, D.C., corrected to October 1, 1939), pp. 26–67 (hereafter cited as *Biog. Reg.*).

[7] After 1939, almost entirely novel problems faced the service: full-scale collaboration with the Allies during the Second World War, the recruitment and later absorption of an auxiliary service of specialists, the postwar demands of collective and internal security, and the amalagmation of the service with the Department of State.

[8] *Congressional Globe*, Part 1, 33 Cong., 2 sess. (February 24, 1855), p. 761 (hereafter cited as *Cong. Globe*).

An examination of the structure of the upper or ministerial level also discloses little. Men usually received their positions late in life and seldom held them for more than a few years.[9] It is true that the period saw a few who held several successive posts, spent much of their lives in diplomacy, and could, by many definitions, be considered "career men." But they were exceptional.[10] The more typical ministers and chargés were politicians in timely exile, statesmen-to-be, wealthy campaign contributors, superannuated generals, and journalists. They either planned to return to their occupations or considered their appointment as a climax to their other careers. The non-professional status of a portion of the upper service, of course, remains (1960) a fact.[11]

Nor is it possible to consider the growth of professional diplomacy as a postscript to developments in the consular service. It is true that many changes in both services occurred simultaneously, that the two services were appropriated for in the same bill, and that they were often confused in Congress as being a single branch of the Department of State. It is also true that the propelling logic behind their development had the same source. However, it is equally true that separate organizations did arise, that the gulfs between them were not only legal but also social and functional, that the logic behind change, al-

[9] An examination of the tenures of *all* upper service appointments made between 1787 and 1906 reveals the following facts. (Tenures were rounded off to the nearest year. For tenures which overlapped the period limits, the total service was included in both periods. Data from *Biog. Reg.* [1937]; percentages were calculated by the author.) A single category served for more than four years at one post: those appointed to minor European posts between 1787 and 1828 served an average of 6.1 years. All of the remaining categories served for less than a Presidential term:

	1787–1828	1829–60	1861–88	1889–1906
Major European	3.8 years	3.0	3.2	3.1
Minor European	6.1 years	3.6	3.4	3.0
South American	2.7 years	3.8	3.0	3.3
Other	None	3.2	3.9	3.6

Further evidence that upper service appointees took their posts with the understanding that they would serve only short periods may be found in a host of autobiographies, biographies, and memoirs: e.g., T. Jefferson Coolidge, *The Autobiography of T. Jefferson Coolidge* (Boston, 1923), p. 141; Royal Cortissoz, *The Life of Whitelaw Reid* (New York, 1921), II, 127–28; Bayard Taylor, *The Life and Letters of Bayard Taylor*, ed. Morse Hanson Taylor and Horace E. Scudder (Boston, 1884), II, 722–23; *New York Tribune*, July 24, 1880, p. 6.

[10] Charles G. DeWitt served as chargé for Central America from 1833 to 1853. William Miller was chargé for Guatemala for twenty-three years (see *Biog. Reg.* [1870], pp. 41, 47). George P. Marsh served twenty-one years as minister to Italy (see George P. Marsh, *The Life and Letters of George P. Marsh*, ed. Caroline Crane Marsh [New York, 1888], *passim*). Only four other upper service appointees served more than ten years.

[11] In October, 1958, 67.5 per cent of all upper service posts were occupied by career officers. Percentage calculated by the author from data found in *Foreign Service List* (Washington: Department of State, 1958), *passim*.

though the same, lagged many years behind in the case of the diplomatic service, and that changes occurred more often separately. One would miss the very real and independent developments in the diplomatic service if he insisted upon viewing the growth of professional diplomacy as an afterthought to the growth of the consular service.

The origins of professional diplomacy can only be found in the developments on the secretarial level, for it was from the secretaries of legation that the career emerged. It is impossible, however, for a person viewing the service from the mid-twentieth century to conceive of the state in which the service found itself throughout the nineteenth century. No feature of the present service existed then: entrance by examination, personnel mobility, emphasis upon qualifications for diplomacy, adequate provisions for salaries and retirement, security of tenure, and promotion by merit.

Three particular aspects of the career's development from the nineteenth century until 1939 will be traced: its professionalization, democratization, and specialization. Professionalization refers to the movement to exempt recruitment, tenure, and promotion from political considerations. It also refers to the development of a career-consciousness within the service. Democratization refers to the movement to open the service's ranks to all who physically and intellectually qualified, regardless of their financial position.[12] Specialization refers to the movement to differentiate and develop the skills necessary for diplomacy. All three were interrelated and coexistent. Their separation in this study is solely for clarity of analysis.

How one entered the service varied in the eighteenth century but had crystallized by the beginning of the nineteenth. Although subsequent practice differed, the Department of Foreign Affairs, under both Robert Livingston and John Jay, had no executive powers of nomination.[13] The secretaries were elected by the members of the pre-Constitution Congresses. The first of the five elected received his commission on October 9, 1779.[14] All commissions were for specific posts, and a change of post, presumably, required a second election. It

[12] The enormous semantic problems involved in using the word "democratization" are recognized by the author. Passing the examination usually required a university education. As this was not universally obtainable, it could be argued that the service was undemocratic. Likewise, even traveling to the Civil Service districts to take the examination worked a financial disability. In this study, the word "democratic" refers to the absence of "unreasonable" qualifications for admission. These would include disabilities on the grounds of sex or color or from the necessity of possessing a private income.

[13] 1 *United States Statutes at Large* 28–29n (hereafter cited as Stat.).

[14] W. C. Ford, *et al.* (eds.), *Journals of the Continental Congress* (Washington, 1904–37), II, 273. See also James Lovell to Richard Henry Lee, September 27, 1779, in E. C. Burnett (ed.), *Letters of Members of the Continental Congress* (Washington, 1921–38), III, 442–43.

was not uncommon for a minister to hire and compensate his own private secretary.[15]

Upon ratification of the Constitution, the diplomatic machinery was continued in force. In 1792, Jefferson wrote to Washington, "Where the new Constitution did not demolish an office, either expressly or virtually, nor the President remove the officer, both the office and the officers remained."[16] Once fresh appointments were required at the secretarial level, however, a practice arose that was recognized neither by established diplomatic usage nor by the Constitution. According to the Constitution, the President has to submit his nominations for all offices created by the Constitution and in subsequent laws, unless otherwise exempted by legislation, to the Senate for confirmation.[17] The Act of July 1, 1790, officially recognized the office of secretary of legation and did not exempt it from senatorial confirmation.[18] But no name was ever placed before the Senate. Instead, the President authorized the appointment of private secretaries. While some of their names appeared on Washington's approved list for possible office-holders,[19] their selection was the prerogative of the minister.[20] A change of post, although it never occurred, would have probably required only the Secretary of State's or the President's approval. Abroad the appointees dropped the domestic distinction and assumed the nomenclature in international usage.[21] They were limited to ministers plenipotentiary and were paid by the Treasury.[22]

Certainly Congress was aware of the situation. In 1800, a second act was passed to ascertain the positions authorized in the expired Act of 1790.[23] Furthermore, the appointees were often from well-known families, and it is scarcely conceivable that their appointments went unnoticed.[24] Both branches apparently considered that the clerical capacity of the secretaries and the discretion of the Executive in foreign affairs kept the practice from being unconstitutional. The practice

[15] Allen Johnson and Dumas Malone (eds.), *Dictionary of American Biography*, IX, 312 (hereafter cited as *DAB*). Henry B. Livingston was John Jay's secretary.

[16] Jefferson to Washington, February 4, 1792, as quoted in Gaillard Hunt, *The Department of State* (New Haven, 1914), p. 104.

[17] Art. 2, sec. 2.

[18] 1 Stat. 128 (July 1, 1790).

[19] Washington to Hamilton, September 25, 1789, in John C. Fitzpatrick (ed.), *Writings of George Washington* (Washington: Government Printing Office, 1931–44), XXX, 413.

[20] A. C. Morris (ed.), *Diary and Letters of Gouverneur Morris* (London, 1899), I, 91.

[21] Thomas Boylston Adams, *Berlin and the Prussian Court in 1798* (New York, 1916), *passim*. Adams assumed the title "secretary of legation" when he left the United States.

[22] *American State Papers: Documents, Legislative and Executive* (Washington, 1832–61), I, No. 62, 137–38 (hereafter cited as *American State Papers*).

[23] 2 Stat. 78 (May 10, 1800).

[24] Thomas Boylston Adams was the son of the President and brother to John Quincy Adams.

also had precedents in other departments.[25] However, the contraction of Executive power under the Jeffersonians ended the policy. In 1802, the names of the private secretaries were brought before the Senate and confirmed as secretaries of legation.[26] Thereafter the President submitted all names to the Senate. By the Act of 1810, which adjusted secretaries' salaries, payments were prohibited to any secretary who had not been confirmed by the Senate. Even interim appointments had to be confirmed at the following session of Congress, and a temporary duty as chargé had to be approved or the increased compensation would be withheld.[27]

It is true that Congress cannot be charged with undue delay in confirming nominations. Throughout the nineteenth century, they were handled with relative dispatch.[28] In addition, only one was ever refused, and then the issue turned on a larger question during Reconstruction.[29] It is, of course, impossible to determine how many nominations were never made because of threatened opposition.

It was the President, in fact, who was usually responsible for any delays. As with all appointments, he used them, particularly after 1828, to gain support for his faction of the party, for his party in a certain section of the country, or for one of his measures. A secretaryship occasionally remained open for several months until the "right" candidate was found.[30] Nevertheless, the machinery for appointments was cumbersome and time-consuming; it permitted extraneous considerations to enter into staffing the service, and it diffused control over the diplomatic service between the Executive and the Legislature.

The problems of appointment were further complicated by congressional control over the size of the service. It stemmed from the House of Representative's power of the purse. But this power was not fully exploited for a generation, and the lump-sum appropriations allowed the Department to send secretaries wherever and whenever it

[25] *Register of Debates in Congress*, VII, 21 Cong., 2 sess. (February 25, 1831), 247. See also Charles R. King (ed.), *Life of Rufus King* (New York, 1895), IV, 272. It was customary for the retiring minister to appoint his own chargé.

[26] *Journal of the Executive Proceedings of the Senate of the United States*, I (January 6, 1802), 401 (hereafter cited as *Executive Proceedings*).

[27] 2 Stat. 608 (May 1, 1810). See also House Executive Document 10, 28 Cong., 2 sess. (December 13, 1844) (hereafter cited as House Exec. Doc.).

[28] The Senate seldom took more than two weeks to approve the nominations. For nominations, see *Executive Proceedings*.

[29] The Senate refused to certify Henry S. Watts as secretary of legation for Austro-Hungary on October 12, 1868 (see *Executive Proceedings*, LXI [October 12, 1868], 412). Many nominations of Johnson's for other offices were also refused. See also *Biog. Reg.* (1874), p. 61.

[30] Seven months passed between William B. Lawrence's resignation from the secretaryship in London and the nomination of Washington Irving. Two years passed between Thomas Barton's resignation from his secretaryship in Paris and Charles E. Anderson's nomination. Data from biographical cards in author's possession.

chose.[31] But once detailed appropriations began, the service became more institutionalized and less flexible. Every increase in personnel had to be submitted for the approval of the House. Even existing secretaryships were annually reviewed — occasionally with unfortunate results.[32] In the twenty years between 1810 and 1830, nine secretaryships were created and five discontinued. The following twenty years saw six created and only one discontinued.[33]

The number of secretaryships during the period was considerably behind the demand. Consequently, many missions were greatly overworked. Early in 1833, Secretary Edward Livingston's report to Jackson included a statement from the chargé in Chile to the effect that he could not "discharge properly the duties of his office without the allowance of an interpreter or secretary." [34] The previous year Colonel Anthony Butler, chargé in Mexico, implored Jackson "that a secretary be allowed me." [35] By no means, however, were complaints confined to those who were without secretaries at their posts. The European legations which were equipped with secretaries often found their staffs insufficient. Abbott Lawrence, minister to Britain, wrote to Webster in 1852, "I cannot close this Dispatch without renewing my testimony to the inadequacy of the provision made by Congress for this Legation." He added, "The duties are more than can be performed by the force allowed." [36] In an earlier statement he assigned the problem to "the increase in the means of intercourse between Europe and North America [which] has brought a corresponding increase in the calls upon the time of the Minister and of the Secretary." [37]

Aid was given to some legations when they were elevated to ministerships plenipotentiary, and clerical help was authorized for China, London, and Constantinople.[38] But these appointments did not meet

[31] *Biog. Reg.* (1874), *passim.* Secretaries were often sent to countries with which the United States was then negotiating a treaty, such as Prussia in 1798–99. Secretaries were also appointed for limited periods to minor European capitals, such as Sweden and the Netherlands.

[32] There was no appropriation for Spain in 1835, Prussia in 1849, and Brazil in 1873 (see *Biog. Reg.* [1874], *passim*).

[33] Between 1810 and 1830, the following secretaryships were discontinued: the Netherlands, Sweden, Chile, Argentina, and Mexico. Austro-Hungary had a secretaryship between 1838 and 1840 (*Biog. Reg.* [1874], *passim*).

[34] House Exec. Doc. 94, 22 Cong., 2 sess. (February 7, 1833), p. 11.

[35] Butler to Jackson, January 2, 1832, in John S. Bassett (ed.), *The Correspondence of Andrew Jackson* (Washington, 1934), IV, 392–93.

[36] Lawrence to Webster, September 30, 1852, in Hamilton A. Hill, *Memoir of Abbott Lawrence* (Boston, 1883), p. 245.

[37] Lawrence to Webster, December 10, 1851, in Beckles Willson, *American Ambassadors to Great Britain* (London, 1929), p. 263. See also Senate Report 209, 34 Cong., 1 sess. (July 10, 1856), p. 2.

[38] Senate Miscellaneous Document 16, 33 Cong., 2 sess. (February 16, 1855), pp. 10, 13 (hereafter cited as Senate Mis. Doc.).

the demand. The report of the Committee on Foreign Affairs in 1855 maintained that "the business transacted at some of our legations makes absolutely necessary an assistant to the minister,"[39] and the law of the same year permitted the appointment of one secretary to each legation.[40] But President Pierce's refusal to execute the law negated the provision.[41] Over the next thirty years, Congress reluctantly permitted the over-all size of the service to double, the institution of the assistant or second secretary to expand, and miscellaneous employees, such as interpreters, to be hired.[42] Nevertheless, many legations remained shorthanded.

To ease the labor problem, as well as to accommodate young Americans abroad, the extralegal custom of appointing attachés arose at the beginning of the nineteenth century. Following European practice, the Department of State authorized the various ministers and chargés to appoint, at their discretion, unpaid attachés.[43] As they were no charge on the Treasury, their positions were liable neither to the scrutiny of the House nor to the senatorial prerogative over appointments. Their existence was recognized only by the Executive and the countries in which the United States had missions.

The functions of the attaché were essentially those of the secretary of legation. Often they supplemented the latter's work or performed it in the absence of a secretary. They assisted the minister in securing information, in conducting correspondence, and in carrying on the business of the legation.[44] They also served a ceremonial function. When Caleb Cushing was departing for China, Secretary Webster advised: "It will add dignity and importance to the occasion if your suite could be made respectable in number by accepting such officers of attendance without expense to the government." Heeding Webster's advice, Cushing selected five attachés to accompany him on his mission.[45] In return for their presence and their labor, all attachés received admission to court functions, an entrée into the capital's society, an opportunity to study and travel, and usually the hospitality of the minister's own residence and table.[46]

While it is not certain that all legations had them, or that the same

[39] *Cong. Globe*, Part 1, 33 Cong., 2 sess. (January 11, 1855), p. 246 (section of report read before Congress by Representative John Perkins).

[40] 10 Stat. 619 (March 1, 1855).

[41] 7 Attorney General's Opinions 186.

[42] *Biog. Reg.* (1870–88), *passim.*

[43] Eugene Schuyler, *American Diplomacy* (New York, 1886), p. 122; John W. Foster, *Practice of Diplomacy* (Boston, 1906), pp. 208–10; Henry M. Wriston, *Executive Agents in American Foreign Relations* (Baltimore, 1929), p. 25. These early attachés should not be confused with military attachés, which were first appointed in 1892.

[44] Andrew D. White, *The Autobiography of Andrew D. White* (London, 1905), I, 449.

[45] Foster, *Practice*, p. 208.

[46] White, *Autobiography*, I, 449.

legation had them all the time, it can be shown that, at various times, all European capitals, China, and a few South American countries had attachés.[47] It was common for ministers, such as Albert Gallatin and Martin Van Buren, to accord their sons the distinction to ease the latters' way into society.[48] Needless to say, the attachés possessed independent incomes. Andrew White described the aspirants for the posts as "young men of sufficient means, generally from leading universities."[49] Scholars, teachers, "fops," and businessmen held the position; only three of them are known to have served later as secretaries.[50] The others used it merely for its social advantages or to pursue another interest abroad.[51] They normally did not remain more than two years.

For the position itself, there were no formal qualifications. Even the absence of a foreign language was tolerated.[52] With this laxity, the number of attachés increased until, in the words of Minister George M. Dallas, "they were plentiful as blackberries." Dallas added, "The minister, always conscious of the invidious nature of selecting from young countrymen, preferred giving his appointments without discrimination and to everyone who asked."[53]

After complaints of misconduct were registered against the attachés, the Department under William L. Marcy moved to abolish the position. Displaying the same scorn as he did over the question of diplomatic dress, Marcy held that the position was pretentious and unrepublican.[54] The laws of 1855 and 1856 expressly repealed "any usage or law whereby any attaché is or may be allowed to any legation."[55] The prohibition was later reaffirmed in the official regulations.[56] Although one exception to the law was recorded, the abolition

---

[47] Great Britain: Richard Rush, *The Court of London — 1819-25* (London, 1873), p. 98; John C. Fitzpatrick (ed.), *Autobiography of Martin Van Buren* (New York, 1920), II, 445; George M. Dallas, *Letters of George M. Dallas* (London, 1870), II, 219. France: *DAB*, XIX, 391; Henry Adams, *Life of Albert Gallatin* (Philadelphia, 1879), p. 622. The Netherlands: *DAB*, III, 63. Russia: White, *Autobiography*, I, 447-49; *DAB*, VII, 299; Abraham Flexner, *Daniel Coit Gilman*, (New York: Harcourt, Brace, 1946), pp. 6-7. China: Foster, *Practice*, pp. 208-10. South America: *DAB*, II, 376. Even Thomas H. Halliburton's Sam Slick was an attaché in London (see Thomas H. Halliburton, *The Attaché* [London, 1843], 2 vols., *passim*).

[48] Henry Adams, *Gallatin*, p. 622; Fitzpatrick, *Autobiography of Martin Van Buren*, p. 445.

[49] White, *Autobiography*, p. 449.

[50] *DAB*, VII, 299; Sarah A. Wallace and Frances C. Gillespie (eds.), *Journal of Ben Moran* (University of Chicago Press, 1948), I, 35, 3.

[51] Rush, *op. cit.*, p. 98; Flexner, *op. cit.*, pp. 6-7; White, *Autobiography*, I, 449.

[52] White, *Autobiography*, I, 448.

[53] Dallas, *op. cit.*, p. 219.

[54] Foster, *Practice*, p. 210.

[55] 10 Stat. 619 (March 1, 1855); 11 Stat. 52 (August 18, 1856).

[56] *Personal Instructions to the Diplomatic Agents of the United States in Foreign Countries* (Washington, 1874), section 45; *Instructions to the Diplomatic Officers of the United States* (Washington, 1897), section 37.

was little objected to.[57] When the indiscretions were forgotten, many people argued for reviving the practice.[58] Objections, however, were too great.[59]

The only other possible solution to the labor problem was also blocked by Congress. All appointments were made to specific posts, and no interchange could occur without the President's securing a second confirmation. The restriction was particularly felt when a legation fell under unexpected pressure.[60] Even in normal times, legations felt the hardship of the inflexible wedding of a man to his post. It made it impossible to shift secretaries with light loads to hard-pressed legations. While noticeable before the Civil War, the problem became more apparent with the addition of personnel during and immediately after the war. Soon a division grew between busy legations, such as London, Paris, and China, and, as Minister John Bigelow called them, the "ornamental secretaryships."[61] For instance, Benjamin Moran in London could work many hours every day, while John Hay in Vienna occupied his time with "excursions or in watching the folklife in the streets, or at the theater and opera" as "his official duties took up little of his time."[62] Considering himself completely dispensable, Hay wrote to Bigelow, "But equally sure am I that no other two American diplomats can catch each other's eyes without mutual guffaws unless they have a power of facial muscle that would put the Roman augurs to shame."[63] President Chester Arthur attempted in vain to alleviate the situation by requesting Congress to provide a secretarial pool.[64] Later Grover Cleveland renewed the request, but it was again denied by Congress.[65]

The officer who chose the nominees varied with every administration. At various times, the President, his Secretary of State, one of the

[57] Wallace and Gillespie, *op. cit.*, p. 35.

[58] Herbert H. D. Peirce, "Our Diplomatic and Consular Service," *Arena*, XVII (May, 1897), 915; White, *Autobiography*, I, 449; Schuyler, *American Diplomacy*, pp. 122–24.

[59] *Congressional Record*, XXXII, 55 Cong., 3 sess. (February 23, 1899), 2207; XXXIII, 56 Cong., 1 sess. (December 6, 1899), 88 (hereafter cited as *Cong. Rec.*). Both bills, S. 5564 and S. 150, were never reported out of committee. They were introduced by Senator James McMillan and were designed to create a corps of "honorary attachés of legation to serve without compensation."

[60] Wickham Hoffman, *Camp, Court, and Siege* (London, 1877), p. 145.

[61] Bigelow to Secretary of State Seward, August 22, 1865, in John Bigelow, *Retrospections of an Active Life* (London, 1909–13), III, 159.

[62] Gillespie and Wallace, *op. cit.*, II, 915, 1103; William R. Thayer, *Life and Letters of John Hay* (Boston, 1915), I, 288, 302; Wickham Hoffman, *Leisure Hours in Russia* (London, 1883), *passim*.

[63] Hay to Bigelow, April 27, 1868, in Bigelow, *op. cit.*, IV, 179.

[64] James D. Richardson (ed.), *A Compilation of the Messages and Papers of the Presidents* (Washington, 1907), VIII, 67 (Message of December 19, 1881).

[65] *Ibid.*, VIII, 337–38 (Message of December 8, 1885). *Cong. Rec.*, XVII, 49 Cong., 1 sess. (June 5, 1886), 5291.

latter's assistants, or the minister himself was instrumental in the decision. After the Civil War, it became less common for ministers to choose and more usual for the decision to be made in Washington. No other significant generalization can be drawn from the evidence.

If the system of appointment was little geared to the needs of diplomacy, those same needs were similarly ignored when it came to determining the qualifications necessary for the position of secretary. Few legal ones existed. A man had to be a citizen.[66] In later years military and naval officers were barred from the service.[67] There were no age qualifications. Above all, no attempt was made to set standards by which to judge a candidate's competency. Knowledge of the appropriate language, of the history and resources of the United States and the country to which the representative was assigned, and of diplomatic usage were not required. Between 1787 and 1888 it was purely fortuitous that a secretary be so accomplished.

The one qualification in force throughout the period was a "connection," often stemming from a filial relationship, with the party in power. Over 21 per cent of the secretaries between 1787 and 1828 were immediately related to their respective ministers; 17 per cent between 1829 and 1860; and 12.7 per cent between 1861 and 1888. It is impossible to determine the relationships with non-ministerial party members, although the instance of Secretary of State Edward Livingston offering a secretaryship to his son-in-law as a wedding present was probably novel only in the circumstances of the gift.[68] Other secretaries received their posts as compensation for political services or because they had attracted the patronage of an important party member.[69]

The events surrounding Rufus King's second ministership to Britain are revealing. Deciding that he would not accept the appointment unless he could be accompanied by his son John in the capacity of secretary of legation, King dispatched another son to take the request to Secretary of State John Quincy Adams. Unfortunately, the holder of the secretaryship, John Appleton, was under the patronage of Adams. The situation was further complicated by the fact that Apple-

[66] 11 Stat. 52 (August 18, 1856). This had also been a qualification during pre-Constituition days (see Francis Wharton [ed.], *The Revolutionary Diplomatic Correspondence of the United States* [Washington, 1889], VI, 786 [March 16, 1784]; Burnett, *op. cit.,* VII, 471). See also House Mis. Doc. 61, 42 Cong., 3 sess. (December 19, 1872).

[67] *Personal Instructions to the Diplomatic Agents of the United States in Foreign Countries* (Washington, 1874), sec. 37.

[68] Charles H. Hunt, *Life of Edward Livingston* (New York, 1864), p. 384.

[69] Hoffman, *Camp, Court, and Siege,* p. 119; Evelyn Schuyler Schaeffer (ed.), *Eugene Schuyler: Memoirs and Essays* (London, 1907), p. 31; Gillespie and Wallace, *op. cit.,* I, 188; John R. Schultz, *The Unpublished Letters of Bayard Taylor* (San Francisco, 1937), pp. 204–5; Thayer, *Hay,* I, 251.

ton had recently vacated his own secretaryship in Madrid to make way for Adams' nephew. After some dickering, Adams agreed to King's proposition, adding that he had "to take the chance of what might offer for Appleton." [70]

Other indices of partisan considerations, at least with the respective ministers, can be found in the state of origin of the secretaries. Between 30 and 40 per cent of all secretaries appointed came from the same state as their superior officers.[71] A large number also had their names submitted to Congress with their superior officer's name.[72] Many assumed and vacated their positions simultaneously with their ministers.[73] Although several previously and subsequently are known to have held some political office, it is impossible to get exact percentages.

Another qualification that was generally constant throughout the period was the ability to supplement one's salary from private resources. Only under the Articles, seemingly, was there a sufficient wage. Secretary Robert Livingston contended that secretaries' salaries were "at least double what they ought to be." [74] He recommended a graduated scale for the existing members and suggested that future secretaries be compensated according to the standard of living required by the courts at which they were in residence. He thought $2,000 per annum sufficient for "southern courts" and $1,000 for "northern courts." [75] He later added, "as a measure of economy," that private secretaries, instead of secretaries of legation, be appointed at lower salaries, and that the salaries should be augmented by the provision of room and board by the minister.[76] The pre-Constitutional period never lacked candidates for secretaryships.

By the Act of July 1, 1790, the salary of "the secretary of any minister plenipotentiary" was set at $1,350 per annum.[77] The figure was confirmed in 1800.[78] Ten years later Congress increased the salary to $2,000, and here the salary remained until 1856.[79] Meanwhile, especially after 1828, several found the amount inadequate. Unlike their superiors, they were denied the addition of outfits and infits, sums which were designed to defray the costs, first, of establishing a

[70] King, *op. cit.*, VI, 604–6.

[71] 1787–1828: 39.1 per cent; 1829–60: 38.1 per cent; 1861–88: 36.2 per cent.

[72] E.g., *Executive Proceedings*, II (May 27, 1813), 346.

[73] 1787–1828: 26 per cent; 1829–60: 28.9 per cent; 1861–88: 24.5 per cent.

[74] Wharton, *op. cit.*, IV, 846.

[75] Ford *et al.*, *op. cit.*, III, 728.

[76] Wharton, *op. cit.*, IV, 846.

[77] 1 Stat. 128 (July 1, 1790).

[78] 2 Stat. 78 (May 10, 1800).

[79] 2 Stat. 608 (May 1, 1810); *Annals of Congress*, XX, 11th Cong., 2 sess. (April 7, 1810), 645.

mission and, then, of re-entering American society.[80] The only money given them from the contingency fund was for the devaluation of the dollar in exchange.[81] When a secretary acted as chargé in the absence of his superior, he was given money only for normal contingencies. Unless he was specifically commissioned by Congress or applied formally through an appropriation, he was even denied the higher salary of the office he held temporarily.[82]

If it was usually necessary to supplement the salary from private resources, then the description of William Henry Trescot as from "one of the old patrician families of the state [South Carolina]" undoubtedly applied to others.[83] But it is wrong to assume that all secretaries were wealthy. It was, thus, not the spoils system alone that discouraged the prolongation of tenure. The strain on finances resulting from the inadequate salary probably forced many to retire prematurely. After only a few months in St. Petersburg, John Lothrop Motley decided that "the expense of living . . . was out of proportion to his income" and prepared to leave the service he had just entered.[84] Others were discouraged even from entering. In his *Autobiography*, Andrew D. White maintained that the service offered an "insufficient salary, unfit quarters, and an inadequate means of discharging my duties."[85] It was even difficult to get recruits for a position as relatively well paid as secretary and interpreter in China. Minister Peter Parker wrote to Webster, "The office has been absolutely declined by the appointee unless the salary is increased."[86]

The Act of March 1, 1855, granted each secretary $2,000 per annum.[87] When the law fell afoul of the President, Secretary Marcy took the opportunity to propose a revised scale.[88] Using the formula of 15 per cent of the upper service's scale, the system which was adopted raised the salaries of secretaries in France and Great Britain to $2,625 and lowered those of the rest. While it eased the position of secretaries at the two major capitals, it affected adversely the other secretaries in all but one respect. The one improvement granted all secretaries

[80] House Exec. Doc. 67, 33 Cong., 1 sess. (March 1, 1854).

[81] Senate Exec. Doc. 13, 34 Cong., 1 sess. (February 5, 1856).

[82] House Exec. Doc. 368, 25 Cong., 2 sess. (May 10, 1838); House Exec. Doc. 10, 28 Cong., 2 sess. (December 13, 1844). See also Jackson to John Randolph, October 24, 1831, in Bassett, *op. cit.*, IV, 363–64.

[83] Gaillard Hunt, "Narrative and Letter of William Henry Trescot," *American Historical Review*, XIII (April, 1908), 528.

[84] Oliver W. Holmes, *John Lothrop Motley: A Memoir* (London, 1878), pp. 37–38.

[85] White, *Autobiography*, II, 355.

[86] Senate Exec. Doc. 22, 35 Cong., 2 sess. (September 27, 1855), pp. 615–16. He recommended an increase of $2,000.

[87] 10 Stat. 619 (March 1, 1855).

[88] House Mis. Doc. 10, 34 Cong., 3 sess. (December 10, 1856).

serving as chargés was 50 per cent of the absent minister's salary without a senatorial confirmation or a formal appeal through an appropriation.[89] The diplomatic service continued through the century with the 1856 scale.

Why did not the financial qualification create a self-conscious, single-class group, such as existed in British diplomacy? The main reason, of course, is that the spoils system militated against it. Other explanations would be too extended for this book, but certain surface observations can be made. Unlike British diplomats, American secretaries, even if a large proportion came from favored areas, were geographically from widely separated regions with different cultural and social traditions. Those entering between 1787 and 1828 came largely from the areas of dominant political influence: Massachusetts, Virginia, New York, and Maryland. Nearly 70 per cent came from the four states. The remainder were scattered among the other seaboard states, with two secretaries—one each from Kentucky and Alabama—coming from the frontier region. Although the trend diminished as one moved southward, the secretaries were generally from urban areas. The succeeding group, 1829–60, had representatives from twenty-four states. From the states on the Atlantic seaboard came 64.4 per cent, with over 47 per cent from the states of New York, Pennsylvania, Massachusetts, and Virginia. More specifically, the New England states had 17.1 per cent; the Middle Atlantic, 36.8 per cent; the South Atlantic, 19.9 per cent; the East North Central, 7.8 per cent; the other southern states, 13.1 per cent; and the state of California, 3.9 per cent. The secretaries came largely from urban areas.

Following the Civil War, representation became more concentrated. It was still, however, somewhat diffused geographically. Over 50 per cent came from the states of New York, Pennsylvania, New Jersey, Maryland, and from the District of Columbia, 31 per cent coming from New York State alone. The remainder was dispersed, percentages for areas diminishing as the distance increased from the Atlantic. But, like their Middle Atlantic colleagues, the other secretaries originated largely in urban areas. New England had 13.7 per cent, 16 per cent from the East North Central group; the 3.9 per cent from the South Atlantic had to await the last four years of the period to be appointed. The 4.9 per cent from the East South Central represented "border" states. Finally, the relatively large 5.8 per cent from the West South Central is attributable to the custom of sending representatives to Latin America and France from Texas and Louisiana respectively.

[89] 11 Stat. 52 (August 18, 1856). The other salary levels were $1,800, $1,500, and $1,125.

Nor did Harvard and Yale graduates have a monopoly of the American diplomatic posts as Oxford, Cambridge and the Public School men dominated the British service. It is true that Harvard and Yale produced 25 per cent of all secretaries in the period; it is equally true that a host of other institutions were represented, and a fair number of secretaries represented no higher educational institution at all.[90] Insufficient data exist on the preparatory school work of the secretaries. Again unlike Britain, the American diplomatic service had neither a period of probation in the Department of State nor a fixed entering time for new members, both of which would have contributed to an *esprit de corps.*

Few entered a secretaryship before the age of thirty. The average known ages of those entering between 1787 and 1828 was 28.6 years; between 1829 and 1860, 36.8 years; and between 1861 and 1888, 32.8 years.[91] Only in the first group, when 17.4 per cent entered before their mid-twenties, may a claim be made that they entered in order to make diplomacy a career, as John Adams Smith did, or as a prelude to a career in the public service, as Alexander Everett had.[92] Most, however, entered the service after experience in other vocations. Politicians, missionaries, journalists, writers, businessmen, and educators entered the service during the period, and it was argued that the experience of competition in other fields stood one well in diplomacy.[93] A few had had experience as attachés, private secretaries to ministers, consuls, and employees of the Department of State.[94]

Reasons for entering the service often had little to do with diplomacy. The most common was the desire for travel, education, or pleasure. More specific reasons emphasize that members looked at their temporary vocation as a means to some unrelated end. Two men entered to find materials for a history of Mexico; another sought to continue his Tibetan studies through a Far Eastern appointment, while a third joined the service to gain residence in Russia in order to learn a Slavonic language.[95] One man entered to secure European medical care for his wife; another, because he was the only na-

[90] On Harvard and Yale graduates alone are accurate percentages available. These were obtained by checking through various editions of "alumni lists." Academic backgrounds for an additional thirty secretaries (14.2 per cent) were obtained through perusal of the volumes listed in the bibliography.

[91] The age averages are based on forty-nine secretaries, or 23.2 per cent of those holding this position.

[92] Percentage based on 39.1 per cent of the secretaries.

[93] *Cong. Globe,* Part 1, 35 Cong., 2 sess. (January 25, 1859), pp. 593–94 (speech by Senator Daniel E. Sickles of New York).

[94] Three had been attachés; three, private secretaries; seven, consular officers; and five, employees of the Department of State.

[95] *DAB,* II, 376; XII, 449; XVI, 66; IV, 608.

tional in a city when a minister was suddenly called away.[96] The tradition, begun in 1845, of a missionary-secretary to China continued throughout the period. Even an opera composer was commissioned to be secretary of legation in Italy; he was only prevented at the last minute from taking the position by a personal complication.[97] The utility of the service was often argued on the ground that a secretary-ship was "one of the few methods incident to our institutions, whereby not only a race of gentlemen, but a class of disinterested, social, artistic, and literary men can be fostered and become intellectual benefactors as well as patriotic representatives of our country."[98]

The exact attitude which the secretaries had toward the service cannot be determined. It is not, however, unfair to infer from the statistics of tenure and the stated reasons for joining the service that it was regarded as an interim experience and not as a career. Other bits of evidence point to the same conclusion. In a letter to John Jay, John Adams claimed that his son-in-law would probably resign his commission as secretary because of its low prestige.[99] Statements were also made throughout the period that permanent tenure would produce a crop of serious young men, implying conversely that the present system did not.[100]. The laxity which some secretaries displayed toward their appointments underlines this assertion.[101] It was not uncommon for a man to refuse an appointment after he had been confirmed by the Senate. There were fourteen cases of this between 1787 and 1888.[102]

Two elements of a professional service, security of tenure and promotion by merit, were almost totally absent from the nineteenth-century diplomatic service. Again, however, distinctions must be made between the groups. Of the five men elected before the Constitution, only two remained after its adoption. Both were promoted and, as far as can be made out, resigned of their own volition.[103] The 1787–1828 group also evidenced many characteristics of a career service. The members stayed an average of slightly over seven years, while somewhat more than one-quarter served fourteen or more years. Over 21 per cent served two successive appointments and a single member

[96] *DAB*, XIV, 555–56; XIII, 524.

[97] *DAB*, VII, 49–50. The composer was William Fry.

[98] "American Diplomacy," *Atlantic*, XXII (September, 1868), 358.

[99] Adams to Jay, January 24, 1787, in Charles Francis Adams (ed.), *Works of John Adams* (Boston, 1853), VIII, 423.

[100] House Exec. Doc. 94, 22 Cong., 2 sess. (February 7, 1833), p. 7.

[101] Senate Exec. Doc. 21, 33 Cong., 2 sess. (January 16, 1855), pp. 1–5. Buckingham Smith, for instance, took a year and three months to assume his post. Ten months passed between R. A. Erving's commissioning and his entering upon his official duties.

[102] *Biog. Reg.* (1874–88), *passim*.

[103] *DAB*, III, 497–98; XVII, 128–29.

three. Finally, over 34 per cent served immediately following their secretaryships, or shortly thereafter, in the position of chargés d'affaires, and 21.7 per cent served as ministers resident or plenipotentiary. None served subsequently in the Department of State or in the consular service.

The introduction of rotation in office and the frequent shifts in power of the parties strongly influenced the service between 1829 and 1860. The average tenure fell to three years, one month, and ten days. The median dropped to three years, and over 43 per cent served two years or less. This meant that representation changed more frequently than once in a presidential term. The rapid rotation merely mirrored the position in the upper service, where the less time one stayed abroad the more profitable was the office.[104]

But the spoils system was not universally in operation. While a vast drop from the previous group's record, 9.2 per cent did hold two successive posts, and one man held three. Furthermore, five members served over ten years each, and their tenures spilled over substantially into the administrations of other parties. Another 9.2 per cent later occupied higher ministerial positions, and 7.9 per cent were appointed chargés. Another 5 per cent had subsequent experience in the Department of State. These exceptions, however, usually occurred in areas considered undesirable or unhealthy by politicians, and the longer tenure is attributable to omission rather than commission.[105]

The long tenure of the Republican party following the Civil War affected the tenure statistics of the secretaries. During the period, secretaries served an average of slightly more than five years, about a year longer than a presidential term. The median was four years. A large number also stayed considerably longer periods in the service. Over 12 per cent remained eleven or more years, and one member claimed twenty-two years of continuous service. On the other hand, secretaries were less frequently serving in the upper service. Only 5.8 per cent received promotions to the upper service. Some 8.8 per cent served two successive appointments, and 3 per cent served three or more. Six secretaries subsequently entered the Department of State and five the consular service.

To leave the service, a man resigned, as Motley did,[106] was forced out of office by an unexpected or unwelcome successor, as Augustus

---

[104] See above, n. 9. In addition to the salary, a minister received an infit and outfit. The maximum salary could be obtained by staying abroad for only two years. Thereafter the total amount annually diminished rapidly (see *Cong. Globe*, Part 1, 33 Cong., 2 sess. [January 11, 1855], p. 246).

[105] The exceptions occurred, almost without exception, in South America.

[106] Holmes, *op. cit.*, pp. 37–38.

Jay was,[107] or was asked to resign when a different party entered office, as most were. Secretaries were even liable to being appropriated out of existence, as Eugene Schuyler was.[108] About this method, a reviewer in the *Atlantic* complained, ". . . the heartless system of legislating men out of office by refusing to appropriate their salaries . . . is perhaps frequent enough to be called a system." [109]

Remaining in office and receiving promotions depended primarily upon being "connected" in Washington.[110] The fate of the patron was the fate of his appointee. If the former fell from influence, or more important influences arose, the secretary's position was in jeopardy. Also, such diverse considerations as one's geographical background entered into the decision of retaining, ejecting, or promoting a secretary.

In 1888, America's changing world relations found the diplomatic service unprepared. The service was tied down by an antiquated system of appointments and a menacing inflexibility. It was chronically either shorthanded or overstaffed. No adequate salary scale existed. Members were not selected for their qualifications for diplomacy, and they, in turn, entered the service for reasons quite apart from desiring to serve the nation. The service was spoils-ridden and could offer no prospect of permanent tenure or promotion by merit.

To understand how the service subsequently responded to the new order, it is first necessary to discover the reasons for the service's administrative malaise. How most late eighteenth- and nineteenth-century Americans felt toward international relations provides part of the answer. Although these views were held for different reasons by different people at different times, certain common presuppositions existed. For many the Revolution had been fought to free America from the entanglements of Europe. Such freedom included the complete diplomatic withdrawal of the United States from European affairs. This unparalleled attempt at isolation and independence was nourished by the geographical separation of the new nation from Europe and dominated the thoughts of many of its early leaders. In 1783, John Adams wrote, "I confess I have sometimes thought that after a few years it will be the best thing we could do to recall every minister from Europe and send embassies only on special occasions." [111] After a ministership to France and a term as Secretary of State, even Jefferson agreed with Adams, something which he was

[107] Coolidge, *op. cit.*, p. 231.
[108] Schuyler to Russell Sturgis, July 23, 1884, in Schaeffer, *op. cit.*, pp. 167–68.
[109] "Schuyler's Diplomacy," *Atlantic*, LVIII (September, 1886), 417–18.
[110] See Gillespie and Wallace, *op. cit.*, I, 796; Schaeffer, *op. cit.*, pp. 154–55.
[111] Adams to Livingston, February 5, 1783, in C. F. Adams, *op. cit.*, VIII, 39.

not often inclined to do.[112] The same position was held by Paine, James Wilson, Gallatin, and Charles Pinckney.[113] When a congress-man from Tennessee inquired of his colleagues, "Situated as the United States are, at a great distance from the transatlantic world, un-ambitious of conquests, and blessed with a Government formed by the people, and highly pleasing to a large majority of them, what have we to do with the politics of Europe?" he echoed the sentiments of a substantial number of citizens and leaders.[114]

While it was possible to argue diplomatic isolation abstractly, it should have been inconceivable to do so in the face of national ex-perience. Independence brought a series of diplomatic episodes which ran counter to the position taken in the earlier period. The quasi-war with France, the Napoleonic Decrees, the British Orders-in-Council, impressment, the War of 1812, the Spanish threat in Florida, and the Russian challenge on the Pacific Coast, all should have subverted the logic of withdrawal. But they were, in the American mind, counter-balanced by the gradual hemispheric retreat of Europe and by the forcefulness of immigrant and frontiersman thinking.

If these events were not convincing, the Civil War should have brought incontrovertible evidence that diplomatic withdrawal was impossible. Maximilian's regime in Mexico and the European in-trigues to profit from the Union's distress showed many people that di-plomacy was a necessary precondition of security. James Russell Lowell wrote, "Our civil war has taught us, among other useful things, how intimate and sensitive are our relations with the Old World." [115] But many Americans remained unconvinced. The post–Civil War vistas of domestic opportunity obscured the realities existing outside the nation.

Several reasons were given at various times for maintaining isola-tion. Some argued that diplomatic relations would invariably involve America in foreign wars, and many incidents during the first few years of independence confirmed the argument.[116] One southern congress-man believed, ". . . it will be a God-send if they do not . . . embroil

[112] Jefferson to William Short, in Henry M. Wriston, *Diplomacy in a Democracy* (New York: Harper & Bros., 1956), p. 26.

[113] Thomas Paine, *Common Sense* (New York, 1776), *passim*; Jonathan Elliot (ed.), *Debates in the Several State Conventions on the Adoption of the Federal Consitution* (Philadelphia, 1861), II, 513 (December 11, 1787); *Annals of Congress*, VII, 5 Cong., 1 sess. (January 19, 1798), 858–59, 865–66.

[114] *Annals of Congress*, VII, 5 Cong., 1 sess. (January 24, 1798), 916–17 (Representa-tive William C. Claiborne).

[115] James Russell Lowell, "Diplomatic Correspondence," *North American Review*, XCVIII (April, 1864), 620. See also "American Diplomacy," *Atlantic*, XXII (September, 1868), 352.

[116] See *Annals of Congress*, VII, 5 Cong., 1 sess. (January 18, 1798 – March 5, 1798), 851–1209. The debate was in response to the XYZ Affair.

us with foreign nations." [117] But most simply felt that foreign relations were unnecessary. They were enjoying the century-long euphoria produced by chance geographical factors and the fortuitous benevolence of a balance of power across the seas. An early congressman could not conceive "what could be benefited by any sort of compact these foreign agents could frame for us." [118] They argued that, while little harm could be done by maintaining relations, there existed "little opportunity for good either." [119] Using a contemporary example, a Kansas representative claimed, "For months there was no Minister at Vienna. I have never heard that there was [sic] any interruptions of the ordinary course of affairs because of it. So I would be willing to take the chances of having no member at London or Berlin." [120]

Not everyone who accepted this viewpoint agreed that a diplomatic service had always been superfluous. Many believed that it had once been very important but that certain political and technological changes, particularly after the Civil War, made one unnecessary. The service was necessary, they argued, "when the world was ruled by monarchs, and when there were but few liberal legislative bodies in existence." [121] But the important nations in the world, they thought, were rapidly becoming controlled by liberals, and the end of monarchial rule meant the end of intrigues and selfish international ambitions.[122] Moreover, advances in transportation and communication provided adequate substitutes for permanent diplomacy. The laying of the Atlantic Cable in 1866 "allowed a minister of foreign affairs, with the telegraphic wire under his hand, [to] treat with the same fuctionary of another state almost as if the two sat on each side of a table." [123] Developments in transportation, they further contended, conveniently permitted foreign ministers to deal directly with each other.[124] With a flourish of late nineteenth-century confidence, a congressman exclaimed, "These and other elements of progress have

[117] *Register of Debates in Congress*, X, 23 Cong., 1 sess. (April 30, 1834), 3881 (speech by Representative W. Ransom Davis of South Carolina).

[118] *Annals of Congress*, VII, 5 Cong., 1 sess. (January 18, 1798), 851 (speech by Representative John Nicholas of Virginia).

[119] Samuel S. Cox, *The Folly and Cost of Diplomacy* (Washington, 1874), p. 6.

[120] *Cong. Rec.*, XX, 50 Cong., 2 sess. (January 28, 1889), 1247 (Representative Preston B. Plumb of Kansas).

[121] *Cong. Rec.*, XVII, 49 Cong., 1 sess. (May 12, 1886), 4443 (Representative John H. Reagan of Texas).

[122] *Cong. Globe*, Part 1, 35 Cong., 2 sess. (January 24, 1859), p. 547 (speech by Representative Owen Lovejoy of Illinois).

[123] Albert Rhodes, "Our Diplomats and Consuls," *Scribners*, XIII (December, 1876), 175.

[124] *Cong. Rec.*, XIII, 47 Cong., 1 sess. (March 2, 1882), 1565 (speech by Representative Andrew Curtin of Pennsylvania).

rendered ministers abroad trifling, expensive, and useless for every purpose of national comity, interest, and glory." [125]

Most Americans, however, discovered early in the Republic's history that diplomatic relations and isolation were not antithetical, and that the former was essential to the latter. During the XYZ Affair, a convert, John Adams, stated the position clearly:

> Although it is very true that we ought not to involve ourselves in the political system of Europe, but to keep ourselves always distinct and separate from it, if we can; yet to effect this separation, early, punctual, and continual information of the current chain of events, and of the political projects in contemplation is no less necessary than if we were directly concerned in them. [126]

In many sessions of Congress, this position was reasserted. It was pointed out that diplomatic withdrawal would jeopardize America's security and that a system of spies would have to be inaugurated in the place of the service. [127]

Still, those who maintained the position of qualified isolationism insisted that relations be minimal. They also maintained that the success of the existing system precluded nearly every administrative change. [128] Legations existed only to gain information about potential threats to the nation, to pursue claims, and to report on the state of commerce. [129] Many even found these functions too wide or felt that a better substitute could be found to perform them. Those who held the former were convinced that a treaty between the United States and another nation would end the necessity for representation. [130] They rejected all advice that treaties needed to be enforced or that episodes

[125] Cox, *op. cit.*, p. 4.

[126] *American State Papers*, I, No. 13, 41 (speech before Congress by President John Adams, May 16, 1797).

[127] E.g., *Annals of Congress*, VII, 5 Cong., 1 sess. (January 24, 1798), 933–34 (speech by Representative Elizur Goodrich of Connecticut). See also *Cong. Globe*, Part 1, 35 Cong., 2 sess. (January 19, 1859), p. 460 (speech by Representative William Barksdale of Mississippi).

[128] See *Cong. Globe.*, Part 1, 35 Cong., 2 sess. (January 25, 1859), pp. 593–94 (speech by Representative Sickles). See also *Cong. Rec.*, XVII, 49 Cong., 1 sess. (June 4, 1886), 5222 (speech by Senator William B. Allison of Pennsylvania). See also "Our Diplomatists," *Nation*, XXVI (March 28, 1878), 209.

[129] See House Exec. Doc. 94, 22 Cong., 2 sess. (February 7, 1833), p. 1; Senate Exec. Doc. 93, 32 Cong., 1 sess. (July 2, 1852), p. 9; Senate Rept. 209, 34 Cong., 1 sess. (July 10, 1856), p. 2; *Register of Debates*, VIII (April 13, 1832), 783 (speech by Senator Henry Clay of Kentucky).

[130] *Cong. Globe*, Part 1, 35 Cong., 2 sess. (January 24, 1859), p. 549 (speech by Representative John Sherman of Ohio).

not covered by a treaty might harm relations between states.[131] One of their number maintained:

> There may be backward nations with which we have communication where a minister resident all the time may be of some service; but with those nations of Europe with whom we are in constant communication, having treaties well understood with each other, there is no more need for and no more importance to be attached than there is to have such agents sent by these states to each other.[132]

As treaties were about the only tangible products of foreign intercourse and as early American history was dominated by usually successful attempts to secure treaties of commerce, it was little wonder that these facts, coupled with the confidence that agreements were self-operating, set the public mind against the need for extensive continuous diplomacy.

If treaties were the most important objects of foreign relations, then the only representatives necessary were those needed to negotiate the treaties. Distilled as well from a fear of a permanent office-holding class and an inbred American distaste for diplomatic conventionalities, the logic of this position appealed to many. They were persuaded that the idea of permanent legations was not of long standing and that the practice of retaining them "had been doubted by many of the wisest statesmen." [133] Fortified with a growing list of precedents, they concluded that the best substitute was the special agent, particularly one formally commissioned by Congress.[134] He was able to be more direct and efficient, "much cheaper and much more in accordance with republican principles." [135] Late in the eighteenth century, Oliver Wolcott tersely suggested, "If we want to do any business abroad, give some good fellow a letter of attorney and let him do it." [136] A century later, when relations between nations were patently more complex, a congressman still urged that "a special commission to settle vexed

[131] *Annals of Congress*, I, 1 Cong., 2 sess., (January 26, 1790), 1085 (speech by Representative William L. Smith of South Carolina).

[132] *Cong. Globe*, Part 3, 39 Cong., 1 sess. (May 16, 1866), p. 2618 (speech by Representative Benjamin F. Wade of Ohio).

[133] House Rept. 166, 28 Cong., 1 sess. (February 15, 1844), pp. 4–5.

[134] *Cong. Globe*, Part 2, 35 Cong., 2 sess. (February 17, 1859), p. 1088 (speech by Senator George E. Pugh of Ohio). See also *Cong. Globe*, Part 1, 40 Cong., 3 sess. (January 6, 1869), p. 220 (speech by Representative Benjamin F. Butler of Massachusetts).

[135] *Cong. Globe*, Part 1, 35 Cong., 2 sess. (January 19, 1859), p. 458 (speech by Representative J. L. M. Curry of Alabama).

[136] Oliver Wolcott, *Memoirs of the Administrations of George Washington and John Adams* (New York, 1846), I, 131.

questions" be appointed "whenever there is a disagreeable complication that has in it a possible casus belli." [137]

The few attempts to provide an adequate diplomatic service in the nineteenth century, particularly at the secretarial level, failed partly because of the prevailing attitudes toward relations with other nations. Jefferson early discovered that a popular form of economy was slicing the appropriation for the service.[138] If minimal relations were the standard, issues such as personnel mobility, the requirement of qualified secretaries, the recognition of training and experience, and freedom from partisan considerations held no importance. From a personnel standpoint, this standard undoubtedly dissuaded good men from entering the service. Competent men wish to deal with important events. The strength of the British diplomatic service in the nineteenth century stemmed partly from a general belief in the importance of foreign policy; the American service, save for the period 1787–1828, was weakened by the absence of such unanimity.

The American attitude toward foreign commerce also helps to explain the state of the nineteenth-century diplomatic service. In 1889, Henry Cabot Lodge concluded that foreign affairs filled "but a slight place in American politics, and excite only a languid interest." [139] Commercial affairs, on the other hand, were always important in American politics and thinking. The connection between continuous diplomacy and foreign commerce shaped many views about the service. But the debate on this connection had many ramifications. Were official agents necessary to superintend the nation's commerce? Were diplomatic, as well as consular, officers required? The position was even argued that the United States should forgo "an uncertain subsistence on the ocean" and all its requisite officials, and pursue "the peaceful cultivation of the soil." [140] But the Arcadian philosophy of the early Jeffersonian was soon silenced by the demands of American merchants.

A few unreconstructed individualists saw no connection at all between commerce and diplomats or any other foreign agent. At the beginning of the Republic, one representative insisted that agents only tended to entangle commerce without rendering it any aid. He recommended that the nation leave its commerce "to seek its own markets totally disembarrassed." [141] After a century of national ex-

[137] Cox, *op. cit.*, p. 5.

[138] Carl R. Fish, *The Civil Service and the Patronage* (New York, 1905), p. 45.

[139] Henry Cabot Lodge, *George Washington* (Boston, 1889), II, 129.

[140] *Annals of Congress*, VII, 5 Cong., 1 sess. (March 5, 1798), 1209 (speech by Representative Claiborne).

[141] *Ibid.* (January 18, 1798), 851 (speech by Representative Nicholas of Virginia).

perience, it was possible to hear public figures argue the same position. In 1886, a congressman maintained:

> If the object is to promote commercial intercourse, the active, vigilant, intelligent merchants of the country are the men who acquire and avail themselves of all the information that is necessary to the successful prosecution of mercantile pursuits.[142]

No matter how laissez-faire advocates talked and sought to act domestically, dealing abroad was generally another question. The European or Asian whom they could not trust politically was even less trustworthy economically, and so the vast majority of members of the Executive and Congress and most publicists had early agreed that some official representation was necessary. Doubters were invariably confronted with the example of Great Britain, for the proponents of agents abroad were convinced that "there is no place where there is a pound sterling to be gathered that she has not some one there to represent her interests."[143] Later they were convinced that the rapid rise in American commerce after the Civil War had been a result of "this very system," and maintained that it was "well known that commerce will not seek a port where there is no representative of the Government of the United States."[144]

For those who believed that foreign representation was essential to commerce, the question remained whether both diplomatic and consular representation were required. Most maintained the need for consular representation alone, and they usually carried the day when cuts were to be made in the diplomatic service's appropriations.[145] They felt that the diplomatic service was a luxury. A middle western congressman claimed:

> Now, I confess to you, sir, that I know of no area of the public service that is more emphatically useless than the diplomatic service — none in the world. For commercial purposes, our consuls discharge all the duties that are re-

---

[142] *Cong. Rec.*, XVII, 49 Cong., 1 sess. (May 12, 1886), 4443 (speech by Representative Reagan of Texas).

[143] *Cong. Globe*, Part 1, 40 Cong., 3 sess. (January 6, 1869), p. 221 (speech by Representative Horace Maynard of New York).

[144] *Cong. Rec.*, IV, 44 Cong., 1 sess. (March 27, 1876), 1971 (speech by Representative Aaron A. Sargent of California).

[145] E.g., House Rept. 23, 44 Cong., 1 sess. (January 28, 1876), p. 1. The appropriation of that year abolished six legations on the grounds that consular representation was sufficient. See also Samuel S. Cox, *The Beauties of Diplomacy* (Washington, 1876), p. 4; *Cong. Rec.*, XVII, 49 Cong., 1 sess. (May 12, 1886), 4444.

quired. The diplomatic ministers discharge no duties of a commercial character.[146]

When Labouchère and Beaumont advocated the abolition of the British diplomatic service,[147] the supporters of the same position for the United States insisted, "If this be true in Great Britain, which commands the commerce of the world . . . , then, a fortiori, it might be true of this country." [148] In general, they agreed that the immediate course "should be expansion in the consular and contraction in the diplomatic service." [149] Thus, the administrative problems of diplomacy were of little moment. And if a young man were interested in commerce, he would probably have become a merchant, possibly a consul, but never a diplomat.

The service's condition was also partly the product of the republican environment in which it had its being. To all the early citizens, the government under the Articles and under the Constitution was a new experiment, unlike anything in the Old World. This sense of uniqueness colored the views of many people who made decisions about foreign policy and who controlled the machinery of diplomatic intercourse. They concluded that republican institutions and diplomacy were either difficult to harmonize or completely incompatible.

This group, however, was not restricted to a lunatic fringe. In his charge to Jay, Washington warned him to have a "horror of finesse and chicane" which he thought dominated European diplomacy.[150] Adams contended that "it is very certain that we shall never be a match for European statesmen in such accomplishments," the accomplishments being "bribes well placed" and "intrigues of pleasure with a woman." [151] Gallatin even made distinctions between the diplomacies of European countries. He believed that in France they "occasionally say what is not true," while in England "they conceal the truth." [152]

[146] *Cong. Globe*, Part 1, 35 Cong., 2 sess. (January 19, 1859), p. 459 (speech by Representative Benjamin W. Stanton of Ohio).

[147] For the Labouchère reference, see Hansard, *Parliamentary Debates*, CXCII, cols. 927–39, May 28, 1868. For the reference to Somerset A. Beaumont, see *ibid.*, CXCIX, col. 549, February 18, 1870. Cox was not wholly correct in his reference to their views. Labouchère was primarily interested in extending parliamentary control over the field of foreign policy. Beaumont, on the other hand, recommended that the Diplomatic Service be abolished.

[148] Cox, *Folly and Cost of Diplomacy*, p. 5.

[149] Rhodes, *op. cit.*, p. 173.

[150] *American State Papers*, I, 497.

[151] Adams to Livingston, February 5, 1783, in C. F. Adams, *op. cit.*, VIII, 39.

[152] Albert Gallatin to James Gallatin, January 13, 1827, in Henry Adams, *Gallatin*, p. 622.

In either case, America's republican virtues and institutions were sorely taxed. The difficulty was also recognized by Alexis de Tocqueville, when he wrote in 1835, "Foreign politics demand scarcely any of those qualities which are peculiar to a democracy; they require, on the contrary, the perfect use of almost all those in which it is deficient." [153]

To argue that diplomacy for republicans was difficult or that perhaps the system of government was poorly adapted for it was one thing; to contend that it was corrupting or completely incompatible with republican institutions was quite another. Throughout the period, the latter theme was persistently labored. Some felt that diplomacy was inherently unrepublican and should be modified to harmonize with American institutions or abolished completely. Referring to the diplomatic service, one congressman claimed, "The growth of institutions directly opposed in principle to our own" had created "great and positive evils." He recommended that the machinery be recast in an American mold.[154] Those who were less indulgent demanded an end to the institution. In 1859, a representative insisted, "Here is the evil, the fungus, the excrescence, a pinchbeck imitation of the pomp and pageantry of royalty, and we should put the knife to it and cut it out." [155] One generation later an opponent of the diplomatic service reasoned that it should be ended because the United States "should not make its salaam before the kings and kaisers of the world." [156] A correspondent to the *Nation* concluded that diplomacy in a republic was an attempt to fuse two opposites — aristocracy and democracy.[157]

What frightened the republicans most was the influence which diplomacy might have on the nation's diplomats or on the nation itself. The members of the Continental Congress were so concerned about the possibility of Europe corrupting the republican simplicity of its members that a resolution was passed permitting diplomats to remain abroad on their commissions for a period of only three years. [158] Even the seasoned John Quincy Adams maintained that the European atmosphere was unhealthy for Americans, and that diplomats after a

[153] Alexis de Tocqueville, *Democracy in America* (London, 1862), I, 299.

[154] *Cong. Globe*, Part 1, 33 Cong., 2 sess. (January 11, 1855), p. 245 (speech by Representative Perkins).

[155] *Ibid.*, Part 1, 35 Cong., 2 sess. (January 25, 1859), p. 593 (speech by Representative Curry). See also *Cong. Rec.*, XVIII, 49 Cong., 2 sess. (February 5, 1887), 1421 (speech by Representative James B. McCreary of Kentucky).

[156] Cox, *Beauties*, p. 4.

[157] "Foreign Legations," *Nation*, XLI (December 24, 1885), pp. 524–25.

[158] Oliver Wolcott, *op. cit.*, I, 281. See also Milledge Bonham, Jr., "Robert Livingston," *American Secretaries of State*, ed. Samuel F. Bemis, I, 183.

few years abroad needed "to be renovated by the wholesome republican atmosphere of their own country." He added that this was also a maxim of Jefferson and Monroe.[159] And a southern congressman complained that diplomats returned "with their heads as full of kings, queens, and knaves, as a pack of cards" and that the system of foreign intercourse was radically wrong, "unsuited to an agricultural, distant, peaceful republic."[160]

The passage of time did not modify this view. Despite the growing belief that Europe was being "liberalized," an author in *Scribner's* wrote, "Some of our diplomatic agents have become so emasculated by the intercourse with royalty as to forget that they represent a nation of simple republicans."[161] Another magazine writer complained that diplomacy spoiled a few Americans each year.[162] Even those who defended the service referred to the corruption argument. In a letter to Seward, Minister George H. Yeamans insisted, "There is probably no instance of any American diplomatic agent having fallen into unrepublican ways of thinking and feeling."[163]

Those who feared diplomacy would corrupt the country itself verged on the demagogic. An early congressman sought to bolt the door against foreign representatives and returning American diplomats "as a necessary precaution to secure our freedom and happiness."[164] This fear did not abate with time either. In a classic of xenophobia, one senator maintained:

> This diplomatic service is working our ruin by creating a desire for foreign customs and foreign follies. The disease is imported by our returning diplomats and by the foreign embassadors sent here by monarchs and despots to corrupt and destroy our American ideals. They should both be quarantined as we quarantine foreign rags through fear of cholera.[165]

Two products of America's republican presuppositions were a fanatical parsimony in public expenditures and a deep dislike for non-elected office-holders. Revenue ultimately came from the pockets of

[159] W. C. Ford (ed.), *Writings of John Quincy Adams* (New York, 1913–17), VI, 357.

[160] *Register of Debates*, X, 23 Cong., 1 sess. (April 30, 1834), 3881 (speech by Representative Davis of South Carolina).

[161] Rhodes, *op. cit.*, p. 176.

[162] *Public Opinion*, VI, (February 9, 1889), 367.

[163] Yeamans to Seward, December 4, 1866, in *Papers Relating to the Foreign Relations of the United States* (Washington, 1867–68), I, 647 (hereafter cited as *Foreign Relations*).

[164] *Annals of Congress*, VII, 5 Cong., 1 sess. (January 24, 1798), 917 (speech by Representative Claiborne).

[165] *Cong. Rec.*, XVI, 48 Cong., 2 Sess. (January 10, 1885), 613 (speech by Senator William E. Robinson of New York).

constituents. Consequently, no waste could be tolerated. Representative Ingersoll sought a substantial contraction in representation in 1844 in order "to reduce their cost, and diminish[ing] that executive patronage which is, in this respect, the most arbitrary and detrimental." [166] Other attempts to economize in the service were made during the period.[167] The standard which republicans applied was summarized in a resolution in 1884 to create a commission "to inquire and report, what changes and consolidations, if any, can be made in the diplomatic service of the United States in foreign countries, with due regard to international comity, and without impairment of the efficiency of the service." [168] International comity and efficiency were always secondary to considerations of economy.

The republican environment affected nearly every aspect of the service's administration. The question of diplomatic dress was settled along republican lines.[169] The republican prejudice against a permanent office-holding class and the belief that extended stays abroad contaminated the secretaries encouraged public approval of spoils and short terms in office. These considerations eliminated most hope that Congress would abdicate its strangle hold over appointments, either with regard to individuals or to general mobility of personnel. Republican opposition ended the system of attachés. Coupled with the prevailing feeling that extensive diplomatic relations were unnecessary and that the consular service was the only important agency of commerce, the fierce sense of republican economy frustrated attempts to expand the service or to improve it if that required money. The inadequate salary scale also had its roots here. A public office was not to be held at a profit. Attempts to point out that it was costing diplomats money to serve abroad were countered with the argument that personal outlays in diplomacy were only to find out "who appeared to the best advantage in the halls of Terpsichore." [170] Such frivolities had, they thought, nothing to do with public duties.

But had these considerations not existed, it would still have been

[166] House Rept. 166, 28 Cong., 1 sess. (February 15, 1844), pp. 4–5.

[167] Senate Rept. 88, 19 Cong., 1 sess. (March 6, 1826), p. 15; House Rept. 166, 28 Cong., 1 sess. (February 15, 1844), pp. 1–6; House Rept. 23, 44 Cong., 1 sess. (January 28, 1876), p. 1.

[168] House Mis. Doc. 135, 49 Cong., 1 sess. (March 1, 1886), *passim*; Cox *Beauties*, p. 4; *Cong. Globe*, Part 2, 35 Cong., 2 sess. (February 17, 1859), p. 1088 (speech by Representative George E. Pugh of Ohio).

[169] E.g., *Cong. Globe*, Part 1, 40 Cong., 1 sess. (March 20, 1867), p. 216. Resolution 39, which was sponsored by Senator Charles Sumner, passed both Houses. It established the "republican criterion" of wearing the uniform appropriate for an audience with the President. See also John B. Moore, "American Diplomacy: Its Influence and Tendencies," *Harper's Monthly*, CXI (October, 1905), 690–96. Moore's article has the only accurate discussion of the dress question.

[170] *Cong. Globe*, Part 1, 35 Cong., 2 sess. (January 19, 1859), p. 459.

unlikely that the service would have achieved a greater degree of organization than it, in fact, possessed in 1888. Other considerations, notably the governmental framework in which the service operated, helped determine its administration. The problems arising from constitutionally shared powers in the field of foreign policy were particularly important. While in most areas of usage the Executive expanded at the expense of the Legislature,[171] the reverse was the case in diplomatic administration, not, however, through the senatorial prerogative over appointments. The House of Representatives was the important agent in widening Legislative control. Through its power over appropriations, it laid whatever legal base existed in the nineteenth century and caused the diffusion of responsibility over administration which prevailed into the twentieth century.

The proponents of the right of Congress to determine the number and destination, as well as the merits, of appointments argued from three positions: that the Constitution had been originally misinterpreted, that there was a conscious conspiracy on the part of the Presidency to deprive Congress of its power, and that the exercise of the power itself was inherent in the powers of Congress. Upholding the first position, Representative John Perkins asserted in 1855, ". . . our early legislation conferred upon the President a degree of discretion over foreign intercourse more in accordance with the spirit of the English than of our own Government." [172] He hoped that the legislation for which he was speaking would restore the original balance. Members who considered Executive control over foreign intercourse as a form of tyranny and part of a conspiracy were the most vociferous. Early in the Republic's history, one representative warned Congress about the "union and consolidation of all its parts [branches] in the Executive" and insisted that there be "constant operation on the part of the Legislature to resist the overwhelming power." [173] Finally, many maintained that foreign policy administration was inherent in the powers of Congress. A western congressman defiantly contended, "I say we have the power to abolish a mission, and I say that any indication or intimation from Congress that a particular agent abroad does not represent the nation, ought to be respected by the State Department and ought to be a law to that Department." [174]

[171] See Wriston, *Executive Agents*, pp. 27–105; Edward S. Corwin, *The President's Control of Foreign Relations* (Princeton, 1917), pp. 49–71.

[172] *Cong. Globe*, Part 1, 33 Cong., 2 sess. (January 11, 1855), p. 245.

[173] *Annals of Congress*, VII, 5 Cong., 1 sess. (January 18, 1798), 849 (speech by Representative Nicholas of Virginia).

[174] *Cong. Globe*, Part 2, 39 Cong., 2 sess. (February 18, 1867), p. 1503 (speech by Representative George G. Fogg of New Hampshire). See also *Cong. Globe*, Part 1, 27 Cong., 1 sess. (April 27, 1841), p. 393 (speech by Representative Ingersoll).

Many resisted the Legislative usurpation of power on the grounds that Congress was incompetent constitutionally to determine anything more than the merits of nominees. While recognizing the power of the purse, they believed that the House should be a trusting Cerberus and that the Constitution did not "mean to give them the use of one power thro' the abuse of another." [175] In a letter to Washington, Jefferson wrote:

> The transaction of business with foreign nations is Executive altogether. It belongs then to the head of that department, except as to such portions of it as are specifically submitted to the Senate. Exceptions are to be construed strictly.[176]

This position was later argued in Congress. When the power was analogized with that to determine the number of judges, one representative reasoned that, while regulating the number of judges was strictly a Legislative act, the "appointment of foreign Ministers was strictly Executive." [177] Following an attempt in 1832 to reduce the service to three roving ministers, a report by the Committee on Foreign Affairs maintained that "this would be an obvious intrusion on the executive province." [178] But the position was most definitively stated by Attorney General Cushing in 1855. Listing an impressive number of historical precedents, he argued that "the President has power by the Constitution to appoint diplomatic agents of the United States at any time in his discretion." [179]

The debate was a deadlock, and reference to the Constitutional authorities adds no decisive weight to either side. But the position emerges from usage. There was a continuous diminution of the Executive's prerogative in foreign affairs administration. By 1888, the number of secretaries, their destinations, and their other characteristics were under the control of the Legislature.

With independence in no way fully assured and the problem of securing commercial treaties continuous, Washington went before Congress in 1790 and stated:

> The interests of the United States require that our intercourse with other nations should be facilitated by such pro-

[175] Jefferson to Washington, April 24, 1790, as quoted in Hunt, *Department of State*, p. 106.
[176] Jefferson to Washington, April 24, 1790, in P. L. Ford (ed.), *Writings of Thomas Jefferson* (New York, 1892–99), V, 161.
[177] *Annals of Congress*, VII (January 24, 1798), 897 (speech by Representative John Dennis).
[178] House Rept. 180, 22 Cong., 1 sess. (January 12, 1832), p. 3.
[179] 7 Attorney-General's Opinions 186.

visions as will enable *me* to fulfill *my* duty in that respect in the manner which circumstances may render most conducive to the public good.[180]

Congress responded with the Law of July 1, 1790. From the duties on "exposts and tonnage," a sum was appropriated annually "for the support of such persons as he [President] shall commission to serve the United States in foreign posts." Among the positions established was that of secretary of legation. The law was in force for a two-year period and was thereafter re-enacted for one-year periods until 1800.[181]

The law was not without its restrictions. There was a maximum compensation for agents beyond which the President could not go. The law was also in force for a limited length of time only. And the President did have to go to Congress for its authorization. But the significant point was not the restrictions it imposed; it was that the law recognized the Executive's prerogative by appropriating a lump sum to be disposed of as the President chose. He was able to compensate his agents at any rate up to the maximum amount. He was able to send as many agents as he wanted within the limits of the appropriation. Their destinations were of his own determining. Part of this latitude was a confidence in Washington's moderation; part came from the pressures of international events and a general ignorance of the needs of a diplomatic service by the early government.[182] Nevertheless, the Executive control was wide and firmly recognized.

The first decade saw the system of the lump-sum appropriations receive the character of extraordinary expenses; the second decade saw the system, in the character of ordinary expenses, placed in the General Appropriations Bill.[183] The salary maximums and the offices were re-established by the Act of May 10, 1800.[184] Under the pressure of the impressment issue and of claims outstanding, Executive control was further increased by the creation of a contingency fund in 1806, which, unlike the extraordinary increase in 1794, made permanent a fund to defray special expenses of foreign intercourse.[185] With the exception of the legitimate and effective objection by Congress in 1802 to the appointment of private secretaries, the Executive power over foreign affairs administration was nearly complete.

[180] *American State Papers*, I, No. 2, 11–12 (emphasis by author).
[181] 1 Stat. 128 (July 1, 1790).
[182] *Cong. Globe*, Part 1, 33 Cong., 2 sess. (January 11, 1855), p. 245 (speech by Representative Perkins); *Annals of Congress*, VII, 5 Cong., 1 sess. (February 28, 1798), 1099 (speech by Representative Joshua Coit of Connecticut).
[183] 2 Stat. 65 (May 7, 1800).
[184] 2 Stat. 78 (May 10, 1800).
[185] 2 Stat. 389 (April 18, 1806); cf. 1 Stat. 345 (March 20, 1794).

In 1810, however, Congress curtailed the Executive power in two ways. Although reluctantly increasing the salary for secretaries, the Act of May 1, 1810, demanded that the payment of a salary for a secretary "was compensation for all his personal services and expenses." This forbade any payment from the contingency fund. Second, it constricted the power over appointments by refusing salaries to any secretary who had not been formally confirmed by the Senate.[186] Congress exercised traditional oversight on both.[187]

The Executive prerogative was still very wide. Only salaries and nominations were controlled by Congress. But the situation was not to last long. The period following the War of 1812 saw a concerted attempt to end almost entirely the Executive's responsibility for appointments. By the Act of April 9, 1818, the lump-sum appropriation was replaced by detailed appropriations which specified the destinations and the amounts payable to each mission.[188] In 1831, a second act constricted the Executive's power further by taking the detailed appropriation one more step and prescribing the amounts to be paid to each position and the destinations for the members of the service.[189] While objections were raised by the President and the Secretary of State over the abolition of specific legations, none were raised over the new state of affairs. Thereafter, it was necessary for new posts to be approved by Congress and old posts to be re-examined annually. Thus, the ultimate responsibility for important administrative matters was shifted from the Executive to the Legislature, and Congress became the important agency for change for the diplomatic service.

It early became apparent to Congress that its new prize could be ignored without immediate danger to national interests. Although resolutions were introduced, reports made, and speeches delivered, no serious consideration was given to the needs of the service.[190] Beginning in 1851, tales of abuses to the infit and outfit and to the position of attaché led to a series of inquiries by the Committee on Foreign Affairs,[191] culminating in 1854 with a bill to remodel the

[186] 2 Stat. 608 (May 1, 1810).

[187] E.g., House Rept. 220, 21 Cong., 1 sess. (February 22, 1830), *passim*; House Rept. 931, 25 Cong., 2 sess. (May 26, 1838), *passim*.

[188] 3 Stat. 433 (April 9, 1818).

[189] 4 Stat. 452 (March 2, 1831).

[190] *Cong. Globe*, Part 1, 31 Cong., 2 sess. (January 31, 1851), p. 403 (resolution by Henry S. Foote of Mississippi). See also *Cong. Globe*, Part 1, 29 Cong., 1 sess. (February 17, 1846), p. 382; Senate Exec. Doc. 93, 32 Cong., 1 sess. (July 2, 1852), *passim*; House Exec. Doc. 94, 22 Cong., 2 sess. (February 7, 1833), *passim*; *Register of Debates*, X, 23 Cong., 1 sess (April 30, 1834), 3881; *Cong. Globe*, Part 1, 27 Cong., 1 sess. (April 22, 1841), p. 393.

[191] Senate Exec. Doc. 21, 33 Cong., 2 sess. (January 16, 1855), *passim*.

diplomatic and consular services.[192] Through a parliamentary tactic the bill was passed over; [193] it was not until the following year that a second bill was introduced and accepted. Representative John Perkins and Dudley Mann of the Department of State collaborated on the bill, which incorporated the recommendations of previous reports and State Department plans.[194] Along with abolishing infits, outfits, attachés, and the formal office of chargé d'affaires, and prohibiting alien appointments, it elevated all lower ministers to "envoy extraordinary and minister plenipotentiary" and provided a secretary of legation for each country listed in the bill. It also raised the clerk at London to an assistant secretary and created a similar office at Paris. All the changes were to go into effect the following July.[195]

Before the bill was passed in Congress, Secretary of State Marcy, who had not seen the bill in its writing stage, wrote to a member of the Committee on Appropriations. He claimed that it was unconstitutional to require the President to appoint diplomatic agents to specific destinations with specific ranks.[196] He and President Pierce, although recognizing the need for the law, resented the further intrusion into the residue of Executive prerogative.[197] Through his Attorney General, Pierce sent to Congress an elaborate refusal to execute the law.[198] The period requiring the reappointments and the changes in rank passed, but Pierce remained adamant. When Congress convened, it retreated by passing a joint resolution on July 28, 1856, making the objectionable provisions of the law "permissive" instead of "mandatory." [199] The following month a second act was passed. It contained all the prohibitions of its predecessor, but it made appointments and promotions in rank permissive. It also added a wage scale of Marcy's devising and delegated to the Department the power to issue administrative orders not inconsistent with the law.[200] The balance was affected, but not turned. Congress still controlled appointments, salaries, and the size of the service. The Executive retained the prerogative to send an agent and to determine his rank. Although the latter's power, considering the Legislative control over appropria-

[192] *Cong. Globe*, Part 2, 33 Cong., 1 sess. (June 7, 1854), p. 1354.
[193] *Ibid.*, Part 3, 33 Cong., 1 sess. (August 1, 1854), p. 2040.
[194] Roy Franklin Nichols, *Franklin Pierce* (Philadelphia, 1931), p. 383; *Cong. Globe*, Part 1, 33 Cong., 2 sess. (January 11, 1855), pp. 244–45 (speech by Representative Perkins).
[195] 10 Stat. 619 (March 1, 1855).
[196] *Cong. Globe*, Part 2, 33 Cong., 2 sess. (March 2, 1855), p. 1100.
[197] Nichols, *op. cit.*, p. 383.
[198] 7 Attorney-General's Opinions 186.
[199] *Cong. Globe*, Part 2, 34 Cong., 2 sess. (July 28, 1856), pp. 1797–99.
[200] 11 Stat. 52. (August 18, 1856).

tions, was more fictional than real, it appeared to be a fiction worth fighting to sustain.

The period between the Civil War and 1888 saw no real change in the position. Save for occasional reiterations of arguments and prohibitions against certain types of positions, only one relevant piece of legislation was passed. Following an abortive attempt under Grant for civil service reform and an aggravated situation produced by the revelation of frauds and nefarious practices in government, the forces of reform pushed through Congress the Pendleton Act of January 16, 1883.[201] The law authorized the President to remove any area of the public service from patronage and put it under civil service rules. While it was not applied to the diplomatic service before 1888, it was the basis for the service's later reform and the device for restoring much of the Executive prerogative.

The struggle between the two branches deeply affected the administration of the service. Congress' insistence upon exercising its control through detailed appropriations wedded the secretary, regardless of the needs of the service, to his mission and prevented any degree of flexibility in administration. It also diffused authority between the Executive and the Legislature. Practice appears settled now, but contemporaries found the distribution poorly defined, especially after the Attorney General's opinion in 1855. This uncertainty frustrated any possibility of vigorous direction. Also, the peculiar position of the State Department as the "President's Office"[202] and the antagonisms engendered during the struggle colored the relationship which the diplomatic service was to have with Congress throughout its history.

Other evidence that the service was limited by its administrative milieu can be found in the prevailing personnel practices. Patronage had always existed in America. Despite statements to the contrary,[203] there was no substitution, as a result of the alleged corrupting influence of democracy, of a civil service based on partisan preference for one based strictly on merit. Political considerations were important from Washington's time onward.[204] When a single party dominated

[201] 22 Stat. 403 (January 16, 1883).

[202] The sense of exclusiveness was graphically shown in Webster's refusal to participate in Senator Hunter's classification program. For Hunter's scheme, see 10 Stat. 189 (March 3, 1853). For Webster's refusal, see Daniel Webster, *Writings and Speeches*, ed. J. W. McIntyre (Boston, 1903), XIV, 552–3.

[203] E.g., White, *Autobiography*, II, 356–57; G. L. Rives, "Our Need of a Permanent Diplomatic Service," *Forum*, XXV (August, 1898), 702.

[204] Washington to Pickering, September 27, 1795, in Fitzpatrick, Washington, XXXIV, 315. "I shall not, whilst I have the honor to Administer the government, bring a man into any office of consequence knowingly whose political tenets are adverse to the measures which the general government are pursuing; for this, in my opinion, would be a sort of political suicide."

for a long period, as the Jeffersonians did, it was natural that some stability was created in the diplomatic service. Yet it is difficult to believe that factions within the party did not compete for appointments. The Republicans after 1860 had a similar long tenure in power. It is significant that this period saw the rise of the civil service movement and stirrings within the diplomatic service.[205]

After 1828, to patronage on the national level was added the doctrine of rotation in office. The doctrine held that no government job required such extensive training as could not be acquired in the briefest time. It further argued that it was salutary and instructive that, usually after two years, an office be vacated and refilled. The doctrine refused to recognize those elements upon which any career is based — experience and training. While there were many exceptions, the rule applied generally to the civil service, and its influence was felt in the diplomatic service.

Rotation was opposed even during Jackson's administration. The opposition swelled but was left powerless by the viciously circular nature of the system. After Lincoln's refusal in 1865 to redistribute the offices, rotation's strength subsided. But political preference continued as the criterion for office — diplomatic or otherwise. With original appointment, promotion, and tenure dependent upon politics, with party changes and factional splits frequently occurring, and with the doctrine of rotation operating through part of the period, many of the service's deficiencies in 1888 can be attributed to the cumulative effects of the personnel practices in all departments of the Executive.

One final element in the administrative atmosphere limited the organizational potential of the diplomatic service. The standards of business efficiency, which were later important, were then being developed and had not yet been popularly accepted. Civil service reform was far more concerned with preventing abuses than in securing efficient administration. The popular figure of the Yankee jack-of-all-trades, who changed his occupation often and unfailingly succeeded, conditioned many to oppose a merit service. An era of wide opportunities for profit and great instability of social stratification was conducive to such a symbol.

Regardless of the opposition to and limited potential of the diplomatic service, it survived. Perhaps it is as important to discover why

[205] See Adelbert Sageser, *The First Two Decades of the Pendelton Act* (Lincoln, Neb., 1935); Fish, *op. cit.*; Ari Hoogenboom, "The Pendleton Act and the Civil Service," *American Historical Review*, LXIV (January, 1959), 301–18; Leonard D. White, *The Republican Era* (New York: Macmillan, 1958), pp. 278–345; Paul D. Van Riper, *History of the United States Civil Service* (Evanston, Ill.: Row, Peterson & Co., 1958), pp. 30–168.

it survived as it is to analyze the sources of its deficiencies. What sustained the service in such a hostile environment? It can be argued that some of the forces which crippled it also sustained it. If the Executive-Legislative struggle succeeded only in diffusing authority over administration, it also established a belief among many that control of the service was strictly Executive and that Congress should not tamper with it excessively. If the spoils system prevented a career from arising, it also prevented the service from being dissolved. Describing the effect of a threatened slash in diplomatic personnel on Congress, one critic wrote:

> Congress did not and does not want such a measure of this kind. At bottom, the majority dislike such a measure, for it cuts off patronage, and each one of them is the center of a group of friends whose political interests have been bound together for years, and any act, promoted by one, tending to withdraw a political benefit from another, is regarded as something akin to crime.[206]

If qualified isolationists favored only minimal relations, they at least recognized that a diplomatic service was probably the best means for conducting them.

The service, however, also had its dedicated supporters. There were, for instance, "diplomatic realists," men who were convinced that the United States was irrevocably linked, for good or ill, to the world. An early congressman sagely remarked, "The project of abolishing our foreign intercourse [is] perfectly chimerical, and when a resolution should be offered to that effect, it should be accompanied by a proposal to encompass our seaboard by a magic circle, and to build a Chinese wall on our frontier." [207] With the struggle for possession of the continent over, "the number of our errant countrymen so much larger," [208] and the irresistible commercial pressures for new markets in the Orient, the argument increased in intensity. During the debate over the Act of 1855, Representative Perkins assumed that "the age of entire national isolation has passed." [209] Near the end of the period, Secretary of State Frederick T. Frelinghuysen argued, "While the United States are separated from most foreign nations by a wide expanse of sea, they are not commercially and politically iso-

---

[206] Rhodes, *op. cit.*, p. 172.

[207] *Annals of Congress*, VII, 5 Cong., 1 sess. (March 2, 1798), 1150 (Representative H. G. Otis of Massachusetts).

[208] "American Diplomacy," *Atlantic*, XXII (September, 1868), 353.

[209] *Cong. Globe*, Part 1, 33 Cong., 2 sess. (January 11, 1855), p. 244. See also *ibid.*, Part 1, 35 Cong., 2 sess. (January 25, 1859), p. 593 (speech by Representative Lawrence M. Keitt of South Carolina).

lated or independent of foreign political and commercial entanglements." [210] Along with the qualified isolationists, the realists outnumbered those seeking to end the service and contributed to sustaining it through the nineteenth century.

Not all who thought about foreign commerce believed that the resourcefulness of the individual entrepreneur or the efficiency of the consular service alone would suffice. Many understood the needs of commerce and knew that only a diplomatic service could deal with crippling tariff walls and arbitrary practices. In the first serious debate on a permanent service, Representative Robert G. Harper asserted, "But those great and general interests of commerce, which form the basis of treaties, and are among the most important objects of national intercourse, and of the law of nations, are wholly above the reach of consuls, and wholly confined to those public agents whom we call Ministers." [211] This position was frequently reiterated by other congressmen, members of the Executive, and publicists. The period which separated these early statements from Representative Jonathan Chace's assertion in 1884 that "when you propose to strike down the diplomatic service, you aim a blow at the commerce of the United States in foreign countries as directly as if you should strike at the consular service," [212] was marked by a stubborn defense of the diplomatic service. Many had come to agree with Secretary Frelinghuysen's conclusion that "the consul aids the individual and protects separate interests, while the minister acts for the nation and guards its general political and commercial welfare." [213]

On a more practical plane of evidence, the one long-standing criterion for continuing a mission was the amount of trade that existed between a specific country and the United States.[214] Although legations were maintained for political reasons as well, it was generally felt that political relations flowed from commercial relations. If trade became negligible, few reasons could be marshaled strong enough to save the mission's appropriation. Often, however, Congress would support a legation, regardless of its gross commercial value, if it were

[210] House Exec. Doc. 146, 48 Cong., 1 sess. (April 28, 1884), p. 1. See also "The Rise of American Diplomacy," *Boston Review*, IV (September, 1864), 463.

[211] *Annals of Congress*, VII, 5 Cong., 1 sess. (January 19, 1798), 871.

[212] *Cong. Rec.*, XV, 48 Cong., 1 sess. (May 15, 1884), 4190 (Representative Jonathan Chace of Rhode Island).

[213] House Exec. Doc. 146, 48 Cong., 1 sess. (April 28, 1884), p. 1.

[214] E.g., *Cong. Globe*, Part 1, 33 Cong., 2 sess. (January 11, 1855), p. 245; House Rept. 23, 44 Cong., 1 sess. (January 28, 1876), p. 1; *Annals of Congress*, VII, 5 Cong., 1 sess. (January 19, 1798), 870–71 (speech by Representative Robert G. Harper of South Carolina); Senate Rept. 154, 40 Cong., 2 sess., (July 2, 1868), p. 13. See also *Cong. Globe*, Part 1, 35 Cong., 2 sess. (January 19, 1859), p. 460; *Cong. Globe*, Part 1, 26 Cong., 1 sess. (May 2, 1840), p. 373 (Representative Edward Everett of Massachusetts).

important commercially to a single region. Further recognition of diplomacy's importance to commerce was in the Act of 1856. It authorized the President to publish "commercial information communicated to him by such diplomatic and consular officers, as he may deem important to the public interest." [215]

Prior to the Civil War, to whom were legations valuable in economic terms? Domestic manufacturers usually had both their supplies and markets within the nation. The country's stable export items, such as cotton and tobacco, were seldom frustrated by adverse tariffs. It was to the nation's shipowners and importers that permanent legations were valuable. Consequently, the diplomatic service's chief commercial support came from large shipping areas — coastal New England, the Middle Atlantic, and a few southern ports. The merchants needed officials with greater authority than consuls to press claims over seizures and defaults in contracts. The diplomatic service alone was capable of dealing with recalcitrant governments and opening world ports to American shipping through advantageous trade treaties. Commercial interests were among the influential forces in the attempted revamping of the service in the 1850's.[216] Whenever drastic cuts in the appropriations were threatened, their representatives were the service's most stalwart defenders. After the Civil War, when manufacturing began to expand abroad and to compete with European goods, the first recourse of the manufacturer was to the consular service to find agents, verify contracts, and insure payments. When tariff doors started to shut, particularly from 1880 onward, manufacturers began turning toward the diplomatic service. The connection between diplomacy and commerce established in the nineteenth century a precedent that was to be important in the service's later professionalization.

Necessity was not the only supporter of the diplomatic service. A deeper irrational force was present. For many proponents of continuous diplomacy, the honor of America as a nation was tightly linked with the service. The act creating the Department of Foreign Affairs in 1781 asserted, "The extent and rising power of these United States entitle them to a place among the great potentates of Eu-

[215] 11 Stat. 52 (August 18, 1856).

[216] *Cong. Globe*, Part 1, 33 Cong., 2 sess. (January 11, 1855), pp. 245–46. Representative Perkins advocated his bill on the grounds "that the commercial interest of the country has repeatedly protested against the incompatibility of many of its provisions and their utter inadequacy to meet the wants of our extended trade." See also *Cong. Globe*, Appendix, 33 Cong., 2 sess. (February 7, 1855), pp. 162–64. It is significant that American shipbuilding reached its pre-1914 peak in 1854–55. See J. G. Randall, *Civil War and Reconstruction* (New York, 1937), p. 84.

rope." [217] This theme was often repeated during the period. In 1868, Senator Patterson was inspired to propose reform of the service partly because of "the continued failure of European governments to recognize in their diplomatic intercourse the position which this Republic is entitled to hold among the first-class powers in the world." [218] E. L. Godkin was convinced that "nothing can prevent us from playing a great part in the future of modern society, in influencing both its manners and ideals; the larger part we play, the more important will our diplomacy become." [219] For them the diminution of the service's strength was unthinkable. Their influence, while hard to assess, affected as well the struggles for higher salaries, ministerial residences, and an ambassadorial class.[220]

Perhaps the single most consistent supporter of the diplomatic service was the President. No matter how a man felt before he assumed office, once he did he began to understand the difficulties and painstaking preparations, irrespective of who signed the document, which preceded any treaty. He began to appreciate the necessity for permanent diplomacy in pursuing claims. He began, above all, to comprehend the fortuitous circumstances which often led to war and the indispensability of an agent and his staff on the spot. Also his executive prerogative over foreign affairs and the fact that the service was his personal representative abroad made him loath to see it curtailed. Finally, no early Executive wished to forgo the patronage opportunity that the service offered him.

Adams' conversion was only the first. Even the Jeffersonian leaders, who opposed the service when they were without office, became its defenders when in power. Madison had sent "abroad nearly every man in America whose pretensions to civil distinction were considerable." [221] Monroe, like his predecessor, brooked no talk about reducing the service.[222] Whenever it faced the paring knife of appropriations, pleas would be made by the administration — usually with success.

Many miscellaneous factors should be considered. The service's absence from the public eye and its infrequent appearance before Congress (and then with other appropriation bills) kept the service

[217] Gaillard Hunt (ed.), *Journals of the Continental Congress* (Washington, 1912), XIX, 42–44. The act was passed on January 10, 1781.

[218] Senate Rept. 154, 40 Cong., 2 sess. (July 2, 1868), p. 25; *Cong. Globe*, Part 1, 35 Cong., 2 sess. (January 25, 1859), pp. 592–93; *Foreign Relations*, I (1867–68), 645.

[219] "The American Diplomatic Service," *Nation*, VI (February 27, 1868), 166.

[220] See below, chaps. two and three.

[221] Henry Adams, *Gallatin*, p. 517.

[222] Ford, *Writings of John Quincy Adams*, VI, 248.

from continuous criticism.[223] Also, no little weight should be given sheer administrative inertia. The task and cost of ending the service were beyond the energies of a single Congress. One attempt to save $40,000 on the service would itself have cost $20,000.[224]

Thus, an amalgam of many forces sustained the service in its hostile environment. Its response to the new world relations was built upon this earlier defense and against the other attitudes and practices prevailing in the nineteenth century.

[223] Oscar S. Straus wrote, "The people are perhaps less familiar with the duties of our diplomatic and consular agents than with any other branch of the public service. This is primarily due to the fact that the duties devolving upon these agents are not performed at home under the eyes of our citizens, but abroad, in foreign lands" (see Oscar S. Straus, "The Reform of the Consular Service," *Proceedings of the National Civil Service Reform League* [1894], pp. 97–106).

[224] House Rept. 166, 28 Cong., 1 sess. (February 15, 1844). Representative Ingersoll sought to abolish ten missions and to amalgamate others.

CHAPTER TWO

REFORM AND THE CHANGING
ADMINISTRATIVE ENVIRONMENT
1860–1906

Voices advocating reform were not entirely silent before 1888. Their first assumption was the necessity of a diplomatic service, and they sought to improve its structure. Early reformers, particularly Secretary Livingston in 1830 and Representative Perkins in 1854–55, wished to gear the service to the trade it served and to remove excesses. The former was concerned with provisions for sufficient salaries, representation, and legation archives, while the latter aimed at perfecting the method of compensation.[1] Later reformers, especially after the Civil War, concerned themselves with the personnel system in the service.

The post–Civil War reformers, however, were by no means the first to object to the spoils system in diplomacy. In 1834, one representative maintained, "They [diplomatic positions] are places merely for the reward of partisans; places of refuge for worn-out, useless, second-rate politicians."[2] Shortly before the war, another congressman asked:

> If they are places to which party mendicants are assigned,
> if they are infirmaries where your inferior and disappointed
> leaders are put, whose fault is it? Is it not the fault of your

[1] House Exec. Doc. 94, 22 Cong., 2 sess. (February 7, 1833); House Rept. 348, 33 Cong., 1 sess. (August 1, 1854).

[2] *Register of Debates*, X, 23 Cong., 1 sess. (April 30, 1834), 3881 (speech by Representative W. Ransom Davis of South Carolina).

parties, the fault of your Administration? Should you not carry your reforming hand where reform is needed?[3]

But the postwar reformers concentrated on the issue of patronage and its ramifications. In the *North American Review*, James Russell Lowell complained that positions in the diplomatic service "had been too often shamelessly peculated in to pay the wages of dirty political work at home."[4]

What reasons did these reformers give for opposing the spoils system? An author in the *International Review* wanted an end to the "whole brood of evils [which] have dishonored our Government abroad," or as the professional reformer John Hoyt called them, "the conspicuous acts which have been in flagrant violation of the most sacred obligations."[5] Others were less polemical. They wanted to put economy into the operations of the service, to increase efficiency, or to place a premium on training, experience, and ability.[6] They wished to avoid what E. L. Godkin had earlier deplored: ". . . that all kinds of men are, for all sorts of reasons, sent to represent us abroad, [who] inevitably lessen the social consideration enjoyed by even our best of ministers."[7] Although one reformer desired a service "as elastic as the progress of civilization itself, and at the same time as watchful and appreciative of the symptoms which reveal the decay of nations,"[8] most sought primarily "to have, always and everywhere, the right man in the right place."[9] Behind this lay the presupposition that members of the service, especially secretaries of legation, "represent the Government and the interests of the United States, not the President nor the interests of any political party."[10]

What struck many of the critics was the apparent inconsistency with the practice assumed to have existed in the past in the armed forces, the judiciary, and in many of the departments of government, including the consular service.[11] Minister Yeamans wrote to Seward in

[3] *Cong. Globe*, Part 1, 35 Cong., 2 sess. (January 25, 1859), p. 593 (speech by Representative Lawrence M. Keitt); *Ibid.* (January 24, 1859), p. 547 (speech by Representative Owen Lovejoy of Illinois).

[4] James R. Lowell, "Diplomatic Correspondence," *North American Review*, XCVIII (April, 1864), 620. See also "American Diplomatic Service," *Nation*, VI (February 27, 1868), 165.

[5] "Diplomacy," *International Review*, VI (January, 1879), 306; John W. Hoyt, *Of Appointment and Removal* (New York, 1884), p. 13.

[6] Senate Rept. 154, 40 Cong., 2 sess. (July 2, 1868), p. 2.

[7] "American Ministers Abroad," *Nation*, IV (February 14, 1867), 133.

[8] Senate Rept. 154, 40 Cong., 2 sess. (July 2, 1868), p. 27.

[9] "American Diplomacy," *Atlantic*, XXII (September, 1868), 356.

[10] Eugene Schuyler, *American Diplomacy* (New York, 1886), p. 131.

[11] E.g., Albert Rhodes, "Our Diplomats and Consuls," *Scribners*, XIII (December, 1876), 170. The progress made in the consular service, although sporadic, is still note-

1866, "The course of our own government in this respect is in marked contrast, not only with the policy of other governments, but with its own care and solicitude to prepare young men for the army and navy."[12] Similarly, E. L. Godkin, after asking that the United States make diplomacy a profession, added, "just as we do the regular navy, the regular army, and the judiciary."[13]

But the system seemed most backward when compared with the diplomatic services of other nations. The Report on Retrenchment in 1868 argued that "to compete successfully with the agents of foreign powers, and to conduct advantageously the political and commercial affairs of our country," it was necessary to adopt the "best in diplomatic . . . policy practiced by the more enlightened governments of Europe."[14] Lowell believed, "We are undoubtedly at a disadvantage, as respects the other great nations, in not having a regular diplomatic service."[15] A New York congressman pointed out that "all leading nations in Europe educate their diplomats," and recommended the United States follow suit.[16]

While Representative Perkins claimed every President, Secretary of State, and minister, both Whig and Democrat, as supporters of his attempt to remodel the service,[17] the later reformers were few in number and usually not in any official capacity. They were independently wealthy, upper middle class, and largely of English descent. They were usually, although not always, Republicans and dwelt in eastern urban areas. Often they were professional men, members of whose families had once been prominent in governing circles. Becoming first alarmed by the expansion of patronage under Lincoln, they fell into a state of panic as they increasingly discovered that the world of Ulysses Grant did not belong to them. This resentment mounted with every report of fraud occurring under the Grant administration. They read the *North American Review*, the *Nation*, the *Independent*,

worthy. The Act of 1856 authorized the appointment of a corps of consular pupils. See 11 Stat. 52 (August 18, 1856). This provision, however, was eliminated the following year. On October 1, 1866, President Johnson issued an Executive Order requiring an examination for appointments to minor consulates. One examination was given, and the scheme was abandoned (see 120.11/22, Minutes of the Board of Examiners of the Consular Service). A second Order was issued by Grant on March 14, 1873. It was based on the first Civil Service Act of March 3, 1871. Again, only one examination was given (see 120.11/22, Minutes of the Board of Examiners of the Consular Service). There were also attempts to establish a career service for consular clerks.

[12] *Foreign Relations*, I (1867–68), p. 650 (letter dated December 4, 1866).

[13] "A Word with Prospective Ambassadors," *Nation* (September 3, 1868), VII, 187.

[14] Senate Rept. 154, 40 Cong., 2 sess. (July 2, 1868), p. 2. See also "American Diplomacy," *Atlantic*, XXII (September, 1868), 354.

[15] James Russell Lowell, *op. cit.*, p. 620.

[16] *Cong. Globe*, Part 1, 42 Cong., 3 sess. (January 23, 1873), p. 808.

[17] *Cong. Globe*, Part 1, 33 Cong., 2 sess. (January 11, 1855), p. 245.

Scribner's Magazine, and the *New York Evening Post*. When the National Civil Service Reform League was organized in 1881, they were its leading members.[18] The diplomatic service did not engage their full attention, but it became a natural area of concern for a group which wished to perfect the entire governmental establishment. A correspondent to the *Nation* wrote, "As we are reasonably confident of having an era of reform in the various branches of the Government service . . . , it may not be amiss to direct attention to the urgent need of change and improvement in a branch of the service which ordinarily receives far less attention than its importance merits — the foreign service." [19] The service's importance increased for them as they took to residing abroad in official and unofficial capacities.

Deep social implications underlay the reformers' insistence upon administrative change. They wished to create a "free trade" in government positions. In such a merit system, which excluded all privilege, they and their immediate descendants would populate the diplomatic service — and the rest of the civil service as well. This demand for merit and competitive examinations was the prerogative of the well-educated alone. And no attempt was made to hide the class origins of the reform movement. Godkin wanted the service filled with "representatives of what is best in American society, of that element in it which gives it its strongest claims to gratitude and respect of the civilized world." [20] He begrudged the right of "the majority of political managers," who were ignorant "of a man's social gifts," to influence the selection of diplomats.[21] In *American Diplomacy*, Eugene Schuyler maintained a similar position:

> One other qualification is absolutely necessary at all events
> in civilized countries, that the person appointed should be
> a gentleman, that is, acquainted with the ways of the world
> and the usages and manners of the best society in each cap-
> ital in which he will be expected to move — that of the gov-
> erning classes.[22]

The reformers, however, were against wealth as the standard of appointment as much as they were against politics. The postwar boom, they thought, had created a class of *nouveau riche* capitalists "who have made fortunes rapidly, and to say the least are not attrac-

---

[18] See Frank M. Stewart, *History of the National Civil Service Reform League* (Austin, Tex., 1929), *passim*. Three of the League's first six Presidents — Joseph Choate, Charles W. Eliot, and Richard H. Dana — showed great interest in the service's development.

[19] Letter to the Editor, *Nation*, XL (March 26, 1885), 259.

[20] "The American Diplomatic Service," *Nation*, VI (February 27, 1868) 165–66.

[21] "American Ministers Abroad," *Nation*, IV (February 14, 1867), 133.

[22] Eugene Schuyler, *op. cit.*, pp. 122–24.

tive in mind and manners." [23] Wealth alone was unacceptable. Education and good breeding were their criteria for office-holding. While these ultimately depended upon wealth, the reformers insisted that, by advancing them, they were not departing from republican thought. They held that an office should be open to all who qualified intellectually for it, and they sought to make the intellectual standard as high as possible. They refused to sanction "the property qualification in diplomacy." [24] The most eloquent spokesman for this view was Representative Robert Hitt, a former secretary of legation and an avid reformer. To Congesses that persisted in denying an adequate wage structure and even supported the concept of an economic elite in government,[25] he declared, "What we want in such a post is not mere wealth but ability, the real merit of the man; we want judgment, experience, information, character, but such men will be barred from this service unless they are wealthy." [26]

Universal among the reformers was an admiration for British institutions. This admiration stemmed partly from praiseworthy administration and partly from the belief that had they been British subjects their claims to leadership would have been recognized. In 1876, Dorman Eaton was assigned by President Hayes, who sympathized with the group, to investigate the British system of civil service administration with an eye toward perfecting the American civil service. Eaton's recommendation for the diplomatic service was the adoption of the English system of examinations, probation, and promotion by merit.[27] This admiration was also displayed by friendly congressmen. Congressman Jonathan Chace observed:

> Whenever a change of administration occurs in Great Britain these [members of the Diplomatic Service] men know that no change will take place in regard to their positions, but all over the world today every man in the diplomatic and consular services of the United States is packing his trunk and engaging his passage preparatory to returning home.[28]

The first proposal of the reformers for the diplomatic service, as it was for the rest of the civil service, was an end to rotation and the

[23] "American Ministers Abroad," *Nation*, IV (February 14, 1867), 133.
[24] Andrew D. White, *Autobiography*, I, 358.
[25] Samuel S. Cox, *Beauties of Diplomacy* (Washington, 1876), p. 8; *Cong. Rec.*, XVIII, 49 Cong., 2 sess. (February 10, 1887), 1592.
[26] *Cong. Rec.*, XV, 48 Cong., 1 sess. (May 14, 1884), 4166.
[27] Dorman B. Eaton, *Civil Service in Great Britain* (New York, 1880), p. 311.
[28] *Cong. Rec.*, XVI, 48 Cong., 2 sess. (January 10, 1885), 615. See also Senate Rept. 154, 40 Cong., 2 sess. (July 2, 1868), p. 4; Lester M. Dorman, "A Century of Civil Service," *Scribner's*, XV (March, 1878), 395.

establishment of security of tenure. While the reformers were not the first to complain about the system,[29] they were the first to incorporate its abolition as part of the general rehabilitation of the service. Yeamans, for instance, asserted, "I avow myself unable to conceive a greater or more apparent error in administration than the theory of rotation in office *merely for the sake of rotation.*" He recommended good behavior as the standard for tenure.[30] This thought was translated into the Report on Retrenchment, which argued, "Continuance is necessary to usefulness in office under our present system of appointments." [31]

The second plank in the professionalization of the service was promotion by merit in a graded service. Again there were several predecessors to the reformers. Secretary Livingston, in his oft-quoted report of 1833, conjectured, if young men "of education" could be attracted through allowances to serve as secretaries to ministers, "they will acquire habits, knowledge, and talents, which will fit them to serve in the higher ranks of diplomacy, according to their merits." [32] Congress also had accepted the grading and classification of clerical positions in the domestic civil service in 1853.[33] But the reformers made it an integral part of their comprehensive program, occasionally insisting that ministerial level be included in the promotion scheme.

On this point, however, the reformers were not in agreement. In 1864, Lowell advocated a system "in which our ministers might be trained to their profession, and in which promotion should be the reward of merit." [34] Patterson's report stated that promotion by merit to the office of envoy extraordinary and minister plenipotentiary would enable the officer "to exercise a far-reaching and transcendent influence abroad and at home." [35] On the other hand, a secretary of legation publicly held, ". . . it is quite as well that the head of the embassy should be a *new* man. He will attach much less importance to trifles, and act more fearlessly in emergencies. . . . The old diplomates grumble, but it is clearly for the advantage of the country." [36] A writer in the *Nation* thought that "a new Administration should fill the chief diplomatic posts with men in hearty sympathy with its purposes." [37]

[29] *Cong. Globe*, Part 1, 33 Cong., 2 sess. (February 24, 1855), p. 761 (speech by Senator John M. Clayton of Delaware).
[30] *Foreign Relations*, I (1867–68), 645–46.
[31] Senate Rept. 154, 40 Cong., 2 sess. (July 2, 1868), p. 1.
[32] House Exec. Doc. 94, 22 Cong., 2 sess. (February 7, 1833), p. 7.
[33] 10 Stat. 189 (March 3, 1853).
[34] Lowell, *op. cit.*, p. 620.
[35] Senate Rept. 154, 40 Cong., 2 sess. (July 2, 1868), p. 4.
[36] Wickham Hoffman, *Camp, Court, and Siege*, pp. 154–55.
[37] "The Diplomatic Service," *Nation*, XL (June 11, 1885), 476.

The third major plank was entrance by examination. Like the other proposals, the system of examinations for offices had several precedents. But the isolation of the well-educated from power after the Civil War made it a more vital proposition to the reformers. Again Senator Patterson's report summarized the position:

> . . . the person nominated for the diplomatic career will not be admitted without examination, and only well qualified persons, equipped with the requisite linguistic and other capacities, being able to pass an examination, the service in the future will be conducted by men who will know how to make the best use of their many opportunities for the public utility.[38]

The seeming success of the examination in the domestic service encouraged the reformers to recommend it for the diplomatic service.[39]

Ridding the diplomatic service of the "baneful influence of politics" by applying the formula of civil service reform was insufficient unless the special qualifications for a professional career were also obtainable. This problem was realized by many reformers, and they frequently pointed out the vocational deficiencies of the existing system, particularly in respect to the knowledge of the appropriate foreign language. They felt that diplomacy on all levels required a mastery of "the laws, customs, industries, and products of our own land . . . and . . . the laws, pursuits, language, and character of the people to whom they [the diplomatists] are accredited." [40] To expect amateurs to succeed at diplomacy, "however able and skillful they may be in other things," was not unlike putting "the unpracticed neophyte in figures upon the Principia or Mechanique Celeste with the expectation that he will understand and enjoy its abstruse deductions." [41] There were two variations on the theme of specialization. Some, led by Senator Patterson, argued for a probationary period in the Department of State for all prospective secretaries of legation.[42] Others, led by Herbert B. Adams and the National Bureau of Education, argued for the establishment of a diplomatic and consular academy to train the members of the lower service.[43] Neither proposal attracted much support. The whole attempt to create a specialized service was subordinated to the more important task of extirpating political considerations from appointment and tenure. Besides, the

[38] Senate Rept. 154, 40 Cong., 2 sess. (July 2, 1868), p. 4.
[39] "The Diplomatic Service," *Nation*, XL (June 11, 1885), 476.
[40] Senate Rept. 154, 40 Cong., 2 sess. (July 2, 1868), p. 2.
[41] *Ibid.*, p. 1.
[42] *Ibid.*, pp. 4–5.
[43] Letter to the Editor, *New York Times*, July 1, 1914, p. 10.

reformers probably assumed axiomatically that the well-educated possessed all the qualifications for diplomacy.

The fact that Americans were "essentially a commercial and navigating people" gave their diplomatic service a much more specific character than was found in the services of other countries.[44] So inextricably linked were commerce and diplomacy for many of the reformers that they advocated the amalgamation of the consular and diplomatic services. The opposition was large. People argued, not without reason, that the services "were as different as the two professions of law and medicine," and that international usage would oppose the consolidation.[45] Social differences undoubtedly influenced some who opposed the move.[46] Others, however, were convinced that the United States should create the precedent and hope that "in Europe . . . the progress of civilization may even there do away with the prejudice." [47] Of all their recommendations, this was the first upon which there was any action. The Patterson bill had proposed amalgamation, but the whole bill was ignored in Congress.[48] In 1876, however, Eugene Schuyler, whose experience had mainly been at semi-commercial diplomatic posts, aided in the drafting of a bill which combined the positions of consul general in many areas with secretary of legation.[49] But its success was due more to its overtones of economy than to its soundness as a principle of administration. Amalgamation as a concept was still premature.

By the 1880's the growing strength of the reformers was mirrored in Executive pronouncements. Many Presidential messages to Congress referred to the needs of the diplomatic machinery.[50] Whenever the reformers saw some of their work take hold, they publicized it widely in the hope of preparing a more favorable atmosphere for their recommendations.[51] However naïve their presuppositions may have

[44] *Cong. Globe*, Part 1, 33 Cong., 2 sess. (January 11, 1855), p. 245 (speech by Representative Perkins).

[45] *Cong. Rec.*, XV, 48 Cong., 1 sess. (May 14, 1884), 4159 (speech by Representative Daniel D. Burns of Missouri).

[46] Gillespie and Wallace (eds.), *Journal of Ben Moran*, I, 580. On August 17, 1859, Moran wrote, "I can state most deliberately that they are as a class [consuls] a most pretentious and ignorant set. . . ." See also Evelyn Schuyler Schaeffer (ed.), *Eugene Schuyler*, pp. 150–51. Eugene Schuyler wrote in 1881, "Generally speaking, in Europe diplomats come from the upper and consuls from the middle class; and this looks like putting a man above his sphere."

[47] Senate Rept. 154, 40 Cong., 2 sess. (July 2, 1868), p. 14.

[48] 40 Cong., 2 sess., S587 (July 2, 1868) (copy obtained from the Library of Congress). See also *Cong. Globe*, Part IV, 40 Cong., 2 sess. (July 2, 1868), p. 3671. The bill was titled "To provide for retrenchment and greater efficiency in the diplomatic and consular service."

[49] 19 Stat. 170 (August 15, 1876). See also Schaeffer, *op. cit.*, pp. 150–51.

[50] J. D. Richardson (ed.), *Messages*, VIII, 242, 506, 783; IX, 33.

[51] "The Diplomatic Service," *Nation*, XL (June 11, 1885), 476.

been, the reformers had formulated over the years a comprehensive program for the diplomatic service. When the time became ripe for doing something about the state of diplomatic administration, their program was the obvious choice.

The post–Civil War period saw significant internal changes take place in the diplomatic service. The increasing tenure and the specific long-term records have been already noted. These long-term members, unlike their predecessors, were not exclusively located in non-European legations. They occupied some of the most important European posts in the lower service.[52] Generally, this difference arose out of the large increase in duties at the European posts and a change in the methods of appointment. Prior to the Civil War, the more important political figures received the ministerships to European capitals and usually selected their own staffs. Less important political figures received non-European posts, and the Department of State could generally resist their patronage demands and appoint others to secretaryships. Because of independent factors, many of these non-European appointments were of considerable duration. While there was no change after the Civil War in the relative importance of the ministerships, there was a change in the position of the secretary of legation. Owing to increased social and work demands at some posts in Europe, the secretaryships became patronage plums themselves. The Department began filling them and shifting the more temporary patronage claims to non-European posts.[53] With one party remaining in office throughout most of the period, it is not surprising that several European secretaries stayed for long terms at their posts. In addition to the tenure statistics, four and five, respectively, entered the service after experience in the Department of State and the consular service. This situation was repeated in terms of post-diplomatic experience with six entering the Department and five the consular service.[54]

Other suggestions of the later career service emerged during the period. The Department of State began emphasizing the continuity of many of its appointments in its *Register*.[55] More significant, how-

[52] Benjamin Moran was in London, Henry Vignaud in Paris, and Nicholas Fish in Berlin. *Biog. Reg.* (1870–88), *passim.*

[53] See John Bigelow, *Retrospections*, II, 556–57; William R. Thayer, *Hay*, I, 251. In a letter to William Cullen Bryant, dated May 16, 1865, Bigelow laments the fact that he does not have the power to select his own secretaries. The entry from Hay's Diary, dated February 2, 1867, describes Secretary Seward offering secretaryships in Europe to Hay.

[54] Numbers found by comparing biographical data in author's possession with *Biog. Reg.* (1870–88).

[55] *Biog. Reg.* (1875–84). 1875: 4; 1876: 5; 1877: 3; 1878: 11; 1879: 9; 1880: 11; 1882: 6; 1883: 14; 1884: 11. The practice ceased after 1884. The *Register* for 1881 was unobtainable.

ever, were the changes in the concept of "service" held by some officers. They began voicing their disapproval of the doctrine of rotation and the refusal of the government to honor experience with continued tenure. They objected to the unceremonious and insensitive means used to end a person's career in diplomacy. In 1866, John Hay wrote to Albert Rhodes, "I leave the service of the ungrateful Republic in a week or two." [56] Henry Adams, while not a member of the service, summed up the position for many secretaries of legation: "He could not buy a post of Secretary at Vienna or Madrid . . . until the next President should do him the honor to turn him out." [57]

Along with the disapproval of rotation came a desire to make the service a career in its fullest sense. The period saw men enter the service determined to make diplomacy a life's work. Through the vagaries of American politics, they somehow maintained for long periods their positions. [58] Chief among them were Benjamin Moran, Henry Vignaud, Nicholas Fish, Eugene Schuyler, and Henry White. All but one of these men entered through political preferment. Benjamin Moran had been private secretary to Buchanan when the latter was minister to Britain; Fish was the son of Grant's Secretary of State; Schuyler entered through the patronage of Andrew Curtin, minister to St. Petersburg; and White had many connections in political circles.[59] Henry Vignaud alone entered on merit. A Louisianian by birth, a Democrat by politics, and a journalist by profession, Vignaud made his way to Paris during the Civil War to serve in the delegation of the Confederacy seeking French recognition.[60] After the war, he remained in Paris, serving briefly as secretary to the Rumanian legation and later as interpreter to the Alabama Claims Commission. While minister to Paris, Elihu Washburne, a Republican, turned to Vignaud for aid and later recommended him for appointment on the strength of Vignaud's ability.[61] He was commissioned in 1876.[62]

All had expressed the intention of remaining in diplomacy and making it a career. Schuyler wrote of his "strong preference for a diplomatic career and his unwillingness to give it up." [63] Henry White maintained:

[56] William R. Thayer, *Hay*, I, 246.

[57] Henry Adams, *Education of Henry Adams* (New York: Modern Library, 1931), p. 210.

[58] Moran served 27 years; Henry Vignaud, 36 years; Fish, 15 years; Schuyler, 14 years; and White, 24 years.

[59] *DAB*, XIII, 151; VI, 400; Schaeffer, *op. cit.*, p. 31; Allan Nevins, *Henry White: Thirty Years of American Diplomacy* (New York, 1930), pp. 42–44. Among them were Seceretarget of State Frelinghuysen, Hamilton Fish, Chauncey Depew, Bayard Cutting, "and others."

[60] *DAB*, XIX, 268–70.

[61] Elihu Washburne, *Recollections of a Minister to France* (New York, 1887), II, 325.

[62] *Biog. Reg.* (1876), p. 14.

[63] Schaeffer, *op. cit.*, pp. 50–51.

I resolved to become the nucleus, if possible, of a permanent service. . . . I had a feeling that it would be possible for the United States to have, as the other leading powers of the world then had, a non-partisan (so far as domestic politics were concerned) service, to which appointments should be made on the basis of fitness only.[64]

Furthermore, all of them were promoted within the service. Moran went from assistant to first secretary in London and then to minister resident in Portugal.[65] Vignaud passed from second secretary to first and remained so until 1909.[66] Fish followed a similar course in Germany, eventually becoming minister to Belgium.[67] Schuyler served in several capacities and rose to minister to Sardinia.[68] White, although he reached his highest success in a later period, held secretaryships in Vienna and London.[69]

Not all of them succeeded in making diplomacy a lifetime career. Moran, Schuyler, and Fish were ousted during Cleveland's first administration. Only White and Vignaud survived. The former was saved through the intervention of friends,[70] and Vignaud was becoming an exception to all rules. While tenure was not guaranteed, while promotion hinged usually on partisan considerations, while longevity depended upon the continuity of a single party in power, the post–Civil War period still saw definite suggestions of a career in diplomacy.

These internal and external movements toward reform occurred in a vacuum. The "climate of opinion" was not yet hospitable to change. The issues of the 1888 election, however, indicated a changing orientation in American interests. The tariff, the Bering Sea controversy, and the Sackville-West scandal, all with foreign policy implications, surprisingly predominated over other issues. Every facet of the new orientation argued that the existing system was inadequate and that to assume the system's past success guaranteed its future efficacy was fallacious. Between 1888 and 1906, not only was a favorable "climate" established but many internal strides were taken toward making the diplomatic service a career.

One profound alteration was in the domestic view of America's

[64] Nevins, *Henry White,* p. 45.
[65] *DAB,* XIII, 150–51.
[66] *DAB,* XIX, 268–70.
[67] *Biog. Reg.* (1882), p. 11.
[68] *DAB,* XVI, 472
[69] Under Theodore Roosevelt, White served as ambassador to Italy and later as ambassador to France.
[70] Nevins, *Henry White,* pp. 58–59.

international position. Publicists increasingly stressed that "America's importance in international politics has been steadily increasing." [71] President Harrison wrote in 1889, ". . . we must be equipped for emergencies, and every now and then, even at the smallest and most remote courts, there is a critical need of an American representative to protect American citizens and American interests." [72] To prove these contentions, Herbert Peirce pointed out that even with a nation as commercially, politically, and geographically isolated from the United States as Russia, a single year's correspondence amounted to 2,300 letters, "many of which were of considerable length." [73]

While the pressures of polyglot immigration and problems of Americans traveling abroad were two of the more obvious manifestations of the new position, the position was not clarified for many until the Spanish-American War in 1898. Thereafter the erstwhile "simplicity of our business" abroad had to give way to more complex considerations. George L. Rives in the *Forum* insisted:

> Whether we like it or not, it is plain that the country is now entering a period in its history in which it will necessarily be brought into far closer and more complex relations with all the other great Powers of the world. We shall now and henceforth be looked upon as having cast aside our traditional attitude of isolation.[74]

This new role, people argued, included membership "in all the great combinations of the world's politics." [75]

Their prediction of America's new diplomatic importance seemed immediately to be confirmed. Referring to Hay's first Open Door note, Representative Adams maintained, "No greater recognition was ever given to any nation upon the earth and no greater evidence of the position that this country has attained in diplomatic relations will be found anywhere. . . . " [76] F. M. Huntington Wilson in 1906 believed that Hay's notes "placed America in the diplomatic world where she had never been before," and added, with reference to the

[71] H. C. Chatfield-Taylor, "American Diplomacy in Europe," *North American Review*, CLXIII (July, 1896), 125.

[72] Benjamin Harrison, *This Country of Ours* (New York, 1889), p. 196.

[73] Herbert H. D. Peirce, "Our Diplomatic and Consular Service," *Arena*, XVII (May, 1897), 911.

[74] "Our Need of a Permanent Diplomatic Service," *Forum*, XXI (August, 1898), 710-11.

[75] Leon Mead, "The New Diplomacy," *North American Review*, CLXVIII (March, 1899), 377.

[76] *Cong. Rec.*, XXXIV, 56 Cong., 2 sess. (February 7, 1901), 2108-9 (speech by Representative Robert C. Adams of Pennsylvania).

Portsmouth Conference, "Had there been any doubts as to America's diplomatic leadership, that leadership was then positively confirmed." [77] Further confirmation of this role came from President Roosevelt. In his Fifth Annual Message, he asked for increased facilities for the Department of State because of "the growth of our present weight in the councils of the world." [78]

From America's new diplomatic importance, many drew a single conclusion. As the United States "will always be an important factor in the management of the affairs of the world," Representative Robert C. Adams warned his colleagues, "our country must equip itself and get ready to occupy that position." [79] More specifically, as George McAneny wrote in the *Century*, "the measure of our success must depend very largely on the fitness and on the special training of the men to whom we intrust the management of delicate foreign relations." [80] Their recommendation was a merit diplomatic service based on specialized training. So important did it seem to Brooks Adams that he exclaimed, "Questions of domestic administration can be relegated to the future to which they appertain; for the moment our foreign relations, which will brook no delay, may well absorb our attentions, for they involve peace and war." [81] Representative Longworth insisted, "It is too late now to allude to our diplomatic service as a luxury and not a necessity." [82]

At the qualified isolationists, who would admit that the new relations required effective responses, but who felt that diplomacy was technologically outmoded or would be vestigial once a treaty was signed, the publicists aimed their fire. A former minister to Britain, Edward Phelps, claimed, ". . . steam, power, the telegraph, invention . . . have brought foreign countries to our door and have carried us to theirs. The telegraph, rather than simplifying relations, had led to their complication." [83] Toward those who were confident that treaties were self-operating, Herbert Peirce trained his guns. "There is," he wrote in *The Arena*:

[77] F. M. Huntington Wilson, "The American Foreign Service," *Outlook*, LXXXII (March, 1906), 500.

[78] Theodore Roosevelt, *Writings*, ed. Herman Hagerdorn (New York, 1931), XV, 340. The speech is dated December 5, 1905.

[79] *Cong. Rec.*, XXXIV, 56 Cong., 2 sess. (February 7, 1901), 2110. See also Alfred T. Mahan, *The Interest of America in International Relations* (Boston, 1910), p. 178.

[80] "How Other Countries Do It," *Century*, LVII (February, 1899), 605.

[81] Brooks Adams, *America's Economic Supremacy* (Boston, 1900), p. 144.

[82] *Cong. Rec.*, XL, 59 Cong., 1 sess. (May 23, 1906), 7326.

[83] Edward John Phelps, *International Relations* (Burlington, Vt., 1889), p. 11. See also Perry Belmont, "The First Line of National Defense," *North American Review*, CCI (June, 1915), 886: "But at the time of these negotiations [Fisheries Question], he [Phelps] told the writer . . . that there was nothing more important to the interests of our Government than the establishment of a permanent diplomatic service."

no competent judicial authority for the interpretation and application of the laws of nations. Each nation interprets for itself at its own capital, the principles of these laws; and it is of the highest importance to each of the other nations to retain upon the spot, at that capital, competent and learned counsel of acknowledged ability, to plead the views of his own government.[84]

As well as in diplomatic negotiations, the new world relationship was felt in other very practical ways. Frequent were the requests from Americans residing abroad for efficient, trained diplomats to take care of their interests.[85] Of a more serious nature was the need for protecting naturalized citizens who were traveling abroad from conscription laws and arbitrary practices of their native states.[86] In 1884, Representative Joseph G. Cannon inquired of a colleague, "Does my friend propose when rights of naturalized citizens of this country or of native-born citizens are in jeopardy in Europe or elsewhere throughout the world we shall have no representative of the government present . . . ?"[87] To answer the question negatively was necessary in view of the situation; to qualify the answer by insisting upon a professional diplomatic service was more in tune with the beliefs of many in the period.

In *Harper's Weekly*, Henry Loomis Nelson wrote, "We are not only growing more than we are eating, but manufacturing more than we are using." This problem of production had been increasing in importance with the expansion of industry after 1861. Well-protected by tariffs and stimulated by an ever-expanding home market, manufacturing thrived. By the 1880's, the domestic market was becoming saturated. American industrialists began looking to Europe and the Orient to absorb the excess. Also, the amount of investment abroad, particularly in Latin America, was multiplying rapidly. Nelson continued his article with the warning, "We cannot threaten a serious competition and remain in political isolation."[88]

The consular service was the first to receive attention. As the cen-

[84] Peirce, *op. cit.*, p. 910.

[85] E.g., "American Diplomacy," *Nation*, LVI (April 6, 1893), 251; "Educated Men in the Foreign Service," *Dial*, XVI (April 16, 1894), 232.

[86] Theodore Roosevelt, *Letters*, ed. Elting E. Morison *et al.* (Harvard University Press, 1951–54), III, 438; IV, 929–30. In his acceptance letter for the second term, Roosevelt quoted Hay's instructions to the effect that "this Department does not discriminate between native-born and naturalized citizens in according their protection while they are abroad, equality of treatment being required by the laws of the United States."

[87] *Cong. Rec.*, XV, 48 Cong., 1 sess. (May 15, 1884), 4160.

[88] "The Need of Trained Diplomats and Consuls," *Harper's Weekly*, XLV (June 15, 1901), 599.

tury neared its close, however, the problems of acquiring information and securing agents diminished somewhat. In their place arose the need for more foreign markets. But this need was being frustrated by the closing of ports and by preferential treaties. A *Forum* contributor lamented, "Meantime many of the manufacturing nations, beaten out of the field, will have retired behind tariff fortifications which they will construct around themselves and their colonies." [89] Treaties, entering wedges of all sorts, became necessary. Here diplomacy was the only tool, a tool "that has proven more and more valuable every year to the great commercial interests." [90]

Brooks Adams, however, insisted that "if we are to turn towards Asia and elsewhere, and enter into the struggle for foreign markets, we must be as well organized as our competitors." [91] Oscar Straus, sometime diplomat, held, ". . . every new market gained by our expanding commerce will accentuate that pressure for reform [of the diplomatic service]." He specifically recommended a system in which appointments were made for fitness and "promotion and fixed tenure on capacity and good behavior reward efficient service." [92] In an article entitled "Our Export Trade," Charles Flint advocated that the service recruit "men of experience and industry, speaking the languages of the countries to which they are accredited." [93] The demand for a service even came from the cotton-producing states, hitherto relatively unaffected by tariffs but now feeling Egyptian and Indian competition. Their congressmen supported appointments that represented "the commercial interests of those sections." [94] Thus, the needs of commerce began focusing attention on the needs of the machinery of diplomacy.

The interest of business in the service also acted to invest it with business standards of efficiency. A contributor to *Lippincott's* in 1905 maintained, "It is intended, in a word, to put the entire diplomatic system on a business basis, and to manage it in the future in accord-

[89] Ulysses D. Eddy, "Our Chance for Commercial Supremacy," *Forum*, XVIII (June, 1891), 426.

[90] *Cong. Rec.*, XXXIII, 56 Cong., 1 sess. (February 5, 1900), 3339. See also Charles Denby, Jr., "America's Opportunity in Asia," *North American Review*, CLXVI (January 1898), 38; Charles Denby, "The Duties of a Minister to China," *Forum*, XXXIII (March, 1902), 31–32.

[91] Letter to the Editor, *Boston Daily Advertiser*, September 23, 1898, p. 4 (quoted in Thornton Anderson, *Brooks Adams: Constructive Conservative* [Ithaca. N.Y.: Cornell University Press. 1951], p. 76).

[92] Oscar H. Straus, "Our Diplomacy with Reference to Our Foreign Service," *Journal of Social Science*, XL (1902), 1–11.

[93] "Our Export Trade," *Forum*, XXIII (May, 1897), 292–94.

[94] *Cong. Rec.*, XL, 59 Cong., 1 sess. (May 29, 1906), 7628 (speech by Representative Albert S. Burleson of Texas).

ance with the principles of sound common sense." [95] Business appreciated training and experience and expected similar standards in the agencies with which it dealt. It looked contemptuously upon the man who "is serenely confident of his capacity to undertake business equally novel, often delicate and difficult, which must be conducted in a foreign country, and generally with people of whose language he is wholly ignorant." [96] Much of this attitude had come through sad experience. An attempt to open a branch of the National City Bank in Argentina failed "because of a lack of men trained to do duty abroad." [97] An article on foreign markets stressed the same point: the need of business for "proper representatives" who "have a knowledge of the language of the country they may visit." [98]

America's excursion into imperialism also improved the chances for reform. The political, psychological, and economic factors which forced Europe to turn outward again in the late nineteenth century operated in America's case as well. These factors drew attention to the agencies necessary for an expansionist policy: a large navy, coaling stations, an interoceanic canal, and a diplomatic service. [99] America, it was argued, was propelled by its "cosmic tendency" for imperialism into world relations. No longer would "single issue" and bilateral diplomacy be the rule. Every move collided with a host of claims and counterclaims. An editorial in the *Century* emphasized that "in view of increasing competition with the other leading nations of the world," there was a "growing appreciation of the desirability of a better consular and diplomatic service." [100] And it was by no accident that the leading journals in the imperialist cause, the *Century*, the *Forum*, and the *Review of Reviews*, devoted significant space to reform of the diplomatic service. Nor was it coincidence that America's

[95] René Baché, "Shuffling the Diplomatic Cards," *Lippincott's*, LXXIX (February, 1907), 223.

[96] Rives, *op. cit.*, p. 702. See also "American Diplomacy," *Nation*, LVI (April 6, 1893), 251.

[97] "That Alliance Against Us," *Nation*, XCVIII (January 1, 1914), 5.

[98] "How to Win Foreign Markets," *Scientific American*, LXXV (October 3, 1896), 269.

[99] Rives, *op. cit.*, pp. 710–11. Rives wrote, "The end of the present war will not improbably find us in possession of Cuba, Porto Rico, the Ladrones, the Carolines, and the Philippines. If we seek to retain the latter, we shall not be met with the indifference that attended our retention of California. We shall become involved at once in all jealousies and rivalries which the partition of Asia has awakened. . . . The acquisition of Hawaii creates many new points of contact with foreign countries. The construction of the interoceanic canal will probably require us to maintain a greatly expanded navy. . . . More than all else, our demonstration of commanding naval strength and skill makes us henceforth an ally or enemy with whom everyone of the other great powers must reckon." See also A Diplomat, "British and Russian Diplomacy," *North American Review*, CLXX (June, 1900), 875.

[100] Editorial, *Century Magazine*, LVII (November, 1898), 154.

leading imperialists, Senator Henry Cabot Lodge and Theodore Roosevelt, were in the forefront of the movement to reform the service.

Expansionist experience also focused attention upon the needs of the diplomatic service in an indirect fashion. For the staffing of the colonial governments, the forces for reform successfully advocated the merit system. They argued that "more will depend upon the class of officials the President sends out than upon any other influence," and recommended the organization of a permanent "quasi-colonial staff." [101] In his acceptance letter of 1904, Roosevelt referred to the progress made in this direction: "Where the merit system was of course most needed was in the Philippine Islands; and a civil service law of a very advanced type has been put into operation and scrupulously observed." [102] This precedent of creating a merit service to deal with a form of foreign affairs undoubtedly encouraged those who felt a similar system should be developed in diplomacy.

But a closer nexus can be found. Many who maintained the importance of a merit service in the colonial sphere considered diplomacy a necessary institution of imperialism. In the *North American Review*, Edward Bourne lamented:

> What Holland, England, France, and Germany are doing to obtain trained men for the diplomatic and colonial services cannot fail to impress every thinking reader with the simple fact that we have entered the race far behind our rivals and critics in preparation for the work. . . . We lack not only trained men, but the belief that training is necessary.

He prescribed "permanency of tenure, the social distinction of an honored profession, and the privilege of retiring after their term of service on an allowance adequate to their comfortable support." [103]

Another element of imperialist thought, "Social Darwinism," was important to professional diplomacy. Social Darwinism has affected American thought in many areas, but in few did it result in such marked activity as in foreign affairs. The conviction of Anglo-Saxon superiority and the nation's mission undoubtedly was part of the inspiration for the territorial acquisitions. [104] The same superiority,

[101] John Barrett, "An American School of Diplomacy," *Harper's Weekly*, XLIV (March 3, 1900), 194.

[102] Roosevelt to Cannon, September 12, 1904, in T. Roosevelt, *Letters*, IV, 930.

[103] "A Trained Colonial Civil Service," *North American Review*, CLXIX (October, 1899), 534. See also "The Imperial Policy," *Nation*, LXVI (May 26, 1898), 396.

[104] See Richard Hofstadter, *Social Darwinism in American Thought* (Boston: Beacon Press, 1955), pp. 170–200.

predicated as it was on the "survival of the fittest," was translated into the language of the merit system. The spoils system was survival by fraud or trick; competitive examinations were the only proof of fitness. An editorial in the *Nation* upheld this position:

> We have no diplomats, while every country with which we have dealings requiring diplomatic action has its body of public servants trained by an education of years and *made effective by careful selection and the survival of the fittest* to perform services which we, if we attempt such an uphill work, are compelled to delegate to men who have all the details of the business still to learn.[105]

Chiefly, however, Darwinism made the critics of the old system picture the necessity for reforming the diplomatic machinery as almost a question of life or death. Articles dealing with reform were invariably sprinkled with phrases, such as "survival," "war between races and states," and "struggles for new spheres." [106] They usually concluded, "Every progressive nation is superior to us in reorganization, since every nation has been reorganized since we began." [107] The irrepressible Brooks Adams contended that if "the United States must shortly bear the burden which England has borne, must assume the responsibilities and perform the tasks which have within human memory fallen to the share of England, it must be equipped shortly." [108]

Religious groups also contributed to the spirit of reform. As an English critic observed, "The foreign policy of the United States is foreign missions." [109] Indeed, much of America's non-European diplomatic business concerned missions, of which the majority were Protestant. Treaties granting equal personal and property rights, as well as the continuous need for protection, brought the American government, usually through the diplomatic service, into contact with missionaries.[110] They, in turn, requested the Department to continue

[105] "American Diplomacy," *Nation*, LVII (November 30, 1893), 408 (emphasis by author).

[106] Rives, *op. cit.*, p. 709; editorial, *Century*, LVII (November, 1898), 154; Robert Adams, "Faults in Our Consular Service," *North American Review*, CLVI (April, 1893), 466.

[107] Brooks Adams, *America's Economic Supremacy*, p. 49.

[108] *Ibid.*, p. 144.

[109] "Missions and Colonization," *Methodist Review*, 5th Series, XXX (September, 1898), 824. The critic was Dr. George Smith.

[110] E.g. *General Index to the Published Volumes of the Diplomatic Correspondence and Foreign Relations of the United States — 1861–99* (Washington, 1902), pp. 833–42. See also Roosevelt to W. W. Rockhill, May 18, 1905, in T. Roosevelt, *Letters*, IV, 1184; see also Lloyd C. Griscom, *Diplomatically Speaking* (Boston: Little, Brown & Co., 1940), p. 134.

certain personnel and memorialized Congress for increased diplomatic protection.[111] Although they made few statements about reform, the *Methodist Review*'s contention that "international relations" was a "class of political duties that ought to be exempt from the odor of partisanship" was probably shared by others, especially in view of the role which religious groups played in the civil service reform movement as a whole.[112] In any case, the frequent demands made on the President and the Department by missionaries helped make them aware of the defects in the service.

Long before the Protestant sects had thought about the service and its role in governmental protection, the Roman Catholics, through their *Catholic World*, had made several relevant statements. Their objective was a neutral service from top to bottom — one which did not take sides on religious questions. Complained one editorial, "The gentlemen whom it has represent us at foreign courts have acted, in numberless instances, and with few exceptions, as if they were emissaries of Protestant or infidel missionary societies rather than emissaries of a government which professes no religion." It concluded by pointing out that, while the United States was represented in nineteen Catholic countries, "not one of our foreign representatives is a Catholic." [113] But if Catholic representation was unobtainable, then the best alternative was a merit service. John McCarthy referred to the dispatches of the quasi-permanent staff as "refreshing oases in the dreary desert of dull verbiage" and criticized the fact that "Americans have not yet quite got over the idea that they are competent to undertake at the shortest possible notice any position calling forth human skill, wit, and activity, no matter how incongruous for such a position a man's antecedents and previous surroundings may have been." [114]

Against this backdrop of changing demands upon the service and widening support, the plan for reform took a significant turn. The reformers were as insistent as ever in replacing entrance through patronage with entrance by examination. They were equally insistent

[111] E.g., *Methodist Review*, LXXXVII (September, 1895), 815; LXXXI (March, 1899), 313; LXXXI (November, 1899), 972–74; *Annual Report of the American Board of Commissioners for Foreign Missions* (Boston), LXIX (1889), lxvii; LXXX (October 11, 1890), viii; LXXXIII (October 10, 1893), xiv; XCIII (October 15, 1903), viii; XCIV (October 11, 1904), x; XCV (September 28, 1905), ix–x. See also Cyrus Hamlin, "America's Duty to Americans in Turkey," *North American Review*, CLXIII (September, 1896), 280–81. See also Correspondence between the Department and the American Bible Society, June 21, 1907 — July 24, 1908, in 14102/6–15, Vol. 876.

[112] "National Politics," *Methodist Review*, LXX (September, 1888), 761.

[113] "A Sectarian Diplomatic Service," *Catholic World*, XXVII (May, 1878), 223–24.

[114] John McCarthy, "A Dish of Diplomacy," *Catholic World*, XXXII (October, 1880), 58, 69.

upon security of tenure and promotion by merit.[115] But now there was a greater stress on the specialized nature of the non-partisan service and the limits that this service would have in the existing hierarchy. After 1888 the argument ran deeper than just the need for men who could speak the appropriate foreign language and have some knowledge of commercial treaties. It insisted "that diplomacy is a business which, like any other, has to be learned." [116] Diplomacy acquired the air of a science, and reformers were wont to prescribe that a person "be not only clever and well-educated, but thoroughly acquainted with the technical details of the business of diplomacy." [117] To support their position they cited the other professions and particularly the increasingly specialized life of the businessman. Peirce again set the tone:

> As we would not put a ship into the hands of a commander ignorant of navigation, an army under the control of a general without military training, a suit at law into the hands of a counsel who had never opened a law book . . . , so we should not put the foreign affairs of our government into the hands of men without knowledge of the various subjects which go to make up the diplomatic science. . . .[118]

Peirce's reference to the military underlines the changed emphasis. Increasingly the reformers argued that the diplomatic profession was very much akin to the military service. A writer in *Harper's Weekly*, for instance, maintained, "Another reason for a trained service is that a diplomatic agent, like an army officer, should have no political future." [119] It was also argued that "above all, dismissal from the service should be permitted only as the result of a hearing, equivalent to the findings of a court martial." [120] The fact that the army was then going through a radical overhaul probably spread the analogy.

A few universities and several congressmen moved to make the prescribed specialized training available. The National Bureau of Education in 1885 was the first to outline proposals for a diplomatic and consular education, and although no evidence can be found on the attempts to actuate the proposals, a correspondent to the *New York Times* maintained that they "attracted considerable attention at the

[115] Rives, *op. cit.*, pp. 709–10 (cf. James G. Whiteley, "Ambassador of Trade," *Forum*, XXXIII [March, 1902], 85–89).

[116] Baché, *op. cit.*, p. 223.

[117] *Ibid.*, p. 216.

[118] Peirce, *op. cit.*, p. 919.

[119] Nelson, *op. cit.*, 599.

[120] Rives, *op. cit.*, pp. 709–10.

time." [121] The establishment of institutions in Paris and Berlin for international law doubtless inspired Herbert Adams in 1885, and it is certain that these institutions influenced the opening of the schools of law and diplomacy in Columbian College at Washington. On November 18, 1898, the President, members of his Cabinet, and judges of the Supreme Court opened the institution which *Harper's Weekly* called "the first school of political science in the New World." It offered training in "the science and practice of diplomacy and international law." The institution, it was felt, would make promotion by merit in the diplomatic service automatic, and "gradually the fruits of this training will be more and more in evidence until the value of having disciplined and experienced men will assist in forming a cumulative and irresistible argument in favor of an established and permanent diplomatic and consular service equal to that of Great Britain, Germany, France, and Russia." [122] No member of the service within the next eight years attended Columbian College.

Other proposals were made. The National Educational Association announced in 1899 a plan similar to Adams', and Leon Mead in the *North American Review* suggested that the Daughters of the American Revolution and the George Washington Memorial Association, which had jointly been planning a national university, should include a diplomatic course in its curriculum. He added that another but unnamed university had been considering such an addition. It was his contention that "hundreds of young men fresh from college and others ambitious to enter public life would flock to such an institution." [123] In Congress a resolution and bill were proposed in 1900 to establish a government-operated academy "at or near Washington" for the purpose. The resolution specifically recommended "the establishment of the United States diplomatic academy." [124] Neither was reported out of committee.

Another significant shift in the reform proposals was one toward the secretarial level of the service. The reformers between 1860 and 1888 were ambiguous about the levels of the service they intended to include. As the century closed, the emphasis was clearly on restricting merit to the lower service and leaving the ministerial level in politics, permitting exceptional secretaries to be promoted occasionally to the upper level. Several insisted that maintaining a professional lower

[121] Letter to the Editor, *New York Times*, July 1, 1914, p. 10. Letter signed "B. T."

[122] Barrett, *op. cit.*, pp. 193–94.

[123] Leon Mead, "The New Diplomacy," *North American Review*, CLXVIII (March, 1899), 377–81; "A Proposed School for Consuls," *Scientific American*, LXXXI (December 16, 1899), 389.

[124] *Cong. Rec.*, XXXIII, 56 Cong., 1 sess. (April 30, 1900), 4888; (March 26, 1900), 3339. The Bill was HR 9990. The resolution was HJ Res. 244.

service, which would carry on the routine of the mission and maintain continuity, permitted the "filling of the more important offices from time to time by men of exceptional capacity and character." [125] Although some reformers still advocated an entirely professionalized service, the appointment of life ministers, and the retention of competent ministers on good behavior, the number who argued the virtues of a mixed system — half career and half political — was significant. An *Atlantic* contributor wrote, "We may well hesitate to establish a profession which would at once deprive us of Motley, Bayard Taylor, Choate, Lowell, and Andrew D. White." [126]

The discussion of the adequacy of compensation also received added urgency with the changing circumstances. Here the focus was chiefly on the ministerial level. The objection was, in essence, that the parsimony of the national government had produced "an office-holding class, a class most repugnant to our democratic institutions, a class of persons who, as a rule, owe their official position not to learning or to ability or to integrity, but to wealth, and wealth alone." [127] This fact was attacked with the growing force of Progressivism, and all the spirits of American political hagiography were invoked. "The great men in the history of our country," claimed Nicholas Longworth, "have been almost without exception poor men, or at least men of very moderate means." [128] Still the secretarial level did not escape notice. Salaries there were compared unfavorably with those of other nations, and it was stressed:

> He [the secretary] must go to court to every function. He must maintain an establishment of considerable expense, and must to some extent entertain company, in order to fulfill his duties properly. If he is married, he cannot with decency live upon his salary in the plainest and simplest manner.[129]

Men had been appointed who looked upon the job for its "great social opportunities" and could pay their own way, "but appointments of

[125] Peirce, *op. cit.*, 919–20.

[126] Francis C. Lowell, "American Diplomacy," *Atlantic*, XCVII (January, 1906), 1–7; Baché, *op. cit.*, pp. 217–18; "Educated Men in the Foreign Service," *Dial*, XVI (April 16, 1894), 232; Theodore Stanton, "Literary Men as Diplomatists," *Lippincott's*, CXIII (July, 1898), 139.

[127] *Cong. Rec.*, XL, 59 Cong., 1 sess. (May 23, 1906), 7324–26 (speech by Representative Nicholas Longworth of Ohio).

[128] *Cong. Rec.*, XLI, 59 Cong., 2 sess. (January 22, 1907), 1528.

[129] Peirce, *op. cit.*, 917. See also "American Diplomacy," *Nation*, LVI (April 6, 1893), 251.

this nature have . . . not been generally very useful or creditable." [130]

No statement was made on any racial or religious qualifications for appointment, and few men were capable of conjecturing publicly about the possibility of women entering diplomacy.[131]

Important in this attempt to educate the public about the need for the service and about reform were the nation's periodicals. Almost every "respectable" American magazine, particularly after 1894, ran one or more major articles advocating reform. Some magazines, such as the *Outlook*, the *Nation, Harper's Weekly*, the *North American Review, Century*, the *Forum*, and the *Review of Reviews*, published articles almost annually. Newspapers contributed their support. After 1893, the organ of the National Civil Service Reform League, *Good Government*, became interested in all developments in the service.[132] None of the muckraker magazines, however, dealt seriously with the issue, contenting themselves understandably with the more sensational exposés.[133] Also important was the fact that many ministers and secretaries of legations, including Herbert Peirce, John B. Moore, Henry Loomis Nelson, Huntington Wilson, Oscar Straus, Andrew White, and John Foster, appeared in print to support reform in the service.[134]

But there were also objections to both the service and the prospects of reform. Champ Clark in 1908 found America's international relations, political and commercial, as simple as did his nineteenth-century predecessors. He argued, "It would be better really to with-

[130] Peirce, *op. cit.*, p. 917.

[131] E.g., Mead, *op. cit.*, p. 378: "But it fairly may be questioned whether even the most advanced woman expects to see the day when members of her sex will serve as ambassadors at the Court of St. James or at Paris or St. Petersburgh." See also Frederic Van Dyne, *Our Foreign Service* (New York, 1909), p. 75: "Perhaps the greatest obstacle to the employment of women as diplomatic officers is their well-known inability to keep a secret."

[132] *Good Government*, XII (January, 1893), 83. Innumerable references appeared subsequently.

[133] In 1909, *Cosmopolitan* ran an article by Charles E. Russell lambasting the service. It concluded: "And in view of the results to the nation, the diplomatic service is surely the wildest extravagance of our government. Why not end it?" See Charles E. Russell, "The American Diplomat Abroad," *Cosmopolitan*, XLVII (November, 1909), 739–46 (quote is on page 746). In one of its subdued periods, *McClure's* ran an article by Maurice Francis Egan supporting reorganization of the Diplomatic Service. See Maurice Francis Egan, "Why We Must Reform Our Diplomatic Service, " *McClure's*, LI (October, 1919), pp. 1–8.

[134] Peirce, *op. cit.*, pp. 909–21; John Bassett Moore, "American Diplomacy: Its Influence and Tendencies," *Harper's*, CXI (October, 1905), 690–96; Nelson, *op. cit.*, p. 599; F. M. Huntington Wilson, "The American Foreign Service," *Outlook*, LXXXII (March, 1906), 499–504; White, *Autobiography*; John W. Foster, *Practice of Diplomacy* (Boston, 1906).

draw the entire diplomatic corps as a general thing, and then when we need a representative at a foreign court, whenever we have need for anyone to attend to these delicate duties . . . pick out a man of the highest capacity in this country. . . ." [135] Twentieth-century republican sensibilities were also piqued by the diplomatic service. As a warning to the special agents who were going to replace diplomats, Mr. Dooley threatened, ". . . if I hear iv ye takin' a cup iv tea with a duchess or visitin' th' tomb iv Shakespeare, I'll have ye hanged as a thraitor." [136]

Those who felt a service necessary but disapproved of the reform platform aired their views as well. Defending the spoils system, Representative James L. Slayden informed the House, "I do not object to having consular and diplomatic posts filled by politicians, but I do believe that the best and most capable politicians available should be chosen." [137] Before the American Historical Association, E. A. Grosvenor argued that American diplomats "in efficiency, in integrity, in ability . . . have stood the equals of their foreign colleagues in royal and imperial courts," and that "there is no better training for the real business of European diplomacy than the practical school of American politics." [138]

The significant fact, however, is not that adverse statements were made but that they were dwarfed by those in support of the service. Defenses considered common in the nineteeth century became uncommon in the twentieth. But many adverse opinions went unheard. Although public attacks on reform were infrequent, the strongest attack was made by the silence of Congress and public apathy.

In response to the changing international circumstances and the demands of the informed, distinct movements within and outside the service took place. Some were only distantly related to the professionalization of diplomacy; others were immediately relevant. Chief among the latter were the legislative attempts to remedy organizational faults and apply the merit service. After 1888, few sessions of Congress met without a resolution calling for an investigation of the two overseas services or legislation to improve their organization. The diplomatic service was usually excluded, but often it was not. And in

[135] *Cong. Rec.*, XLII, 60 Cong., 1 sess. (April 18, 1908), 4926. See also *Cong. Rec.*, XXIII, 52 Cong., 1 sess. (April 26, 1892), 3663 (speech by Representative Blount of Georgia).

[136] F. P. Dunne, "Mr. Dooley on Diplomacy," *American Magazine*, LXVI (June, 1908), 111.

[137] *Cong. Rec.*, XXXVI, 57 Cong., 2 sess. (January 19, 1903) 969 (speech by Representative James L. Slayden of Texas).

[138] E. A. Grosvenor, "American Diplomacy," *Annual Report* (New York: American Historical Association, 1898), p. 293.

the most important attempt in the nineteenth century, the Morgan bill, the service was included — though relegated to secondary importance.

Perhaps most significant about the bill was not that it attempted to apply professional standards to the two services, but that it demonstrated the desire of officials within the Department of State to achieve a more permanent structure. In 1891, Wilbur J. Carr entered the Department and began a career that was to stretch until World War II and embrace within it the development of the Consular and later the Foreign Service. While in the Bureau of Indexes and Archives, Carr became associated with François Jones, who was later to serve in the diplomatic service. After long discussions, they evolved a plan which they felt would prove the best remedy for the services' malaise — the absence of a career.[139]

The remedy was calculated to end the reformers' objections and to increase administrative efficiency. Concerning administrative efficiency, the bill provided that reorganization would be placed under the aegis of the President, who would also fill in the bill's details. It provided appointment to grade, rather than to post, and authorized transfers, at the President's discretion, without reduction in salary and at the government's expense. Lateral transfer was permitted between the services and the Department with the stipulation that the appropriate examination would precede each change. Finally, it authorized the appointment of a paid attaché, between the ages of eighteen and twenty-one, for every embassy and legation as a means of obtaining simultaneously a probationed trainee and an alleviation of the work-load.

The reform provisions included, among other things, examinations for both entrance and promotion. The former required a knowledge of the history "of the most important treaties" of the United States, Constitutional, international, and commercial law, geography, arithmetic, at least one foreign language, and a mastery of English composition. A person passing the examination was appointed to either the consular or the diplomatic service. The promotional examination was "chiefly, but not exclusively, related to the duties and the work of the consular and diplomatic service" with the proviso that promotion to the highest class in either "shall require the passing an examination in a second foreign langauge." A Board of Examiners, composed of three members of the Civil Service Commission and two from the

[139] "Who's Who — and Why?" *Saturday Evening Post*, CXCVII (January 27, 1923), 62. The author was unable to obtain the papers of Wilbur Carr. An account of his career can be found in Katharine E. Crane, *Mr. Carr of State* (New York: St. Martin's Press, 1960).

Department, was established to devise, administer, and mark the examinations. Age limits were set at twenty-one and forty-five. Definite classes were established and promotion was possible to the rank of "secretary of embassy of the first class." Presumably, one applied to take the promotional examination when one felt prepared. Under any circumstance, six months had to be passed in a single class. A graduated salary scale, beginning at $2,000 for a secretary of legation of the second class and rising to $3,500 for the top position, was also created.[140]

The follies of the bill are plain enough. The ranks allowed no expansion within the service. No quotas for classes could be established as long as promotion was contingent upon examinations. The new salary did not ease substantially the financial disability. Finally, while arranging for the existing consular service to take an examination within three years to confirm their positions, no provision was made for the existing diplomatic service.

Although the Department remained aloof from the proceedings, Carr and Jones secured its permission to show the bill to a friend of Jones, Senator John T. Morgan of Alabama.[141] Morgan, who had already demonstrated his imperialist inclinations and interest in diplomacy, agreed to introduce the bill. It cannot be imagined, however, that Morgan entertained expectations of its success. He introduced the bill on April 3, 1894, pointing out that the "bill was prepared by a gentleman [Jones] who is and has been for some time in employment of the State Department, and has made a very thorough study of the matter."[142] The bill, along with a report, was submitted to the Committee on Foreign Relations.[143] Later, Bellamy Storer, who subsequently served in many diplomatic capacities, introduced the same bill in the House.[144] In neither case was the bill reported out within the session. However, as soon as the next session began, Senator Lodge, who would long take an interest in commercial expansion, imperialism, and reform in both services, introduced a similar bill.[145] The Morgan bill was reported out on February 6, 1895.[146]

The accompanying report had been prepared by Carr and Jones. It

[140] 120.11/22, Minutes of the Board of Examiners of the Consular Service. Copy of S1854, dated April 3, 1894. 1st class: $3,500; 2d class: $3,000; 3d class: $2,500; 4th class: $2,000.

[141] "Who's Who — and Why?" p. 62.

[142] *Cong. Rec.*, XXVI, 53 Cong., 2 sess. (April 3, 1894), 3411.

[143] *Ibid.*, p. 3410.

[144] *Ibid.* (April 24, 1894), p. 4104.

[145] *Cong. Rec.*, XXVII, 53 Cong., 3 sess. (December 18, 1894), 386.

[146] *Ibid.* (February 6, 1895), p. 1825.

argued the established positions. The report maintained that the bill would "encourage our best classes of people to qualify themselves for this important service by giving them just compensation for their work, and by securing them in these offices during good behavior." The report deplored that the two services were the only branches of the public service used for gratification of the incumbents "without regard to their capacity to render efficient service to the country." And it drew the inevitable comparisons with the military service, insisting that amateur diplomacy was similar to "constructing a navy to defend the country and to entrust its command to a landsman." Although the report's primary focus was on the consular service, these arguments referred to both. [147]

Public attention, too, was primarily directed at the consular service. Memorials to Congress and editorials were chiefly concerned with the commercial branch. Some notice, however, was given to the diplomatic service in the better journals. An editorial in the *Dial* welcomed the bill "as a step in the right direction" and asserted that "the measure proposes to take the foreign service out of politics and make of it a professional career that may be chosen by a young man just as he chooses law or divinity." [148] A writer in the *Arena* supported the move toward professionalization but questioned whether the pending bill, excluding as it did the ministerial level, would be "a tempting inducement to men of such calibre as should constitute the diplomatic service of a great nation." [149]

Morgan, realizing the probability of opposition, immediately asked that the bill be laid on the table. He then claimed, "Although the bill meets the approval of the majority of the committee, there are some members who do not feel committed to it entirely." [150] His strategy was to have the bill offered as an amendment to the annual appropriation bill. To increase support Lodge ceremoniously withdraw his bill in preference to Morgan's.[151] But still the Senate balked at the procedure and refused the amendment on a voice vote.[152]

Cleveland and his Secretary of State, Richard Olney, both of whom had shown some interest in the measure by permitting Carr and Jones to submit their bill to Morgan and who were anxious to rectify the error they had committed against the consular service in 1893,[153] were

[147] Senate Rept. 886, 53 Cong., 3 sess. (February 6, 1895), pp. 1–8.
[148] "Educated Men in the Foreign Service," *Dial*, XVI (April 16, 1894), 232.
[149] Peirce, *op. cit.*, pp. 919–20.
[150] *Cong. Rec.*, XXVII, 53 Cong., 3 sess. (February 6, 1895), 1825.
[151] *Cong. Rec.*, XXVII, 53 Cong., 3 sess. (February 9, 1895), 1985.
[152] *Ibid.*, p. 1986.
[153] See Adelbert Sageser, *op. cit.*, pp. 186–87. In the first year of Cleveland's second term, 117 out of 317 consular officers were discharged. Business groups strongly protested against this move.

disappointed at the fate of the consular service provisions.[154] Encouraged by memorials and favorable editorials, Olney used the summer to prepare an Executive Order.[155] It provided that all vacancies in the consular service commanding a salary less than $2,500 should be filled either by applicants passing a prescribed examination or by transferees from the Department. On September 20, 1895, Cleveland approved the order, claiming, "It being of great importance that the consuls and commercial agents of the United States shall possess the proper qualifications for their respective positions, etc." [156]

The Executive Order did not include the diplomatic service. The reason for the lack can partly be seen in Cleveland's attitude toward diplomacy. Although the preparation of the Order coincided with the events in the Venezuela dispute, it is clear that Cleveland opposed overseas commitments of most sorts. In his chapter on the controversy, Allan Nevins concluded, "American public opinion, suddenly awakening to the importance of the nation in world affairs, accepted a new bias toward vigorous action in foreign relations and the acceptance of overseas responsibilities—a bias thoroughly distasteful to Cleveland." [157] He opposed imperialism and was generally uninterested in diplomatic affairs. The economic depression during his administration proved to be one of the forces which required manufacturing to look abroad, but such was not yet the case. While he deplored the lack of information over Venezuela, he never thought that the man he was to send there needed any special training. But the major reasons for the diplomatic service's absence were the existence of glaring problems in the consular service, about which Cleveland twice asked Congress for reform,[158] the urgent demands of business for consular reform, and Cleveland's desire to win again the support of the reformers.

Senator Lodge reintroduced the bill the following year.[159] He argued that Cleveland's order "does not diminish the need of the comprehensive reorganization proposed by the accompanying bill." [160] But the bill even failed to reach the Senate floor. A subsequent attempt also failed.[161] By this time, however, the diplomatic service provisions had been dropped.

[154] *New York Times,* July 13, 1895, p. 11; July 29, 1895, p. 12.

[155] Henry James, *Richard Olney: His Public Service* (Boston, 1923), p. 173n.

[156] 121.11/22, Minutes of the Board of Examiners of the Consular Service. Copy of the Executive Order of September 20, 1895.

[157] Allan Nevins, *Grover Cleveland: A Study in Courage* (New York: Dodd, Mead, 1932), p. 648.

[158] James D. Richardson, *Messages,* VIII, 506, 783.

[159] *Cong. Rec.,* XXVIII, 54 Cong., 1 sess. (May 27, 1896), 866. The Bill was S3230.

[160] Senate Rept. 1073, 54 Cong., 1 sess. (May 27, 1896), p. 7.

[161] *Cong. Rec.,* XXIX, 54 Cong., 2 sess. (January 23, 1897), 1104.

The decade following Lodge's attempt to have Morgan's bill approved saw no year pass without the introduction of a bill to reform the consular service. A session often would see two or three such bills introduced. Measures "to increase the efficiency," "for the improvement of," "to remodel," "to reorganize," "to grade," and "to appoint a commission to investigate" were sent to the appropriate committees.[162] Some were reported out and debated; most were never heard of again. The bills generally followed the Morgan proposals but concentrated on the consular service's archaic fee system. The leaders of the movement were Senator Lodge and Representative Adams, and they had the continuous support of the Presidency. After the passage of a modified reform bill in April, 1906, Adams claimed that the legislation climaxed sixteen years of his own active support.[163]

In 1899, an author in the *North American Review* predicted, "The Consular Service will be organized in all probability long before the Diplomatic Service is submitted to that much-needed and important process." [164] Why was this the case? Why was the consular service reformed before the diplomatic service? The answer is simple: the consular service was in worse shape and touched more directly powerful interest groups.

The consular service was a mixture of a limited merit service, a salaried service, and one based on fees for compensation. This chaos was further aggravated by the right of those compensated by fees to engage in business.[165] Inequities were rife. The consular service, furthermore, was much larger than the diplomatic service, and this personnel potential made it a prime target for spoils. In a letter to Cleveland, Secretary Olney reported, "Complaints of the consular service of the United States, of the incompetency of consuls, and of injurious consequences to great public interests, are not infrequently brought to the notice of the Department." [166] This situation enlisted the support of the National Civil Service Reform League. Its Committee on Consular Reform worked steadily to develop a public aware-

[162] *Cong. Rec.*, XXXV, 57 Cong., 1 sess. (December 2, 1901), 52 (HR 84); XXIX, 54 Cong., 2 sess. (March 1, 1897), 2591 (HR 10375 and HR 5683); XXXV, 57 Cong., 1 sess. (December 4, 1901), 123 (S223); XXXVI, 57 Cong., 2 sess. (January 21, 1903), 611 (HR 16023); XXXVIII, 58 Cong., 2 sess. (February 10, 1904), 1822 (S4267).

[163] *Ibid.*, XL, 59 Cong., 1 sess. (March 19, 1906), 3975.

[164] Francis Butler Loomis, "The Foreign Service of the United States," *North American Review*, CLXIX (September, 1899), 358.

[165] See Wilbur J. Carr, "The Consular Service of the United States," *American Journal of International Law*, I (October, 1907), 891–912. See also Chester Lloyd Jones, *The Consular Service of the United States* (Philadelphia, 1906), *passim*. See also "Consuls," *Nation*, II (January 25, 1886), 104.

[166] 120.11/22, Minutes of the Board of Examiners of the Consular Service, September 17, 1895.

ness of the service's deficiencies.[167] Finally, on strictly theoretical grounds, the consular service had the better claim to political neutrality. Although the presuppositions of foreign policy were generally agreed upon, their application was susceptible to party variations. Both parties agreed that commerce should be expanded. George McAneny summarized the view:

> To change the whole personnel of the corps whenever there is a change in the political character of the government at Washington must be considered a proceeding no more sensible than would be a removal of the manager of every commercial house in the city of New York on the election of a Tammany or anti-Tammany mayor.[168]

But, most important, the consular service had the power behind it of America's number one interest — business. A writer in the *Outlook* believed, "It was from this source that the demand for the reorganization of that service on a permanent, efficient basis emanated. The work of the consular service touched the pockets of the people, they responded with a demand for results, and, to that end, for organization." [169] The bewildered American businessman trying to secure an opening abroad found the consul his best friend. The consul's reports taught him how to deal with foreign buyers and how to cater to their wants. Diplomacy was also needed, but the conviction that a trained diplomatic service was necessary was only then growing. Petitions from hundreds of boards of trade, chambers of commerce, and individual companies, flooded Congress and the State Department. The President of the National Association of Manufacturers insisted, "We must encourage the government to broaden the work so as to apply to all countries and all products we sell."[170] A National Committee on Consular Reorganization was even formed, "representing the interests of nearly all the chambers of commerce and similar commercial bodies throughout the country." [171] With such reasons and pressures behind it, it is not difficult to see why the consular service was reformed before the diplomatic service. Indeed, the difficulty is perhaps in understanding why it took so long for the former to be reformed. The answer, of course, is the tenacious refusal by Congress to give up

[167] Jonathan Lane, "Results of Recent Agitation for Consular Service Reform," *Proceedings of the National Civil Service Reform League* (1895), pp. 63–75; "Report on the Committee on Consular Reform," *ibid.* (1903), 60–74; (1905), pp. 88–93; (1906), pp. 76–81.

[168] McAneny, *op. cit.*, p. 605.

[169] Editorial, *Outlook*, CVI (September 16, 1915), 534.

[170] James W. Van Cleave, "What America Must Do to Make An Export Business," *Annals of the American Academy*, XXIX (1907), 471–72.

[171] Whiteley, *op. cit.*, p. 86.

patronage and the apathy of the non-commercial sections of the country — reasons which also applied to reform in the diplomatic service.

By no means, however, did Congress completely ignore the diplomatic service. After the failure of Morgan's and Lodge's bills, other attempts were made to reorganize both services, or at least to appoint a commission to investigate the possibilities of reform. Representative Samuel W. McCall spearheaded the latter.[172] Legislation was also proposed to remedy some outstanding problems. In 1895, McCall unsuccessfully attempted to secure the appointment of language assistants for missions.[173] Representative James McMillan twice proposed the appointment of honorary attachés to ease the work-load.[174] In 1904–5, Senator Shelby M. Cullom, who was later to participate in service reform, recommended a bill which would permit diplomatic and consular officers to be transferred from post to post at the President's discretion.[175] None received congressional assent.

A movement indirectly related to professionalization was one which culminated in the appointment of America's first ambassadors. The struggle over the question of diplomatic rank had been raging since Washington's unsuccessful attempt to appoint only chargés d'affaires.[176] Thereafter it was a continuous push for higher ranks — chargé d'affaires to minister resident to minister plenipotentiary and so on. Through the years, by virtue of laws, resolutions, debates in Congress, and Executive exhortations, the majority of posts had "envoys extraordinary."[177] But congressional members were particularly insistent that the process should not stop, accompanying their injunctions with accounts of small nations snubbing America in the diplomatic hierarchy, tales of eminent American diplomats being treated shabbily in foreign capitals, and pleas by ministers, retired and active, and secretaries.[178] On March 1, 1893, a rider was attached to

[172] *Cong. Rec.*, XXVIII, 54 Cong., 1 sess. (April 2, 1896), 3531 (HR 7863); XXX, 55 Cong., 1 sess. (May 15, 1897), 21 (HR 42).

[173] *Ibid.*, XXVII, 53 Cong., 3 sess. (February 8, 1895), 1955.

[174] *Ibid.*, XXXII, 55 Cong., 3 sess. (February 23, 1899), 2207 (S 5564); XXXIII, 56 Cong., 1 sess. (December 6, 1899), 88 (S 150).

[175] *Ibid.*, XXXVIII, 58 Cong., 2 sess. (April 9, 1904), 4550 (S 5441).

[176] Washington to Senate, February 18, 1791, in J. C. Fitzpatrick (ed.), *Writings of George Washington*, XXXI, 219–21.

[177] E.g., 11 Stat. 52 (August 18, 1856); House Mis. Doc. 110, 50 Cong., 1 sess. (January 16, 1888); *Cong. Globe*, Part 1, 27 Cong., 1 sess. (August 27, 1841), pp. 393–94; Richardson, *Messages*, IX, p. 33; on March 1, 1893, there were thirty-one envoys extraordinary, five ministers resident, and one agent (see 27 Stat. 496 [March 1, 1893]).

[178] See *Cong. Globe*, Part 3, 39 Cong., 1 sess. (May 16, 1866), p. 2617; *Cong. Rec.*, XIX, 50 Cong., 1 sess. (May 21, 1888), 4484. See also T. Jefferson Coolidge, *The Autobiography of T. Jefferson Coolidge* (Boston, 1923), p. 221; Peirce, *op. cit.*, p. 912.

the regular diplomatic and consular appropriation.[179] The events preceding the amendment were without partisan coloring, and the amendment passed "both chambers without a word or comment." Although both Foster and Moore contended that the President and his Secretary were opposed and that no need had been demonstrated for the move, Cleveland managed to sign the bill anyway.[180]

The law granted that "whenever the President shall be advised that any foreign government is about to be represented in the United States by an ambassador, [etc.], he is authorized, in his discretion, to direct that the representative of the United States to such Government shall bear the same designation." The riders prohibited any change in the duties, powers, or compensation.[181] On March 30, 1893, Britain became the first to designate an ambassador. By 1906, nine ambassadorships had been created.[182]

The effect of the ambassadorial question on professionalization was twofold. First, it drew from the same source, and, in turn, focused greater attention on diplomacy. Political, commercial, and religious forces had found the old rank inhibiting and demanded more immediate access to governments. The imperialists' sense of American dignity also demanded diplomatic parity. On the other hand, the long-run effect, particularly as the measure provided no increase in compensation, was to remove the office of ambassador from the hands of the prospective professional diplomat, unless he was prepared to cover the higher expenses of an embassy from his own pocket.

But changes in size, in the existing hierarchy, and in the standards of compensation took place subtly through the appropriation process. The effects of the commercial, political, and religious expansion were felt especially in the size of the service after 1898. For many years the number of first and second secretaries had remained at twenty-four. Slowly, particularly in Europe and South America, the number rose. On March 9, 1898, four new secretaryships were created; four more came the following year. By March 3, 1905, there were forty-eight — an increase of 100 per cent in little more than a decade.[183] The implica-

[179] *Cong. Rec.*, XXIII, 52 Cong., 1 sess. (March 1, 1893), 2457.

[180] John W. Foster, *The Proper Grade of Diplomatic Representation* (Washington, 1904), pp. 6, 24; John Bassett Moore, *op. cit.*, pp. 691–96.

[181] 27 Stat. 496 (March 1, 1893).

[182] Wilbur J. Carr to Representative Foss, in *Cong. Rec.*, LVII, 65 Cong., 3 sess. (January 21, 1919), 7. France: April 8, 1893; Germany: September 14, 1893; Russia: February 11, 1898; Mexico: December 8, 1898; Austro-Hungary: May 27, 1902; Italy: October 20, 1903; Brazil: January 13, 1905; Japan: January 25, 1906. By 35 Stat. 672 (March 2, 1909), the provision was repealed. Thereafter, ambassadorships had to be approved of by both Houses.

[183] 30 Stat. 263 (March 9, 1898); *ibid.*, 824 (February 9, 1899); 33 Stat. 916 (March 3, 1905).

tions of this rise were great. The President could no longer insure competent patronage appointments to such a large number, and the increased size encouraged the feeling of participating in a service, rather than that of being isolated secretaries.

Congress also provided for changes in the clerical staffs of the posts. Interpreters were created for Persia, Korea, and Siam, in 1894.[184] In 1902, with Roosevelt's support, the Department requested the creation of a body of ten student interpreters for the Chinese legation to study the language "with a view to supplying interpreters" for a potential tenure of ten years. Included was a significant provision:

> That said student interpreter shall be chosen in such a manner as will make the selections non-partisan so far as may be consistent with aptness and fitness for the intended work.[185]

In 1906, this program, including its merit provisions, was extended to the Japanese embassy. The only modification was that the number authorized was six, and both schemes had their tenure limits reduced to five years. The same appropriation also authorized the appointment of clerks at embassies and legations.[186] The new personnel released the secretary from the more onerous tasks and permitted him to engage in the more agreeable but demanding chores of representation. The merit principle applied to student interpreterships also marked a further commitment to the idea of non-partisan service.

Another change through appropriations was the continued development of a hierarchy in the service. In 1894, the first appointments were made of secretaries of embassy.[187] Later, on behalf of the Department, Lodge amended the appropriation for 1900 to include provisions for appointing third secretaries of embassy to Berlin, Paris, and London. The position was subsequently extended to Mexico and Russia.[188] Second secretaryships were also created for six posts, mostly European but including Turkey and Cuba.[189] The emerging hierarchy was stabilized by a differential wage structure.[190]

A few successful attempts were made to relieve the problems of compensation. The creation of the third secretaryship was accom-

---

[184] 28 Stat. 142 (July 26, 1894).

[185] 32 Stat. 78 (March 22, 1902).

[186] 34 Stat. 288 (June 16, 1906).

[187] 28 Stat. 142 (July 26, 1894).

[188] *Cong. Rec.*, XXXII, 55 Cong., 3 sess. (January 10, 1899), 527. See also 30 Stat. 824 (February 9, 1899); 31 Stat. 61 (April 4, 1900); 34 Stat. 287 (June 16, 1906).

[189] They were Italy (1898), Turkey (1901), Austro-Hungary (1902), Cuba, (1903), Mexico (1896), and Russia (1898).

[190] 34 Stat. 287 (June 16, 1906). This applied only to secretaryships in embassies. First secretaries of legation received $2,625, second secretaries $1,800.

panied by a new wage schedule: $3,000 for first secretaries, $2,000 for second secretaries, and $1,200 for third secretaries. This, however, did not apply in all cases.[191] A second remedy came through the proportional increases on the secretarial level whenever a minister or ambassador's salary was increased.[192] Early in 1890 the appropriation provided payments of salaries "for periods actually and necessarily occupied in receiving instruction and making transits to and from their posts . . . ," ending the strictures imposed in 1856.[193] A second great problem was overcome in 1906. In that year Congress agreed to "pay the cost of transportation of diplomatic and consular officers in going to and returning from their posts, or when traveling under the orders of the Secretary of State, at the rate of five cents per mile, but not including any expense incurred in connection with leaves of absence." [194] While the changes did not permit a man without a fixed income comfortably to enter the service, they did ease the load in that respect.

A vocation which offered an opportunity to travel in foreign lands, mingle with the wealthy and refined governing classes of Europe, and be of some value to the nation, naturally appealed to many. Roosevelt wrote to von Sternberg about the situation:

> There are a large number of young fellows who are upright and gentlemanly, who know French and German and very possibly law, and who are extremely desirous of getting in as secretaries to some of the legations. . . . there is great pressure for them.[195]

An anxious candidate in 1904 had to wait until 1909 before he was appointed.[196] And Roosevelt's correspondence indicates that a waiting list existed.[197]

In most cases, however, the salary scale necessitated that each member contribute from private sources. When the highest salary paid was much less than that paid the equivalent British position,[198] the service

[191] *Ibid.*

[192] The first secretary in Vienna received an increase to $2,250 when his minister received an increase in salary (see 32 Stat. 77 [March 22, 1902]).

[193] 26 Stat. 272 (July 14, 1890).

[194] 34 Stat. 288 (June 16, 1906).

[195] Roosevelt to Ambassador Herman von Sternberg, March 18, 1901, in T. Roosevelt, *Letters*, III, 21–22.

[196] Roosevelt to William Bayard Cutting, September 13, 1904, in *ibid.*, IV, 943–44.

[197] Roosevelt to von Sternberg, March 18, 1901, in *ibid.*, III, 21–23. "It is in some ways the hardest position for which to try, because the qualifications demanded are such as many young men possess; there is great pressure for them."

[198] See *Foreign Office List*, ed. Sir. Edward Hertslet (London 1890), pp. 26–41, 231. The British First Secretary in Paris received the equivalent of $5,000 in salary and $1,000

understandably was staffed with sons of old-line American families, such as the Roosevelts or Peirces, or the scions of recently wealthy industrialists, such as the Fergusons of Pittsburgh.[199] Although exact evidence cannot be found for each member, certain conclusions about their financial resources can be drawn.

There are statements made by the secretaries referring to their own incomes. William Phillips described himself as "financially independent, in contrast to most of my friends who were planning to concentrate their efforts on the dollar." [200] Hugh Wilson volunteered, "I inherited an income sufficient to follow my inclinations." [201] Henry White's private income ranged from $35,000 to $50,000 per annum.[202] Other evidence can be found in statements made by members of the service about their colleagues. Selden Chapin, for instance, estimated that 99 per cent had private incomes.[203] William Sands referred to his colleagues as "wealthy young men wanting posts at European courts for the sole purpose of making acquaintances there which would advance them socially at home." [204] Finally, the character with which the public dubbed the members was that of wealthy, dilettantish young men, a character which must have had some basis in fact. Various congressmen described secretaries as "fops," "dietetic or dinner-table diplomats," or as "members of an office-holding aristocracy based on wealth." [205] Journalists made the same point. René Baché, writing in *Lippincott's*, contended:

> Quite a good deal of social prestige attaches to such employment, and partly on this account, as well as for the sake of enjoying a residence abroad under the circumstances otherwise agreeable, young men of the leisure class have hitherto monopolized to a great extent the secretaryships at our legations.[206]

Further evidence may be inferred from their associations with other men of the time. The connections with the reformers, particularly

in housing allowance. He also received his own traveling expenses and those for one servant. The exchange rate was roughly £1 to $5 (see Joseph Whitaker [ed.], *An Almanack* [London, 1890], p. 631).

[199] F. M. Huntington Wilson, *Memoirs of an Ex-Diplomat* (Boston, 1945), p. 103.
[200] William Phillips, *Ventures in Diplomacy* (London: John Murray, 1955), p. 2.
[201] Hugh Wilson, *The Education of a Diplomat* (New York, 1938), p. 1.
[202] Nevins, *Henry White*, p. 42.
[203] "The United States Foreign Service," *Fortune Magazine*, XXXIV (July, 1946), 198.
[204] William Franklin Sands, *Undiplomatic Memories* (New York, 1930), p. 3.
[205] See *New York Times*, April 29, 1900, p. 6; *Cong. Rec.*, XLII, 60 Cong., 1 sess. (April 18, 1908), 4923; XLII, 4920; XXIII, 52 Cong., 1 sess. (April 26, 1892), 3681.
[206] Baché, *op. cit.*, p. 214.

with Roosevelt and Lodge, were many.[207] Indeed, one receives the impression that secretaries of legation were part of a network of social relationships. Robert Lincoln wrote to Roosevelt in support of Larz Anderson's application for a secretaryship, "You know his antecedents and surroundings so well that I need say nothing about them" [208] Not atypical of the claims made in memoirs and autobiographies was the assertion of William Sands:

> I felt that it was hardly respectable not to be on easy terms
> with Presidents and Secretaries of State. Had not Presi-
> dents, from Grant on, been frequent and informal visitors
> in my grandfather's house (except Chester Arthur, who was
> not approved of and not received)? [209]

Other evidence exists. Of all secretaries 15 per cent had previously served as private secretaries to ministers or ambassadors. These positions were unpaid and demanded their holders to participate in "the season." [210] Over 60 per cent of the secretaries of 1888–1906 for whom information on higher education was obtainable attended Harvard, Yale, or Princeton. This figure must be compared with the percentage from state universities, which was less than 12 per cent. The high proportion from the three institutions does not conclusively prove the existence of a fixed income, but it does argue that the men came from homes where relatively more costly education was within the family's means. No reliable information was obtainable on secondary school backgrounds. Finally, 36 per cent of the secretaries were elevated to ministerial positions. These promotions, in almost every case, required expenditures greater than the amount of the salary.

Were they all attracted solely for the social opportunities which the service offered? The answer is no. *Noblesse oblige* motivated many. Larz Anderson's biographer noted, "Public service was deeply rooted in the Anderson family tradition and showed itself in a variety of ways." [211] Others were part of a return to government by the wealthier classes witnessed at the turn of the century. Hugh Wilson remarked:

> Ease and a measure of education had encouraged us to be-
> lieve that life should have a wider scope than business alone
> could offer. So when I broached to my father's friends my

[207] E.g., Phillips, *op. cit.*, *passim*; Post Wheeler and Hallie Ermine Rives, *Dome of Many-Coloured Glass* (New York: Doubleday, 1955), p. 203.

[208] Larz Anderson, *Letters and Journals of a Diplomat* (New York, 1940), p. 69.

[209] Sands, *op. cit.*, p. 3.

[210] Phillips, *op. cit.*, p. 2.

[211] Anderson, *op. cit.*, p. 13.

idea of entering the diplomatic service, I found a chasm separated the two generations.[212]

Particularly instrumental in this return was Theodore Roosevelt's own example and preaching. William Phillips unhesitatingly attributed "T.R.'s call to youth" as the factor that lured him to a public career.[213]

The evidence, however, will not support the conclusion that *all* secretaries were wealthy stewards of the people.[214] The dictates of patronage demanded that geographical factors be considered as well. While the concentration in the Middle Atlantic states continued, there were rises in representation from the New England and East North Central regions. From these three areas, 81 per cent of the appointments originated.[215] The West North Central, however, contributed 7.5 per cent; the South as a whole, 8.2 per cent; and the Mountain and Pacific regions, about 3 per cent. That the places of origin were somewhat diffused was still the product of the patronage system. The pattern of concentration, however, can be attributed to the greater demands, brought on by an awareness of the need for diplomacy, for positions, the more greatly stratified society which sought class differentiations, and the heavier weight which the three areas had in elections and representation.[216]

Without examinations, the criterion for appointment remained a man's political beliefs and demonstrated support of them. For instance, Arthur Beaupré's "prominence in local and state politics induced McKinley to appoint him." [217] Applying for a secretaryship, Huntington Wilson was armed with letters from leading politicians, including ones from Senators Mann, Hanna, and Cullom.[218] When John Riddle returned on leave from Constantinople, he was employed by the Republican national headquarters. His letter of introduction assured Graeme Stewart that "the young man is a

[212] Hugh Wilson, *Education of a Diplomat*, p. 4. See also F. M. Huntington Wilson, *Memoirs of an Ex-Diplomat*, p. 45; Griscom, *op. cit.*, p. 26.

[213] Phillips, *op. cit.*, p. 2.

[214] Even among those who were elevated to the ministerial level, there were those who lived on their salaries, or with only a small additional private income. John Ridgely Carter resigned his ministership for lack of funds (see Emily Bax, *Miss Bax of of the Embassy* [Boston, 1939], p. 198).

[215] New England: 21.2 per cent.
Middle Atlantic: 42.4 per cent.
East North Central: 17.4 per cent.

[216] The concentration occurred in regions with major population centers, areas of manufacturing that required overseas trade, and the largest shipping areas.

[217] *DAB*, II, 110. See also F. M. Huntington Wilson, *Memoirs of an Ex-Diplomat*, pp. 46–47.

[218] *Ibid.*, p. 46. See also Griscom, *op. cit.*, pp. 127–28; Herbert Hagerman, *Letters of a Young Diplomat* (Santa Fe, N.M., 1937), p. 11.

Republican." [219] While serving Ambassador Joseph H. Choate as his private secretary, William Phillips attempted to enter the service. He realized, although "I was a Republican and had made the acquaintance of Senator Lodge . . . I had no claim whatsoever upon a Republican administration." [220] Still, men received positions without partisan connections. William Bayard Cutting, while not a Republican, received a secretaryship. He had to wait a long time, and when he first applied, he was warned that "one of the legitimate considerations to be taken into account is what a man had done in politics." [221] Roosevelt also told von Sternberg that the latter's protégé "ought to have some Senator or Congressman behind him, and of course it is difficult to get such backing when one resides in the District of Columbia." [222]

Politics also played a role in questions of tenure and promotion. Although less frequently employed, the service's crude system of appointing a "faithful" to a post held by an "infidel" without informing the latter persisted. [223] Although increasingly less the case, continued tenure was dependent upon the same party remaining in power. In the case of promotion or transfer, party members intervened on behalf of secretaries. Trained and superior employees with long experience in one spot were denied transfers or promotion because "they were not among a clique of those who were the President's pet, had strong friends in the Department, or commanded special political influence." [224] And this influence was exploited at every turn. Huntington Wilson's wife, for instance, "made some good friends among the Taft group . . . and sailed back . . . to try to secure my promotion." [225]

Many of the other problems remained. No adequate training was yet given by the Department. Herbert Hagerman's "in-service training" was a day's visit to the "Bureau of Diplomacy where the whole recent diplomatic correspondence with Russia was set before me." [226] About his own experience, Wilson concluded, "I was thrown into diplomacy . . . without due preparation or advice, just as I had earlier been thrown into the water to learn to swim." [227] The problem of insufficient staffs continued to plague many of the posts. About the

[219] Roosevelt to Graeme Stewart, July 27, 1900, in T. Roosevelt, *Letters*, II, 1366.

[220] Phillips, *op. cit.*, p. 6.

[221] Roosevelt to Cutting, September 13, 1904, in T. Roosevelt, IV, 943–44.

[222] Roosevelt to von Sternberg, March 18, 1901, in *ibid.*, III, 21–22.

[223] F. M. Huntington Wilson, *Memoirs of an Ex-Diplomat*, p. 51.

[224] *Ibid.*, pp. 100–102. See also Roosevelt to Henry White, October 5, 1896, in T. Roosevelt, *Letters*, I, 561.

[225] F. M. Huntington Wilson, *Memoirs of an Ex-Diplomat*, p. 136 .

[226] Hagerman, *op. cit.*, p. 11.

[227] F. M. Huntington Wilson, *Memoirs of an Ex-Diplomat*, p. 48.

British mission, Griscom claimed, "The Embassy was so short-handed that the work was months behind." His experience at Constantinople was similar, although work at the new post was even more in arrears. [228]

Within this framework, however, the tendencies toward a merit service continued with ever greater success. Men enthusiastically entered the service intending to make it a career. Griscom, Wilson, Phillips, Carter, Jackson, Peirce, Riddle, and others, entered with this intention.[229] Increasingly, signs confirmed their expectations. Over 25 per cent of those holding either a ministerial or secretarial post in 1905 had entered the service between 1888 and 1895, while the remainder had entered before 1904. Another 61.4 per cent had succeeded in serving under two parties. Exactly 40 per cent received appointments to two or more posts or promotions within their own post. The number achieving the ministerial rank also was increasing.[230] In this case, however, the rates of promotion were so uneven that generalizations cannot be drawn. Only 13 per cent were immediately related to, or from the same state as, the superior officer. A large number also entered the service after experience as a private secretary or from the Department or the consular service.[231] Moreover, secretaries were even receiving their commissions at an earlier age, the average being 31.1 years.[232]

All this needed a sympathetic administration. From 1888 to 1906, almost every President and his Secretary of State publicly supported the merit service for diplomacy and privately sought to insure tenure for competent secretaries. Much of their support, however, stemmed from sheer necessity. Faced with the geometrically increasing foreign business of the United States, the ministers and ambassadors depended upon the experience of their secretaries. The attempt to replace Vignaud in 1893 brought forth protests from the inexperienced ambassador James B. Eustis that he was helpless without him.[233] Lincoln, Hay, and Choate, found White, and later John Ridgely Carter, ab-

[228] Griscom, *op. cit.*, pp. 28, 133.

[229] E.g., *ibid.*, p. 69; F. M. Huntington Wilson, *Memoirs of an Ex-Diplomat*, p. 45; Phillips, *op. cit.*, p. 2; *DAB*, XI, 612.

[230] In 1906, nearly 31 per cent of all upper service appointees had had previous experience as secretaries of legation or embassy.

[231] In addition to the number of private secretaries, seven had had previous experience in the consular service and one in the Department of State. Information obtained from official and biographical records.

[232] Average based on 58.3 per cent of all secretaries.

[233] T. Jefferson Coolidge, *op. cit.*, p. 231.

solutely indispensable.[234] A correspondent to the *Nation* observed, "We have gotten so far towards an establishment as to have appointed some secretaries of legation who hold from one minister to another because otherwise the new minister would be as helpless as a new-born babe." [235]

When Benjamin Harrison entered the Presidency, he was relieved of the necessity "to turn the rascals out." His predecessor, Grover Cleveland, had not let them in initially and had been generally true to his civil service predilections. Of those secretaries holding office in 1888, 70.8 per cent remained during Harrison's first year and 54.1 per cent during the second. If a one-year grace period is assumed as necessary to break in a new minister, then, barring all other variables, such as voluntary resignation, over half of Cleveland's lower diplomatic staff served under Harrison. Harrison's support of longer tenure for secretaries was probably reinforced by his appointment of John W. Foster, an avid reformer and erstwhile diplomat, to succeed James G. Blaine as Secretary of State.[236]

Cleveland's re-election in 1892 did not alarm the members of the service.[237] His readiness to reward experience was well known. However, under the influence of Walter Q. Gresham and Josiah P. Quincy, he authorized certain removals. By 1893, almost half of the secretary-ships had changed hands; a year later 68.3 per cent had. Of the former, 63.6 per cent had originally been appointed by Harrison. Thus, Cleveland generally spared the longer-tenured and removed the more recent appointments. But there were some prime exceptions. Henry White, already a *doyen* of diplomacy, and Augustus Jay were among the experienced secretaries who were dismissed. Adverse publicity on these removals, as well as public disapproval of the ministerial appointments, informed Cleveland of his *gaffe*.[238] He later repented White's dismissal. During the Venezuelan crisis, Ambassador Thomas Bayard was without contacts in English governing circles. Cleveland enlisted White's unofficial aid, and White, as Roosevelt wrote to his sister, was "trusted as no man not in official position has before been trusted." [239]

Further reliance upon "career men" was demonstrated by Cleveland's appointments to the Assistant Secretaryship of State. After 1893, two out of four appointed had previously served as secretaries

[234] Edward S. Martin, *Life of Joseph Hodges Choate* (London, 1920), II, 212. See also Royal Cortissoz, *Life of Whitelaw Reid*, II, 352.

[235] "American Diplomacy," *Nation*, LVI (April 6, 1893), 251.

[236] John W. Foster, *Diplomatic Memoirs*, I, 214.

[237] *Good Government*, XII (October 15, 1892), 47; T. Jefferson Coolidge, *op. cit.*, p. 34.

[238] *Good Government*, XIII (January, 1894), 50.

[239] T. Roosevelt, *Letters*, I, 574. Letter is dated January 8, 1897.

of legation.[240] The President also made gestures toward establishing a more efficient service within the framework of patronage. Gresham's successor, Richard Olney, devised a plan to train new secretaries. Condemning "the tendency of young American diplomatic officers to deteriorate in the atmosphere of our European courts," Cleveland and Olney agreed to appoint men initially to South America or the Far East so that they might "study the workings of concession diplomacy generally, away from attractions of courts, to watch European diplomacy in the raw, in regions where presently American interests would be greatly affected." [241] This experience was to be supplemented by a tour of duty in an American university and the State Department. The secretary was then equipped — even for a European post! The first secretary under this scheme, William Sands, was appointed in 1896 and began his service in Japan.[242] The following year, however, William McKinley became President and the plan lapsed.

But McKinley was not opposed to continuing secretaries on good behavior. Indeed, "business government" had as its essence "administrative efficiency." Almost 60 per cent retained their positions, and most of those departing did so before McKinley took office. The argument that they left in the face of a changing administration is contradicted by the small percentage, 12 per cent, of Cleveland's appointees who were among those departing. The long-term members who left, presumably of their own will, probably were discouraged with the limited opportunities for advancement, the problems of compensation, or decided to cash in on their experience by taking employment with businesses expanding overseas. But this is not to argue that McKinley was above partisan appointments. Quite the contrary, he made several of a decidedly partisan nature, although his Secretary of State, John Sherman, was sympathetic to reform.[243] Sherman's successor, John Hay, while generally weak in administrative matters pursued a policy of retaining all able secretaries in the service.[244]

McKinley's successor embodied the movement toward the merit service in diplomacy. Theodore Roosevelt had long been interested

[240] Cleveland's Assistant Secretaries of State were W. W. Rockhill and Edward H. Stroebel.

[241] Sands, *op. cit.*, pp. 3–5. See also *idem, Our Jungle Diplomacy*, (Chapel Hill, N.C.: University of North Carolina Press, 1944), pp. 225–27. The two citations are the only evidence that such a plan existed. Perusal of the official documents during May, 1896, reveals nothing.

[242] *Cong. Rec.*, XXVIII, 54 Cong., 1 sess. (May 27, 1896), 5800.

[243] *DAB*, II, 110; Roosevelt to Bellamy Storer, in T. Roosevelt, *Letters*, III, 218; Adelbert Sageser, *op. cit.*, p. 208.

[244] Editorial, *Outlook*, LXXXI (November 25, 1905), 685; A. L. P. Dennis, *Adventures in Diplomacy* (New York, 1928), p. 522; Roosevelt to Lodge, January 28, 1909, in T. Roosevelt, *Letters*, VI, 1496–97. See also Nevins, *Henry White*, p. 326.

in civil service reform generally and had outlined as early as 1894 the need for the merit principle in foreign affairs administration.[245] While President, he extended the classified civil service to cover the Department of State and supported the program for student interpreterships.[246] He was the first President to think in global terms, and his administration of foreign affairs made him vitally aware of the need for information from trained observers.[247] He was an intimate of White and had often supported the latter's attempts to remain in the service.[248] The attrition rate of secretaries during his first year as President fell to 27 per cent. Once a man had demonstrated fitness, he need not fear for his position.[249] Roosevelt was equally determined that effective secretaries would be rewarded by promotions to the ministerial level. In 1906, nearly 31 per cent of all higher appointments were of men who had previous experience as secretaries.

The movement for professional diplomacy had much in common with other Progressive campaigns of the day. Its emphasis on civil service reform was only one such element. The Progressive interlude also saw a shift to the Executive for leadership in the reform of national life. This shift coincided with congressional abdication of the responsibility for administrative reform in favor of the President. Too, the movement for a career service, if the aggregate of the statements made by people interested in a question can be considered a movement, was characteristically populated by professional men. Their stress on the specialized nature of diplomacy was hardly coincidental. Finally, the pattern of reform approximated the pattern followed in other areas. First there was the exposé of defects in the service, followed by moral exhortations. But, in the case of the diplomatic service, the ripples never extended far from the source. Unlike most other Progressive campaigns, a favorable public and congressional opinion, followed by action, was not forthcoming. Al-

[245] T. Roosevelt, *Letters*, I, 369; Albert H. Washburn, "Some Evils of our Consular Service," *Atlantic*, XCIV (August, 1894), 249–50. See also T. Roosevelt, *Works*, XIV, 152.

[246] 120.11/22, Minutes of the Board of Examiners of the Consular Service (copy of Executive Order of April 15, 1903).

[247] E.g., T. Roosevelt, *Letters*, IV, 119, 1253; Henry Cabot Lodge (ed.), *Selections from the Correspondence between Theodore Roosevelt and Henry Cabot Lodge* (New York, 1925), II, 209. Letters deal with Roosevelt's need for information about events in Russia and Venezuela.

[248] Roosevelt to Henry White, letters of March 19, 1894, and March 8, 1897, in T. Roosevelt, *Letters*, I, 369, 583. For his attitude to Rockhill, see Roosevelt to Cecil Spring Rice, August 13, 1897, in *ibid.*, I, 649.

[249] T. Roosevelt, *Letters*, IV, 1249; V, 28. The first letter is to Taft, dated June 21, 1905; the second is to Archibald J. Sampson, dated September 16, 1905. For reformer's evaluation of Roosevelt on this score, see Richard Henry Dana, "President Roosevelt's Civil Service Record," *Boston Transcript*, October 8, 1904, p. 4.

though referring to a related subject, Roosevelt summarized the problem:

> As for opening out of all possible new channels of trade by diplomatic activity and by positive legislation, I can only say that here again it is astonishing how little public feeling there is for any such effort. I have tried once or twice to make such an opening by diplomatic activity, and have had to fight tooth and nail to get either Democratic or Republican senators to so much as even consider the treaties I have sent in, and generally they have rejected them, while popular interest has been nil.[250]

Hay's successor, Elihu Root, subscribed to Roosevelt's policy of encouraging competent secretaries through retention in office and advancement. His appointment was also made with a view to reorganizing the administration of all branches dealing with foreign affairs. As Secretary of War, he had learned the need to modernize outdated administrative machinery.[251] His control over the nascent colonial service had introduced him to the possibilities of a merit service. In his report of 1899, he wrote, "No officer, high or low, has been appointed upon anyone's request, or upon any personal, social or political considerations." [252] He, like Roosevelt, was aware of the need for trained observers abroad, especially in Latin America.[253]

The commitment to reform by Roosevelt and Root was more than shared by their Department of State. Two of the three Assistant Secretaries of State, Herbert Peirce and Francis Loomis, had publicly supported the merit service for diplomacy.[254] The third, Alvey Adee, and the chief of the Diplomatic Bureau, Sydney Smith, while good civil servants who kept silent on public affairs, were living testimonials to a career service. After eight years as a secretary of legation, Adee entered the Department in 1877.[255] Smith began his career in 1882.[256]

The President and his Secretary of State were faced in 1905 with the cumulative pressures for reform from businessmen dealing in foreign commerce, imperialists, missionary societies, and members of the Na-

[250] Roosevelt to Nicholas Murray Butler, September 24, 1907, in T. Roosevelt, *Letters*, V, 806.

[251] Philip C. Jessup, *Elihu Root* (New York: Dodd, Mead, 1938), I, 240–64; II, 100.

[252] Elihu Root, *The Military and Colonial Policy of the United States* (Cambridge, 1916), p. 266.

[253] For Root's attitude toward Latin America, see Jessup, *op. cit.*, I, 468–92.

[254] Peirce, *op. cit.*, pp. 909–21; Francis Butler Loomis, *op. cit.*, pp. 349–61.

[255] *Biog. Reg.* (1877), p. 7. He had previously been secretary of legation in Madrid. See *Biog. Reg.* (1870), p. 12.

[256] *Ibid.* (1882), p. 8.

tional Civil Service Reform League. There was a nascent service growing without the protection of legislation. Many members of the Department of State were wedded to the career principle, and both Root and Roosevelt, like most of their predecessors after 1888, had approved of and supported its application. While most congressmen and the largest segment of public opinion were opposed, theirs was the opposition of apathy. Against this interplay of forces, the first step was taken toward placing diplomacy on a firm career basis.

CHAPTER THREE

THE PROFESSIONALIZATION OF THE SERVICE

1905–1915

Throughout Hay's service to Roosevelt, the President retained control over appointments for both the diplomatic and consular services.[1] During the Secretary's final year, Roosevelt practically ran the Department.[2] These facts, coupled with Roosevelt's interest in civil service reform and international affairs, made him sympathetic toward congressional attempts to reorganize the foreign service, particularly the consular branch. Preceding his Fourth Annual Message, he gathered together many proponents of professional diplomacy, including Secretary William Howard Taft and Senator Philander Knox, to discuss the recommendations he should make to Congress for the service.[3] The meeting's results, however, did not convince Roosevelt that a strict merit service was desirable, and he finally made no reference to it in his Message, concentrating instead on the consular service.[4]

Months passed and Congress refused all consular legislation. Secretary Root, whom publicists had associated with reform in the machinery of foreign affairs, was also being frustrated in his project by the priority demanded by international complications. Still, both he and the President decided to adopt a consular reform measure that

[1] Hay to Roosevelt, May 5, 1902, as quoted in A. L. P. Dennis, *Adventures in Diplomacy* (New York, 1928), p. 521.

[2] Roosevelt to Lodge, January 28, 1909, in Theodore Roosevelt, *Letters*, VI, 1496–97.

[3] Oscar H. Straus, *Under Four Administrations* (Boston, 1922), p. 184.

[4] Theodore Roosevelt, *Writings*, XV, 242–43 (Message of December 6, 1904).

would give a lead to Congress. The prospect of reform through an Executive Order appealed to Roosevelt, especially as he could anticipate three more years in office and he could satisfy some of the mounting pressures from business groups.[5]

Root worked on the directive during the autumn of 1905. It was his plan to extend the merit provisions of Cleveland's order to all consuls salaried at more than $1,000.[6] Meanwhile, Ambassador George Meyer consulted with Root and convinced the Secretary that the opportunity could also be used to initiate the merit system in diplomacy.[7] The assignment to draw up the provisions for the diplomatic service was probably given to career diplomat and Assistant Secretary of State Herbert Peirce.[8] Roosevelt subsequently accepted both Orders and promulgated them on November 10, 1905. It is perhaps not without significance that Root and Roosevelt were then preparing for the Algeciras Conference, a meeting at which the United States was to be represented by career diplomat Henry White.

The Order for the diplomatic service provided that vacancies be filled either through "transfer or promotion from some branch of the foreign service" or "by the appointment of a person, who, having furnished satisfactory evidence of character, responsibility, and capacity, and being thereupon selected by the President for examination, is found upon such examination to be qualified for the position."[9] To supplement this, Root issued a departmental order on the same day establishing a Board of Examiners composed of the Second Assistant Secretary of State, the Solicitor, and the chief of the Diplomatic Bureau, "whose duty it shall be, by appropriate exam-

[5] The "mounting pressures" may be seen by analyzing the memorials sent to Congress by businesses and business organizations. See *Cong. Rec.*, XXXIX, 58 Cong., 3 sess. (December 5, 1904 — March 4, 1905), 95, 117, 186, 395, 508, 618, 766, 998, 1113, 1161, 1216, 1276, 1563, 1619, 1664, 2053, 2054, 2142, 2705, 3357, 3712, 3819, 3925, and 4041.

[6] 120.11/22, Minutes of the Board of Examiners of the Consular Service (copy of the Executive Order of November 10, 1905).

[7] Mark A. De Wolfe Howe, *George von L. Meyer: His Life and Public Service* (New York, 1919), pp. 220–21.

[8] No evidence can be found as to the exact authorship of the Order. Root was undoubtedly busy with Algeciras. Peirce was known to have been interested in a professional service (see Herbert H. D. Peirce, "Our Diplomatic and Consular Service," *Arena*, XVII [May, 1897], 909–21). He had also been in charge of the research project to study comparative career services for consular officers (see 1102–4, Vol. 183). Peirce's successors were the authors of subsequent orders and bills.

[9] 120.11/22, Minutes of the Board of Examiners of the Consular Service (copy of Executive Order for the consular service, dated November 10, 1905). See also Minutes of the Board of Examiners of the Diplomatic Service (copy of the Order for the diplomatic service, dated November 10, 1905). The second set of Minutes, for which there is no National Archive number, will hereafter be referred to as Minutes, followed by the appropriate year. The material may be found in the Record Center of the Department of State.

ination, to determine the qualifications of persons selected by the President therefor, to be appointed secretaries of embassy or legation." The examination was to be given "from time to time" in Washington, a reasonable notice having been given. The examination was to be both oral and written, consisting of questions on international law and diplomatic usage. The knowledge of one foreign language was also required. The language was to be either French or "the language spoken in the country in which the embassy or legation is located." [10]

Two things were accomplished by the Order. Fitness for office, demonstrated either by experience or by examination, was established as a principle. And second, a Board of Examiners was granted the authority to see that the examination provision was carried out. By implication, the Order also embraced security of tenure. While posts were not guaranteed, the requirement of transfer, promotion, or passing an examination eliminated much of the threat of the spoils politician. Also by implication, if tenure was secure, then promotions from within the service could, a fortiori, be expected. Both, however, relied upon the probable intentions of Roosevelt and Root.

The Order was still a considerable distance from the demands of the reformers. It was binding, though not legally, on Roosevelt alone. The required examination was merely a qualifying test. Also the fact that it was administered only to those prescribed by the President permitted partisan considerations to continue. It was given whenever the Department chose, and was confined exclusively to practical subjects, ignoring completely economics, geography, or history. The required language could be the appropriate one of the post, and this provided little possibility for interpost mobility. There was no attempt at grading secretaryships according to salary or importance in order to establish clear-cut avenues of promotion. Finally, the provisions permitting transfer or promotion from another branch violated the career principle, for "new blood" could always be transfused into the service over the heads of existing members.

If Roosevelt was so internationally minded and sympathetic to civil service reform, why was the Order short of the reformers' demands? The President, above all, felt that the service had too much "bad timber" in it. To perpetuate these men in office would be wrong. In a letter to Richard Harding Davis, Roosevelt wrote, "But there are a large number of well-meaning . . . secretaries, who belong to what I call the pink-tea type, who merely reside in the service instead of working in the service, and these I intend to change whenever the

[10] Minutes (1905) (copy of Departmental Order of November 10, 1905).

need arises." [11] He also believed that a career as a secretary should be "for three or four years and then come back here as they ought to go into business or politics or something of that kind." He further felt that a completely closed system would prevent him from appointing men from the outside.[12] A final reason was his realistic view toward reform. In a letter to William Hale, he wrote:

> One of the disadvantages of needed reforms is that together with the good they do they also now and then work an irritating limitation on the power to do some specific act which would be good in itself, but the performance of which is incompatible with the general scheme.[13]

The Root-Roosevelt Order attracted little attention. Among the supporters of professional diplomacy, however, it was warmly greeted. A writer in *Lippincott's* claimed, "The recent executive order . . . will be a sad blow to the fashionable people who have been accustomed to billet their idle sons and brothers upon the diplomatic service." [14] Shortly after the Order's promulgation, Horace Porter wrote in the *Century*, ". . . the excellent rules established for the examinations of candidates for secretaryships, in languages and other qualifications for entering the diplomatic service, are daily making their advantages manifest." [15] John Foster also supported the Order, but cautioned others to realize that political considerations had not been wholly removed.[16] Roosevelt's standby, the *Outlook*, commended the move, holding, "All this is closely in line with the best English and Continental practice." [17]

The most significant support was forthcoming from the nation's universities. Several institutions had early indicated interest, but it was not until after the Executive Orders for both services that the larger insitutions became attracted. In January, 1906, the National Business League assembled in Chicago presidents of different universities "to improve training and awareness of the American foreign service." During the next three years, eighteen universities, including Harvard, Yale, Columbia, and the universities of Wisconsin, Michigan, and California, announced their plans to provide preparation for

[11] Roosevelt to Davis, January 3, 1905, and to Meyer, December 26, 1904, in T. Roosevelt, *Letters*, IV, 1089–90, 1079.

[12] Roosevelt to Francis Cabot Lowell, January 8, 1906, in *ibid.*, V, 129. See also Arthur Sherburne Hardy, *Things Remembered* (Boston, 1923), p. 46.

[13] Roosevelt to Hale, December 3, 1908, in T. Roosevelt, *Letters*, VI, 1407.

[14] René Baché, *op. cit.*, 223.

[15] Horace Porter, "Should the Government Own Its Embassies," *Century*, LXXVII (March, 1909), 782.

[16] John W. Foster, *Practice of Diplomacy*, p. 11.

[17] Editorial, *Outlook*, LXXXI (November 25, 1905), 686.

men interested in entering the service. The George Washington University and Yale schemes were financed by New York business firms. Yale and Columbia maintained a joint program — Yale providing the instruction in languages and Columbia in political science.[18] Charles W. Eliot of Harvard keynoted the movement, maintaining, "The Universities of the country can perform a service of increasing value in training men for diplomatic and consular positions." [19] And Eliot's Harvard was one of the first to attempt establishing diplomatic training in the curriculum. In late 1906, Roosevelt received a solicitation for funds for a diplomatic, consular, and colonial service school at Harvard. The letter said that Root and Mrs. Hay supported the venture.[20] Although the Harvard attempt failed, other institutions continued in liaison with the State Department over modifications in university curriculums and suggestions about examinations.[21]

Those who opposed the application of merit to the diplomatic service remained silent. Concerning its application to both services, Root wrote to Seth Low:

> I supposed there would be a tremendous row about the change, but I have been agreeably surprised to find comparatively few violent objections. I think we are going to maintain our position without very serious controversy throughout this administration.[22]

The support the Order received was scarcely merited. Primarily the measure was an expression of good intentions. In operation, it did not end political or personal considerations. Nor was the examination seriously adhered to. Post Wheeler's wife's cousin, Speaker Cannon, was the instrumental party in Wheeler's appointment. Wheeler subsequently performed an act of political faith and received Roosevelt's designation.[23] The names of approving senators appeared next to the names of designees in the examiners' books.[24] On a purely personal level, Henry White convinced the President of the wisdom of designating his brother-in-law for a secretaryship.[25] Also, Joseph

[18] National Business League of America, *American Universities and an American Foreign Service* (Chicago, 1909), pp. 1–36.

[19] *Ibid.*, p. 36.

[20] E. H. Wells to Roosevelt, December 8, 1906, in 2108/136.

[21] Philip C. Jessup, *Elihu Root*, II, 108. Letters from Dr. Richard S. Harlan (April 5, 1907) of George Washington University and Professor Andrew F. West (January 25, 1909) of Princeton.

[22] Root to Low, December 24, 1906, in *ibid.*, II, 107.

[23] Wheeler and Rives, *Dome of Many-Coloured Glass*, p. 203; see also Hugh Wilson, *Education of a Diplomat*, p. 8.

[24] Minutes (1906–8).

[25] Roosevelt to White, July 21, 1906, in T. Roosevelt, *Letters*, V, 335.

Grew was brought to the attention of Roosevelt by the Storers and thereafter dealt personally with the President.[26]

Correspondence also reveals that "the geographical needs of the situation" entered into decisions. These "needs," however, differed from those of previous periods. While Roosevelt and Root sought to prevent a concentration of office-holders in only a few of their supporters' states, they also sought to assuage some public criticism of the sectional character of their appointments.[27] In response to ten years in the patronage wilderness, the southern Democrats attempted to use the administration's support of the merit principle to force appointments of southerners to both services. The section's commercial situation, they thought, made these appointments particularly imperative. Senator Albert S. Burleson of Texas was the most vocal of them. He insisted:

> In a republican form of government the diplomatic officer is the representative of his country, and is in no sense the personal representative of the Chief Executive. Such being the case I do not believe there is a man within the sound of my voice who would contend for one minute that the appointment of our diplomatic officers should not be equitably and fairly distributed between the various sections of our country.[28]

Although the reformers pointed out the contradiction between the merit principle and distributing positions equitably among the states, subsequent appointments by Roosevelt recognized the Southern claims. To William Dudley Foulke, Roosevelt wrote, ". . . appointments in the diplomatic and consular services . . . have been made without regard to politics; . . . more Democrats than Republicans having been appointed, as we are trying to even up the quotas of the Southern States."[29] In practice, 26 per cent of all appointed under the 1905 Order came from states nominally considered Southern. Roosevelt's correspondence and the sectional percentage are significant for three reasons. They first show a growing interparty belief that the development of the service should be along non-

[26] Roosevelt to Maria Storer, January 9, 1905, in *ibid.*, IV, 1096; Joseph C. Grew, *Turbulent Era*, ed. Walter Johnson (Boston: Houghton Mifflin Co., 1952), I, 13.

[27] Roosevelt to William Dudley Foulke, February 7, 1908, in T. Roosevelt, *Letters*, VI, 927; Roosevelt to Lodge, April 10, 1905, in IV, 1166–67. Although the letter was written before the Executive Order, it reveals the seriousness with which Roosevelt treated the question of states' representation.

[28] *Cong. Rec.*, XL, 59 Cong., 1 sess. (May 29, 1906), 7628.

[29] Roosevelt to William Dudley Foulke, February 7, 1908, in T. Roosevelt, *Letters*, VI, 927.

partisan lines. They also reveal the greatest personnel problem facing a federal system. If the service was filled with men whose basic qualification was residence in a certain state, then all pretenses to a career must be abandoned. Finally, Roosevelt's letter to Foulke, while admitting to the sectional appointments, also inferred that a candidate's political preference was known before the appointment.

The fact that partisan and geographical considerations were important mitigated the potential influence of the examination system on appointments. That two "career men," Adee and Smith, were members of the Board of Examiners was encouraging. Their setting the passing mark at 80 per cent was also encouraging.[30] But it was soon apparent to the Board that "designation" was synonomous with "approval," and that admission to the service was not necessarily contingent upon success in the examination. In an undated letter to Adee, Smith wrote, "Mr. Peirce sails next Thursday and desires Mr. L. to accompany him, so that there is not much time left to complete the papers."[31] The establishing of qualifications in languages was equally meaningless. Reporting favorably on a candidate, Adee wrote, "As to his knowledge of languages, I find that he does not now possess a working knowledge of any modern tongue. . . . I find that he was carefully educated in Latin and Greek, and this . . . will doubtless make a practical acquisition of the French tongue easy."[32] Smith took to calling the process "the needful" examination.[33]

Although Post Wheeler contended that "no Princeton, Yale, or Harvard senior could have passed it with a grade over 65," the examination was considerably less difficult than his statement implies.[34] As it was primarily of a "short-answer" nature, its reliance on memorized facts made it easily crammed for. During this period, a textbook, Van Dyne's *Our Foreign Service*, was published to fill any lacunae in knowledge.[35] A "cram-school" was also reported to be in operation.[36] Furthermore, the examination was not substantially changed during Roosevelt's Presidency. A new passage occasionally appeared for language translation, but the sections on diplomatic usage and international law remained essentially unaltered. Nor was any formal procedure adopted for conducting the prescribed oral examination.

[30] Minutes (1906).
[31] Minutes (1906).
[32] Minutes (November 5, 1906).
[33] Minutes (July 5, 1906).
[34] Wheeler and Rives, *op. cit.*, p. 204.
[35] Frederic Van Dyne, *Our Foreign Service* (New York, 1909).
[36] Hugh Wilson, *op. cit.*, p. 10. A statement in Wilson's book is the only evidence that such a school existed. Wilson wrote, "He [Huntington Wilson] advised me to stay away from the cramming school and go to the École Libre des Sciences Politiques."

Finally, only two out of the twenty-five taking the examination failed it.[37] It is probably not coincidental that one of the failures was from the South and the second from a state in the hands of the Democrats.[38]

But other evidence must be considered before a judgment can be made on the Roosevelt-Root diplomatic service. While the recruitment showed a more apparent than real gain, other aspects, more or less directly relevant, revealed genuine advances in the direction of professionalization. One of these was promotions within the service. To succeed Herbert Peirce as Assistant Secretary of State, Roosevelt, under the pressure of Taft, promoted career officer F. M. Huntington Wilson.[39] This appointment provided a continuity for the service's point of view in the administration of the Department. A more significant trend was in the question of ministerial appointments made from within the service. Betwen 1906 and 1908, the percentage of these promotions rose from 31 to 39.3 per cent. Over 64 per cent of all members remaining in the service from before 1901 had risen to the upper level. Men like Griscom, Riddle, Jackson, and Peirce constituted a solid nucleus of career ministers.[40] Even those not promoted to ministerships received, with few exceptions, promotions to one or more posts or positions.[41]

Two qualifications, however, must be registered. An average of only 9.4 years passed between entering the service and reaching the ministerial level. This meant that ministers were relatively young and had had, by present standards, fantastically rapid promotion.[42] The speed, though, was very uneven, and many worthy secretaries were passed by. This problem would become less frequent once the channels of promotion were worn down through career stability. The second qualification is that political pressures operated here also.[43] An unqualified claim that merit was the sole element in these promotions cannot be defended. Nevertheless, amidst continuing debate about their advisability, widening opportunities for promotion were created under Roosevelt. The *Outlook* in 1907 appropriately commented, "Merit — that is, character, attainments, and proved efficiency of serv-

[37] Minutes (1906–9) (copies of examinations given for admission into the Diplomatic Service).

[38] They were from Florida and Missouri.

[39] *Biog. Reg.* (1906), p. 9. Wilson received his commission on June 22, 1906.

[40] Griscom was then ambassador to Japan; Riddle was ambassador to Russia; Jackson was minister to Persia, and Peirce was minister to Norway.

[41] Only one secretary who was appointed before 1905 had not received a promotion by the end of Roosevelt's second term.

[42] Griscom was twenty-nine and had served two years as a secretary when he was promoted to the ministership in Persia. John W. Riddle, on the other hand, was forty-five and had served thirteen years as a secretary before his promotion.

[43] Roosevelt to Albert J. Beveridge, November 12, 1907, in T. Roosevelt, *Letters*, V, 844–45.

ice — has been increasingly emphasized by President Roosevelt's foreign appointments." [44]

The principle of security of tenure also gained. That people were promoted, a fortiori, implies that they retained their membership in the service. Exactly 15 per cent of the lower service consisted of secretaries appointed before 1902, many of them even before 1896. Personnel turnover was about 7 per cent annually, new appointments stemming from recently created secretaryships.[45] To Redfield Proctor in 1907 Roosevelt boasted that he made fewer original appointments "than almost any other President within the same length of time, because I have continued in office all good men." [46]

Even the "needful" examination process was not without improvements before Roosevelt's retirement. In 1906, the function of grading examinations was assumed by the independent and impartial Civil Service Commission.[47] Designees were officially discouraged from attending the cram-schools, and the system of administering the examination at legations and embassies was inaugurated in 1908. Designees, however, were required to return to Washington for the oral examination.[48]

Although less immediately relevant to professionalization, several events occurred after the 1905 Order that had long-term effects on the diplomatic service. Each was the product of Legislative-Executive co-operation. No Secretary of State had been more effective in his relations with Congress than Elihu Root.[49] Comparing his relations with Hay's, Roosevelt claimed, "As soon as Root came in the situation changed as if by magic." [50] The Secretary's aim was to be as co-operative as possible on some issues. For instance, when Representative Charles C. Bennett in 1908 attempted to organize a commission to investigate the overseas facilities, Root indorsed the move:

> I think that a visit by such a commission as is proposed to
> our diplomatic and consular officers abroad for the purpose
> of becoming more familiar with the ways in which their

[44] "Merit and Diplomacy: Some Personal Impressions," *Outlook*, LXXXV (January 26, 1907), 211.

[45] Cf. *Foreign List for 1912* (London, 1913), p. xxii. The resignation rate in 1912 for the British Service was 1.2 per cent.

[46] Roosevelt to Proctor, June 13, 1907, in T. Roosevelt, *Letters*, V, 689.

[47] Peirce to Proctor, January 4, 1906, in 120.1121/159.

[48] Hugh Wilson, *op. cit.*, p. 10; Minutes (1908).

[49] A Diplomatist, *American Foreign Policy* (Boston, 1909), p. 177. Lewis Einstein observed, "Of late there has been a fortunate disappearance of that lack of sympathy which long existed between Congress and the Department of State." The disappearance was temporary. When Root resigned, the antagonisms began afresh, and, with the possible exception of Charles Evans Hughes, no subsequent Secretary has had great success in securing support for administrative matters.

[50] Roosevelt to Lodge, January 28, 1909, in T. Roosevelt, *Letters*, VI, 1497.

work is done, their needs, their deficiencies, their capacity for improvement, and the best way to improve them, would be very useful.[51]

He was also always ready to testify at congressional hearings.[52] In return, Congress usually granted the Secretary's requests. Particularly important to diplomacy was congressional approval for expansion in the number of posts. Twelve new secretaryships, many located significantly in Central and Latin America, were authorized by Congress.[53] The lower service now stood at sixty secretaryships.

Another example of these relations was the successful passage in April, 1906, of a law reorganizing the consular service. While it was partly a synthesis of previous bills on the subject, it was framed afresh by Root and Lodge.[54] Their final draft enlarged the bill's scope, retaining the merit and classification provisions, but adding a system of inspection and several administrative prohibitions relating to hiring and accounting.[55] The law as accepted eliminated the merit provisions and diluted the mechanism of classification.[56] Upon the advice of Root, Roosevelt supplemented this with the Executive Order of June 27, 1906, which established a Board of Examiners, an examination based on a wide range of subjects for entrance to the lowest class, promotions by demonstrated merit, and the abolition of partisan considerations from appointment or promotion.[57] The significance of the new Order is twofold. First, the Order provided a yardstick and continuous precedents for similar developments in the diplomatic service. And second, the administration of the Order was placed temporarily in the hands of Huntington Wilson. This experience, coupled with his studies of foreign service administration in other countries, later guided his reorganization of the diplomatic service.[58]

The 1905 Order was enforced for such a short period that it is

[51] Root to Charles Landis, February 21, 1908, in House Rept. 1696, 60 Cong., 1 sess. (May 12, 1908), p. 1.

[52] E.g., House Rept. 2008, 61 Cong., 3 sess. (January 28, 1911), p. 2. Extracts of testimony by Root before the Committee on Foreign Relations in 1906.

[53] 35 Stat. 172 (May 21, 1908). Those in South America were Brazil, Bolivia, Costa Rica, Dominican Republic, Ecuador, Honduras, Nicaragua, Panama, Paraguay, and San Salvador.

[54] Jessup, *op. cit.*, II, 100–106.

[55] 120.11/22, Minutes of the Board of Examiners of the Consular Service (copy of S 680).

[56] 34 Stat. 99 (April 5, 1906).

[57] *Biog. Reg.* (1907), pp. 84–85 (copy of Executive Order of June 27, 1906).

[58] F. M. Huntington Wilson, *Memoirs of an Ex-Diplomat*, pp. 157–58; *Foreign Relations* (1906), II, 1362–63; Emily Bax, *Miss Bax of the Embassy* (Boston: Houghton Mifflin Co., 1939), p. 119; 1702–4, Vol. 183.

impossible to generalize about its effects on the service. A few letters and dispatches from secretaries suggest that a sense of identity and uniqueness as professionals was being developed.[59] Statistically, over 39.1 per cent of those appointed had seen service either as a private secretary to a minister or ambassador or as a member of the consular service. The latter were not, however, cases of lateral transfer. They had taken positions in the consular service to await vacancies in the diplomatic.[60] It can be argued from this statistic that those who were best acquainted with the diplomatic service had confidence in its future as a carer. The average age remained at thirty years. Only 16.6 per cent had attended public secondary schools. Exactly half of those appointed had been educated at Harvard, Yale, or Princeton. A further 25 per cent had received education abroad.[61] Study abroad, particularly at the École Libre des Sciences Politiques, was often recommended by members of the Department to aspirants.[62] Only three secretaries received an education at state universities, while none were without a university education. Over 65 per cent had taken some course of postgraduate work.

Before retiring from the Secretaryship, Root obtained from his successor an assurance that the Orders would remain in force.[63] A guarantee, however, was unnecessary, for the election of 1908 sustained the Republican party in power. The diplomatic service continued to function as if nothing had occurred in November. Only two secretaries resigned after the election, and Roosevelt's Department held an examination in January, 1909, to fill the posts.[64] William Phillips was appointed by Acting Secretary Bacon to the Third Assistant Secretaryship with the expectation that he would continue in office under Taft.[65] Public opinion was not alarmed either. Journals stressed the number of career appointments under Roosevelt and anticipated further progress under Taft.[66]

[59] Norman Hutchinson to Root, September 18, 1908, in 15864, Vol. 938. Hutchinson complained that his politically appointed superior ignored his career officers in "diplomatic business and social affairs." On the other hand, Lewis Einstein maintained, "The remembrance of a former and purely political method of recruitment of all officials still causes our diplomatic posts abroad to feel perhaps too isolated from one another, and not as parts of one great system bound together by common action inspired by a common purpose." See A Diplomatist, *American Foreign Policy*, p. 164.

[60] Grew, for instance, served a consularship in North Africa before he received his appointment. See Grew to Edward Bell, January 4, 1910, in Grew, *op. cit.*, I, 63.

[61] This percentage includes both the undergraduate and graduate levels.

[62] Hugh Wilson, *op. cit.*, p. 10; Hugh Gibson, *Hugh Gibson*, ed. Perein G. Galpin (New York: Belgian-American Educational Foundation, 1956), pp. 159–60.

[63] Jessup, *op. cit.*, II, 107.

[64] Minutes (1909).

[65] *Biog. Reg.* (1909), p. 90. The date of commission was January 11, 1909.

[66] E.g., Editorial, *Outlook*, XCII (May 15, 1909), 93.

This confidence in the service's future came partly from the fact that the same party remained in power and partly because Roosevelt's successor, William Howard Taft, was also heir to his policies. As Governor General of the Philippines and Secretary of War, he appreciated the career nature of the military and colonial services. These experiences also made him keenly interested in questions of administration. In 1904, he was among those whom Roosevelt consulted about applying the merit principle to the diplomatic service.[67] Finally, the aims of Taft's diplomacy made a professional service indispensable. From the outset, he was wedded to the concept of official assistance in extending American commerce abroad.[68] He was also toying with the idea of negotiating compulsory arbitration treaties.[69]

Less was known about the attitudes of Taft's Secretary of State, Philander Knox. He had officiated at the birth of the Carnegie Steel Corporation and the Department of Commerce and Labor and thus presumably had an interest in administration.[70] He also was consulted by Roosevelt in 1904 on the question of merit in the diplomatic service.[71] And it is fair to assume that his appointment meant that he agreed with the views of the President.

Nevertheless, the early acts of the new administration contradicted these assumptions. In a letter to Whitelaw Reid, Henry Adams reported, "Knox did not know enough diplomacy to organize his Department, which he has thrown into confusion." [72] Of greater significance was Taft's forcing the resignations of five of Roosevelt's seventeen career ministers. Among them were Henry White and John Riddle. The reformers, as well as former President Roosevelt, were shocked and indignant.[73] An editorial in the *Nation* believed that the removals were "not an encouraging example to the young American who aspires to fit himself thoroughly for diplomacy." [74] But much of this criticism was unwarranted. Lloyd Griscom had only qualified claims to having "come from the ranks," and Roosevelt personally had recommended the dropping of Spencer Eddy.[75] Also one man was

[67] Straus, *op. cit.*, p. 184.

[68] See William Howard Taft, *Presidential Addresses and State Papers* (London, 1915), pp. 463–64 (Message to Congress, dated December 7, 1909).

[69] Foster Rhea Dulles, *America's Rise to World Power* (London: Hamish Hamilton, 1955), pp. 79–80.

[70] See Herbert B. Wright, "Philander C. Knox," *American Secretaries of State and their Diplomacy*, IX, 303.

[71] Straus, *op. cit.*, p. 184.

[72] Harold Dean Cater, *Henry Adams and His Friends* (Boston: Houghton Mifflin Co., 1947), p. 637. The letters is dated February 15, 1909.

[73] Roosevelt to George Otto Trevelyan, October 1, 1911, in T. Roosevelt, *Letters*, VII, 368.

[74] "The Diplomatic Service," *Nation*, LXXXIX (October 28, 1909), 398.

[75] Griscom had served only two years as a secretary. Furthermore, he had not expected

reappointed to the service.[76] However, Taft's major *gaffe*, White's and Riddle's expulsion, is beyond intelligent explanation.

To solve the organizational problems of the Department and ameliorate reformers' criticisms, Taft appointed as First Assistant Secretary Huntington Wilson.[77] No one was better equipped to restore order to the Department than he. Wilson was acquainted with the problems and had attempted earlier to improve the administration. He was also a long-time advocate of reform in the diplomatic service. In 1906 he maintained:

> But the ideal foreign service for which the way is now open needs for its accomplishment the support of an active, not passive, public opinion; and it needs the cooperation of the Senators and Representatives entrusted with the President and the Secretary of State, and with some of those who have studied the service from within. The foreign service of all countries must be studied and examined. What is good must be adopted, or what is better must be devised.

He generally believed, "Examinations will insure the special knowledge, a permanent service will supply the experience, promotion for meritorious work will secure the zeal." [78] Finally, his administration of the Executive Order for the consular service showed him the possibilities of reform. It was he, for instance, who insisted upon and subsequently devised an equally weighted oral examination in 1906.[79]

Wilson's first task was to fill the vacancies created by the elevation of some secretaries to ministerships and by recent resignations. Although the examiners set virtually the same written examination as before, Wilson used the opportunity to institute the formal criteria used in the consular service's oral examination. The criteria were "character and disposition," "personality," "general intelligence," and "experience and business capacity." Each heading was subdivided into more specific headings, such as "address," "judgment," "discretion," and "resourcefulness." [80]

Twenty-six ultimately took the examination. The situation over ministerial expulsions apparently did not discourage applicants, for the total was larger than it had ever been. Fourteen passed the examin-

to be retained by Taft. See Lloyd C. Griscom, *Diplomatically Speaking*, p. 305. Roosevelt to Taft, December 31, 1908, in T. Roosevelt, *Letters*, VI, 1454 (letter concerning Eddy).

[76] H. Percival Dodge was reappointed to a secretaryship.

[77] *Biog. Reg.* (1909), p. 104. The date of his commission was March 5, 1909.

[78] F. M. Huntington Wilson, "The American Foreign Service," *Outlook*, LXXXII (September 16, 1906), 501, 504.

[79] F. M. Huntington Wilson, *Memoirs*, pp. 155–56.

[80] Minutes (1909).

ation. Only seven of the successful, however, achieved the requisite 80 per cent. The remaining seven received a bonus of 5 per cent. Twelve were subsequently appointed.[81]

Wilson then moved to the question of in-service training. A period of instruction in the Department prior to an assignment had long been advocated.[82] Wilson had complained about his own inadequate training.[83] Using the 1890 provision that allowed compensation for diplomatic officers receiving instructions, Wilson inaugurated in June a month's instruction in the Department for the new appointments.[84] A similar scheme had been established two years earlier in the consular service.[85]

In a letter to Representative Perkins, Knox described the training:

> The candidates worked during the Department's office hours (9–4:30) with two talks upon different matters with which they should be familiar before going to posts in the diplomatic service. They are also taught to write dispatches and an effort is made to familiarize them with all the forms and procedures of diplomacy.[86]

Members of Congress were among the speakers.[87] On the scheme the *New York Times* commented, "As the Young-Men-Who-Would-Be-Ambassadors have nothing to do but absorb the lectures and look happy, there is every reason to believe it will work out to a triumphant finish." [88]

Wilson's third task was the reorganization of the Department. On July 22, Knox asked Congress for $100,000 to carry out Wilson's plans. With the support of career diplomat Chandler Hale's father, Senator Eugene Hale, the appropriation was granted two weeks later. Although many aspects of the reorganization, such as the geographical regrouping of reporting units, had long-term effects on the service, the more extensive application of the merit principle was alone of immediate relevance.[89] Little can be discovered about the framing of the Executive Order, but the fact that it could draw on the experiences of the 1905 and 1906 Orders suggests that there was little diffi-

[81] Minutes (1909).

[82] E.g., William Franklin Sands, *Undiplomatic Memories*, pp. 3–5.

[83] F. M. Huntington Wilson, *Memoirs*, p. 48.

[84] *Ibid.*, p. 188.

[85] James B. Stewart, "Foreign Service Officers Training School," *American Foreign Service Journal*, X (June, 1933), 224–27.

[86] In 20345, Vol. 1085, June 22, 1909.

[87] Knox to Senator S. M. Cullom, June 23, 1909, in 20346, Vol. 1085.

[88] *New York Times*, June 20, 1909, p. 12.

[89] See *Reorganization of the State Department*, II (1911). See also F. M. Huntington Wilson, *Memoirs of an Ex-Diplomat*, pp. 181–93.

culty in its preparation. In October, an editorial in the *Nation* contended, "When Mr. Taft returns to Washington he will find nothing more pressing than the reorganization of the diplomatic service." [90] On November 26, 1909, President Taft signed the measure.[91]

Briefly, the Order extended the provisions of the Pendleton Act of 1883 to the diplomatic service without placing the service's personnel under the jurisdiction of the Civil Service Commission. A Board of Examiners was established within the Department, composed of the Assistant Secretary of State, the Solicitor, the chief of the Diplomatic Bureau, the chief of the Bureau of Appointments, and the chief examiner of the Civil Service Commission. It was given authority to issue notices about, make rules for, and hold examinations, "at such time as the needs of the service require." Presidential designations were to cease thirty days before the examination, and "reasonable notice" had to be given to the candidates. The Order also stipulated that "neither in the designation . . . or certification for appointment . . . will the political affiliations of the candidates be considered." The examination was to be in two parts. The written part required a knowledge of international law; one modern language; [92] "the natural, industrial and commercial resources and the commerce of the United States, especially with reference to the possibilities of increasing and extending the trade of the United States with foreign countries"; American history, government, and institutions; and the modern history since 1850 of Europe, Latin America, and the Far East. The object of the oral examination was to "determine the candidate's alertness, general contemporary information, and natural fitness for the service." The parts were to count equally, and a score of eighty on a scale of one hundred was the passing mark. The eligibility of successful candidates was to last for two years.

The Order further prescribed admission only to the lowest positions, security of tenure, and promotion by merit. Original appointments were confined to the positions of third secretary of embassy, second secretary of legation, or first secretary in a single-secretary legation. In these appointments, "due regard will be had to the rule, that as between candidates of equal merit, appointments should be made so as to tend to secure proportional representation of all the States and Territories." Vacancies in higher secretaryships were to

[90] "The Diplomatic Service," *Nation*, LXXXIX (October 28, 1909), 398.

[91] Civil Service Commission, *Twenty-Sixth Report* (Washington, 1909), pp. 120–22.

[92] *Ibid.* The language could be French, German, or Spanish. Cf. Departmental Order of November 10, 1905. It stipulated that "familiarity with at least one foreign language will be required. This language may be either the language spoken in the country in which the embassy or legation is located, or French" (see Minutes [1906]).

be filled by promotions. Except for those earning more than $1,800 annually, transfers from the Department and the consular service required an examination; no preferential treatment, "unless the exigencies of the service imperatively demand it," was to be shown transfers. The only condition stipulated for remaining in the service was "maintaining a degree of efficiency well up to the average high standard which the interests of the service demand." A secretary was able to leave the service for one year and be reinstated,[93] and temporary duty in the Department was permitted without loss of rank. A record of efficiency of every officer was to be kept "so that there may be no promotion except upon well established efficiency shown in the service." To facilitate promotions all secretaryships were graded "according to the importance, volume, difficulty, or other aspects of the work done by each mission in proportion to the number of men allotted to it." Finally, the Order directed the Secretary of State "to report from time to time to the President, along with his recommendations, the names of those secretaries of the higher grades in the Diplomatic Service who by reason of efficient service have demonstrated special capacity for promotion to be chiefs of mission."

When compared with the 1905 Order and the 1906 Order for the consular service, many advances and similarities emerge. In the case of the 1906 Order, several of its administrative features, such as efficiency records and the scope of the examination, were borrowed for the diplomatic service. Even the phraseology of their provisions was similar.[94] Over the 1905 Order, the 1909 measure primarily insured a politics-free lower service. Although the examination remained a qualifying examination, it was more intelligently conceived and better geared to the commercial aims of American diplomacy. A minimal concession only was made to geographical representation, while demonstrated efficiency became the sole criterion for promotion — even to the ministerial level — in a graded system. And established as the keystone of the new merit system was the cumulative efficiency record of every secretary.

On the other hand, for reasons both within and beyond the control of the Executive, many administrative barriers to sound career development were created or maintained by the 1909 Order. Age limits of twenty-one and fifty were established for candidates. They permitted men to enter the service after failures in other vocations and

[93] *Ibid.* This provision was dependent upon the willingness of the President to reinstate the secretary and on the existence of a vacancy.

[94] See *Biog. Reg.* (1907), pp. 84–85. Clause ten for the consular service and the paragraph dealing with promotions in the diplomatic service are, to a large extent, the same. The state representation clauses are also the same.

too late to make it a "lifetime" career. The system of holding the written examination only in Washington hindered those living in distant areas from taking it. Also, by not specifying a general date for the examination, the Order prevented potential applicants from making long-range plans for suitable preparation. Lateral transfers had not been completely abolished. Above all, stopping the promotional ladder below the ministerial level erected a ceiling over the service, past which only special cases could go. There were now "the service" and "the ministers and ambassadors."

Beyond control of the Order were the inadequate wage structure and the absence of retirement provisions. Also untouchable was the senatorial control over the movements of secretaries from one post to another and up the promotional ladder. Finally, the Order was not legally binding on the President. Without legislation, Taft's successor could simply ignore it.

Shortly after its promulgation, Huntington Wilson moved to secure the necessary public opinion behind the Order. On November 29, under the Secretary's signature, Wilson sent copies of the Order to 125 newspapers and periodicals. Knox's accompanying letter claimed:

> At the present time, when the commercial rivalry between nations is so keen and when political questions of great importance are constantly arising, it is necessary that the efficiency of the American foreign service . . . should be considerably increased.

It then suggested that "any publicity which you may find space and inclination to give the subject of this Order . . . will be a useful public service." [95]

The response came as expected. A Seattle newspaper held, "Secretary Knox's changes in the regulations of the diplomatic and consular service ought to work a healthy and hopeful revolution." [96] The *New York Times* thought ". . . the improvements in the lower offices of the service will be beneficial, on their own account, and doubtless many young men of good character and education will be attracted to the diplomatic career." [97]

In his first Message to Congress on December 7, Taft claimed:

> In modern times political and commercial interests are interrelated, and in the negotiation of commercial treaties,

---

[95] In 22629, Vol. 1136, November 29, 1909.

[96] Editorial, *Seattle Post-Intelligencer*, December 7, 1909, p. 6. See 22629, Vol. 1136.

[97] Editorial, *New York Times*, December 6, 1909, p. 8. See also editorial, *Outlook*, XCIII (December 18, 1909), 851.

conventions, and tariff agreements the keeping open of opportunities and the proper support of American enterprise,
our Diplomatic Service is quite as important as the Consular Service to the business interests of the country.

For this reason, he contended, he had signed the Executive Order
which assured securing competent personnel. He concluded by
recommending that Congress consider safeguarding the merit system
through legislation.[98]

Agreeing with Taft's argument and appreciating the need for
legislation, Representative William H. Wiley communicated with the
President about putting the Executive Order into a statute. Taft
turned the matter over to Knox, who, along with Wilson, thought
that a law so soon after the Order would not permit the kinks to
emerge before they were set into legislation. Both further felt that the
Republican party had at least three more years in power and that more
propitious times were yet to come.[99] But Wiley persisted and introduced the bill on January 7, 1910. The bill was sent to the Committee on Foreign Affairs and died there from lack of support.[100]

Meanwhile, Wilson was preparing for the first examination under
the new Order. Although applications were slow in coming, he
was encouraged by the continuing interest shown by the universities.
L. F. Rowe, for instance, wrote to Wilson that "an increasing number
of students at the University of Pennsylvania . . . desire to enter the
diplomatic and consular service." [101] By the beginning of February,
however, only eleven had applied and were designated for examination. Of the nine who took the examination, six passed it and were
appointed. But more distressing yet was the fact that only two had
achieved the requisite 80 per cent. Bonus percentages had to be added
to the scores of the other four.[102] For a second time, the number of
places to be filled exceeded the number of successful candidates.

If the Executive Order were to establish the service on a career
basis and consequently attract qualified candidates, the first examination showed that it failed. The number was small and their quality
dubious. To exacerbate things further the *New York Times* in October reported that the courses at Yale and Columbia for training
graduate students for the service had proved a failure. Only one stu-

[98] Taft, *op. cit.*, pp. 463–64.
[99] Knox to Taft, December 18, 1909, in 22629, Vol. 1136.
[100] *Cong. Rec.*, XLV, 61 Cong., 2 sess. (January 7, 1910), 409. Copy of the bill was
found in Library of Congress, HR 17270.
[101] Rowe to Wilson, February 1, 1910, in 2108/137.
[102] Minutes (1910).

dent had taken the examination.[103] The cause, which was later confirmed by a Columbia official, was "the belief of men, who might otherwise select the course, that political and personal influence rather than individual merit and record is still the mechanism for obtaining a diplomatic appointment."[104] More important still, the Republicans lost control of the House of Representatives in the 1910 election. In order to insure that the Order would not be rescinded by a hostile administration in 1912 and to overcome the hesitation of potential applicants, a law was needed. And it was needed before the new Congress took office. The time was also ripe for putting the consular service's merit provisions on a legislative basis.

On December 6, 1910, Taft urged Congress to enact the merit provisions for both services into law. He insisted that the extension of the merit principle had had "excellent results" and to codify it would "effect further improvement." He thought it would serve to attract candidates of a high quality and "maintain that degree of efficiency which the interests of our international relations and commerce demand." Without referring to the consular service, whose position was then beyond doubt, Taft concluded by maintaining that the diplomatic service was "devoid of partisanship."[105]

Representative Frank Lowden, who was simultaneously interested in legation legislation, agreed to sponsor the necessary bill. With Wilson and Carr, he drafted a measure which put the merit provisions of the two Executive Orders into statutory language.[106] The Boards of

[103] *New York Times*, October 23, 1910, p. 3.

[104] William Harris Douglas to Knox, November 11, 1910, in 120.1/-. Cf. Foster, *op. cit.*, p. 11.

[105] 120.1/24A, Copy of Taft's Message to Congress, December 6, 1910.

[106] House Rept. 2008, 61 Cong., 3 sess. (January 28, 1911), p. 11; F. M. Huntington Wilson, *Memoirs of an Ex-Diplomat*, p. 189; 120.11/22, Copy of HR 31170, January 11, 1911. Lowden's legation legislation is worthy of some attention here, for it had long-term effects on the democratization of diplomacy. The necessity for a minister to provide his own official quarters had been protested for many years (e.g., House Exec. Doc. 94, 22 Cong., 2 sess. [February 7, 1833], pp. 5–6). The salary by no means permitted a minister to conduct his social business and maintain an adequate legation without private financial assistance (e.g., Charles R. King, *Life of Rufus King* [New York, 1895], II, 73; Caroline G. Marsh, *Life and Letters of George P. Marsh* [New York, 1888], pp. 177–78). When outfits and infits were abolished in 1855–56 (10 Stat. 619 [March 1, 1855], 11 Stat. 52 [August 18, 1856]), the problem increased enormously. After the Civil War, especially after the creation of ambassadorships, it became virtually impossible for a man without an independent income to take an upper service post (e.g., Elsie P. Mende, *Horace Porter: An American Soldier and Diplomat* [New York, 1927], II, 180). Drawing on democratic sentiment, publicists began agitating in the 1890's for government ownership of buildings as a means of ameliorating the financial burden (e.g., Edward J. Phelps, *International Relations*, p. 27; Julien Gordon, "Proper Grade of Diplomatic Representation," *North American Review*, CLXXX [January, 1905], 63; Baché, *op. cit.*, p. 218. Herbert H. D. Peirce, "The American Diplomatic Service,"

Examiners for both services, the scope and method of their examinations, the requirement for reporting to the President the names of particularly qualified candidates for promotion, the efficiency records, and the self-denying ordinance on partisan considerations, were all to be legally established. The bill also proposed many other needed features. The posts were arranged into five classes, according to salaries,[107] and appointments thereafter were to classes, not posts. To Congress the concession was granted of announcing the results of the examinations and geographical representation of the service annually. But, upon Lowden's insistence, no concession was made on the question of appointments or promotions.[108] Congress could not force the President to appoint anyone who passed the examination or promote anyone who had served within the ranks. Although all features of the bill facilitated such appointments or promotions, the Constitutional prerogative was not surrendered.

The bill was introduced on January 11 and was referred to the Committee on Foreign Affairs.[109] Meanwhile, Knox and Wilson attempted to aid the measure's passage. Letters indorsing the bill were sent to influential congressmen. Knox wrote to Representative David J. Foster, "I cannot overstate my belief that Mr. Lowden's bill is exactly what is demanded by the best interests of the foreign serv-

Putnam's, V [February, 1909], 530–35; "The Ambassadorship Muddle," *Nation*, LXXXVI, [April 2, 1908], 298). To this was added the force of the growing chauvinist sentiment. Many people argued that an American legation occupying the upstairs of a grocery shop endangered the national honor (e.g., Gustav Steinberg, "America's First Embassadorial Building in Berlin," *Overland Monthly*, XL [August, 1902], 139; Herbert H. D. Peirce, "Our Diplomatic and Consular Service," p. 921; Horace Porter, "Should the Government Own its Embassies," p. 782; *Cong. Rec.*, XLII, 60 Cong. 1 sess. [April 18, 1908], 4925). Furthermore, it was becoming increasingly apparent that proper representation had a dollar value. Using this as its theme, an American Embassy Association was established to further the movement (e.g., American Embassy Association, *American Embassies Mean Better Foreign Business* [New York, 1913]; Ellery C. Stowell to Phillips, November 21, 1919, in 121.1/32:1140).

After several unsuccessful attempts and with the continued support of the Executive (James D. Richardson, *Messages*, IX, 648; T. Roosevelt, *Letters*, V, 150; *Abridgement* [Washington, 1913], XI, 8), Lowden finally obtained congressional approval on February 23, 1911 (see *Cong. Rec.*, XLIII, 61 Cong. 3 sess. [February 23, 1911], 3210). The law allowed the construction of government-owned embassies, legations, and consulates up to $500,000 per building. The passage of the law, however, did not immediately alter the situation (e.g., Burton J. Hendrick, *Life and Letters of Walter Hines Page* [Garden City, N.Y., 1922–25], I, 233; Paul S. Reinsch, *An American Diplomat in China* [London, 1922], p. 20; William Graves Sharp, *War Memoirs* [London, 1931], p. 56). Although it is impossible to evaluate accurately the influence which the progress under the act had toward democratizing the upper service, it is safe to argue that it was an important step in that direction.

[107] 120.11/22, Copy of HR 31170, January 11, 1911. Class one: $3,000; Class two: $2,625; Class three: $2,000; Class four: $1,800; Class five, $1,200.

[108] F. M. Huntington Wilson, *Memoirs*, p. 189.

[109] *Cong. Rec.*, XLVI, 61 Cong. 3 sess. (January 11, 1911), 813.

ice." [110] The Department also sent copies of the bill to newspapers and trade associations.[111]

In the Senate on January 23, Lodge introduced a bill "for the improvement of the foreign service." [112] While it was basically similar to Lowden's, it required the President to appoint all who passed the examination and promote only those within the service.[113] The fate of Lodge's friend Henry White probably persuaded him to include the mandatory provisions.

Five days later the House Committee reported out the Lowden bill.[114] Although it included a series of statements complimenting the services and a long list of diplomatic achievements by "professionals," the accompanying report dealt primarily with the Constitutional issue raised by the bills. Lowden believed:

> It thus becomes necessary to examine anew the question of whether or not it is competent for Congress to require the President to appoint to the lower classes of the foreign service only such as have passed an examination, and to limit the President's power of appointment to the higher grades to those who have served in some lower grade.

He concluded that, regardless of the beneficial nature of the examination system, "to limit the President's power of appointment to the higher grades . . . is a direct and positive limitation of the power of appointment." [115]

The public support came from the expected sources. Before the National Board of Trade, Wilbur Carr was asked to speak about the legislation. He emphasized that the bill would "accomplish the desired results not only in the consular service but in the diplomatic service as well." He went on to praise both services for their aid to business enterprise.[116] The *Outlook* saw the Lowden Bill as a safeguard for the Executive Orders of Taft and Roosevelt "from the peril" of spoils. *Good Government* also indorsed the measure.[117]

[110] Knox to Foster, January 14, 1911, in 120.11/22.

[111] Letter from Knox, January 14, 1911, in 120.11/22. It was sent to seventeen periodicals and three trade associations.

[112] *Cong. Rec.*, XLVI, 61 Cong., 3 sess. (January 23, 1911), 1277.

[113] 120.11/22, Copy of S 10368, January 23, 1911. See also Knox to Cullom, February 23, 1911, in 120.11/22.

[114] *Cong. Rec.*, XLVI, 61 Cong., 3 sess (January 28, 1911), 1618.

[115] House Rept. 2008, 61 Cong., 3 sess. (January 28, 1911), pp. 8, 11.

[116] *Ibid.*, p. 21. Extract from statement by Carr made before the National Board of Trade on January 18, 1911.

[117] Editorial, *Outlook*, XCVII (February 4, 1911), 252; *Good Government*, XXVIII (February, 1911), 25. See also Standard Varnish Co. to Taft, February 11, 1911, in 122.1/177.

But no congressional support could be mustered. Taft's relations were poor with Congress anyway, and the measure's aims were not considered vital. When Congress adjourned, no action had been taken. Thus, a Republican House retired and one dominated by a patronage-hungry Democratic party took office.

The National Business League was as insistent in obtaining statutory permanence for the consular service as the Department was for both services. Soon after the new Congress convened, the League secured the sponsorship of Senator Shelby M. Cullom and Representative Foster for a bill drafted by the organization. The bill required compulsory appointment and promotion in the consular service and made no mention of the diplomatic service.[118] The Department would not settle for this and refused its support. The bill died in committee.

For the third time Taft included the needs of the two services in his Annual Message. On December 7, 1911, the President maintained that the entire foreign service organization "is being improved and developed with especial regard to the requirements of the commercial interests of the country." He recommended higher salaries and "a wider and more permanent extension of those principles [civil service] to both branches of the foreign service." He felt that the existing rules had served "to bring about a zealous activity in the interests of the country which never before existed or could exist." He also sought to placate the new House by insisting that:

> Available statistics show the strictness which the merit system has been applied to the foreign service during recent years and the absolute non-partisan selection of consuls and diplomatic secretaries, who indeed far from being selected with any view to political considerations have actually been chosen to a disproportionate extent from States which would have been unrepresented in the foreign service under the system which it is hoped is now permanently obsolete.[119]

The National Business League immediately revived its bill. Through Senator Knute Nelson and Representative George E. Foss on December 11 and 15, respectively, it was reintroduced.[120] This time, however, a provision for grading secretaryships was included.

[118] *Cong. Rec.*, XLVII, 62 Cong., 1 sess. (April 6, 1911), 101; 120.1/24, Copy of HR 4422, April 12, 1911. See also Burnham to Wilson, April 19, 1912, in 120.1/25.

[119] 120.1/24A, Copy of Taft's Message of December 7, 1911.

[120] *Cong. Rec.*, XLVIII, 62 Cong., 2 sess. (December 11, 1911), 184; (December 15, 1911), p. 411.

Retained for the consular system were the compulsory appointment and promotion provisions of the previous bill.[121] Again Knox refused his approval, claiming that the Department had not been consulted and was not wholly in agreement. His objection, aside from his hope of securing better coverage for the diplomatic service, was the measure's strictures on the power of the President to appoint "outsiders." [122]

Encouraged by resolutions from the National Civil Service Reform League and the American Chambers of Commerce in Paris and the Levant favoring continued action along the Lowden lines, Knox turned to Representative William Sulzer for aid.[123] The Secretary outlined what he thought the bill should include. In effect, it was substantially the Lowden bill. It was the Secretary's conviction "that the further extension of the merit system by legislation would automatically give to this country a foreign service as able in every respect as that of any great power." [124] Sulzer's bill was introduced on February 13.[125]

Support and opposition arose almost immediately. Businessmen wrote to the Department in advocacy of the Sulzer Bill.[126] On February 28, the *New York Times* claimed, "These provisions have been partly in force under executive orders for from three to six years, and have worked admirably. They should have the force of law, which is given them by Mr. Sulzer's Bill." [127] But the National Business League, which had authorized the Nelson-Foss bill, was unprepared to abandon its measure in favor of a constitutionally more refined but less mandatory bill. On the Constitutional issue, the *Record Herald* of the League maintained, "There are those who doubt its constitutionality. We advise them to leave that question to the Supreme Court."[128]

Ignoring the opposition, Wilson embarked on a campaign to align business interests behind the Sulzer Bill and to secure public support. With a letter beginning, "In view of your interest in the extension of

[121] 122.1/194, Copy of HR 15925, December 15, 1911.

[122] Knox to Representative William Sulzer, December 28, 1911, in 120.1/13A.

[123] 120.1/11, Copy of resolution of January 27, 1912, by the National Civil Service Reform League, February 13, 1912; 120.1/19, Copy of memorial of the American Chamber of Commerce in Paris, February 10, 1912; 120.1/120, Copy of memorial from the American Chamber of Commerce for the Levant, February 9, 1912. See also 120.1/16, Resolution of February 8, 1912, of the American Chamber of Commerce, February 8, 1912.

[124] Knox to Sulzer, February 12, 1912, in 120.1/17A.

[125] *Cong. Rec.*, XLVIII, 62 Cong., 2 sess. (February 13, 1912), 2032. See also Sulzer to Knox, February 14, 1912, in 120.1/18.

[126] E.g., Chandler and Price Co. to Knox, May 23, 1912, in 120.1/30; J. K. Stauffer to Wilson, February 17, 1912, in 120.11/27.

[127] Editorial, *New York Times*, February 28, 1912, p. 16.

[128] Editorial, *Record Herald*, March 7, 1912. See Burnham to Wilson, April 19, 1912, in 120.1/25.

the commerce of the United States with foreign countries and the development of an efficient foreign service capable of rendering substantial assistance to American manufacturers and exporters . . . ," Wilson sent copies of the bill to 1,130 Chambers of Commerce and Boards of Trade and nearly 1,500 newspapers.[129] From all evidence, his campaign paid off. Business organizations from all parts of the nation wrote in support of the bill.[130] Many newspapers were also obliging. The *Brooklyn Eagle* argued, "What is now custom should become law." [131] The *Indianapolis News* thought, "There ought to be a public opinion strong enough to bring this reform to pass." [132] The *Journal of Commerce* contended, "Important as have been the gains which by successive Executive Orders have been made in establishing a uniform rule of fitness in the service, no President or Secretary of State has yet been able to keep its prizes from being clutched by politicians." [133]

The National Business League, however, was unwilling to see its legislation scrapped, and its President George Sheldon wrote to the Department to object to the Sulzer bill and to criticize Knox's dropping the Nelson-Foss, Cullom-Foster, and the Lodge bills.[134] In a reply in which condescension and hostility were mixed, Wilson answered Sheldon:

> . . . those officials who have for many years had the actual direction of the foreign service, who, I am sure, are the most enthusiastic and constant advocates of foreign service, whose business in life this is, and who should therefore be given the credit for knowing what they are talking about, are abundantly convinced [the Sulzer bill] is on the whole decidedly better for the service than . . . the other bills.

He insisted that the Department dropped the other bills only after long study of their constitutional implications. Wilson recognized the limitations of the Sulzer bill, but hastened to add that public opinion, "made effective through organizations like your own," would deter any President from returning to the spoils system. The Assistant Secretary moved to clinch the argument by pointing out that the "Department is receiving from all parts of the country expressions of

[129] Wilson letter, March 11, 1912, in 120.1/21C.

[130] House Rept. 840, 62 Cong., 2 sess (June 5, 1912), pp. 12–33. Statements summarized in Report.

[131] 120.11/22, *Brooklyn Eagle*, March 13, 1912.

[132] 120.11/22, *Indianapolis News*, March 23, 1912.

[133] House Rept. 840, 62 Cong., 2 sess. (June 5, 1912), pp. 20, 46. See also *New York Times*, March 14, 1912, p. 10; *Good Government*, XXIX (March, 1912), 41.

[134] George Sheldon to Wilson, March 12, 1912, in 120.1/21A.

cordial approval of the Sulzer bill," that the only organization which disagreed was the National Business League, and, finally, that Senators Cullom, Lodge, and Root and Representative Foss agreed with him.[135]

Two days after Wilson's reply the committee hearings on the Sulzer bill opened. Statements approving the measure came from executives of business groups, reforms groups, and Henry White. Knox, Wilson, and Carr also testified. Their statements emphasized the importance of both services to commerce, the insufficiency of the spoils system, and the Constitutional problem.[136] Wilson, for instance, argued, "You can't carry on the business of promoting foreign commerce with an amateur, catch-as-catch-can foreign service." [137] With a sense of the historical, Knox pointed out, "This bill is in harmony with the disposition manifest throughout the country to improve the machine of government and raise the standard of efficiency on the part of the officers and employees." [138]

But all was not going smoothly for the legislation. Sulzer admitted:

> I have had the greatest difficulty in obtaining the support of my Democratic colleagues for even my limited bill. They foresee a Democratic president in the White House after March, 1913, and they don't want to throw away all the patronage in the foreign service which would result from the enactment of a strict merit rule bill.[139]

Strong opposition to the bill developed among proponents of the merit system, too. Representatives of the National Business League, unswayed by Wilson's letter, insisted upon appearing before the hearings. One League official felt that the proposition was whether "the capable sons of American businessmen . . . who have been especially equipped by the commercial schools of our great universities, shall, after a crucial test of examinations, enter the foreign service for successful life careers, or this Nation be represented abroad by appointees whose only claim to recognition lies in party fealty." [140] The League carried the attack on outside the hearings as well. In the *Record Herald,* an editorial writer insinuated:

> The State Department is throwing its influence upon the side of the Sulzer bill, but Secretary Knox, head of the State

[135] Wilson to Sheldon, March 18, 1912, in 120.1 / 21A.
[136] House Rept. 840, 62 Cong., 2 sess. (June 5, 1912), *passim.*
[137] House Rept. 840, p. 15, testimony given March 27, 1912.
[138] *Ibid.,* p. 117
[139] Burnham to Wilson, April 19, 1912, in 120.1/25.
[140] House Rept. 840, p. 89.

Department, comes from Pennsylvania, and he reflects in various ways the low political standards of the commonwealth from which he stems.[141]

Later Sheldon wrote to Wilson, "The Sulzer bill was an attempt to permit the Republicans to be continued in office."[142] The League wrote to other business organizations and condemned the Sulzer bill.[143] Even the members of the service were contacted.[144]

Flagging interest in the bill led Wilson to reappear before the Committee on April 5. While he conceded certain advantages to the League's measure, he felt the Constitutional question outweighed all others. He concluded his testimony, "Without the Sulzer Bill, the whole new system rests on executive orders, to be set aside by a stroke of a pen."[145] His appearance seemed to turn the tide. Sulzer wrote to Carr, "We are making a splendid record."[146] Newspapers continued to support the Department.[147]

Although the League made a last-ditch stand with the reintroduction of the Nelson-Foss bill,[148] the Sulzer bill was reported out of committee on June 5.[149] The accompanying report exhorted Congress to accept the measure. Sulzer maintained, "It was prepared and introduced in response to a strong public opinion and an insistent demand upon the part of commercial organizations and businessmen of the country that the American Diplomatic and Consular Services shall be brought to the highest practicable standard of efficiency." Sulzer, who wrote the report, argued that great thoroughness and a high level of non-partisanship had been attained through the Executive Orders, and that his bill would provide mobility without constricting the President's Constitutional powers. The report was filled with statements of approval by business organizations and newspapers and with extracts of testimony from members of the Department.[150] But all was for nought. The bill never could be maneuvered to the floor for a vote. The combined forces of those opposed to the merit system

[141] Burnham to Wilson, April 19, 1912, in 120.1/25. The *Record Herald* issue is dated March 23, 1912.

[142] Sheldon to Wilson, March 25, 1912, in 120.1/24.

[143] Chicago Chamber of Commerce to Knox, March 24, 1912, in 120.1/24.

[144] Copy of letter sent by National Business League to member of service, March 23, 1912, in 120.1/27.

[145] Wilson to Sulzer, April 5, 1912, in 120.1/25A.

[146] Sulzer to Carr, April 6, 1912, in 120.1/26.

[147] E.g., editorial, *Chicago Daily News*, March 23, 1912. See 120.1/25, copy of editorial.

[148] *Cong. Rec.*, XLVIII, 62 Cong., 2 sess. (May 22, 1912), 6934. Bill was numbered S 6927.

[149] *Ibid.* (June 5, 1912), p. 7737.

[150] House Rept. 840, 62 Cong., 2 sess. (June 5, 1912), *passim.*

or continuous diplomacy, patronage-hungry Democrats, and the divisions among the reformers defeated the Sulzer bill.

Because the Democrats won both Congress and the Presidency in the 1912 election, Taft's valedictory as President in December stressed the non-partisan nature of the diplomatic service, the fact that men "were chosen for ascertained fitness without regard to political affiliations." To pacify the now powerful South and West, Taft claimed that only a dearth of candidates from these areas "made it impossible thus far completely to equalize all the States' representation." Concluding his Message with the aims of his diplomacy, Taft indicated why he so wholeheartedly supported a professional service:

> The nation is now too mature to continue in its foreign relations those temporary expedients natural to a people to whom domestic affairs are the sole concern. . . . We are now in a larger relation with broader rights of our own and obligations to others than ourselves.[151]

How far did Taft's administration go in replacing the "temporary expedients" with the more solid foundations of a career service? Irrespective of Taft's initial expulsions, about which many qualifications must be made, his administration continued Roosevelt's policy of promoting men from the lower service to the ministerial level. Of the twelve "career ministers" of Roosevelt retained by Taft, eight remained in 1912.[152] Of the eight original appointments from the service made under Taft, six remained in 1912. One of the resignees was John Ridgely Carter. He had found the salary too small.[153] Exactly 35 per cent of Taft's ministers had come from secretaryships. Like those under Roosevelt, Taft's appointments had served slightly more than nine years in the lower service.

Where they were sent is as important as how many were appointed. Constituting more than 60 per cent of American representation in the area, 85.7 per cent of all career ministers were posted in Latin America. Latin America, "where our relations are close and our interest is great," was one of the prime targets of Taft's "dollar diplomacy," and his appointing professionals there was consistent with his views.[154] Taft's administration also followed Roosevelt's precedent and appointed a diplomatic secretary to an executive post in the Department. Huntington Wilson, William Phillips, and Chandler

[151] *Abridgement* (Washington, 1913), pp. 7–8, 28–29.
[152] Philip M. Brown and Herbert Squires resigned in 1910, and Herbert H. D. Peirce and Fenton McCreary resigned in 1911.
[153] Bax, *op. cit.*, p. 198.
[154] *Abridgement* (Washington, 1913), pp. 7–8. Speech by Taft, dated December 3, 1912.

Hale, all three career men, served as Assistant Secretaries of State in Knox's Department. The first had charge of the entire reorganization of the Department and its drive for service legislation, while the latter two were responsible for the administration of the diplomatic service after the Department's reshuffling. On the basis of external evidence, the four years under Taft strengthened the concept of professional diplomacy on the ministerial level and in the executive posts of the Department.

But a service was not to be built on promotions alone. Under Taft's administration, the officials of the Department, particularly Wilson, strove to obtain better qualified candidates for the service, to eliminate traces of partisanship, and to develop a sense of career confidence. The first of these was primarily dependent upon the examination system. The written examination established the areas of knowledge and the degree of their acquaintance which it was important for future officers to have, while the oral examination determined those traits of personality which it was desirable for secretaries to possess. That great attention was paid to the mechanics and content of both examinations is hardly surprising.

The aim of the written examination, especially that of 1910 and after, was to permit the passing of those who, as well as knowing a language and diplomatic usage, understood international law, appreciated the workings of foreign commerce, and had a wide knowledge of world economic history.[155] The questions, which were changed after each examination, stressed the location of American imports, the mechanics of the balance of trade, and the means of extending American commerce. Even the history sections dwelt on commercial controversies and their solutions. By the December, 1911, examination, the Board of Examiners had determined the respective weight to give the various subjects prescribed in the Executive Order.[156] In the two-day examination period, six papers were taken. International law characteristically had the greatest weight, counting one-quarter of the total score. On the other hand, diplomatic usage counted only one-tenth. It was probably assumed that it could be easily acquired "on the job." Together, however, the questions on modern European and American history and "the natural, industrial, and commercial resources and the commerce of the United States" counted nearly one-half. The language section, which had both oral

---

[155] Minutes (1910–12), Copies of examinations given in 1910–12.

[156] Minutes (1911). International law: 5; diplomatic usage: 2; modern language: 4; natural, industrial, and commercial resources of the United States: 3; American history: 3; modern European history: 3.

and written parts, was one-fifth the total score. Although the questions were mostly factual and easily crammed for, they were designed to favor the candidate with an economic orientation. About their quality, Hugh Wilson wrote, "The written tests were exhausting, but they were only different in degree from what I had become accustomed to in school and university." [157]

But of greater importance to the service than recruiting men with a knowledge of economics was recruiting men with the flexibility of mind that characterized the "generalist." The ideal secretary was one who was capable of handling all types of reporting and every duty of representation.[158] For this reason, Wilson believed the oral to be the more important examination.[159] As well as possessing the usual desirable personality traits, the successful candidate in the orals was resourceful in his conversation and equipped with a wide and accurate knowledge of contemporary affairs.[160] In describing the procedure for the orals, Wilson wrote:

> . . . each member of the board had a printed sheet on which he would jot down his rating of each candidate opposite each item in the long list of qualifications we were endeavoring to appraise. Many hypothetical questions were asked, designed to evoke replies that would be self-revealing, both in substance and the manner of the answer. Usually the candidates were examined three at a time, because comparison facilitated judgment. After each lot the members of the Board would compare notes and, after discussion, agree on the marks to be given. Later we would meet all the candidates together in another room and chat with them informally, in order to see how they appeared when at ease, with no possibility of "stage fright." After this the final marks were set down and the names of the successful were placed on the eligible list.[161]

[157] Hugh Wilson, *op. cit.*, p. 28. Cf. Grew, *op. cit.*, I, 62. The Pendleton Act had prescribed that the examinations be practical in character and relevant to the skills which they would use if employed (see 22 Stat. 403 [January 16, 1883]).

[158] See Department of State, *Information Regarding Appointment and Promotions in the Diplomatic Service* (Washington, 1912), p. 7. Among the diverse specific duties of the secretary, the Department listed that secretaries "are expected to perform such other duties of an official character as may be required of them by their chief of mission." On April 10, 1912, Hugh Gibson wrote, "I have developed into combination diplomat–office boy–social secretary–lord-chamberlain–undertaker–train despatcher–headwaiter–gum-shoe detective–bouncer–ground-and-lofty mental acrobat." See Gibson, *op cit.*, p. 151. See also Peirce, "Our Diplomatic and Consular Service," pp. 913–14.

[159] F. M. Huntington Wilson, *Memoirs*, p. 188.

[160] Minutes (1909).

[161] F. M. Huntington Wilson, *Memoirs*, p. 188.

The oral originally was given at the same time as the written examination. As the numbers increased, however, a later date, usually two weeks after the examination, was set.[162] Evaluating the experience, Hugh Wilson claimed,

> The oral tests were a real ordeal. It is not easy to appear before a jury of five or six senior men in the service and do yourself justice. . . . Anyhow, they were exceedingly polite and asked, to my surprise, questions that demanded thought and careful presentation, rather than facts.[163]

To encourage applicants, the Board of Examiners publicized the dates of the examinations in Civil Service Districts, in newspapers, and at American missions abroad.[164] There was also a general willingness on the part of members to accept invitations from universities to speak on the subject.[165]

Banishing all traces of partisanship from appointments and promotions was the second problem confronting those who wished to replace "temporary expedients" with a career service. In addition to the 1909 self-denying ordinance that political affiliations would not be considered in appointments, other methods were used to insure that selection would be on the basis of merit alone. The Board of Examiners adopted the policy of identifying candidates by numbers during both the written and oral examinations. Identities remained unknown until after the ratings were made.[166] The Board itself consisted of three career men and a member of the Civil Service Commission, while its only political figure was J. Reuben Clark, the Solicitor.[167] All examinations were marked by the Civil Service Commission.[168] A further step was taken on December 23, 1910, when Taft signed an Executive Order forbidding members of the Department to give instruction to candidates.[169] To the charge that senatorial indorsements were tantamount to partisan considerations, Wilson replied that indorsements were simply assurance that a name would pass the Senate.[170] For promotions, the efficiency record existed. Although

---

[162] Minutes (1910–12).

[163] Hugh Wilson, *op. cit.*, p. 28.

[164] *Biog. Reg.* (1909), p. 108.

[165] E.g., L. F. Rowe to Wilson, February 1, 1910, in 2108/137.

[166] House Report 840, 62 Cong., 2 sess. (June 5, 1912), p. 15.

[167] Two were career members in the Department: Sidney Y. Smith and Miles Shand. Huntington Wilson was the third.

[168] Minutes (1910). The Civil Service Commission marked the papers on American history, government, and institutions; modern European history; and natural, industrial, and commercial resources and commerce of the United States. International law, diplomatic usage, and the foreign language papers were marked by the Department.

[169] 120.11/22, Copy of Executive Order of December 23, 1910.

[170] House Rept. 840, 62 Cong., 2 sess. (June 5, 1912), p. 78.

political ministers evaluated members of the service, partisan considerations of this sort were beyond all control. A member was still able to discuss his record with a member of the Department.[171]

Unless confidence in the career's future could be instilled in its members, all other steps were futile. The administration sought to encourage confidence through career appointments to the ministerial level. The guaranteeing of tenure and regular promotions on the basis of merit were other ways of building an *esprit de corps*. Wilson's month of instruction in the Department was also partly used for this purpose. Finally, candidates were encouraged to think of themselves as applying for positions in a service. A Department pamphlet read:

> A candidate is not designated for examination with a view
> to his appointment to a particular post, but in order to
> determine his eligibility for appointment to such a post as
> in the judgment of the Department his services would best
> serve the public interest.[172]

How successful was the drive to obtain qualified candidates? Although the difficulties in answering this are nearly insuperable, certain statements can be made. Some evidence argues that recruitment between 1909 and 1912 was very successful. Only 40.3 per cent of the candidates succeeded in passing the examination, and not all of the successful candidates received appointments. In terms of the formal educational qualifications of the candidates, the drive was also successful. Of those appointed 87.5 per cent possessed a university degree. Of these, 62.8 per cent had had experience on the postgraduate level as well. Only one appointee had never attended a university. Finally, a high percentage had had previous experience in positions related to diplomacy. Nearly 30 per cent of the successful candidates had been private secretaries to ministers or ambassadors. Several had also served as consular officers or in the Department of State.[173]

Other pieces of evidence modify this conclusion somewhat. An average of only 20.8 candidates took each examination. The totals for the examinations fluctuated so that no pattern of increasing interest in the service can be established.[174] Of those who qualified, only 52.3 per cent legitimately attained the requisite 80 per cent. The others required a five point bonus.[175] Finally, although not necessarily re-

---

[171] *Biog. Reg.* (1909), pp. 108–9.

[172] Department of State, *Information Regarding Appointments and Promotions in the Diplomatic Service* (Washington, 1912), p. 5.

[173] Three had been in the consular service, and one had served in the Department.

[174] Minutes (1909–12). Examination of May 17–19, 1909: twenty-six candidates; March 1–3, 1910: nine; January 16–18, 1911: twenty-nine; December 4–6, 1911: twenty-two; and May 27–29, 1912: eighteen.

[175] *Ibid.* Twenty-two legitimately achieved 80 per cent; twenty candidates did not.

ferring to this period alone, testimony given by diplomats during the hearings on the Rogers Act indicates that there was not complete satisfaction with recruitment.[176]

How successful was the drive to eliminate partisanship in appointments and promotions? Again the problem is enormous. Particularly important here are the unobtainable efficiency records of secretaries. From external evidence, however, an attempt can be made at an answer. The period saw no sons of ambassadors or ministers appointed to the service. If there were relatives, it is not known. Furthermore, no secretary listed "politics" as a previous occupation. Private secretaries alone may be seen as having a definite partisan connection, although this was not universally true.[177] It cannot be determined if the private secretaries received the bonus points. The non-partisan reputation of those appointed after an examination led one pre-examination secretary to take the examination and be recommissioned.[178] One possible area of partisanship was in the appointment from those certified as qualified. Five out of forty-two were not appointed. One had passed away; one was in poor health; and a third was involved in a scandal.[179] No facts are known about the other two. Only one person was appointed without an examination. Edward Williams, a missionary qua student interpreter, was assigned briefly to Peking.[180] With Williams and the two unappointed candidates as possible exceptions, it can still be argued that there was no apparent attempt to insure that Republicans alone were appointed.

Indeed, the reverse can be argued. The Department was continually plagued by the problem of states' representation. Often these sectional pressures had political overtones. If the Department surrendered to these pressures, then the merit system was not in full operation. Letters from congressmen, particularly southerners, complained that too few from their state or section were appointed as secretaries. Representative D. Thompson Morgan of Oklahoma, for instance, wanted to know why there were no secretaries from his state when it was entitled to 1.94 secretaries.[181] Representative Cordell Hull of Tennessee spearheaded the southern movement to remedy "the lack of

---

[176] House Committee on Foreign Affairs, *Foreign Service of the United States*, Hearings on HR 17 and HR 6357, 68 Cong., 1 sess. (January 14–18, 1924), p. 85.

[177] Hugh Wilson had been a private secretary to career minister Edwin V. Morgan. See Hugh Wilson, *op. cit.*, p. 18.

[178] *Biog. Reg.* (1912), pp. 24, 110.

[179] Minutes (1909–12).

[180] *Biog. Reg.* (1912), pp. 21, 106. Williams had also been a consul general in Peking and assistant chief in the Division of Far Eastern Affairs. The Executive Order had provided for such an exception.

[181] Morgan to Knox, February 21, 1911, in 120.1/13.

representation in the foreign service of the cotton-growing areas." [182] Resolutions and debates in Congress on this subject reached Knox's ears. His response, in public, was to point out that "the foreign service deals with American interests in foreign countries of every character and affecting every section of the United States." [183] In private, he was more conciliatory. Writing to Hull, Knox insisted, "But the Department has not been successful in obtaining many suitable candidates from the Southern States for the Diplomatic Service." [184] In practice, Knox and other members of the Department made requests "of educational institutions and of Senators of the States to suggest candidates for the examination." [185] With service legislation pending in Congress, Knox could not afford to offend an important section.

Is there evidence that the South or any other region received undue consideration in appointments? If it can be assumed that the same proportion from each area of those taking the examination pass it, then two areas exceeded their proportion — the Middle Atlantic and the three southern regions considered as a whole. All other areas had a smaller proportion qualifying than took the examination. [186] The Middle Atlantic superfluity may partly be explained by the propensity of candidates from other areas to take instruction in the District of Columbia and to assume residence there. The only conclusion for the southern case, aside from coincidence, is that the Board of Examiners was excessively solicitous with southern candidates. If this is true, then Taft's administration can be charged with limited partisanship of a very perverse sort.

Without access to the efficiency records, no statement can be made on partisan considerations in promotions. Most secretaries during the period had one change of post, and many of them can be considered as promotions. But an attempt to correlate geographical backgrounds with promotions proved only that they had no influence.

The necessity to add to one's salary from private means remained constant throughout the period. Indeed, the problem increased as the service assumed the characteristics of a lifetime career. There were even unofficial financial prohibitions on the man who wished to apply. The examination required not only a trip to Washington but also at least a two-week stay there. Both were costly without a guarantee of employment. It is, however, unknown if the Board ever

---

[182] *Cong. Rec.*, XLV, 61 Cong., 2 sess. (February 10, 1910), 1753.

[183] House Rept. 2008, 61 Cong., 3 sess (January 28, 1911), p. 14 (statement by Knox).

[184] Knox to Hull, March 12, 1910, in 120.11/22.

[185] House Rept. 840, 62 Cong., 2 sess. (June 5, 1912), p. 17.

[186] The Middle Atlantic should have had 17.4 successful candidates; it had twenty. The three Southern regions: 2.8/4. New England should have had 4.6; it had 4. East North Central: 6/4; West North Central: 1/2; Pacific: 4.2/2; Mountain: .35/1.

inquired into a candidate's financial position. Also the suggestion that candidates be limited to college graduates was opposed by Knox as unwise and imposing a financial restriction inconsistent with democracy.[187] Nevertheless, the financial prerequisite determined the social composition of the service. Over 70 per cent of all secretaries attended private boarding schools, while 22.5 per cent attended public secondary schools. The same pattern was repeated on the university level. Attending Harvard, Yale, or Princeton were 51.3 per cent. State universities, on the other hand, provided a scant 7.6 per cent. There was no other concentration in a single category of institutions.[188]

What evidence is there that the attempt to create a greater career confidence succeeded? There are statements made by secretaries about the service, such as one by Joseph Grew in a letter to his father-in-law:

> Every new executive order of the kind recently issued [Taft's 1909 Order] will make it just so much harder for a new administration to overturn things and reclothe the Service in its former character of a Congressional plum orchard. This is very gratifying.[189]

There are also inferences from statistics. If it can be assumed that a person leaves the service because he feels it does not provide a secure future, then it can be argued both that the secretaries had little faith in the service and that they had great confidence in it. An average of 8.6 per cent resigned every year.[190] This meant that Taft's four years as President saw the resignation of over a third of the diplomatic service. Yet, 21 per cent of the secretaries in 1912 were appointed between 1890 and 1905. Also, over 60 per cent of the post–1905 Order group remained, while only four of Taft's appointments had resigned. The period, however, was too short to permit substantial generalizations to be made from statistics.

A greater test of the service's future as a career was appearing on the horizon. The election of 1912 gave control of the Executive and Congress to the Democratic party, a party that had been in the patronage wilderness for sixteen years. Members of the service naturally were apprehensive. Their merit system rested on an Executive Order

[187] Knox to William Harris Douglas, January 3, 1911, in 120.1/–. See also *Biog. Reg.* (1909), p. 108.

[188] Other Ivy League: 7.6 per cent.
    Eastern Private: 17.9 per cent.

[189] Grew, *op. cit.*, I, 63; Hugh Wilson, *op. cit.*, p. 38; Norval Richardson, *My Diplomatic Education* (New York, 1923), p. 313.

[190] The rate should again be compared with that of the British Service, where in 1912 only 1.2 per cent resigned. See *Foreign Office List* (1913), p. xxii.

that was not binding on succeeding Presidents. The Order had only been in effect for three years. Unlike its commercial cousin, the diplomatic service had not yet established a non-partisan reputation in the public mind. Without even the protection of having taken a qualifying examination were 21 per cent of the secretaries. The career ministers were similarly placed, and, by custom, they had to submit their resignations to the new President. To add to this apprehension, a solicited statement from Wilson on reform did not mention the diplomatic service.[191] Between the election and Wilson's inauguration, five secretaries resigned. Those remaining awaited a decision from Wilson.[192]

Observers knew that Wilson had long been an advocate of civil service reform, serving once as a vice-president of the National Civil Service Reform League. They knew that he, as an educator, appreciated the need for career specialization. They also knew that the Democratic party's platform claimed that "merit and ability should be the standard of appointment and promotion rather than service rendered to a political party." [193] On the other hand, although the President was personally in political debt to few, he was faced with the problem of being a minority President and head of a minority party. Patronage was a long-standing method of remedying this position. Furthermore, his approach to foreign affairs conflicted with Taft's. He opposed his predecessors' policies toward Latin America, the Caribbean, and the role of government in extending foreign trade.[194] These counter-policies called for a reduction in diplomatic activity. Finally, the "New Freedom" was a program of domestic reform, not foreign involvement. This fact made Wilson less interested in the administration of foreign affairs.

The secretaries were particularly apprehensive about Wilson's Secretary of State — William Jennings Bryan. Bryan was never a friend of civil service reform and appreciated even more than the President the patronage needs of his party. In fact, no man in either party had greater demands upon him than Bryan. With the Democratic party, particularly its southern wing, expecting a patronage feast, he was appointed the chef. Bryan's aim in foreign affairs, such as

---

[191] *Good Government*, XXIX (November, 1912), 105–6.

[192] Some evidence suggests that many secretaries were confident that any tampering with the merit service would only be temporary. See Frederic R. Dolbeare to Hughes, January 25, 1921, in 121.1/49:1140.

[193] *Cong. Rec.*, LII, 63 Cong., 2 sess. (April 2, 1914), 6167 (speech by Representative John Jacob Rogers).

[194] Wilson to Charles W. Eliot, September 17, 1913, in Ray Stannard Baker, *Woodrow Wilson: Life and Letters* (London, 1932), IV, 42. See also Ray Stannard Baker and William E. Dodd, *Public Papers of Woodrow Wilson* (New York, 1925), I, 143 (speech by Wilson in Philadelphia on July 4, 1914).

it was, was the negotiating of conciliation conventions with the major powers, but he did not envisage them requiring professional diplomats for negotiations or enforcement.

The course of the new administration toward the diplomatic service emerged slowly. Pressures to determine that course, however, began shortly after Wilson's election. Many of Wilson's friends, such as Henry B. Fine of Princeton, wrote him in support of the merit principle and continuing career ministers.[195] Others sought to dissuade Wilson from following his predecessor's example. Chief among them was Senator John S. Williams of Mississippi. In a letter to Wilson, Williams contended that Taft's 1909 Order was a sham. Republicans alone, he argued, were designated for the examination. To prove his point, he cited "the egregiously sectional character" of Taft's appointments, maintaining that the South should have the same proportion of diplomats as it had population. From this stand, however, Williams did not propose a more strict observation of the merit service; he advocated a wholehearted return to the spoils system.[196] With this Bryan was substantially in agreement. Regardless of public or private statements to the contrary, the Secretary warmly supported any move to increase the patronage opportunities for deserving Democrats.[197] But Wilson's civil service predilections, shored up by the support of Colonel House, checked the Secretary in his attempt to restore spoils to the secretaryships.[198] Yet, no assurance that their positions were safe was issued by the Department to the secretaries. They remained apprehensive and expectant.

Owing to the verbal conduct of these administrative matters, there is no evidence to suggest how and when the decision to retain the merit system for the secretaryships took place. But events subsequent to the inauguration suggest that a bargain was struck, probably in February, between Wilson and Bryan.[199] Wilson approved of the merit system for the lower service, as he did for the consular service.[200] Bryan did not. Although secretaries in the major posts abroad were individually

[195] Reverend Hugh White to Wilson, April 8, 1913, in 121.1/5:1139. See also Seward W. Livermore, "Woodrow Wilson and the Foreign Service" (Unpublished article, Historical Division, Department of State, 1951), pp. 4–5. The author is indebted to Dr. Livermore in several places in his argument. There is, however, only a minimum amount of overlapping. Dr. Livermore construes "Foreign Service" much more widely than does the author.

[196] Williams to Wilson, December 28, 1912, in 121.1/5:1139.

[197] See *New York Times*, April 13, 1913, Sec. 3, p. 8.

[198] Charles Seymour, *The Intimate Papers of Colonel House* (London, 1926), I, 183–84. Diary excerpts of April 18, 1913 and January 16, 1914.

[199] Bryan was in Europe until then. See Gibson, *op. cit.*, p. 153. See also Livermore, *op. cit.*, p. 7.

[200] Grew to Thomas S. Perry, March 9, 1914, in Grew, *Turbulent Era*, I, 119.

evaluated, no secretary was dropped from the service. Second, Wilson wished to appoint men of the highest caliber, irrespective of their politics, to the upper level.[201] Bryan opposed these appointments on several grounds and wished to have the party faithful rewarded.[202] Appointments of high caliber were made only to the major European capitals and China; the other appointments were party hacks. Therefore, Wilson must have agreed that Bryan could dispose of the lesser ministerial positions as spoils rewards in return for agreeing to superior appointments for the major capitals and the retention of the merit system for the lower service.

At the first hint of nominations, the secretaries breathed a sigh of relief. It was announced that ambassadorial appointments had been offered to men like Dr. Eliot and Richard Olney.[203] But the sighs were premature, for both Eliot and Olney refused the appointments on financial grounds, touching off anew the debate on the adequacy of higher diplomatic salaries.[204] Subsequent appointments to European posts, however, were of high quality.[205] And as yet, no career minister had been displaced. On this fact, the *Outlook* issued a caveat: "It would be deplorable should President Wilson consent to any general dismissal of those who have risen from the ranks to the grade of Minister." [206]

The appointments to the Department had been disconcerting for the secretaries. Save for the counsellor, John Bassett Moore, no man associated with the reform movement for the service, let alone a member of the service, was made an Assistant Secretary. A spoils politician, Dudley Malone, assumed administrative control over the service.[207] By mid-July further evidence of the administration's intentions appeared. The nominations for the remaining ministerial and ambassadorial posts began. When the dust cleared, only three career ministers had survived the slaughter. Morgan, Garrett, and Fletcher alone remained, and it was only through the personal intervention of House that Fletcher was saved.[208] Except for William Heimke, who

[201] Burton J. Hendrick, *Walter Hines Page*, I, pp. 112–13.

[202] Bryan to Wilson, June 22, 1914, in Ray Stannard Baker, *Wilson: Life and Letters*, IV, 40.

[203] *Ibid.*, pp. 28–34.

[204] E.g., "Rich and Poor Ambassadors," *Literary Digest*, XLVI (April 5, 1913), 760.

[205] Walter Hines Page was appointed to Britain; Thomas Nelson Page received Italy, and James W. Gerard was appointed to Germany.

[206] Editorial, *Outlook*, CIV (January 28, 1913), 402.

[207] Arthur S. Link, *Wilson: The New Freedom* (Princeton, N.J.: Princeton University Press, 1956), pp. 7, 168.

[208] Seymour, *op. cit.*, I, 183.

was transferred to the Department, no mercy was shown to the ejected eleven career ministers.[209]

To their places an odd assortment of state politicians, supporters of "sixteen-to-one," minor campaign contributors, and preachers were appointed. None had had diplomatic experience. The career men whom they displaced had each served an average of more than nine years at several posts.[210] Yet, they were on the average five years junior to the political appointees. Perhaps the most absurd changes came in Turkey and Greece. To replace W. W. Rockhill, who was first appointed in 1884, was the chairman of the Democratic Finance Committee, Henry J. Morgenthau. John B. Jackson's successor in Greece was a Chicago brewer, Charles Vopicka.[211]

Still, Bryan was beyond the charge of setting a precedent in regard to appointments. He was guilty of using appointments, without attention to qualifications, to satisfy the geographical needs of patronage and to increase the prestige of party members.[212] But his general course was the accepted practice whenever there was a change in parties. To the argument that many of the displaced were non-partisan, Bryan could reply that this was doubtful and irrelevant. Furthermore, Taft had shown himself not averse to ejecting career ministers. Even the charge that Bryan reinstituted rotation in office can be countered with similar evidence for Roosevelt.[213] Above all, the new administration was pursuing a different tack in foreign policy. In a letter to Dr. Eliot, Wilson explained, perhaps apologized for, the situation:

> We find that those who have been occupying the legations and embassies have been habituated to a point of view which is very different, indeed, from the point of view of the present Administration. . . . I have been genuinely distressed at the necessity of seeming to act contrary to the spirit of the merit system in any case or particular, but these are circumstances which seem to me make a certain amount of this necessary at the opening of a new order of things.[214]

[209] *Biog. Reg.* (1914), p. 83. William Heimke was made chief of the Division of Latin American Affairs.

[210] George Harvey, "The Diplomats of Democracy," *North American Review*, CXCIX (February, 1914), 171–72.

[211] *Biog. Reg.* (1914), pp. 22–25.

[212] Bryan to Wilson, June 22, 1914, in Baker, *Wilson: Life and Letters*, IV, 40. See also Bryan to Wilson, April 4, 1913, in Livermore, *op. cit.*, p. 19; Bryan to Wilson, August 4, 1913, in Baker, *Wilson: Life and Letters*, IV, 39.

[213] Bryan to Wilson, September 25, 1913, in Baker, *Wilson: Life and Letters*, IV, 41. Cf. Roosevelt to Hay, December 17, 1904, in T. Roosevelt, *Letters*, IV, 1073.

[214] Wilson to Eliot, September 17, 1913, in Baker, *Wilson: Life and Letters*, IV. 42.

While Bryan set no precedents, the public did. The public dis-approval of the appointments was great. In a letter to a friend, Joseph Grew observed:

> There has, however, so far as I am aware, never been such a row in the press all over the country over this looting of the Service. Formerly it was taken for granted that every single official would be changed; now it is spoken as a scandal that those ministers who have worked their way up from the ranks should be turned out.[215]

Much of the criticism was partisan, lauding the Republican party's progress and condemning the Democratic party's regress.[216] Some criticism was inspired by disappointed office-seekers, such as George Harvey.[217] But even many of Wilson's supporters were dissatisfied with the administration's course.[218]

All agreed that Bryan's wholesale dismissals had demoralized the service completely. The critics vied with each other in their descriptions of the process and its results. Harvey in the *North American Review* claimed, ". . . a clearer case of partisan debauchery cannot be imagined."[219] James Whelpley described the service as "notoriously disorganized";[220] the *Journal of Commerce* believed it was "demoralized."[221] Regardless of the adjective, the critics felt that the remaining secretaries were in a state "of alarm and insecurity" because "men outside of the service have been offered places in which it has been supposed the present occupants would be retained, or that, if changes were made, men already in the corps would be selected."[222] They contrasted it with the atmosphere under Taft when secretaries "no longer feared that the work of years might crumble overnight before the intrigues of some powerful but ignorant politician."[223]

While the critics agreed that the administration was unfaithful to its 1912 platform, they did not agree on whom the blame should be placed. As typical reformers, the majority tended to charge the man

---

[215] Grew to Thomas S. Perry, March 9, 1914, in Grew, *op. cit.*, I, 119–20.

[216] See "Last Refuge of the Spoilsman," *Atlantic*, CXIII (April, 1914), 433–45; editorial, *Review of Reviews*, XLIX (March, 1914), 348–49.

[217] George Harvey, *op. cit.*, pp.161–74.

[218] "Senator James Hamilton Lewis," *Literary Digest*, XLVII (November 22, 1914), 992–93 (editorial from *New York Evening Post*).

[219] George Harvey, *op. cit.*, p. 172.

[220] James D. Whelpley, "Our Disorganized Diplomatic Service," *Century*, LXXXVII (November, 1913), 126.

[221] See *Literary Digest*, XLIX (August 29, 1914), 331.

[222] James D. Whelpley, *op. cit.*, p. 125.

[223] An American Diplomat, "The Diplomatic Service and Its Organization and Demoralization," *Outlook*, CVI (March 7, 1914), 536–37.

least like themselves—Bryan. The *New York Sun* maintained, "It is this miserable state of things that Mr. Bryan has what can only be called the impudence of pretending that the motive to it has been a desire to improve the Diplomatic Service. A more brazenly and shamelessly false pretense was never made."[224] The *Herald Tribune* claimed, "He is the only Secretary of State in our time who has ever set out openly to loot the foreign service."[225]

Wilson received relatively little of the blame. Most congressmen and publicists believed that "Wilson handed over the appointments of the State Department and the appointments of most ministers to the tender mercies of Mr. Bryan as the price of protection of the consular, and the partial protection of the lower grades of the diplomatic service. . . ."[226] The *New York Sun,* which bitterly excoriated Bryan, held that "Credit must be given the President for staying the hand from the consulates and secretaryships."[227] Others, however, were less indulgent. On the floor of Congress, Representative John Jacob Rogers claimed, "We felt confident that a man of his record [Wilson] could be absolutely depended upon to root out the last hint of Jacksonism, in the Diplomatic Service at least. But to how low a degree has the service been brought within the short space of a year."[228] The *New York Evening Post* lamented, "At least, thinking people everywhere will regret that Woodrow Wilson is not to have the credit of once and for all placing the diplomatic service where it belongs."[229] The *Outlook* was even more to the point:

> Upon the President's shoulders rests the ultimate responsibility for the demoralization of the Diplomatic Service, for our consequent loss of prestige abroad and for the present menace to our foreign relations, and it is of no avail to attempt to shift it to Mr. Bryan, who perhaps knows no better.[230]

A mark of the changing times was the paucity of statements, both in Congress and in periodicals, in support of Bryan. Periodicals, of course, were generally owned by Republicans and pro-service people. But it is still surprising that no newspaper and only one magazine said

[224] *Cong. Rec.,* LII, 63 Cong., 2 sess. (April 2, 1914), 6166 (speech by Representative Rogers). Editorial, *New York Sun,* December 21, 1913.

[225] The *Tribune* editorial is dated June 16, 1915.

[226] "Last Refuge of the Spoilsman," p. 435.

[227] Editorial, *New York Sun,* December 21, 1913.

[228] *Cong. Rec.,* LII, 63 Cong., 2 sess. (April 2, 1914), 6167.

[229] "Senator James Hamilton Lewis," *Literary Digest,* XLVII (November 22, 1914), 992–93 (an undated *New York Evening Post* editorial extract).

[230] An American Diplomat, "The Diplomatic Service and Its Organization and Demoralization," p. 537.

anything in his favor. *Collier's*, which alone supported his move, maintained, "Mr. Bryan does not feel that Civil Service principles extend to ministers or ambassadors, and until Congress passes a law covering them . . . he will continue the practice he has established of appointing such men as he sees fit and as he deems qualified for these posts." The article further contended that the merit service was not so meritoriously applied under Taft.[231] This same point was also made in Congress.[232]

This barrage continued intermittently for over a year and a half. It was sustained by reports of fraud committed by Bryan's appointees, indiscretions on the part of the Secretary, such as the Vick letter, and the indefatigable snooping of the National Civil Service Reform League, which had even established a special committee to investigate Wilson's diplomatic service.[233] It resurrected all the old arguments for and against continuous diplomacy and the merit system.[234] Against this barrage, the President and the Secretary adopted entirely different means of defense. Bryan simply ignored it, contending that it was an insignificant coalition between Dr. Eliot and the New York newspapers.[235] The less thick-skinned President attempted to explain the situation and to plead for patience. In a letter to Dr. Charles Sweet, Wilson wrote:

> I admit the force of what you say about our diplomatic appointments, but I am sure that I could put a somewhat different light upon the whole matter if I had the time and opportunity to lay before you the inside bearing of the whole matter. I hope sincerely that in the course of my administration something satisfactory can be worked out by way of the beginning of a system.[236]

[231] Edward G. Lowry, "Bryan's Diplomatic Appointments," *Collier's Weekly*, LII (February 7, 1914), 9.

[232] *Cong. Rec.*, LII, 63 Cong., 2 sess. (April 2, 1914), 6167 (speech by Representative Robert N. Page of North Carolina); *ibid.* (January 17, 1914), p. 1877 (speech by Representative George E. Gorman of Illinois).

[233] Ansley Wilcox, "Report from the Special Committee on Reform in the Consular and Diplomatic Services," *Proceedings of the National Civil Service Reform League* (1913), pp. 114–18.

[234] E.g., Alvard L. Bishop, "The Promotion of American Commerce," *Atlantic*, CXIII (May, 1914), 612; David Jayne Hill, "Why Do We Have a Diplomatic Service?" *Harper's*, CXXVIII (January, 1914), 188–97; *idem*, "Shall We Standardize Our Diplomatic Service?" *Harper's*, CXXVIII (April, 1914), 690–98; *idem*, "Can Our Diplomatic Service be Made More Efficient?" *Harper's*, CXXX (January, 1915), 190–98; *idem*, "The Material Needs of Our Diplomatic Service," *Harper's*, CXXX (February, 1915), 448–56; Judson C. Welliver, "Making Over the Diplomatic Service," *Munsey's*, L (October, 1913), 3–13; *Cong. Rec.*, LII, 63 Cong., 2 sess. (January 17, 1914), 1877.

[235] Bryan to Wilson, January 16, 1914, in 121.1/16:1139.

[236] Wilson to Sweet, December 17, 1913, in Livermore, *op. cit.*, p. 26.

The administration's first opportunity to restore confidence in its civil service intentions came in the midst of the controversy over Bryan's appointments. Although the President and Ambassador Page were anxious to hold examinations for the vacancies in the secretaryships as soon as the nominations for the upper level had been made, Bryan was not to be moved.[237] But the storm outside penetrated even Bryan's protection enough to make the Secretary wish for more calm. He agreed finally that an examination should be held in mid-November.[238]

Save for Malone, the Board of Examiners' personnel had remained unchanged since Taft's administration, and they followed the course set four years earlier by Huntington Wilson.[239] By the beginning of October, fifty-two men had applied and were designated for the examination. A Board memo claimed, "All seemingly well-qualified candidates were designated without regard to state apportionments." This was the highest number yet to apply. The cause of the rise was twofold. Over a year and a half had passed since the last examination and a considerable backlog had been created. More important, holding the examination implied that the administration intended to honor the merit system. Of the thirty-six who finally took the examination, ten passed it and six were appointed.[240]

Further opportunities arose to give the administration a chance to redeem itself. On top of the continuing criticism, John Bassett Moore, overworked and exasperated by Bryan, resigned as counsellor.[241] This resignation confirmed the worst suspicions of the service's supporters. The *Literary Digest* wrote, "The whole service, from its uncertain chief paltering platitudes and coddling cheap politicians to his incompetent horde of retainers in foreign capitals, is the despair of men trained in diplomacy like John Bassett Moore." Although the article appreciated Moore's reasons for resigning, it lamented the absence of a man with the service's best interests at heart in the highest councils of the Department.[242] The subsequent reshuffling of the Department, however, created a vacancy in the Third Assistant Secretaryship. To it Wilson appointed, against Bryan's wishes, career diplomat William Phillips.[243] The move attracted much favorable comment.[244]

The second opportunity resulted from the resignation from Haiti

[237] *Ibid.*, p. 9.
[238] Minutes (1913).
[239] *Biog. Reg.* (1913), pp. 110–11; Minutes (1913).
[240] Minutes (1913).
[241] *Biog. Reg.* (1914), p. 9. See editorial, *Literary Digest*, XLVIII (March 14, 1914), 539.
[242] Editorial, *Literary Digest*, XLVIII (March 14, 1914), 539.
[243] *Cong. Rec.*, LII, 63 Cong., 2 sess. (March 13, 1914), 4817.
[244] E.g., Grew to Thomas S. Perry, March 9, 1914, in Grew, *op. cit.*, I, 120.

of Bryan's appointee. To his post Wilson used the opportunity to appoint a second career man — A. Bailley Blanchard. Although nominally a Democrat, Blanchard was first appointed by McKinley and was considered a *diplomate de carrière*.[245]

One of Phillips' first tasks was to prepare for the service legislation codifying the merit provisions of 1909.[246] This was a further attempt by Wilson to restore the confidence of the supporters of civil service. With the help of Carr, Phillips drafted a measure for both services along the lines of the Lowden and Sulzer bills. Among its features for the diplomatic service were the formal establishment of the Board of Examiners and the examination system, the efficiency records and compulsory reporting, and the appointment of secretaries to classes in a graded system.[247] While Bryan was away on the Chautauquan circuit, the bill was submitted to Representative Henry D. Flood and Senator William S. Stone. It was introduced on May 19 in the House and on the following day in the Senate.[248] When Bryan returned, he discovered that the bill included the merit provisions. He objected to them in a letter to Wilson. The President, wishing to avoid a further rift on the subject of civil service reform, replied:

> I agree with you about the clause to which you called my attention in the bill prepared by Mr. Phillips. I think it would perhaps be unwise to make the examinations for the diplomatic and consular services a matter of law, and if it is not too late to change the bill in that particular I would think it would be wise to change.[249]

As the bill was far from the hearing stage in both committees, Bryan needed to be in no hurry to alter the measure.

Action was slow. With the Dominican scandals and the Phelan investigations dominating all thought about diplomacy, little was done. By the end of June, Bryan had still not advised Stone or Flood to change the bill and had even gone on record to Marsh of the National Civil Service Reform League in favor of the measure as it stood.[250] The events of late July and August, however, provided the catalyst needed for bringing the bill to the attention of Congress. In the opening days of the European war, the American legations and embassies

[245] *Cong. Rec.*, LII, 63 Cong., 2 sess. (May 22, 1914), 9044.
[246] William Phillips, *Ventures in Diplomacy*, pp. 64–65.
[247] 63 Cong., 2 sess., HR 16680, May 19, 1914 (copy of original bill found in Library of Congress).
[248] *Cong. Rec.*, LII, 63 Cong., 2 sess. (May 19, 1914), 8864; *ibid.* (May 20, 1914), p. 8872.
[249] Livermore, *op. cit.*, p. 27. Bryan to Wilson, May 22, 1914, in Bryan Papers, Letter Books, March, 1913 — November, 1914.
[250] Carr to Marsh, July 10, 1914, in 120.1/47.

were swamped with requests from nationals and belligerent governments. American tourists caught without passports or sufficient currency, the endless requests to locate nationals abroad, and the problem
of stabilizing exchange rates, all fell to the missions. To these were
added the business of the German, Austrian, British, Russian, and
French legations.

The staff of every European mission was inadequate. Secretaries,
ministers, and ambassadors worked exhausting hours. Trained assistance was paid for out of the superior officer's pocket.[251] Private organizations of resident Americans were established to aid the legations
and embassies.[252] Page alone required six additional secretaries. He
wrote, ". . . these . . . should be sent as soon as possible in as much
as the volunteer staff which has been so ably assisting the embassy
during the last fortnight will soon have returned to the United
States."[253] Within the service, however, was much of the potential
needed to deal with the situation. If secretaries could be appointed
to classes instead of posts, then their services could be shifted to where
they were needed.

Bryan wrote to Flood and Stone on August 21 emphasizing that
the President had hoped that the bill would "become law at the earliest possible moment." Bryan added, "The President feels that the
responsibilities of the American Government in its relations with the
belligerent nations makes it essential that the staffs of our embassies,
legations, and consulates in certain capitals should be enlarged and
equipped so as to ensure the highest degree of efficiency. . . ." Flood
agreed with Bryan. He was also anxious to amend the existing measure to conform with Bryan's wishes on the merit service, but the latter
counseled him against any course that would delay the bill.[254] Nevertheless, both Stone and Flood eliminated the merit provisions in
bills.[255]

Throughout the measure's congressional hearing the emphasis was
not on the long-range needs of the service. It was on its immediate

[251] See Ray Stannard Baker, *Woodrow Wilson: Life and Letters* (Garden City, N.Y.,
1931), V, 58; James W. Gerard, *My Four Years in Germany* (London, 1917), pp. 96–152;
Hugh S. Gibson, *A Journal From Our Legation in Belgium* (London, 1917), pp. 50–51;
Burton J. Hendrick, *Life and Letters of Walter Hines Page* (London, 1923), I, 301–26;
Henry Morgenthau, *Ambassador Morgenthau's Story* (Garden City, N.Y., 1918), pp. 123–46
and 232–53; Sharp, *op. cit.*, pp. 66–106; Brand Whitlock, *Belgium Under German Occupation* (London, 1919), I, 35; *idem, Journal of Brand Whitlock*, ed. Allan Nevins (New
York, 1936), pp. 12–20.
[252] Senate Rept. 772, 63 Cong., 2 sess. (September 2, 1914), p. 2.
[253] *Ibid.*
[254] Bryan to Flood, August 21, 1914, in 120.1/48A.
[255] *Cong. Rec.*, LII, 63 Cong., 2 sess (September 2, 1914), 14612; *ibid.* (September 3,
1914), p. 14705.

administrative problems. The report declared, "Great and increasing responsibilities have devolved upon the representatives of the United States abroad because the nations engaged in the present conflict in Europe have entrusted the interests of their subjects and citizens to American diplomatic and consular officers." [256] The bill was unanimously reported out of committee.[257]

No action was taken on the measure until October. An attempt was then made in the Senate. Senator James A. O'Gorman argued that "The State Department will be embarrassed very much in its work until the bill is passed." A southern senator, however, objected that the Senate would abdicate its authority over appointments if the bill were passed. And the bill was ignored.[258] When the objecting senator was satisfied, a second attempt was made. This time the bill was again ignored in order that consideration could be given to the Alaska Coal Lands legislation.[259] After receiving a few amendments, the bill finally passed the Senate unanimously on the fifteenth.[260]

Flood's attempts in the House began five days later. He was countered by the traditional congressional query: "Does this increase the cost?" [261] Other questions sought to discover why Flood had eliminated the merit provisions from his first bill. He answered, though incorrectly, that "the bill could not become law with those provisions in it." He expressed the fear that an attempt to insert them would endanger the bill's passage.[262] No action, however, was taken because of confusion over the shifting of appropriations.

Meanwhile pressures began to accumulate. The State Department needed the legislation immediately. Phillips, through Joseph Tumulty, secured the President's aid for the bill. In a letter to Flood, Wilson wrote:

> At the present time when so many responsibilities are thrown upon our Foreign Service not only in caring for the interests of many other governments but also in seeking new ways in which to enlarge our commerce; it seems to me that nothing should be allowed to stand in the way of making both the diplomatic and consular services, thoroughly adaptable to the new and changed conditions.[263]

[256] House Rept. 1141, 63 Cong., 2 sess. (September 4, 1914), p. 3.
[257] Senate Rept. 772, 63 Cong., 2 sess. (September 2, 1914), p. 1.
[258] *Cong. Rec.*, LII, 63 Cong., 2 sess. (October 9, 1914), 16377.
[259] *Cong. Rec.*, LII, 63 Cong., 2 sess. (October 14, 1914), 16595.
[260] *Ibid.* (October 15, 1914), p. 16667.
[261] *Ibid.* (October 20, 1914), pp. 16830–31. The answer to the query was "yes." The increase for the diplomatic service was $17,000 and $31,000 for the consular service.
[262] *Ibid.*, p. 16832.
[263] Wilson to Stone and Flood, December 10, 1914, in Livermore, *op. cit.*, p. 28.

On January 18, 1915, the bill was revived in the House. The co-incidence in time with appropriation legislation made its passage mandatory.[264] This fact led the proponents of reform, particularly in the Republican party, to offer the discarded merit provisions as amendments. Representative Carl C. Mapes introduced the amendments and claimed that he was acting on the behalf of the National Civil Service Reform League. Flood argued that the bill would be rejected by the Senate if the amendments were adopted. He also argued that the Executive Orders could adequately protect the merit system in the face of any assault by spoils. Many of Mapes's Republican colleagues agreed with Flood, and the amendments were defeated.[265]

Two amendments, however, were accepted. Representative Rogers successfully proposed an amendment to permit assignments to the Department of State without loss of grade, class, or salary. Flood inserted an amendment requiring promotions from class to class to be approved by the Senate.[266] On January 19 the bill was passed.[267] The President signed it on the fifth of February. Later that same day the Department submitted the nominations for classes to the Senate.[268]

The years between the 1905 Executive Order and the Stone-Flood Act witnessed the establishment, in most respects, of a career in diplomacy. A system of examinations for entrance was instituted, and these tests attempted to obtain candidates with the service's particular qualifications. On the secretarial level, security of tenure and promotion by merit were fully accepted. They were no longer even affected by changes in power of the two parties. However, after a promising beginning, the prospect of promotion to the ministerial level was all but choked off by Wilson's administration. Yet, the exceptions kept the prospect alive. And in the long run, one product of the Democrats' action was the stabilization of the ranks and the rates of promotion. In all the steps forward, there was the influence of the career diplomat: Peirce, in 1905; Huntington Wilson, in 1909 and in the legislative attempts; and Phillips, in the Stone-Flood Act. The period also saw the service transformed from one arranged in separate units of representation to one organized by classes and affording personnel mobility. Above all, evidence was appearing that the secretaries were beginning to respond favorably to the career concept and that a substantial body of public opinion existed to prevent, if possible, any violations of the merit principle. On these foundations, the American Diplomatic Service faced the challenges of the nation's growing responsibilities in world affairs.

CHAPTER FOUR

THE FIRST WORLD WAR:
FUSION AND DEMOCRATIZATION
1915-1924

T HE influence of the First World War on the Diplomatic Service was profound. The nation's view of the war's causes, conduct, and consequences required an opinion on professional diplomacy as well. Social forces released by the war demanded recognition by the service in its personnel policies and career concept. The revolution in America's world trading position, accelerated by the war, transformed the traditional questions of diplomacy and necessitated a radical structural reorganization of the entire foreign affairs establishment. And directly, the war affected every administrative aspect of the service and the attitudes which its members had toward the career.

Between 1914 and 1918, the long-range requirements of a career in diplomacy had to give way to the exigencies of the war. The main problem posed by the increasing demands upon the service was to secure sufficient personnel for the embassies and legations. Ordinarily, a sudden call for more overseas personnel could have been met by shifting departmental personnel, via senatorial confirmation, into the service or by drawing from the eligibility list. Neither was possible. The Department was equally swamped.[1] And to draw from the eligibility list, first of all, required congressional authorization.

The problem was partially solved by certain institutional changes,

[1] Graham H. Stuart, *The Department of State* (New York: Appleton-Century, 1948), p. 244.

temporary expedients, and pure good fortune. Authority to utilize personnel from overstaffed missions in those which were particularly hard-pressed was the first major accomplishment. Through the provisions in the Stone-Flood Act in which a secretary was appointed to a grade rather than to a post, this mobility was achieved. One postwar commentator on the Act insisted, ". . . many close students of the subject believe that during war conditions the conduct of our international relationships would have been dangerously impeded if the old practice had been continued." [2] When the United States entered the war, closing the missions to the Central Powers released further personnel, but they were quickly absorbed in co-ordinating the relations between America and the Associated Powers.[3]

Temporary expedients were still necessary. One of these was to request former career ministers, whom Wilson ousted, to serve without compensation at the major capitals. Four accepted.[4] Good fortune was also with the service. Throughout the war period, resignations and the death rate were low. Their combined percentage, including adjustments for promotions to the ministerial rank, reached a high point of 7 per cent in 1917, while the following year it constituted only 3 per cent.[5] The low rate for resignations is probably attributable to the patriotic appeal of the service, the exemptions from military duty granted by the War Department to those holding or about to hold diplomatic secretaryships,[6] and certain reliefs on the salary position. In 1916 Congress authorized "special allowances by way of additional compensation" for both consular and diplomatic officers in belligerent countries "to adjust their official income to the ascertained cost of living. . . ."[7] Two years later these allowances were extended to all posts.[8]

Vital as all these factors were the only practical solution was a permanent expansion in personnel. Between 1914 and 1918, Secretary Robert Lansing secured an increase of 38.5 per cent in the number of secretaryships — from seventy to ninety-seven places. The previous decade had seen a rise of only 45.6 per cent. When he appeared before Congress, he never varied in his complaint:

[2] House Rept. 646, No. 1, 67 Cong., 2 sess. (February 2, 1922), p. 2.

[3] *Cong. Rec.*, LVI, 65 Cong., 2 sess. (February 5, 1918), 1710 (speech by Representative Flood).

[4] *Biog. Reg.* (1915), *passim*. They were H. Percival Dodge at Paris, Lewis D. Einstein at Constantinople, John W. Garrett at Paris, and John B. Jackson at Berlin.

[5] The rate in 1914 was 5.7 per cent; in 1915, 2.7 per cent; and 1916, 5 per cent.

[6] House Committee on Foreign Affairs, *Hearings on Diplomatic and Consular Appropriations for 1919*, 65 Cong., 2 sess. (January 8, 1918), p. 84.

[7] 39 Stat. 252 (July 1, 1916).

[8] 40 Stat. 634 (July 1, 1918).

It has recently become strikingly apparent that the government is seriously handicapped in the conduct of its foreign relations because the number of secretaries in the diplomatic service is wholly inadequate to meet the requirements.

He was able to illustrate his point by referring to the fact that, while America had six more missions than Britain, it had nineteen fewer secretaries.[9] Before the conclusion of the war, Lansing and Phillips calculated the required increase in personnel for the immediate and postwar needs at twenty-five secretaryships. This last increase was obtained without opposition, raising the total number of secretaryships to one hundred and twenty-two.[10]

Thus, in four years, the service was confronted by the necessity to recruit fifty men. Using the last peacetime examination of November, 1913, as a base, it is possible to draw certain conclusions about recruitment under war pressures. The 1913 examination, owing to Bryan's long postponement of it, attracted fifty-two candidates. Of these, roughly 70 per cent took the examination. Only 27.7 per cent of them passed it. Sixty per cent received appointments. Thereafter the number applying to take the examination steadily decreased. Only 65.4 per cent of the total number who applied in 1913 applied in 1914; 50 per cent, in 1915; 48.7 per cent, in 1916; 53.8 per cent, in 1917; and 21 per cent and 11.5 per cent, for the two examinations in 1918. The number taking the examination also declined: 58.3 per cent, in 1914; 50 per cent, in 1915; 52.7 per cent, in 1916; 52.7 per cent, in 1917; and 27.7 per cent and 13.9 per cent, in 1918.

The reverse situation existed in the percentages for those passing the examination. The percentage of those who took the examination and passed it steadily increased: 27.7 per cent, in 1913; 42.8 per cent, in 1914; 44.4 per cent, in 1915; 63.1 per cent, in 1916; and 100 per cent, in 1917. Only in 1918 was there a decrease, the proportion falling to 50 per cent. A similar situation prevailed in the percentage of certified candidates who received appointments. In 1913, 60 per cent received them; 77.7 per cent, in 1914; 87.5 per cent, in 1915; 91.6 per cent, in 1916; and 100 per cent, in 1917. The percentage in 1918 was 85.7 per cent.[11] If it can be assumed that the proportion of qualified men remains about the same in each examination group — or at least does not quadruple! — then the only conclusion possible is that the pressures of war necessitated the admission into the service of candidates who would have been ordinarily rejected.

[9] *New York Times*, February 26, 1916, p. 6.
[10] *Cong. Rec.*, LVI, 65 Cong., 2 sess. (February 5, 1918), 1709–11.
[11] Minutes (1913–18).

What factors account for this decrease in applicants? It cannot be that the examinations were held at too irregular intervals. Never since has such regularity been attained: June, 1915; April, 1916; June, 1917; and June, 1918.[12] The answers must be found elsewhere. Two possibilities exist. Before America entered the war, the reports of administrative difficulties in the missions discouraged men from entering the service, while the business boom encouraged them to enter business. Once America was engaged in the conflict, potential applicants probably preferred to join the more patently patriotic armed forces. Anyway, the service would be a possible career after the war was over.

Does this imply that the examination system had broken down? Before the war, there was evidence that the system was being improved. The oral particularly was strengthened through the addition of a session with career secretaries to ascertain a candidate's fitness for the more practical side of diplomacy.[13] But this ceased when the war began in earnest. The examinations from 1916 to 1918 were either the same or had only minor changes in the questions.[14] A note on the June, 1918, examination admitted, "Owing to the small class to be examined and the volume of work before the Department, it was decided to use questions from previous examinations." [15] Although this fact was not known beforehand to the candidates, the repetition, undoubtedly, aided the cram-schools and those who had previously taken and failed the examination. Furthermore, it highlights the cavalier attitude which the Department took toward the examination. The period also saw examples of accommodating the examination to the convenience of the candidates.[16] Nevertheless, despite these facts, the examinations of 1916 and 1917 had eight private secretaries as successful candidates. This was an unusually high percentage of candidates who had already some experience. It is possible, albeit unprovable, that this factor was taken into consideration — at least at the orals. It was also true that two who had been certified were not appointed. Some even failed.[17] Finally, the examiners felt that those selected were adequate. A typical description of a class appeared in the 1915 minutes: "They are all men of intelligence, well-

[12] Minutes (1915–18).
[13] Minutes (1913).
[14] Minutes (1916–18).
[15] Minutes (June, 1918).
[16] A special examination was held in 1914 at Lanier Winslow's convenience (cf. Minutes [1914]). Prior to the written examination in 1917, three candidates received their oral and physical examinations (cf. Minutes [1917]). This extraordinary procedure emphasizes the perfunctory character of the written examination during the war period.
[17] Minutes (1914–18).

informed on current events and matters of diplomatic history and usage." [18]

The breakdown of the examination systems was not accompanied by a return to partisanship. Only one secretary was appointed to the service by an Executive Order.[19] All other secretaries entering between 1914 and 1918 at least went through the motions of taking an examination. The candidates were known by numbers, and anyone could apply. When a congressman made a charge of partisanship, Secretary Lansing replied, "There are four examiners. As it happens two of them are Democrats and two are Republicans." [20] Moreover, the practice of including the names of indorsers on the examination report ceased after 1914.[21]

Aside from the question of private secretaries, in which an assertion can be made but not proved, data on state representation alone provides possible evidence. However, in areas where the Democratic party was strongest, the disparity between the number who applied and the number appointed was the greatest. The entire South required thirty-four candidates to produce five successful appointments — sixteen more than was mathematically necessary. Only two areas showed a large superfluity: the East North Central and the Pacific regions.[22] Neither was necessarily a stronghold for Wilson. Even the career's congressional guardian John Jacob Rogers could refer in 1918 to Lansing's "scrupulous regard for the merit system in the appointment and retention of secretaries and consuls." [23] Although the standards were not maintained, this fact by no means implies that partisanship re-entered the service.

The war's influence on the other aspects of the service's administration encouraged a secretary to think in terms of a career in diplomacy. The delay between certification and appointment was minimal. The 1917 examination group, for instance, wasted less than two months.[24] The authorizations for new secretaryships, coming as they did in sizable increases, permitted induction in groups often as large as ten men.[25] Promotions from class four to class three usually

[18] Minutes (1915).

[19] Minutes (1918). Charles D. Tenney was appointed by an Executive Order. See also William Dudley Foulke, *Fighting the Spoilsman* (New York, 1919), p. 232.

[20] House Committee on Foreign Affairs, *Hearings on Diplomatic and Consular Appropriations for 1919*, 65 Cong., 2 sess. (January 8, 1918), p. 92.

[21] Minutes (1915–23).

[22] New England should have had 3.6 men; it had four; Middle Atlantic: 19.4/20; East North Central: 6.9/11; West North Central: 4.1/1; South: 9.4/5; Mountain: 2.5/2; and the Pacific: 3/6.

[23] *Cong. Rec.*, LVII, 65 Cong., 3 sess. (January 21, 1919), 1827.

[24] The examination was held June 25–27 (cf. Minutes [1917]). The commissions were all dated August 23 (cf. *Biog. Reg.* [1917], *passim*).

[25] *Biog. Reg.* (1916 and 1917), *passim*.

occurred within three years. Secretaries came more often in contact with each other because of the mobility facilitated by the Stone-Flood Act and by its provisions for limited assignments in the Department. The war also gave them a sense of participating in a vital occupation.

Encouragement was greatest on the issue of higher promotions. During the war, the Department, particularly under Lansing, increasingly recognized the value of professional diplomacy. To insure a concentration of authority in the larger missions, Lansing secured congressional authorization for the President "to designate and assign any secretary of class one as counselor of embassy or legation." [26] While not providing additional compensation, the position allowed a further recognition of career diplomats and brought American practice closer to European. In appointments to the ministerial level as well, the career's interests were advanced. There were few opportunities to make ministerial appointments, for the political appointees retained their positions. However, in three out of the four vacancies that did occur between 1915 and 1918, career men were appointed.[27] The fourth was Page's successor at the Court of St. James. Finally, Lansing utilized career men in important positions within the Department. Aside from Phillips, J. Butler Wright was co-opted to be chief of the Latin American Affairs Division, Jordan Stabler to be his successor, Frederick Seibing to be chief of Western European Affairs Division, and Leland Harrison to be the very important chief of the Division of Secret Intelligence. From December, 1917, the Department of State had twelve career men in its employ.[28]

These factors served to knit the service more closely together. Hugh Wilson dated his first thoughts of the service as a lifetime career to the war period.[29] So evident to all observers was this heightened *esprit de corps* that Brand Whitlock in 1916 could write in his diary, "I don't wish any more personalities like Gibson or in general any of those young or old young sparks who belong to the Secretaries'

[26] 39 Stat. 252 (July 1, 1916).

[27] They were Hoffman Phillip, W. W. Russell, and John W. Garrett (cf. *Biog. Reg.* [1918], *passim*). Garrett was one of the career ministers ousted by Wilson in 1913.

[28] *Biog. Reg.* (1917), *passim*. That Lansing was cognizant of the value of diplomatic training for those filling positions in the Department of State can be seen in his description of William Phillips in his *War Memoirs*. Lansing thought Phillips "was especially equipped because of his long experience in the diplomatic service and also as an official of the Department of State." See *War Memoirs of Robert Lansing, Secretary of State* (London, 1935), p. 361.

[29] Hugh Wilson, *The Education of a Diplomat* (New York, 1938), p. xiii. See also Grew to J. Butler Wright, January 18, 1920, in Joseph C. Grew, *Turbulent Era*, ed. Walter Johnson (Boston: Houghton Mifflin Co., 1952), I, 409: "I feel a new lease on life and a joy in work and living that I have not experienced for over a year; in fact I feel gathered once again in the arms of my father and mother, the Service."

Union and look on all Ministers as 'untrained diplomats,' that is scabs."[30]

While the service attempted to adjust to wartime conditions, its character and tools of trade were attracting growing public attention. An editor's note in a 1916 issue of the *Bookman* explained the reprinting of an essay on the service from a 1906 issue on the grounds that the subject "has an interest now that it did not then have." [31] Before 1914, this interest was in speculation about the service's political and commercial potentialities. However, the war, its causes and portents, transformed speculation into opinions upon concrete realities.

On this new situation, those who had advocated earlier the political necessity of professional diplomacy in a world of nation-states used the war as evidence for their major premise. "The resistless currents of a new age," the argument ran, "had swept over us and destroyed our traditional isolation forever." [32] The reason for this, in the words of Roland Usher, was that "the vital developments of the nineteenth century in science and industry have already robbed our strategic position of a part of its former invulnerability, while the European war threatens seriously to alter the more important of its other features. . . ." [33] The resulting exposure made the Diplomatic Service "the first line of national defense." [34] And it was no coincidence that the periodical *Forum*, "the magazine of constructive nationalism," was a supporter of a stronger service.[35] On the other hand, the more idealistically inclined, who were introduced to diplomacy by the war, considered the conflict to have had its origins in the failures or cabals of professional diplomats. A statement by Senator Borah was typical of this view. In 1918, he wrote, "The greatest war of all history was begun not to preserve liberty, but to destroy it, and the scheme was hatched in the chancelleries of Europe." [36] It was John Dewey's opinion that "secret diplomacy," as it was popularly tagged, "carries with it all the signs of a class so personally and professionally

[30] Brand Whitlock, *The Journal of Brand Whitlock*, ed. Allan Nevins (New York, 1936), p. 269. The entry is for June 4, 1916.

[31] George Barr Baker, "The American Diplomatic Service," *The Bookman*, XLIV (September, 1916), 87n.

[32] Robert W. Bruère, "Changing America," *Century Magazine*, CXXXVIII (February, 1919), 290. Although Theodore Roosevelt made no specific reference to the service during the war, he did call for a more intelligent handling of America's foreign affairs (see Theodore Roosevelt, *America and the World War*, [London, 1915] p. 243).

[33] Roland G. Usher, *Pan Americanism* (London, 1915), p. 98.

[34] Perry Belmont, "The First Line of National Defense," *North American Review*, CCI (June, 1915), 889.

[35] "Our Diplomatic Service: The Facts," *The Forum*, LVI (November, 1916), 611–18.

[36] William E. Borah, "The Perils of Secret Treaty Making," *The Forum*, LX (December, 1918), 661.

set apart that it moves in a high inaccessible realm whose doings are no concern of the vulgar mass." [37] A contributor to the *Annals* complained, "The diplomacy of Europe is still the diplomacy of the eighteenth century. It is controlled by the aristocracy. It does not think in terms of people; it thinks in terms of its own narrow interests." [38] And G. Lowes Dickinson, writing in the *Atlantic*, warned Americans to beware of "the growth of an expert diplomatic service." [39]

It still remained a moot point whether or not American practice smacked of Europe. According to the editor of the *Nation*, "The proposal of 'Democratic control' of diplomacy is only what is settled practice of the United States." [40] However, a writer in the *Atlantic* maintained, "The people of the United States know no more about the international policy of their government than the English or Germans knew of the plans of their Foreign Offices." [41] In either case, the accepted connection between professional diplomats and the causes of the war demonstrated the power of diplomacy and established it as a subject of public importance.

Commercial questions also attracted more attention to the service. Here again, on account of the war, the process transforming America from a debtor to a creditor nation and from an exporter of raw materials to one of manufactured goods had been greatly accelerated. It was increasingly believed that "if we do not establish permanent outlets for our excess production we will surely suffer an industrial setback at the termination of hostilities." [42] American merchants, realizing that the "competition for the world's markets will be fiercer than it has ever been before in the world's history," [43] turned to the government for aid. This aid included securing "government contracts, concessions, participation in loans, the safeguarding of patent rights, and the opposition to laws inimical to the extension of

[37] John Dewey, "The League of Nations and the New Diplomacy," *Dial Magazine*, LXV (November 16, 1918), 402.

[38] Frederic C. Howe, "Democracy or Imperialism," *Annals of the American Academy*, LXVI (July, 1916), p. 252–53.

[39] G. Lowes Dickinson, "Democratic Control of Foreign Policy," *Atlantic*, CXVIII (August, 1916), 151–52.

[40] "Secret Diplomacy," *Nation*, CI (December 30, 1915), 765. See also Roland Huggins, "The United States: Crusader," *The Open Court*, XXXI (June, 1917), 340.

[41] Arthur Bullard, "Democracy and Diplomacy", *Atlantic*, CXIX (April, 1917), 491. See also Briareus, "A Suggestion for Open Diplomacy," *Nation*, CVII (December 28, 1918), 801–2.

[42] Theodore E. Burton, "What Chance Has America After the War," *System Magazine*, XXIX (March, 1916), 243.

[43] Edward A. Filene, "Cooperative Pioneering and Guaranteeism in the Foreign Trade," *Annals of the American Academy*, LIX (May, 1915), 330.

trade." [44] Furthermore, in the words of a trade association, "the interests of American foreign trade demand that our diplomatic and consular representation throughout the world should be provided with greater facilities for the anticipation and analysis of the new commercial policies of the great powers and their colonies." [45] In all these duties there was a general agreement on the division of labor. A contributor to the *Banker's Magazine* summarized it: "These measures should be founded on the principle that diplomats establish cordial relations, that commercial agents act as trade emissaries." [46]

The war period also brought encomiums to the Diplomatic Service for the work it was doing. An article in the *Nation* claimed, "The whole record of the work of American diplomats during the past few months should help us to a better notion of their duties and their usefulness." [47] Although referring to the entire foreign affairs establishment, Representative Flood voiced similar sentiments before Congress in 1918. "In no instance," he maintained, "has a single bureau failed to give a good account of itself." [48]

The recommendations for the service which flowed from these varied considerations differed little from those of the previous period. With the editor of the *Independent*, many argued that "foreign affairs should recognize no party" and that "diplomacy should allow a career." [49] Particularly among foreign policy realists, there was a belief, in the words of Henry White, that "the United States never would assume its place in the family of nations until politics ceased to play an important part in the selection of American diplomats." [50] The Wilsonian purge of professional diplomats in 1913 became an election issue in 1916.[51] The *New York Times* contended throughout the period:

> One Bryan in the State Department can do more harm in a brief period to upset any plans for the improvement of our diplomatic service and discourage young men of the right sort from devoting their lives to it, than three Administrations can do to build up an intelligently devised system.[52]

[44] *Ibid.*, p. 325.

[45] National Foreign Trade Council to Lansing, June 19, 1916, in 120.1/50. The quotation came from a pamphlet circulated to congressmen and trade associations. It was entitled "Urgent Needs of the Diplomatic and Consular Services of the United States."

[46] Arthur Reynolds, "Some of the Elements of Success in International Trade and Banking," *Bankers' Magazine*, XCVII (November, 1918), 535.

[47] "Brighter Side of Diplomacy," *Nation*, XCIX (December 10, 1914), 681.

[48] *Cong. Rec.*, LVI, 65 Cong., 2 sess. (February 5, 1918), 1709.

[49] "Our Diplomatic Service," *Independent*, LXXXI (March 29, 1915), 446.

[50] *New York Times*, April 12, 1916, p. 6.

[51] *New York Times*, August 6, 1916, Sec. 7, p. 2.

[52] *New York Times*, February 27, 1916, Sec. 1, p. 16.

And the advocates of professional diplomacy could claim, contrary to the objection to "secret diplomacy," that a greater reliance upon career men might have avoided the war. Their evidence was the public statement of Prince Lichnowsky that politicians had kept professional diplomats from avoiding the conflict.[53]

It was also argued that diplomacy should not only be a career but one with a specialized training. Before the Navy League, W. H. Slayton recommended the European system because "a man is educated to be a diplomat and stays in the service practically all his life. He is in short a trained diplomat."[54] To a similar point made by Henry White, the *Nation* insisted, ". . . there can be little disagreement."[55]

The desired training was never discussed in detail. It can be argued, however, that the predominance of political issues during the war would have demanded a course emphasizing the process of negotiation and political analysis. At no time was there a suggestion that diplomats should have experience at consular posts. The nearest approximation was the opinion held by the opposition to "secret diplomacy" that commercial scrutiny over diplomacy would be salutary.[56]

The period's most important recommendation, however, was that the service should be democratized. A writer in *Forum* maintained this for the very practical reason that "U.S. Diplomats are the poorest paid, least representative servants of any nation on the globe."[57] But the consideration that actuated most writers was the dangers inherent in recruiting a service from a social elite. The main danger was that the demands of the majority on foreign policy might be ignored. No doubt this in part came from the cosmopolization of Progressive thought. Significantly, though, no writer advocated the abandonment of the service. One lamented, "Even in the United States diplomacy partakes of the aristocratic flavor of Europe."[58] But the solution always lay in providing sufficient salaries to permit the "people's representatives" to enter the service. A writer in the *Nation*, referring to the war, believed that this was "the best possible guarantee that nothing of the sort shall happen again. . . ."[59]

[53] *Good Government*, XXXIX (1918), 83.

[54] "Our Diplomatic Service: The Facts," *Forum*, LVI (November, 1916), 613.

[55] "Diplomacy and Arms," *Nation*, CII (April 20, 1916), 428.

[56] See Walter Lippmann, *The Stakes of Diplomacy* (New York, 1915), p. 194. See also Dewey, *op. cit.*, p. 402.

[57] "Our Diplomatic Service: The Facts," p. 611. See also "Diplomatic and Consular Careers," *Nation*, C (January 28, 1915), 98.

[58] Howe, *op. cit.*, p. 253. See also Edward A. Filene, "Democratic Organization of the Coming Peace Conference," *Annals of the American Academy*, LXXII (July, 1917), 225.

[59] "Responsible Diplomacy," *Nation*, CVII (December 28, 1918), 793.

With the cessation of hostilities, there was no diminution of pressures upon the service. Many of the responsibilities assumed by the Department of State from the temporary war agencies involved the overseas services as well. The preparations for the Peace Conference, the recognition of new states and governments, and the re-establishment of missions in the Central Powers multiplied the existing burdens. To cope with these Congress had authorized the expansion of the service by twenty-five secretaryships.[60] But the record on wartime recruitment permitted little encouragement. Furthermore, dissatisfaction was appearing among existing members. On the issue of salaries, Joseph Grew wrote to Butler Wright, "Certainly many men in the Service will resign unless some hope can be held out of higher salaries or better allowances." [61] Promotions posed another problem. William Phillips insisted in the *Forum*, "I am seeing constantly the look of discouragement upon the faces of men who deserve the highest consideration from their country for their efficient and loyal service." [62] Added to both was the growing competition for the service's personnel by commercial groups. Before a congressional hearing, Phillips acknowledged this threat, admitting, ". . . we have lost, and are continuing to lose, some of the best men we have." [63]

Secretary Lansing, along with the service's spokesman Assistant Secretary William Phillips, was at no loss to know what was needed. To combat the threat from business and to secure the widest possible selection of personnel, it was necessary, in the words of Lansing, "to make the salaries of secretaries ample, thereby opening these positions to all persons who may possess the necessary qualifications, irrespective of the amount of their private fortune." Post allowances, too, were important. To insure the sustained interest of the secretaries, it was essential, again in the words of Lansing, "that young men in choosing the diplomatic career should be inspired in their work by the hope of promotion to the highest office the service presents. . . ." [64]The increases in salary, however, were not to end with secretaries of class one. To permit promotion through to the ministerial level at least, it was vital to secure government residences and post allowances for those in the highest ranks as well. On this point, Phillips commented, ". . . the Government should require its representatives to adopt a standard of living of suitable dignity and this

[60] 40 Stat. 634 (July 1, 1918).

[61] Grew, *op. cit.*, I, 409. The letter is dated January 18, 1920.

[62] William Phillips, "Cleaning Our Diplomatic House," *Forum*, LXIII (February, 1920), 169.

[63] *Cong. Rec.*, LVI, 65 Cong., 2 sess. (February 8, 1918), 1879. The quotation appears in a speech by Representative Rogers.

[64] House Rept. 511, 66 Cong., 2 sess. (January 21, 1920), p. 7.

can be accommodated only by requiring its representatives to occupy a governmental residence and by making it possible for a poor man, through an increased allowance, to live there as well as a rich man." [65]

Apart from an increased reliance by the Executive on career men to serve in ministerial capacities, these solutions rested solely with Congress. Increasing salaries, purchasing residences, authorizing post allowances, putting the Board of Examiners on a statutory basis, classifying ministerships, and providing a formal means for promotions to the upper level, all these were in the competency of Congress alone.

With war fervor still prevailing and an opportunity existing to mobilize some of the attention and good will toward the service engendered by the war, the immediate postwar period appeared as the ideal time to put the service on the firmest base possible. And the initial signs were encouraging. Particularly so was the interest demonstrated by Congressman John Jacob Rogers from Massachusetts. Upon entering the House, he became its staunchest advocate for professional diplomacy and was concerned with every suggestion to advance this concept. He bitterly denounced Wilson's purge in 1913.[66] His amendments to the Stone-Flood Act insured the best interests of the career members. Although a Republican, he drew support from both parties.[67] And while he was not averse to using his support of the service to help his own political position, he was absolutely sincere in recommending career appointments to a Republican President.[68] Rogers' own philosophy of international relations was similar to Senator Lodge's. He was a nationalist who opposed the groundless idealism of the League.[69] But his opposition to internationalism and his support of professional diplomacy were not contradictory. They were, in fact, complementary.

Rogers introduced his first measure on January 16, 1919. It was a bill "to provide a system of promotion of efficient secretaries in the Diplomatic Service to vacancies arising in the rank of minister." The proposed system had its germ in the 1909 Executive Order and the Stone-Flood Act. Rogers' bill, however, sought specifically to create

---

[65] Phillips, *op. cit.*, pp. 169–70.

[66] *Cong. Rec.*, LI, 63 Cong., 2 sess. (April 2, 1914). 6162–66.

[67] "An Appreciation," *American Consular Bulletin*, VI (July, 1924), 241.

[68] Carr to Secretary Hughes, October 12, 1922, in 111/104: "I think Mr. Rogers would greatly appreciate having this letter of approval of his bill as early as practicable while his campaign for re-election is on." Rogers to President Harding, October 17, 1923, in 121.31/16: "I will hope that it will not be deemed an impertinence if I suggest that you consider promoting on a merit basis from men now in the service." The communication refers to vacancies in three ambassadorial positions.

[69] Karl Schriftgiesser, *The Gentleman from Massachusetts: Henry Cabot Lodge* (Boston: Little, Brown & Co., 1945), p. 315.

a board charged with the responsibility of recommending to the President, at definite intervals, the names of secretaries for promotion to the ministerial ranks. A Civil Service "rule of three" was to be required for all recommendations.[70]

Although there is no evidence that Rogers was yet in touch with the Department, its career officers certainly approved of the measure. The ministerial level was more seriously infected with spoils. The measure would constitute a permanent thin wedge into the system. Its mere proposal would encourage members of the service. While the session closed without any action being taken, Congressmen Rogers and J. Charles Linthicum, representatives of both parties, urged support of the bill.[71]

There were favorable steps in the direction of higher compensation and more promotions as well. Secretary Lansing, whose tenure was marked by attempts to secure a more adequate salary for the service,[72] was successful in persuading Congress in 1919 that it was financially responsible for paying the transportation expenses for secretaries' families and effects.[73] Along with the post allowances achieved in 1916 and 1918, this travel grant offered an extra incentive in the face of the great shifts in personnel required by the conclusion of the war. In April, 1919, the career was also recognized when the first postwar ministerial appointment, the ministership to Poland, was filled by career officer Hugh Gibson.[74]

The real test, however, had not yet come. It was whether or not the service had a future in recruitment. The operating premise was that "there are returning to the United States thousands of men who have served abroad . . . who have realized as never before what the Diplomatic and Consular Service really does and means." [75] From these returning servicemen, the Diplomatic Service was to be recruited. Interviews taken in 1957 of officers who entered in the immediate postwar years validate almost unanimously this premise.[76] And, according to the autobiographies of the men of this period, a very important factor in their decisions about the service was the new international role which they felt America must play. For instance, Jefferson Patterson claimed, ". . . it was, at any rate, during the im-

[70] *Cong. Rec.*, LVII, 65 Cong., 3 sess. (January 16, 1919), H.R. 14561, p. 1579.

[71] *Ibid.* (January 21, 1919), pp. 1826–28.

[72] Lansing to Representative Rogers, February 2, 1923, in House Rept. 157, *Report on a Bill for the Reorganization and Improvement of the Foreign Service of the United States*, 68 Cong., 1 sess. (February 5, 1924), p. 8.

[73] 40 Stat. 1325 (March 4, 1919).

[74] *Biog. Reg.* (1919), p. 43.

[75] National Civil Service Reform League, *Report on the Foreign Service* (New York, 1919), pp. 266–67.

[76] Interviews at Diplomatic and Consular Officers Retired (DACOR) with retired members of the Foreign Service, July 15–September 6, 1957 (transcripts in author's possession.)

mediate aftermath of war that my thoughts were first turned toward the possibility of a career in diplomacy." [77] Only the conjectured number was wrong.

The first examination was scheduled for mid-May. With the resignation rate running at about 5 per cent and the number of new secretaryships at 25, nearly thirty vacancies were to be filled. The State Department "made every effort to incite interest" in the examination. At first the premise about postwar recruitment seemed to be confirmed. A number of inquiries were made by prospective candidates.[78] One anxious applicant, who was over the age limit, persuaded Wilson to issue an Executive Order permitting him to take the examination.[79] But when the designated period ended, only seventeen had applied and were designated.[80]

Neither the long-run interest of building a strong service nor the short-run need to reduce pressures on personnel was advanced by the number designated for the May examination. To advance both, Butler Wright suggested that an examination be held in Paris to attract men still stationed abroad.[81] On April 28, Phillips agreed. A temporary Board of Examiners was created from the service's staff at the Peace Conference.[82] The armed forces' newspaper *Stars and Stripes* was used to publicize the examination. The dates were fixed for the twenty-sixth to the thirty-first of May. No indorsers were required. For the examination, 266 candidates appeared. Eighty-five withdrew after the particulars of the examination were explained; 107 completed it. No copies of the examination can be found, but the stated standards for the oral did not depart from previous practice.[83]

The examiners were dissatisfied with the results of both examinations. Only ten candidates appeared in Washington to take the earlier one. Eight had passed it, a ninth establishing eligibility abroad.[84] Phillips considered this examination a failure.[85] But even the Paris

---

[77] Jefferson Patterson, *Diplomatic Duty and Diversion* (Cambridge, Massachusetts: Riverside Press, 1956), p. 3.

[78] Phillips, *op. cit.*, p. 166.

[79] Minutes (May 19–21, 1919). By the Executive Order of April 21, 1915, Wilson lowered the maximum age limit from 50 to 35. See National Civil Service Reform League, *Report on the Foreign Service*, p. 258.

[80] *Ibid.*

[81] Grew, *op. cit.*, I, 385. In the absence of evidence to the contrary, it can be assumed that Wright made the original recommendation. Writing to him on April 24, 1919, Grew stated, "Your point that a great many Americans returning to the United States would be glad to endorse the Service if their attention were called to the importance of doing so, is well taken." This letter implies a previous letter from Wright on the point of recruitment. Several days later Phillips agreed to the Paris examination.

[82] Phillips to Wright, April 28, 1919, in 121.11/31:1140.

[83] Minutes (May 26–31, 1919).

[84] Minutes (May 19–21, 1919).

[85] Phillips, *op. cit.*, p. 166.

examination, with ten times the number of candidates, was similarly considered. Although twenty-two established eligibility, only eleven were appointed.[86] When the problem of the remaining ones arose, Phillips wrote, "It was decided sometime ago that it was not advisable to appoint any more from the Paris list without the Department having the opportunity to see them."[87] None were subsequently brought to the Department. William Phillips later admitted in the *Forum* that the Paris examination "was a little more successful."[88]

Meanwhile Representative Rogers had reintroduced his bill. This time, however, his belief in the primacy of economic questions in postwar diplomacy and his appreciation of the more favorable position which the Consular Service had with Congress led him to expand his bill to permit consuls general to be appointed to the ministerial level as well. The mechanics of the measure otherwise remained the same.[89]

While the Diplomatic Service preferred the original measure, the situation for the service was becoming crucial. Without a continuous stream of potential applicants and with the threats from resignations and higher salaries from business, the service had to create a demand for the career and encourage existing members simultaneously. To Secretary Lansing, then in Paris, Undersecretary Polk wired, "Phillips, Carr, and I are strongly in favor of the general idea contained in the bill and believe that only by the adoption of some such method may the future of the Diplomatic Service be made secure."[90] Events thereafter moved in two directions. They moved, first, toward strengthening the service's career position, and, second, paradoxically, in the direction of forcing the service to compromise its independence of the Consular Service.

This dual movement received impetus from the National Civil Service Reform League. The League considered the postwar period an appropriate time for a full-scale assault on the remaining aspects of patronage in the overseas services. As most domestic battles had been won, the League could afford to concentrate all its attention on the problem. It had used the war period to educate public opinion about the needs of both services. Resolutions demanded the formal enactment of the merit provisions. Editorials deplored the sacrifice

[86] Minutes (May 26–31, 1919).

[87] Phillips to Board of Examiners, December 20, 1919, in 121.11/86:1140.

[88] Phillips, *op. cit.*, p. 166.

[89] *Cong. Rec.*, LVIII, 66 Cong., 1 sess. (May 23, 1919), 195. The second bill HR 2709, was entitled "To amend an act entitled 'An act for the improvement of the foreign service' so as to provide a system of promotion of efficient secretaries in the Diplomatic Service and consuls general to vacancies arising in the rank of minister." The first, HR 14561, provided for "efficient secretaries in the Diplomatic Service" only. Cf. supra.

[90] Polk to Lansing, June 5, 1919, in 121.1/29:1139.

of diplomatic offices to campaign contributors.[91] When John Davis succeeded Page in London, *Good Government* inquired, "If in times like these we can dispense with the publicity value of such names as Choate, why not appoint a career man?"[92] Finally, on April 10, 1919, the League announced the formation of a committee, headed by Ellery C. Stowell of Columbia University, to investigate and make recommendations for the reform of the entire foreign service.[93] After consulting with the service's representatives in the Department, the League published an interim statement for congressmen, the press, and trade associations. In September the full report was published.[94] The following December the League joined the National Foreign Trade Council and the American Manufacturers' Export Association "to carry out the League's recommendations by drafting and securing the passage of appropriate legislation by Congress."[95]

In almost every respect, the report's recommendations would have advanced the interests of the Diplomatic Service. To professionalize the service further, the report suggested that secretaries should enter, after an examination and suitable probation, at the lowest rung before the age of thirty, and that Presidential and congressional designations and state quotas be abolished. It advocated that examinations be held at a set time, preferably at the end of the academic year, and that they be administered in the "principal cities where civil service examinations are held." It also suggested that names of worthy members of both services be submitted regularly to the President for merit promotions, and that ministers be appointed to grade and not post. To democratize the service, the report recommended the usual remedies: higher salaries, residences, pensions, and post allowances. It added, however, the novelty of government provision of transportation expenses to Washington for orals' candidates. To further specialization, the report proposed that lateral transfer be permitted, after an examination, between the services.[96] These recommendations, save for lateral transfer and the traveling expenses for orals' candidates, were ones which no observer of the service could fail to

[91] *Good Government*, XXXIV (January, 1917), 3; XXXIV (March, 1917), 16.

[92] "Who Is Davis?", *Good Government*, XXXV (September, 1918), 147.

[93] National Civil Service Reform League, *Report on the Foreign Service*, p. 17. The members of the committee were Ellery C. Stowell, Richard H. Dana, George T. Keyes, Ogden Hammond, and Ansley Wilcox. For a more detailed discussion of the League's activities for reform in both services, see Frank M. Stewart, *History of the National Civil Service Reform League* (Austin, Texas, 1929), pp. 202–4.

[94] Stowell to Polk, June 3, 1919, in 120.1/57. "Allow me to express to you the appreciation of the Committee for the cordial cooperation of the State Department in answering all inquiries and facilitating the preparation of the necessary material for our report." See also Stewart, *op. cit.*, pp. 202–3.

[95] *Good Government*, XXXVIII (April, 1920), 34–35.

[96] National Civil Service Reform League, *Report on the Foreign Service*, pp. 18–20.

make. But the report gave them currency and, more particularly, encouraged public thinking along its most radical recommendation from the service's viewpoint — lateral transfer.

Lateral transfer by examination compromised the concept of professional diplomacy; fusion of the two services was an unqualified abandonment of this principle. Shortly after the League's report, the latter possibility arose. Its advocate was the consul general in London, Robert P. Skinner. Skinner, who had entered the Consular Service in 1897, was then, except for Carr, probably the most influential member of that service. As early as 1916, he raised the question with Phillips of fusing the two services. Using an English periodical's argument about the same move, he contended, "The effect of fusion, if accomplished under proper conditions, would be extremely beneficial to both branches of the Foreign Department." [97] The question, however, was dropped by Skinner during the war period.

During the summer of 1919, Representative Rogers visited Europe. He was then concerned with Department of Commerce's intention to establish an independent corps of commercial attachés. While in London, Rogers sought Skinner's views on a bill he had drawn placing the attachés under the aegis of the Department of State. Skinner was able to convince Rogers that this issue was unimportant compared with the problem of the existing relations between the Diplomatic and Consular Services, and that an effective foreign service might eliminate the necessity for attachés. Maintaining the basic similarity of the problems dealt with by the services, Skinner held that "they could advantageously be fused into one far more effective organization." [98] Rogers agreed and asked Skinner to put his ideas into the form of a bill.

Skinner's measure, which Rogers introduced on November 15, 1919, had three major provisions. It incorporated the Diplomatic Service into the Consular Service, using the terms "consuls" and "vice-consuls" to refer to members of the new service. With salaries approximating the existing range of Consular Service salaries, the posts were then subdivided into consuls of four classes and vice-consuls of two. A Board of Examiners was proposed to deal with questions of recruitment and promotion. Second, adopting the League's suggestion about the classification of ministers, Skinner's bill created two classes of ministers and included them in the promotional hierarchy. Finally, the measure recommended the creation of a system of scholarships in which university students of two years standing would re-

[97] Skinner to Phillips, July 17, 1916, in 120.1/52.
[98] Hon. Robert P. Skinner to author, November 13, 1957. See also Skinner to Grew, October 8, 1925, in 120.1/151.

ceive, after an examination, a government grant of tuition and subsistence for another two years in return for five years of service.[99]

The reaction of the Department's career diplomats was strong and immediate.[100] Furthermore, it should have been predicted. When Skinner first wrote to Phillips in 1916, the latter had opposed his suggestion. Although he admitted the value of consular experience, he was not convinced of the merits of fusion in the lower ranks.[101] Three years later, in response to the League's suggestion about lateral transfer, Phillips substantially repeated his stand. He claimed, ". . . there should be no attempts to combine the Services until the Diplomatic Service is sufficiently strong to stand on its own feet." Although he again appreciated the value of commercial experience, he feared that, if the plan were adopted, "the Diplomatic Service would disappear and become merged with the Consular Service." Most important in Phillips' mind was maintaining the independence of the Diplomatic Service.[102] This objective was shared by the other career men in the Department. A clash was in the offing.

A possible avenue for compromise, although still leading toward the abandonment of an independent service, was provided by the director of the Consular Bureau, Wilbur Carr. While he had always been particularly interested in the Consular Service, he had nevertheless a greater general grasp of administration than either Skinner or the career diplomats. His aim in reorganization, as expressed in a memo to Undersecretary Polk, was to move in the direction of a "single working-unit." [103] He had held this idea since the Morgan bill.[104] The stage before the single unit was one of interchangeability of personnel between the two services. And this had to be preceded by making "the scales of compensation more or less the same." [105]

When the clash appeared imminent, Carr persuaded Rogers that it could be avoided by maintaining the functional separation of the two services and creating a general personnel classification of "Foreign Service officer." This new classification would have the added advantage of being capable of circumventing the Constitutional restriction against binding the President's power of choice. "Foreign Service officer" was not included in the Constitution, and thus requirements

[99] *Cong. Rec.,* LVIII, 66 Cong., 1 sess. (November 15, 1919), 8614; 120.1/64, Copy of HR 10587, November 15, 1919.

[100] Skinner to author, November 13, 1957. See *American Consular Bulletin,* II (March, 1920), 3, for line reaction.

[101] Phillips to Skinner, July 31, 1916, in 120.1/52.

[102] Phillips and Carr to Polk, June 4, 7, 1919, in 120.1/57.

[103] Carr and Phillips to Polk, June 4, 7, 1919, in 120.1/57.

[104] See chapter two.

[105] Carr and Phillips to Polk, June 4, 7, 1919, in 120.1/57.

for it could be established. In his drafted measure, which Rogers consented to introduce on December 10, Carr retained Skinner's classification of ministers, most aspects of his scholarship scheme, and the enactment of the merit provisions. However, he substituted a general classified personnel hierarchy of nine grades for Skinner's "consuls" and "vice-consuls." An officer entered, via an examination, the lowest grade, advanced by ascertained merit, and was assignable to either consular or diplomatic posts.[106]

Consular officers would have accepted either measure. Their reasons, though seldom made explicit, can be surmised. In many ways, the Consular Service was faced with the same problems as the Diplomatic Service. While salaries were much higher in the former, business firms represented threats to consular personnel as well. While many more applied to enter the Consular Service, there was still dissatisfaction with the quality of the men recruited. By increasing the promotional opportunities and widening the responsibilities of the Consular Service, existing personnel, it was hoped, would be retained and, in the words of Skinner, ". . . we should then get uniformly attractive men in the lowest grades of the Consular Service." [107]

There were also other reasons. Particularly irritating to the consuls was the social schism that kept them, the representatives of commerce, from the diplomatic world in each capital. Although never admitted by consuls as a motivating factor for reorganization, it was observed by others. Miss Emily Bax of the London embassy recalls in her memoirs, "The Consular Service seemed to suffer from an inferiority complex, and the Rogers Act . . . was probably at least in part inspired by disgruntled Consuls who wanted their share in the limelight." [108] Similarly, Representative Tom Connally observed, "It is urged that officers in the Consular Service desire a unified service so that social distinctions may be abolished." [109] Finally, both measures were administratively sound in terms of the problems that were to occupy American foreign affairs after the war. They would also unify administration and provide definite economies.

The Diplomatic Service was not to lose completely on the measure adopted. When writing to Phillips in 1916, Skinner summarized the state of congressional opinion. He claimed, "As a proposition in prac-

---

[106] *Cong. Rec.*, LIX, 66th Cong., 2 sess. (December 10, 1919), 387; 120.1/64, Copy of HR 11058, December 10, 1919. Carr's authorship of the compromise is based on inference. The resulting draft was very similar to what he proposed in the memo to Polk; the career diplomats opposed interchangeability at the outset, and general service opinion acknowledged Carr's hand in the bill's earliest stages (see *American Foreign Service Journal*, XII [October, 1935], 550).

[107] Skinner to Phillips, July 17, 1916, in 120.1/52.

[108] Emily Bax, *Miss Bax of the Embassy* (Boston, 1939), p. 169.

[109] *Congressional Digest*, III (January, 1924), 125.

tical politics, I do not believe that we can get legislation which will put the Diplomatic Service, root and branch, upon a permanent footing without fusion with the Consular Service." Fusion would align congressional and business opinion behind the new service. The questions of salaries and promotions would then be answered. According to Skinner, fusion would increase the quality of the service's personnel by discouraging "the mental idlers from joining as a means of engaging in diplomatic work." [110] And no one could doubt the value of commercial experience for all overseas representatives.

Furthermore, the two measures were not revolutionary. Although no precedents existed in Europe, the United States had not historically maintained both services absolutely distinct. Schuyler's reform instituted the dual commission, and the establishment of legations in the Baltic States after the war saw consuls serving simultaneously as secretaries of legation.[111] It was also by no means uncommon for a consul to be elevated to a ministerial position.

Nevertheless, the Diplomatic Service preferred to remain independent. The reasons were many. From a very practical standpoint, the career diplomats feared being swallowed up by the numerically larger and better organized Consular Service. When the new relationship was authorized in 1924, the ratio was greater than four to one.[112] And organization had progressed to the point in 1919 where an American Consular Association and a monthly journal were established.[113] The higher resignation rate in the Diplomatic Service and its greater relative expansion permitted much more rapid advancement than in its commercial cousin. Competition, too, would be increased for upper service posts.

Emotional issues existed as well. A strong *esprit de corps* had been developed in the service, and this discouraged fusion and interchangeability. Most secretaries also believed, in the words of Minister Charles Ingersoll, that "it would take a very exceptional Consul to make a proper diplomatic representative."[114] The consul's training, education, and general background, the diplomats argued, made him unsuitable for diplomacy. Above all, the diplomat wished to avoid the possibility of consular duty. The world of the consul was

[110] Skinner to Phillips, July 17, 1916, in 120.1/52.

[111] *Biog. Reg.* (1920), *passim.*

[112] 511 officers from the Consular Service to 122 diplomats.

[113] James Barclay Young, "The Twenty-Fifth Anniversary of the Foreign Service Association," *American Foreign Service Journal*, XX (March, 1943), 134–37. The first issue of the *American Consular Bulletin* was published on March 15, 1919. See also Chauncey Depew Snow, "Governmental Foreign Trade Promotion Service in the United States," *Annals of the American Academy*, XCIV (March, 1921), 110.

[114] George Pratt Ingersoll to the Committee, May 29, 1919, in National Civil Service Reform League, *Report on the Foreign Service*, p. 139.

comparatively pedestrian. Assignments were often in industrial cities or unhealthy ports. Associations were generally limited to other consuls, businessmen, and an occasional drunken sailor. Invoices, visas, and passports filled the day. While the diplomat did not avoid routine, he lived in a much more prestigious and exciting world. He met the "best people" in each capital and was part of the social life of the *Corps Diplomatique*. Even in dreary Central American posts, he was still an honored part of the European colony. To this world the consul usually had no access; from the world of invoices the diplomatic secretary was immune. Skinner's bill raised all these specters. The saving aspect of Carr's measure for the diplomat was its maintenance of the functional separation of the two services. In this way, the diplomat might at least avoid a consular assignment.

An independent service, however, was preferred by the career diplomats, and the job of sustaining and strengthening the service was assumed by William Phillips and Butler Wright. The former used the public press, while the latter collected suggestions on strategy from his colleagues. Between them there was general agreement. Before appeals for increased salaries could be made, the public had to be educated to appreciate the necessity for the service. But the defense of diplomacy that would be appropriate in Europe had little relevance for a nation heading toward "normalcy." Joseph C. Grew summarized the problem and its solution:

> The public doesn't care about the political situation in Silesia or what is happening on the Lithuanian frontier or the Danzig question. The only element of the Foreign Service that appeals to the public is the ability of the Service to ensure business, better business, and bigger business. We must get it out of the mind of the public that the Consular Service is the only one that looks after that side.[115]

In his *Forum* article, Phillips stressed: "It is a popular concept that the diplomat leaves to the consul all questions dealing with trade and commerce. This is very far from the truth. The economic and political relations of states are so closely allied that the line of demarcation is almost invisible." Later he referred to the Diplomatic Service as the one "without which consular activities cannot function." [116]

The year 1920 was not encouraging for the future of an independent Diplomatic Service. On January 26 another examination was held. Nineteen applied and were designated; only twelve appeared to take the examination.[117] Simultaneous with this consistently bad

[115] Grew to Wright, January 18, 1920, in Grew, *op. cit.*, I, 410–11.
[116] Phillips, *op. cit.*, pp. 167–68, 172.
[117] Minutes (January 26–28, 1920).

showing was the first public support by the Secretary of State of the principle of interchangeability. In replying to a Senate resolution, Lansing maintained, "It is generally to be desired that our Diplomatic and Consular Services should be brought closer together and given an interchangeable character." [118] To confuse the matter, the Secretary argued earlier that the two elements should "be fused and converted to their appropriate uses." [119] But his position was primarily designed to appear to an economy-minded Congress. While Lansing agreed that interchangeability was a desirable goal, he first wished to see the salary scale of the Diplomatic Service increased, considering the existing standard as undemocratic. [120] To secure congressional approval for the increase, Lansing, having failed in previous years in this respect, used the strategy of associating diplomacy with commerce and eventually with the Consular Service.

Congress responded with a general increase of one thousand dollars for each class, starting with $2,500 for secretaries of class four and rising to $4,000 for secretaries of class one. [121] This scale, however, remained considerably below the consular scale. Nor was it authorized without opposition. Postwar retrenchment dominated congressional thinking. That this raise failed to expand the potential selectivity in recruitment was revealed the following autumn. In the October examination, twenty-six were designated and only eighteen took the examination. [122]

Public opinion also militated against an independent service. It did so partly by confusing the State Department and the two services as one unit, or at least the overseas services as a single unit. The term "Foreign Service" was increasingly employed to refer to both services. [123] When Georgetown University, for instance, established its program for overseas training in 1919, it was called the "School of Foreign Service." [124] Moreover, although the Diplomatic Service as such had the advantages of escaping the war-guilt charge and of having

[118] House Doc. 650, *Foreign Trade Promotion Work of the Government*, 66 Cong., 2 sess. (January 26, 1920), p. 48. Although the report was contained in a House publication, it was first authorized by a Senate resolution of October 3, 1919.

[119] Lansing to Porter, January 21, 1920, in *American Consular Bulletin*, I (February, 1920), 3–4.

[120] *Ibid.*, p. 4.

[121] 41 Stat. 739 (June 4, 1920).

[122] Minutes (October 18–20, 1920).

[123] See Walter Lippmann, "For a Department of State," *New Republic*, XX (September 17, 1919), 195; editorial, *New York Times*, November 5, 1920, p. 14; Arthur Sweetser, "Why the State Department Should Be Reorganized," *World Work*, XXXIX (March, 1920), 511; "Reorganize the State Department," *World's Work*, XXXVIII (August, 1919), 351, and Professor Hiram Bingham to Secretary Lansing, January 13, 1920, in 121.1/34:1140.

[124] Coleman Nevils, S.J., *Minatures of Georgetown* (Georgetown, D.C., 1934), p. 14.

a definite niche in the League of Nations, nevertheless the public was convinced that commerce would be the most important issue in international relations.[125] If America failed to enter the war because of strategic considerations of *Realpolitik*, it could hardly be expected to analyze the postwar scene in terms of power alignments.[126] Furthermore, the war had not destroyed the nation's sense of hemispheric security. Besides, the defeat of German militarism, most people thought, eliminated the possibilities of a future war. That there was a commercial emphasis was not surprising in another respect. America's position in international commerce had become a vital domestic question. A contributor to the *Annals* maintained, "The future index of domestic prosperity of the United States will be the volume of the exports of its manufactures."[127] War loans, development funds, overseas expansion by American firms, exports, and investments, all needed protection. The war had introduced American capitalists to the importance of government in this work. The report of the National Civil Service Reform League held, ". . . we look to our foreign representatives as the vanguard in this work of trade expansion."[128]

Here again there was confusion. Writers often referred to this work as the province of the entire Department of State or of a fictitious "Foreign Service."[129] Reform was then demanded for the whole establishment, not for part of it. But when specific roles were understood, their importance in a pre-eminently commercial venture made fusion or interchangeability sensible. Arthur Sweetser maintained, "The questions of the future will originate, not in dynastic or monarchistic struggles, but solely in the struggle for markets and wealth, in which an efficiently organized foreign service will greatly benefit

[125] On the war-guilt question, see Sweetser, *op. cit.*, p. 511: "All that tangled skein which was to result in the Secret Treaties was largely hidden from us because our Foreign Service was so small. . . ." For the importance of the service in the event America joined the League, see Lippmann, "For a Department of State," p. 196, and "Reorganize the State Department," p. 351. In the latter he claimed, "Our influence in the League of Nations will depend to a large degree upon the efficiency of our State Department and foreign service." Curiously enough, the service also escaped any of the stigma associated with the League. See Sweetser, *op. cit.*, p. 512: "The worst loss to the Foreign Service came when all the work of preparations for the negotiations was turned over to Colonel House." See also "American Diplomacy Justified," *Independent*, CVII (November 12, 1921), 158.

[126] See Robert Endicott Osgood, *Ideals and Self Interest in America's Foreign Relations* (University of Chicago Press, 1953), pp. 111–304.

[127] Walter F. Wyman, "Readjustment of American Industries Through the Development of Foreign Trade," *Annals of the American Academy*, LXXXII (March, 1919), 19. See also F. W. Gehle, "The Future of America's Foreign Trade," *Bankers' Magazine*, CI (August, 1920), 255.

[128] National Civil Service Reform League, *Report on the Foreign Service*, p. 11.

[129] E.g., Charles W. Collins, "Organizing For American Export Trade," *South Atlantic Quarterly*, XVIII (July, 1919), 225.

us." Because of these facts, he felt there was "no reason why the two [the Diplomatic and Consular Services] should be watertight." [130] This latter idea was attracting attention from commercial groups as well. The American Chamber of Commerce in London wrote the Department in February, 1920, in support of Skinner's measure.[131] The previous September the Foreign Trade Convention was "in favor of reorganization and establishment of the foreign service under a unified supervision." [132] A month later a similar resolution was passed by the American Manufacturers' Export Association.[133]

All things pointed toward the end of an independent Diplomatic Service. The existing career attracted few candidates. The wage increase was small, reluctantly granted, and had little visible effect on recruitment. Support for interchangeability was given by the Secretary of State, and the bills authorizing it and fusion were sponsored by the one man who otherwise was the service's best friend in Congress. Public opinion also thought in terms of consolidated administration and of the primacy of commercial questions in postwar diplomacy. Phillips and Wright correctly divined the approach which would appeal, but here, too, the logic of their position undermined the independence of the service. If commerce were the chief subject of diplomacy, then diplomats should equip themselves best to handle commerce — through interchangeability or fusion. On October 13, 1920, when it appeared that Skinner's bill was going to succeed in Congress, Phillips informed Sumner Welles that Butler Wright, who had finally assumed direction for the service's strategy, was not "disposed to antagonize the first bills." Although he realized that Skinner's measure was "not so desirable from a diplomatic standpoint as the other," he also believed it "far more desirable than no legislation at all would be." [134]

The decision to accept interchangeability if possible and fusion if necessary was accompanied by the conviction that in the event of either solution the Diplomatic Service would be found entering the new unit in as strong a position as possible. Events in 1920 and early 1921 led in this direction. Although recruitment was in a bad state, the state of existing personnel was good. A Diplomatic Personnel Committee was established in September, 1920, to facilitate a closer personal touch between the Department and the service members

[130] Sweetser, *op. cit.*, p. 515. See also Will Irwin, "Business in Diplomacy," *Saturday Evening Post*, CXCIII (August 14, 1920), 69.

[131] American Chamber of Commerce in London to Colby, February 20, 1920, in 122.1/399.

[132] *American Consular Bulletin*, I (October, 1919), 2.

[133] *New York Times*, October 18, 1919, p. 17.

[134] Phillips to Welles, October 13, 1920, in 120.1/64.

overseas. Appointments and transfers also came under its jurisdiction.[135] Secretaries were encouraged by the administration's policy toward ministerial appointments. No appointment made after the Armistice came from outside the Diplomatic Service. Beside Gibson, four other career diplomats were elevated, a fact that caused the *New York Times* to remark "a refreshing change since Bryan." [136] Resignation rates were low. The average for 1919–20 was 4 per cent. There was some recognition for the service's political importance from various publicists.[137] The Penfield bequest established a scholarship fund "calculated to turn the thoughts of capable young Americans toward diplomacy as a profession." [138] And some progress was made, particularly after the intervention of Representative Stephen Porter in 1921, toward extending the program of mission construction.[139]

When Congress adjourned in March, 1921, it had taken no action on either bill. The rush of last-minute legislation left no time for their consideration. Also the nature of America's future foreign relations was very much in doubt. Even if this had not been the case, changes in the Secretaryship of State had resulted in a caretakership by Bainbridge Colby. With a Republican Presidential and congressional victory in November, Rogers was undoubtedly willing to postpone action until the new administration had formulated its intentions. Thus, the Diplomatic Service was given a brief reprieve until those intentions became clear.

When the new administration entered in March, the questions of fusion and interchangeability temporarily became of secondary importance. Of primary importance was the fact that the concept of professional diplomacy was again at stake. The issue raised by every new administration, particularly those involving a change in party, was the fate of the career diplomats who had been elevated to the upper service. The settlement of this issue was bound to affect not only the men directly involved but also the morale of every officer and of men who were contemplating applying. As in the past, the proponents of professional diplomacy made their warnings clear to the President-elect. Editorials and articles stressed, in the words of Nich-

[135] *American Consular Bulletin*, II (October, 1920), 6.

[136] *Biog. Reg.* (1920), *passim*. They were H. Percival Dodge, Joseph C. Grew, William Phillips, and Peter A. Jay. See *New York Times*, May 2, 1920, Sec. 6, p. 11.

[137] See "The Leak in Our Constitution," *New Republic*, XIX (June 25, 1919), 236; *New York Times*, January 2, 1921, Sec. 6, p. 2; and "Reorganize the State Department," *World's Work*, XXXVIII (August, 1919), 351.

[138] *Good Government*, XXXVII (August, 1920), 111.

[139] See particularly 41 Stat. 1204 (March 2, 1921).

olas Roosevelt, "If the men who have been appointed Ministers from the ranks of the diplomatic service . . . are removed by the new Administration, it is the end of the diplomatic service." [140] To raise the issue to one of national importance, other writers emphasized the dangers which Wilson exposed the nation to in 1914 by having manned the posts with amateurs.[141] Associations of merchants, such as the Manufacturers' Club of Philadelphia, and individual capitalists intervened in support of the professional diplomats.[142] In Congress, Representative Rogers reintroduced his measure providing a formal channel of promotion for "efficient secretaries . . . and consuls general to vacancies arising in the rank of minister." [143]

The warnings were hardly necessary. The Republican party had been historically the one to favor professional diplomacy. In the election of 1920, it was committed to government aid in the expansion of trade, and the Diplomatic Service was an important tool in fulfilling this commitment. While its President-elect, Warren G. Harding, had few ideas of his own about foreign policy, he was advised by two of the service's oldest friends — Root and Knox.[144] Harding's opposition to the League left the diplomatic machinery as America's only means of international communication. Harding was also elected by a majority large enough to free him from many political debts. Above all, Harding had gone on record as early as January, 1921, in support of professional diplomacy.[145] He later repeated his stand, claiming, "American diplomatic appointments should not be regarded as mere temporary results of political football in the United States." [146]

Harding's choice for Secretary of State should also have inspired confidence. Charles Evans Hughes came to the office with considerable administrative experience, particularly as a reform governor of New

[140] Nicholas Roosevelt, "Removals from the Diplomatic Service," *Outlook*, CXXVII (March, 1921), 382. See also Maurice Francis Egan, "Your Move, Mr. Harding," *Colliers*, LXVII (February 5, 1921), 28.

[141] *New York Times*, February 22, 1921, p. 6; W. W. Nichols, "Organization of the Foreign Service," *Proceedings of the Academy of Political Science* (February, 1921), IX, 307, and Egan, *op. cit.*, p. 11.

[142] Charles L. Guilland to Hughes, March 22, 1921, in 121.1/43:1140. The Club had unanimously passed a resolution "to fully and completely support the Administration at Washington in its endeavor to effect a radical change in the State Department and Diplomatic Service by removal of appointments of envoys from party politics." 121.1/46: 1140, Transcript of interview with Bacon by representatives of fruit companies, July 13, 1921. The men emphasized the "necessity of appointing competent and experienced men in the various Central American countries in order that prestige of the United States be upheld and the commercial interests advanced as much as possible."

[143] *Cong. Reg.*, LXI, 67 Cong., 1 sess. (April 11, 1921), 96. The bill, HR 2284, had the same title as HR 2709.

[144] *New York Times*, February 22, 1921, p. 6.

[145] *Ibid.*, January 10, 1921, p. 15.

[146] *Ibid.*, August 20, 1921, p. 16.

York. He was a known advocate of the merit system.[147] When he opposed Wilson for the Presidency in 1916, he used as one of his issues Wilson's purge in 1913 and the jeopardy in which America was placed by it.[148] He was an internationalist at heart and had supported the League with qualifications. When the people repudiated the League, Hughes undoubtedly realized that this made the service doubly important. Finally, the President's lack of interest in foreign affairs made Hughes the key to the future of the career.

No evidence can be found that the career diplomats holding upper service posts before the election submitted their resignations, as was the practice, to the new President. This would substantiate a report in the *New York Times* which claimed that the career ministers were expressly planning to test the sincerity of Harding's stand on professional diplomacy by withholding their resignations.[149] The record shows that all those holding upper service posts in 1920 retained them. Commissions were all dated with reference to the original appointment. The only names appearing before the Senate were those of career diplomats who were appointed to new ministerships, such as Joseph Grew, who was transferred from Denmark to Switzerland.[150]

Certain qualifications must be made. Although resignations were not submitted, it would have been unreasonable for Harding to assume anything but political loyalty from them. Commenting on Rogers' initial attempt to facilitate merit promotions to the ministerial level, Representative Flood charged:

> The gentleman [Rogers] is a believer in the idea that all our diplomats, our ministers, and our ambassadors should be appointed from the list of rich secretaries, whom under the Republican Party during the administrations of Presidents Taft and Roosevelt were appointed secretaries.[151]

When the issue arose again in 1921, Brand Whitlock contended, "If they succeed, it will only be by the exercise of political 'pull.'"[152] Evidence that this was so appeared in later promotions. Writing to Hughes in 1922, Undersecretary Phillips reminded him, "There are certain Secretaries in Class One who have been in the Service for fifteen years and upwards, all of whom have originally entered the Service through a Republican administration, and who are now

---

[147] *Good Government*, XXXIX (August, 1922), 112: "President Harding is furthermore deserving of commendation in that he has selected for Secretary of State a man of the highest qualifications and one devoted to the merit principle."

[148] *New York Times*, August 6, 1916, Sec. 7, p. 2.

[149] *New York Times*, January 10, 1921, p. 15.

[150] *Biog. Reg.* (1922), pp. 36–41.

[151] *Cong. Rec.*, LVII, 65 Cong., 3 sess. (January 22, 1919), 1873.

[152] Brand Whitlock, *Journal of Brand Whitlock*, p. 656. Entry was for April 5, 1921.

worthy of being considered in the selection of Ministers." [153] Nevertheless, the fact that the administration selected these men in preference to political appointments was a victory for professional diplomacy.

The preference was shown in subsequent appointments as well. In 1922, 35 per cent of all higher posts were held by career men, a high proportion reached before only under Taft. These posts were in all parts of the world and included three ambassadorships.[154] Hughes's appointments to executive posts in the Department were equally encouraging. Henry P. Fletcher, Fred M. Dearing, and Robert W. Bliss, all career men, were Hughes's first assistants. Fletcher and Dearing were succeeded by William Phillips and Leland Harrison. On their succession, the *American Consular Bulletin* remarked: "their appointment is generally accepted as further evidence of a policy on the part of the present administration of filling important positions by promotions within the Service rather than appointments from outside." [155] Thus, in 1922, the Undersecretary and two of the three Assistant Secretaries were career diplomats. Three chiefs of the Department's divisions were also career men.[156]

Although there were charges of partisanship, the public was generally satisfied with the administration's record. This was particularly manifest in a report made by the National Civil Service Reform League on Harding's first year in office. The report concluded, "An examination of the records of appointments in the diplomatic service . . . seems to indicate that an earnest effort has been made to retain the service of men with experience and to appoint to diplomatic posts persons with qualifications in diplomacy." [157] In a letter to Carr, Harry W. Marsh, the report's author, repeated this conclusion. He wrote, "As far as I have gone into the records of the administration they show excellent compliance with the spirit of the merit system." [158]

But the Executive was limited in what it could accomplish for the service. What was needed still fundamentally depended upon Congress, and here the movement continued in the direction of some form of structural reorganization. When the new Congress convened, Rogers introduced only one measure. It was Carr's.[159] His reasons for

[153] Phillips to Hughes, October 7, 1922, in 121.31/19:1141.
[154] *Biog. Reg.* (1922), pp. 36–41.
[155] *American Consular Bulletin*, IV (May, 1922), 187.
[156] *Biog. Reg.* (1922), pp. 36–41.
[157] *Good Government*, XXXIX (August, 1922), 111. The report was titled, *The Foreign Service: A Report on the First Year of the Administration of President Harding* (New York, 1922).
[158] Marsh to Carr, June 6, 1922, in 120.31/3.
[159] *Cong. Rec.*, 67 Cong., 1 sess. (April 11, 1921), p. 87. The bill, HR 17, was titled "For the reorganization and improvement of the foreign service of the United States, and for other purposes." See also 111/106, Copy of HR 17, April 11, 1921.

abandoning Skinner's plan were many. The new administration would undoubtedly have opposed any reorganization that harmed the Diplomatic Service, functionally or in terms of morale. Second, the men surrounding Hughes were career diplomats who would not have been content with Skinner's plan. Third, Carr had been actively engaged in persuading Rogers and the public to accept his measure. This persuasion had included an article in the *Independent*.[160]

The new bill did not differ substantially from Carr's first version. The two services would remain functionally separate but would draw from a common personnel source. In three respects, however, the bill differed. A retirement system was included. The scholarship scheme was dropped.[161] The provision incorporating the ministerial level into the promotional hierarchy was introduced as a separate bill.[162] The decision to separate this provision probably was the result of disagreement within the Department about the major reorganization provisions. The ministerial section, upon which there was agreement, could then capitalize on the sentiment for professional diplomacy evinced at the beginning of the new administration and not be delayed until there was agreement on the reorganization sections. In any event, the administration was so occupied by the Washington Naval Conference that it could give no lead, and the session closed without any action being taken.

Early in 1922 a degree of co-ordination between Rogers and the Department entered into the movement toward acceptable legislation. While discussions were being held on the nature of the reorganization, Rogers introduced a bill bearing the distinct stamp of the Department. In addition to many technical provisions dealing with appropriations, it contained a provision by which ministers would be appointed to classes instead of posts.[163] This was an extension of the Stone-Flood principle to the ministerial level. Its framers had two thoughts in mind. The bill should facilitate career promotions without implying that the entire upper service was going to be professionalized. Prevailing opinion preferred a flexible balance between amateur and professional.[164] The second thought was to avoid

[160] Wilbur J. Carr, "To Bring Our Foreign Service Up-to-Date," *Independent*, CV (February 26, 1921), 207, 220–21.

[161] 111/106, Copy of HR 17, April 11, 1921.

[162] *Cong. Rec.*, LXI, 67 Cong., 1 sess. (April 11, 1921), 96. The bill, HR 2284, had the same title as HR 2709.

[163] *Cong. Rec.*, LXII, 67 Cong., 2 sess. (January 21, 1922), p. 2019. The bill, HR 10213, was titled "Relative to the foreign intercourse of the United States." It was favorably reported out of the Committee on Foreign Affairs on February 2, 1922. See House Rept. 646, 67 Cong., 2 sess. (February 2, 1922).

[164] Typical of prevailing opinion is the following quotation from *World's Work*. "A complete merit system would of course be undesirable. . . . But we can more closely

impairing the President's Constitutional power of appointment. Had the bill been passed, it would not have done this. But it, too, failed to receive any action. It was later obscured by the attention shown the reorganization bill, and it was not reintroduced in the Sixty-eighth Congress.

Consultations, particularly between Carr and Wright, continued until early May. By then the representatives of both services were agreed that interchangeability was their best course of action. On May 3, 1922, Wright wrote to Secretary Hughes, "It is my understanding that these organizations, these individuals, Representative Rogers, and the entire staff of the Diplomatic and Consular Services, stand ready to aid in the achievement of these ends as soon as they may learn that the idea meets with your approval." [165] Before deciding, Hughes requested Phillips' opinion of the plan. It, too, was favorable.[166] In a speech before the United States Chamber of Commerce, Hughes accepted the decision and outlined what the new career necessitated:

> The patent fact is that you cannot have an efficient Foreign Service without having trained men and you cannot obtain trained men without an adequate system for their selection and maintenance; and you cannot keep men who have been properly selected and trained and are invaluable to their country unless you offer reasonable opportunities for promotion.[167]

Why did the representatives of the Diplomatic Service agree to Carr's plan? In short, it had become apparent that the things which were needed to strengthen an independent service could be achieved only by surrendering that independence. Foremost among them was a steady supply of qualified men from which to recruit. In 1916 Wil-

approximate the system which has made the British service the best in the world, while still flexible enough to send a Lord Grey to this country." Sweetser, *op. cit.*, p. 515. See also Andrew Ten Eyck, "The Supreme Court of American Diplomacy," *Outlook*, CXXVII (March, 1921), 384; Irwin, *op. cit.*, pp. 66, 69; and Maurice Francis Egan, "Telling the Diplomatic Truth," *Colliers*, LXX (September 9, 1922), 16.

There were, however, still a few who contended that a complete patronage system was preferable. See House Rept. 646, Part 2, 67 Cong., 2 sess. (Feb. 9, 1922). One passage in the minority report claimed: "The distinctive feature — the very essence — of our political system is the assumption that in the body of the people can always be found the agents who can accomplish most effectively all the purposes of government [p. 4]." The minority report received no public or congressional currency.

[165] Wright to Hughes, May 3, 1922, in 121.11/56. "Organizations" refers particularly to the National Civil Service Reform League and the United States Chamber of Commerce; "individuals" refers to the departmental personnel.

[166] Phillips to Hughes, May 8, 1922, in 121.31/19.

[167] Charles Evans Hughes, *Pathway of Peace* (New York, 1925), p. 261. The speech was delivered on May 18, 1922.

liam Phillips insisted that the "mental idlers" were disappearing.[168] However, subsequent recruitment and the necessity to make a decision on interchangeability forced the career diplomats to be honest about their colleagues. Before Congress, Hugh Gibson admitted, ". . . we are far too largely dependent upon the class of men who are not only incompetent in the service, but who could not make a decent living in private business if they had to." [169] In a memo to Hughes, Phillips was equally frank. He wrote, "The diplomatic service is not what it should be, principally for the reason that it does not attract to it the best young men of the country."

The reason for this was also apparent. Phillips pointed out, "There does not appear to be sufficient career to justify a man of ambition to enter it." [170] This fact was seen in the number applying for and taking the examination. It was expected that the wartime recruitment base would be small. Its continuation in peacetime, however, convinced the career diplomats that the existing structure had to be changed in order to attract a large group of candidates. The examination of 1919 and 1920 were disappointing. So were the ones held in 1921 and 1922. Fifty-one applied in 1921 and forty-eight in 1922, while forty-two and thirty-seven, respectively, took the examination.[171] Both represented an increase over the years immediately following the war, but neither was sufficiently large to satisfy the career diplomats. Furthermore, often when it was necessary to hold an examination, considerable delay was experienced until enough candidates applied.[172]

But the need for men continued. Resignations, which were running at about the same rate as 1919–20, and promotions, required an average of eleven men each year. Because the recruitment base was small and the need continuous, the written examination standard was correspondingly low. This fact was admitted by Gibson, when he testified, "As a matter of fact they are not nearly as hard as they ought to be." [173] Estimates of their difficulty varied. In the *New Republic*, a former secretary wrote, ". . . that the present examinations are a farce is proved by the fact that but three weeks' preparation suffices in order

[168] Phillips to Skinner, July 31, 1916, in 120.1/52.

[169] House Committee on Foreign Affairs, *Foreign Service of the United States*, hearings on HR 17 and HR 6357, 68 Cong., 1 sess. (January 14–18, 1924), p. 18.

[170] Phillips to Hughes, May 8, 1922, in 121.31/19.

[171] Minutes (July 11–15, 1921, and July 10–13, 1922). A special examination was held August 16–18, 1922. See Minutes (August 16–18, 1922). The figures for 1922 include both examinations.

[172] Phillips to Hughes, May 8, 1922, in 121.31/19: "At sometimes there are no applications for entry into the Service; at other times there are just enough to fill the existing vacancies."

[173] House Committee on Foreign Affairs, *Foreign Service of the United States*, p. 85.

to pass with flying colors." [174] Most, however, agreed that they "were not dissimilar in character from the requirements for entrance into one of the more exacting American universities." [175] Comments by educators sent copies of the examination included "put too great an emphasis upon pure memory" and "too elementary." [176]

To conclude from the small base and the evaluation of the written examination that all who entered between 1919 and 1922 were unsuited for their work would be wrong. Along with his other statements, Gibson maintained, "We get a surprising number of able men who are willing to pay their own way." [177] It was also true that the percentage of those passing the examination was steadily decreasing: 66.6 per cent, for both examinations in 1920; 40.4 per cent in 1921; and 37.8 per cent, in 1922.[178] Finally, the examiners placed greater weight on the oral than on the written examination. If a patently incompetent person passed an examination, he would probably fail the oral. And many who passed the former failed the latter.[179] All autobiographical accounts, as well as congressional testimony, confirm the stress placed on the oral.[180]

Nevertheless, even with these qualifications, the career diplomats' original judgment stood. In accepting interchangeability, they assumed, "It is manifest if we had two hundred or three hundred candidates to fill those six or eight places that we would get a much better type of man." [181] Evidence that this was true existed in the case of the Consular Service. With its better salary scale and longer tradition of

[174] Henry Carey, "To the Honorable Charles Evans Hughes," *New Republic*, XXXI (June 21, 1922), 106.

[175] Patterson, *op. cit.*, p. 5. See *infra*.

[176] 120.1121/1½, Replies to Carr's letter. Replies were received from Amherst College, Columbia, Yale, Harvard, New York, Princeton and Leland Stanford universities, and the universities of California and Illinois.

Carr's letter (same National Archive number) indicated that the Examiners' criteria for the examination was "to make the examinations thoroughly practical and effective in keeping out of the Service persons who are not qualified for foreign service work, and at the same time be not so difficult as to discourage men whose entrance into the Service would be advantageous to the Government."

[177] House Committee on Foreign Affairs, *Foreign Service of the United States*, p. 18.

[178] Minutes (1920–22).

[179] Minutes (1919–22).

[180] See Edwin F. Stanton, *Brief Authority — Excursions of a Common Man in an Uncommon World* (New York: Harpers, 1956), p. 2; Patterson, *op. cit.*, p. 5; House Committee on Foreign Affairs, *Foreign Service of the United States*, pp. 66–67, 87. Wright described the oral's objectives as follows: "We were able not only to determine the character of the man in question, his address, and factors that constitute character and personality; but, in addition to that, his oral replies to more abstruse or more elastic questions, such as those concerning international law, showed his depth of knowledge. [pp. 66–67]."

[181] House Committee on Foreign Affairs, *Foreign Service of the United States*, p. 34 (statement by Gibson).

merit appointments, it received in the period 1920–22, 6.6 times the number of applications the Diplomatic Service received.[182] What seemed to be overlooked was the fact that the Consular Service was interested in the new relationship to improve its own personnel.

The increase in numbers would have probably also meant broadening the geographical base of representation. Compared with the Consular Service, the Diplomatic Service was drawn from a very restricted area. Primarily this can be attributed to the operation of the state quota in the Consular Service. As so few applied to the Diplomatic Service at one time, Taft's provision for states' representation was practically inoperable. Southern representation shows this particularly. The geographical representation from the South for those entering the new Foreign Service in 1924 from the Consular Service was 21.1 per cent; the southern representation among those recruited into the Diplomatic Service between 1914 and 1922 was 9.8 per cent. The concentration for the Diplomatic Service was in the Middle Atlantic and the East North Central regions. From the two regions came 64.3 per cent, while 42 per cent came from the Middle Atlantic alone. The same regions constituted 46.7 per cent of the Consular Service with 31 per cent coming from the Middle Atlantic.[183] To secure a service more representative of America and by it to encourage congressional support also motivated the career diplomats in their decision.

It was hoped that, in addition to the purpose of attracting more qualified and representative personnel, the decision would lead to certain administrative improvements. Economies were expected from the consolidation of the personnel source. It was thought that interchangeability would reduce intradepartmental friction. Above all, the new relationship would assure a more comprehensive training for diplomats as well as consuls.[184]

But in this thought considerable confusion existed between Carr

[182] Minutes of the Board of Examiners of the Consular Service (1920–22). There were 954 applications to the Consular Service and 144 to the Diplomatic Service.

[183] Geographical distribution of the services:

	Consular Service (per cent)	Diplomatic Service (per cent)
New England	9.6	10.7
Middle Atlantic	31.0	42.0
East North Central	15.7	22.3
West North Central	10.2	5.3
South Atlantic	9.6	5.3
East South Central	7.3	0.9
West South Central	4.2	3.6
Mountain	4.4	1.8
Pacific	7.5	8.0

[184] Wright to Hughes, May 3, 1922, in 121.11/56:1140.

and the career diplomats. The concept of putting the right man in the right place, irrespective of whether he was in the Consular or Diplomatic Service, was appealing to both sides. The career diplomats, however, assumed that interchangeability of personnel was to be the exception. Carr assumed it would be the rule. In their public and private statements, this confusion can be seen. Carr argued for "free interchangeability" and looked at the arrangement "more in the relation which it bears to a service composed of trained officials than in the matter of mere convenience in mechanism." [185] Even Rogers was unclear as to what the principle meant. He referred to it as "freer interchangeability between the two sides of the Service as the interests . . . make appropriate." [186] On the other hand, career diplomat Hugh Wilson believed, "While interchangeability is essential it should not be carried to such a point as to destroy the independent existence of the two Services." [187] Smilarly, Butler Wright, who was the leading diplomat in reaching the decision, advocated "reasonable interchangeability of personnel." [188] Wright later attempted to end the confusion. After meeting with Rogers and Carr, Wright was still at variance with Carr's interpretation.[189] Wright wrote to A. L. P. Dennis, "Interchangeability be accepted, but not the fusion of the Services." [190] The confusion continued past the enactment of the measure. Indeed, part of the unanimity with which the two services supported the measure was owing in part to their misunderstanding about its cardinal feature.

Without the support of public opinion for independence, the career diplomats could not but accept interchangeability. Commercial issues remained pre-eminent in most thinking on foreign affairs.[191]

[185] Carr, *op. cit.*, p. 220; Carr to Merrill Moore of the Committee on Foreign Affairs, April 20, 1922, in 120.3/10A.

[186] John Jacob Rogers, "The Foreign Service Reorganization Act," *American Journal of International Law*, XVIII (October, 1924), 792.

[187] *American Consular Bulletin*, II (March, 1920), 3.

[188] *Ibid.*, VI (June, 1924), 220.

[189] Wright to Rogers, November 8, 1923, in 111/155C. A memo by Wright on the previous day (111/155, Wright, November 7, 1923) claimed that there was considerable disquietude among diplomats, "for the Service felt that the responsibilities would be even more defined and no overlapping would exist."

[190] Wright to A. L. P. Dennis, November 23, 1923, in 111/165. Cf. A. L. P. Dennis, "The Foreign Service of the United States," *North American Review*, CCXIX (February, 1924), 181.

[191] See Herbert Corey, "He Has Jobs for Rising Young Men," *Colliers*, LXXII (November 3, 1923), 14; Maurice Francis Egan, "More Business in Diplomacy," *Colliers*, LXIX (February 4, 1922), 10; Maurice Francis Egan, "Telling the Diplomatic Truth," *Colliers*, LXX (September 9, 1922), 33; Glenn Frank, "Do We Need a Super Senate?" *Century*, CI (April, 1921), 797; Herbert Adams Gibbons, "The International Whirlpool," *Century*, CI (March, 1921), 656; Snow, *op. cit.*, pp. 110–11; "America's Prosperity and Foreign Trade," *Bankers' Magazine*, CIV (February, 1922), 289.

This fact would permit no argument for an independent service. Support for interchangeability was increasing among trade associations. When the decision was made, the National Association of Manufacturers, the Merchants' Association of New York, and the American Exporters' and Importers' Association had already indicated their interest.[192] So had the American Chamber of Commerce in London. Its newspaper *Anglo-American Trade* insisted, "We look upon the present service as archaic . . . and depriving the young secretary of any opportunity to gain experience in those practical commercial or political matters." [193] Wright had correctly thought that through interchangeability "the support of the commercial organizations of this country may be attracted for the Diplomatic Service, which has hitherto conspicuously failed in its appeal to such interests." [194] Finally, what debate there was on the political responsibilities of the Diplomatic Service was decidedly antagonistic toward professional diplomacy. Recriminations had set in about America's role in the war. One publicist characteristically wrote: "If the world had learned anything at all from civilization's cataclysm, it should have learned that professional diplomacy brought on the war, and failed to prevent the war, and was unable to end the war, and proved unequal to restoring the peace." [195]

Upon the creation of an adequate salary scale and the greater development of the system of promotions rested the possibility of attracting a sufficiently wide base for recruitment. These improvements depended, first, upon public opinion and, second, its expression in congressional action. On the Diplomatic Service, congressional thought reflected external opinion. There was, hence, no attempt to sponsor legislation sustaining the independence of the service. The service's best supporters, Rogers and Senator Lodge, were either committed to interchangeability or otherwise engaged. Any attempts at piecemeal improvements through appropriations ended with their transfer from the Committee on Foreign Affairs to a separate Committee on Appropriations. The decision taken by the career diplomats on May 3, 1922, was in almost every respect inescapable.

The decision was also taken with a full understanding of the social problems involved. A loathing to abandon one's career was not the only element in the diplomats' initial dissatisfaction with inter-

[192] American Chamber of Commerce in London to Hughes, April, 1921, in 120.1/61.
[193] *Anglo-American Trade*, V (April, 1921), 153.
[194] Wright to Hughes, May 3, 1922, in 121.11/56.
[195] William T. Ellis, "Frank Words on the 'Trained' Diplomats," *Outlook*, CXXVII (March 9, 1921), 383. See also Bruce Bliven, "The Diplomat as High Priest," *New Republic*, XXIX (January 4, 1922), 145; Hugh E. Willis, "The Road to World Peace," *American Law Review*, LVIII (Winter, 1922), 558.

changeability and fusion. It came as well from a feeling by career diplomats of social superiority over consuls. This feeling has been admitted by every possible source. Retrospective accounts of the period by consuls and diplomats emphasize the social schism.[196] Contemporary statements referred to it. In an address to the members of both services, Grew predicted "the eventual breaking down of any possible misunderstanding or feeling of prejudice that may hitherto have existed between the diplomatic and consular careers." [197] Likewise Congressman Rogers believed, "We shall get rid of the caste system, of a system where the diplomatic side of the service sometimes looks down on the consular side." [198]

What was the reason for this schism? Partly, of course, it was bound up in the nature and functions of the two careers. But the schism ran deeper. The man who entered the Diplomatic Service, with very few exceptions, had private means of support. Flowing from this were a host of social prejudices. Before Congress, Secretary Hughes maintained, "It is not a good thing for the diplomatic service to be recruited, even on a merit basis, exclusively from men of families of fortune." [199] Whether good or not, the Diplomatic Service drew primarily from this source.

The reason for this has been made clear throughout this study: the wage scale for the Diplomatic Service was inadequate. To his normal domestic expenses the secretary had to add those connected with the social side of his work. For him to ignore the latter would have been tantamount to his failing in his responsibility. It is impossible, owing to differences in posts and costs of living, to estimate the amount required by a secretary of legation or embassy. But certain conclusions can be drawn. Compared with domestic salaries the wages paid were small. A writer in the *New Republic* pointed out that a secretary of legation in Bucharest received $2,800, while "the lowest living wage in New York City for a day labourer's family is $2600." [200] Prior to the raise in 1920, the National Civil Service Reform League reported that the cost of living had increased 2.79 times since the service's previous increase in salary.[201] The raise in 1920 made only a dent in this disparity. When compared with other diplomatic services, the American

[196] E.g., Willard L. Beaulac, *Career Ambassador* (New York: Macmillan, 1951), p. 88; Hugh R. Wilson, *Diplomat between the Wars* (New York: Longmans, Green, 1941), *passim.*

[197] *American Consular Bulletin*, VI (September, 1924), 350.

[198] *Cong. Rec.*, LXIV, 67 Cong., 4 sess. (February 4, 1923), 3145. See also Snow, *op. cit.*, p. 111.

[199] House Committee on Foreign Affairs, *Foreign Service of the United States*, Hearings on HR 12543, 67 Cong., 4 sess. (December 11–19, 1922), p. 8.

[200] Carey, *op. cit.*, p. 106.

[201] National Civil Service Reform League, *Report on the Foreign Service*, p. 82.

service was poorly paid. A first secretary in the British Diplomatic Service earned more than twice as much, including housing and representational allowances, as did his American counterpart.[202]

The examiners did all that was possible to impress the fact of the salary inadequacy on the candidates. If one inquired about the necessity of private means, the Department would reply, ". . . the experience . . . is that at the present remuneration . . . is unfortunately not such as to enable the department to assure them that they will be able to live on their salaries at all posts to which they may be sent." [203] The gigantic exodus from the Paris examination probably stemmed from similar information. Occasionally a candidate who was negligent in inquiring was forced to resign his eligibility. One such successful candidate wrote to the examiners, "I find that the financial obligations which are incumbent upon me would be greater than I can discharge at this time." [204] A contributor to the *Forum* publicly claimed, "I was given to understand that unless I had a private income of my own, it would be next to impossible to make the Diplomatic Service a career." [205] Even taking the examination involved a considerable capital expenditure. It was necessary to travel to Washington, usually to hire a tutor, and often to wait several months before an appointment was made.[206] This is not to argue that there were no exceptions. Butler Wright testified, "I know that there are certain officers in the diplomatic service at present who have no private means." He hastened to add that this was possible only through "rigid economy" and "because they are, by fortuitous circumstances, at posts where the rate of exchange is favorable. . . ." [207]

Other evidence confirms the service's reliance on the independently wealthy for recruitment. A by no means atypical diplomat was Jay Pierrepont Moffat. He claimed the Jays, the Pierreponts, the Livingstons, the Constables, and the Lows as immediate relations.[208] The examiners' notes also included statements that can only be interpreted in the light of the argument on private means. One candi-

---

[202] Using the exchange rate of £1 to $5, a top first secretary in the British Service in October, 1922, earned $12,000. See Godfrey E. P. Hertslet, *Foreign Office List* (London, 1923), pp. 435–39. It was also expected, although no longer required, that a British diplomat possess private means.

[203] House Committee on Foreign Affairs, *Foreign Service of the United States*, HR 17 and HR 6357, p. 57.

[204] 121.11/20:1140, communications to the Board of Examiners, July 23, 1923.

[205] "Our Diplomatic Service," p. 615.

[206] See Patterson, *op. cit.*, p. 5, Jay Pierrepont Moffat, *The Moffat Papers: Selections from the Diplomatic Journal of Jay Pierrepont Moffat*, ed. Nancy H. Hooker (Harvard University Press, 1956), p. 9.

[207] House Committee on Foreign Affairs, *Foreign Service of the United States*, HR 17 and HR 6357, p. 57.

[208] Moffat, *op. cit.*, p. 1.

date was described as having "engaged in management of personal and family affairs, legal matters." Another had "managed family estate since 1914." [209] The conclusion can also be upheld by the large number of private secretaries who later entered the service.

The social aspects of diplomacy required a type of man that had had all the opportunities money could bring. Butler Wright was so frank as to admit that men who possessed private means might be "better equipped, by birth and training and environment, for this work than others. . . ." [210] Examiners' comments frequently mentioned the social graces. One successful candidate was described as "polished with a considerable reserve." [211]

In another respect, however, the Diplomatic Service was more democratic than the Consular Service. Democracy can refer to the sexes as much as to classes or educational backgrounds. Along with other vocations, the pre-eminently masculine calling of diplomacy was exposed after the war to the onslaught of the liberated and newly-enfranchised American woman. Her attack was preceded by resolutions from feminist societies and by letters from reform organizations and deans of women's colleges.[212] For instance, Mrs. Abigail Fleming of the Ohio Federation of Women's Clubs submitted in 1921 the resolutions of her organization's annual convention. One read: "First, the introduction of women into the diplomatic service since questions involving the welfare of women and children often demand the more intimate knowledge of trained women." [213] In July, 1921, one woman took the examination. She failed both her written and oral. [214] The following year three women made the attempt and one succeeded.[215] There were no women in the Consular Service.

The facts for the Consular Service were very different. To the consul the aristocratic world of diplomacy was closed. Its social presuppositions, undoubtedly, irritated him. Furthermore, the Consular Service had an adequate salary scale and, in the words of former Secretary Lansing, "was, therefore, open to men without independent means." [216] The salary scale, according to Rogers, "begins where the secretary's stops." [217] Finally, the experience prior to appointment

[209] Minutes (July 11–15, 1921); Minutes (January 26–28, 1920).

[210] *American Consular Bulletin*, VI (June, 1924), 222.

[211] Minutes (November 17–21, 1913).

[212] See Carr to Harry W. Marsh, July, 1922, in 120.1/69; Dr. Bernice V. Brown, Dean of Radcliffe College to Wright, January 23, 1924, in 121.31/18:1141.

[213] Fleming to Hughes, December 7, 1921, in 121.1/50:1140.

[214] Minutes (July 11–15, 1921).

[215] Minutes (July 10–13, 1922).

[216] Robert H. Lansing, "The Proposed Consolidation of the Diplomatic and Consular Service," *American Journal of International Law*, XVII (April, 1923), 286.

[217] *Cong. Rec.*, LVII, 65 Cong., 3 sess. (January 21, 1919), 1827.

for the consul differed greatly from that of the diplomat. These differences can best be illustrated by comparing the educational backgrounds of all the members of the Consular Service receiving designations as "Foreign Service officers" in 1924 with the group recruited in the Diplomatic Service from 1914 to 1922.

The vast majority of diplomats received private secondary education, usually of the boarding-school type. The vast majority of consuls received public education. More specifically, 72.3 per cent of all diplomats attended residential private secondary schools. Only 16 per cent attended public schools. On the other hand, 73.2 per cent of all consuls were educated at public schools, while only 13.9 per cent attended private residential secondary schools.[218] And this contrast can by no means be explained by the geographical concentration alone.

It was also much more common for the diplomat to have been to a university and to have received a degree. The Diplomatic Service's examiners regarded, albeit unofficially, a college degree with favor.[219] Compared with 14.5 per cent in the Consular Service without any university experience, the Diplomatic Service had only 3.5 per cent. Of all diplomats, 84.8 per cent had taken degrees, while 68.7 per cent had done so in the Consular Service. In the case of those with university experience but without degrees, the Diplomatic Service had 11.6 per cent and the Consular Service had 16.6 per cent.

There was a vast difference in the specific university or college attended. Harvard, Yale, and Princeton provided 63.8 per cent of all diplomats, 32.4 per cent attending the first alone. An additional 13.8 per cent did postgraduate work at Harvard. On the other hand, 9.2 per cent attended state-supported universities. The Consular Service reversed the emphasis. Of all consuls 32.2 per cent attended state-supported universities, and 26 per cent attended eastern private colleges and universities, these ranging from municipal institutions to small New England colleges. Attending Harvard, Yale, and Princeton were 14.7 per cent, 5.4 per cent attending Harvard. An additional 3.1 per

[218] Comparison of secondary school backgrounds:

	Consular Service (per cent)	Diplomatic Service (per cent)
Public School	73.2	16.0
Educated Abroad	2.9	11.6
Private Tutor	1.5	3.5
Military Academy	2.7	1.7
Boarding School	13.9	72.3
Country Day School	9.1	9.8

Many officers attended more than one category of secondary educational institution.

[219] Patterson, *op. cit.*, p. 5.

cent did postgraduate work at Harvard.[220] To mix these very different backgrounds was a problem considered not insoluble by those who made the decision for interchangeability.

Bridges existed as well as gulfs. Across these the career diplomats thought the new service would have to travel. The Consular Service could claim, with greater force than the Diplomatic Service, a virtually unsullied record of merit recruitment and promotion. The student interpreters and consular assistants, who were associated with the scheme, were capable of making the same claim. All consuls had also spent extended periods abroad and were as adept with languages as diplomats. Finally, there were areas in which the backgrounds of members of both services were remarkably similar.

One of these was the number proceeding to do postgraduate work before entering the services. Some 55.6 per cent of all diplomats and 49.1 per cent of all consuls had had further formal study after their bachelor's degrees. In both services, most proceeded to a Master of Arts: 24.8 per cent in the Consular Service and 28 per cent in the Diplomatic Service. On one category, however, the two services diverged. While none had done so in the Diplomatic Service, 8.7 per cent of the Consular Service's postgraduate study group had taken some sort of formal training in "Foreign Service" subjects.[221] A partial corrective for this can be found in the fact that 11 per cent of all diplomats had some experience in a university abroad. Often this experience was at an institution such as the École Libre des Sciences Politiques,

[220] Comparison of collegiate backgrounds:

	Consular Service (per cent)	Diplomatic Service (per cent)
Harvard	5.4	32.4
Yale, Princeton	9.3	31.4
Other Ivy League	9.5	10.1
Eastern private	26.0	10.1
Middle Western private	9.7	1.8
Western private	2.0	1.8
Southern private	7.9	1.8
Military academy	3.6	1.8
Abroad	3.6	2.7
Harvard graduate	3.1	13.8
State university	32.2	9.2

Many officers attended more than one category of institution of higher learning.

[221] Comparison of postgraduate studies:

	Consular Service (per cent)	Diplomatic Service (per cent)
Foreign Service Subjects	8.7	0.0
M.A.	24.8	28.0
Ph.D.	4.8	1.7
Other degrees	31.8	19.3
Experience without degree	33.5	59.6

Many officers pursued more than one course of graduate studies.

in which such courses were available. It is not known if the diplomats took these courses.

Another area of similarity was in the occupation held before entering the services. Of all diplomats 82.1 per cent and 89.5 per cent of all consuls were engaged in some occupation before entering their respective services. Of these 39.3 per cent in the Consular Service and 35.8 per cent in the Diplomatic Service had been engaged in business. The only marked difference was that 29.2 per cent of all diplomats with previous occupational experience had had it as a private secretary or in the Department of State. The Consular Service had 17.9 per cent with experience in the Department, as student interpreters, or as consular assistants.[222]

To have made a decision about the acceptability of one plan over another was still a long way from turning that decision into legislation. The months and years following May, 1922, were filled with activity in this direction. Throughout it all the advocates of reorganization maintained certain presuppositions about the nature of America's international relations and the type of reform that was needed in the two services.

None disagreed with the fact that America's international position had radically changed since 1914. Nor did they disagree with the assumption that America should participate internationally either as a nation-state among nation-states or as part of a supranational personality like the League. Although the majority of Americans now distrusted the world, the advocates of reorganization argued that America's withdrawal would be tantamount to a situation in which "the respectable element should refuse to go to the polls because there were so many cheap politicians."[223] Because of this distrust, according to Gibson, "for us to get along with a makeshift foreign service is just about as foolhardy as it would be for a powder factory to get along with fire extinguishers."[224] Even attempts to remove dis-

[222] Occupational background before service:

	Consular Service (per cent)	Diplomatic Service (per cent)
Dept. of State (Diplomatic or Consular)	17.9	29.2
Government	16.6	15.2
Education	23.6	17.3
Law	15.5	17.3
Business	39.3	35.8

Many officers were engaged in more than one category of previous experience.

[223] Arthur C. Elliott, "America and International Peace," *Bankers' Magazine*, CVI (November, 1923), 870.

[224] House Committee on Foreign Affairs, *Foreign Service of the United States*, HR 17 and HR 6357, p. 18.

trust, such as disarmament, gave no cause to decrease the Foreign Service's strength. Charles Evans Hughes believed, "It is a poor patriot who would scrap both his ships and his diplomats at the same time." [225]

Primarily, however, America's foreign relations were commercial in nature. Representative Rogers claimed, "Today every question of international politics involves a question of business, a question of expanding or protecting trade." [226] Expanding and protecting trade, it was argued, were functions requiring both services.[227] And these functions were vitally important. A southwestern congressman insisted, "If we are to have employment for our people, if we are to secure prosperity in this country, we must have foreign markets." [228] With the other nations reorganizing their services to compete more effectively for foreign markets, the advocates of reorganization could point out, "Unless this measure . . . is passed we will continue in the future, as to a large extent we have been heretofore, at a disadvantage in competition with our principal competitors." [229] And specific items in their program were defended on the ground that they were provided "in the case of every first-class power, and in almost every second-class power as well." [230]

From these assumptions, the aim of reorganization was clear. It was, in the words of Gibson, "to secure for the Government the best possible foreign service." [231] This was to be accomplished in two ways. There was first to be an improvement in the quality of personnel, an improvement which was to stem from an increased number of people applying for a somewhat fixed number of posts. Before Congress, Representative Rogers maintained, "The wider the field of selection the better should be, and I believe will be, our personnel and repre-

[225] Charles Evans Hughes, *op. cit.*, p. 260. Speech before the United States Chamber of Commerce on May 18, 1922. See also Dennis, *op. cit.*, p. 184; Carey, *op. cit.*, p. 106. Carey argued that the money saved on naval disarmament should be applied to reform of the service.

[226] *Cong. Rec.*, LXV, 68 Cong., 1 sess. (April 30, 1924), 7634.

[227] E.g., Dennis, *op. cit.*, p. 185; W. F. Lineberger, *Diplomatic and Consular Service of the United States* (Washington: Committee on Foreign Affairs, 1924), p. 16; House Committee on Foreign Affairs, *Foreign Service in the United States*, HR 17 and HR 6357, p. 41.

[228] *Cong. Rec.*, LX, 66 Cong., 3 sess. (January 29, 1921), 2263 (speech by Representative McKeown of Oklahoma).

[229] *Cong. Rec.*, LXIV, 67 Cong., 4 sess. (February 6, 1923), 3163 (speech by Representative Moore of Virginia). See also *American Consular Bulletin*, III (March, 1921), 2–4; *Cong. Rec.*, 68 Cong., 1 sess. (April 30, 1924), 7568; House Committee on Foreign Affairs, *Foreign Service of the United States*, HR 17 and HR 6357, p. 41; Rogers, *op. cit.*, p. 794.

[230] *Cong. Rec.*, LXIV, 67 Cong., 4 sess. (February 8, 1923), 3273 (speech by Representative Rogers). See also *American Consular Bulletin*, II (December, 1920), 3.

[231] House Committee on Foreign Affairs, *Foreign Service of the United States*, HR 17 and HR 6357, p. 17.

sentation." [232] To this end the advocates had several plans. Wilbur Carr testified, "We would add the advantages of higher salaries, which would widen the range of selection by interesting men who cannot now, because of lack of sufficient private means, aspire to careers in the diplomatic service." [233] However, increased salaries alone would not secure the wider range. Pensions were needed as well. Former Secretary Lansing wrote, "One of the great deterrents to continuance in the service by men with small means . . . is the thought of the time when they must retire without a competency and without the ability, because of the infirmities of age, of earning a livelihood." [234]

These measures might increase the potential personnel source, but they could not guarantee the quality that was desired. A career in its fullest sense had to be assured. To Rogers, Secretary Hughes wrote, "If young men of the greatest ability and intellectual ambitions are to be attracted to the Service there must be the prospect of career recognition, and distinction." He added that this included "promotion to the higher grades." If this were to be the case, then salaries for the ministerial and ambassadorial levels had to be supplemented to permit "the promotion of trained officers to these posts." [235]

Second, once the personnel was obtained, it was then necessary to train them according to the broad intentions of American foreign policy. Consul General Skinner recommended, "Select your young material and form it to your purposes." [236] These purposes were essentially commercial. In 1923, Lansing wrote, "We must presume that our future relations with other nations will be chiefly economic, and the men serving this country in a diplomatic capacity should be trained in these subjects as our consular officers are at present." [237] This would be achieved by the interchangeability of personnel from the diplomatic to the consular side and vice versa. To facilitate interchangeability a common salary scale would be established for a consolidated personnel source.[238]

[232] *Cong. Rec.*, LXIV, 67 Cong., 4 sess. (February 6, 1923), 3144.

[233] House Committee on Foreign Affairs, *Foreign Service of the United States*, HR 12543, p. 42.

[234] Lansing, *op. cit.*, p. 286. This position was argued from an administrative viewpoint as well. Hughes claimed that smooth working of a new service required the pensioning off of the older members who could not retire without a competency. See *Congressional Digest*, III (January, 1924), 122.

[235] Hughes to Rogers, October 13, 1922, in House Rept. 1479, *Report on a Bill for the Reorganization and Improvement of the Foreign Service of the United States*, 67 Cong., 1 sess. (January 30, 1923), pp. 7-8. See also Rogers, *op. cit.*, p. 793.

[236] House Committee on Foreign Affairs, *The Foreign Service of the United States*, HR 12543, p. 77.

[237] Lansing, *op. cit.*, p. 285.

[238] House Rept. 1479, *Report on a Bill for the Reorganization and Improvement of the Foreign Service of the United States*, p. 2.

How far did the Rogers Act go in fulfilling these demands? Since their advocates played a substantial role in the bill's conception, the finished product met most of them.[239] In order to attract the widest possible selection of personnel, the salary scale was increased, beginning at $1,500–$3,000 for the unclassified group and rising to $9,000 for class one. This salary, while unable to compete fully with those offered by business, was larger than the Consular Service's salary and was considered by the Department to be adequate.[240] Traveling allowances were formally authorized as well. There was also instituted a retirement and disability scheme much more generous than the regular civil service scheme.[241] This plan alone was rewritten five times.[242] Sixty-five years of age, with a possible extension to seventy, and at least fifteen years of service were necessary to receive a pension; a maximum pension of $5,400 per annum was set, and special recognition was given for service at unhealthful posts.

To insure further the attraction of qualified personnel, the merit provisions of the Executive Orders were formally enacted. Thereafter new officers would enter, via an examination and a probationary period, the unclassified group. Exceptions to this were limited to Department of State employees with five years' standing. According to the *American Consular Bulletin*, "This puts an end to political appointments; for, although the President may still appoint a consul or diplomatic secretary under his constitutional powers, such an appointment would not be made part of the career." [243] The legislating of requirements for appointment, otherwise unconstitutional, was permitted by adopting the non-Constitutional classification of "Foreign Service officer." The Rogers Act also recognized promotion by merit through the service's ten classes. The only limitation to this was a legislatively imposed restriction on the percentage of the total number of officers in any one class.[244] Statutory leaves were authorized for officers with three years of continuous service abroad. This provision guaranteed for the first time a post upon his return for any officer seeking a short respite from official duties.[245] Prior to the re-

[239] 43 Stat. 140 (May 24, 1924). Subsequent section citations refer to this version.

[240] *American Consular Bulletin*, IV (November, 1922), 314; VI (July, 1924), 241. Hughes claimed that the Act "eliminate[d] the necessity for private incomes."

[241] Robert Patterson, "Historical Relationship Between the Department of State and the Foreign Service," (unpublished article, Advisory and Review Branch, Historical Division, Department of State, August, 1949), p. 7.

[242] *American Consular Bulletin*, VI (July, 1924), 263.

[243] *Ibid.*, p. 233.

[244] Class one: 6 per cent; class two: 7 per cent; class three: 8 per cent; class four: 9 per cent; class five: 10 per cent; and class six: 14 per cent.

[245] When Phillips sought a year of "disponsibilité" in 1913, the Department was unable to guarantee him an appointment upon his return. See William Phillips, *Ventures in Diplomacy* (Boston: Beacon Press, 1952), p. 24.

classification of all officers under the Act, dismissals of incompetent personnel were authorized. Finally, promotions to the ministerial rank were facilitated by the re-enactment of the Stone-Flood provisions. To enable service men to accept these and ambassadorial positions, the Act allowed appropriations for representation allowances. There was, however, no immediate intention of the Department to request allowances.[246]

Apart from the new wage scale and the retirement system, the Act's most important sections dealt with the interchangeability of personnel. This principle was achieved by making the two services part of a superstructure called the "Foreign Service." After a reclassification by existing ranks, the officers, which included not only diplomats and consuls but also vice consuls of career, consular assistants, interpreters, and student interpreters, were assignable "to duty in either the consular or the diplomatic branch." [247] No section, however, was included which prescribed a formal "Foreign Service" education. Even the concept of consular assistants, which was vigorously upheld by Hughes, was abandoned in the law's final form.[248]

The drawbacks to the Rogers Act were many. Most, however, were unavoidable. The Executive-Legislative struggle over foreign affairs administration spilled over into the Act. In order that interchangeability could operate, Congress required that a commission in either branch was to have the advice and consent of the Senate. A Foreign Service officer, therefore, would receive first a commission to be a consul. If he were later assigned to a diplomatic post, he would then need a second commission. The law also failed to clarify the exact relationship of the two services to the new Foreign Service. This was, of course, due to the confusion on the part of the drafters. Read one way, the Act asserted the superiority of the new service. Read another, it emphasized the continuation of separate services. Separate commissions and the recognized breakdown of the new classifications abroad were part of the latter. Finally, the provision, introduced as a separate measure, by which the ministerial level was to become part of

[246] Hughes to Harding, August 22, 1922, in 120.1/70A.

[247] Class one: counselors of embassy and consuls-general of classes one and two; class two: secretaries of class one designated as counselors of legation and consuls general of class three; class three: secretaries of class one, consuls general of class four and consuls general at large; class four: secretaries of class two, consuls general of class five, consuls of classes one, two, and three, and Chinese, Japanese, and Turkish secretaries; class five: consuls of class four; class six: secretaries of class three, consuls of class five, and Chinese, Japanese, and Turkish assistant secretaries; class seven: consuls of class six; class eight: secretaries of class four and consuls of class seven; class nine: consuls of class eight and class nine; unclassified: vice-consuls of career, consular assistants, interpreters, and student interpreters.

[248] House Rept. 1479, *Report on a Bill for the Reorganization and Improvement of the Foreign Service of the United States*, p. 9.

the promotional hierarchy, was dropped, partly because of the Department's decision to concentrate all attention on the Rogers' measure and perhaps as much because of deep congressional opposition to handing virtually every ministerial position over to career men. This meant that the Rogers Act made no adjustment for a man to take a ministerial appointment and to retain his place in the career. To accept the former required a resignation from the latter. This, of course, left the career minister open to danger in the event of there being an administration unsympathetic to professional diplomacy. There was, however, provision for him to retain his retirement benefits.[249]

Nevertheless, the Rogers Act was overwhelmingly beneficial. At the cost of independence, the Diplomatic Service secured entrance by examination for all who could intellectually and physically qualify, security of tenure, and promotion by merit. The Act also brought gains to the Consular Service. And between the two, the principle of interchangeability promised that the most effectively trained man would have the right assignment.

Characterizing the movement for the legislation was a high degree of co-operation between the Executive, Congress, and external pressure groups. Throughout the period, however, the Department of State led. Although Rogers publicly claimed that he "wrote more of it than anyone else," the bill itself refutes this.[250] The decisive role of Carr in the early stages of the bill has already been noted. The large number of technical matters dealt with in the subsequent drafts and the separate bill dealing with the promotional hierarchy points unmistakably to the Department's hand. The bill's amendments, for the most part, were also of a technical nature that only the Department would have considered vital, such as changing the title of the Director of the Consular Service to Assistant Secretary of State. The Department's role can also be seen in certain provisions which reflect the internal disagreement over the intentions of the new relationship. Rogers would not have been at pains to insist that "all official acts of such officers while on duty in either the diplomatic or consular branch of the Foreign Service shall be performed under their respective commissions as secretaries or consular officer." [251] The disagreement, along with the continuing Executive-Legislative struggle over foreign affairs

---

[249] Section. 18. One criticism of the Act was that it failed to go far enough. Former Secretary Lansing believed that the departmental officers, excluding the clerical personnel, should have been included. See Lansing, *op. cit.*, p. 285–87. His suggestion was thirty years premature.

[250] *Cong. Rec.*, LXIV, 67 Cong., 4 sess. (February 6, 1923), 3143.

[251] Section 4.

administration, explains the bill's provision for separate commissions prior to interchangeability.

There is also more concrete evidence. Once the May decision was taken, the bill went through an entire redrafting by Carr and Wright, who were deputed as representatives of the two services with the responsibility for the measure. This fact is shown by an interdepartmental memo dated June 15, 1922, in which Carr hesitated to encourage Chamber of Commerce support "until it is determined in what form that the Bill should take." [252] The form that was finally accepted in the Department was the one Rogers later introduced.[253] Carr and Wright also selected the personnel for the two hearings.[254] They even determined in one case substantially what the individual would testify.[255] The Department provided the material for Rogers' other bills and for his reports.[256] Specific meetings were held, at the Department's instigation, to determine strategy. On October 23, 1923, Wright wrote to Rogers, "I feel very strongly that you and Carr and I should have a discussion as to ways and means, policy, etc., before very long." [257] The decisions on public relations were made by the Department. For instance Carr wrote to Phillips, ". . . no additional steps should be taken in the way of renewed activity on behalf of the bill until after it is on the Calendar." [258] None were.

Part of the strategy was to capitalize on Secretary Hughes's reputation. To Phillips, Carr suggested, "I think if we can attach Mr. Hughes's name to every step that is taken in forwarding this measure

[252] Carr to Phillips, June 15, 1922, in 111/218.

[253] Hughes to Rogers, October 13, 1922, in 111/108: "The bill, H.R. 12543, which was introduced by you on September 1, 1922, is a careful revision of your former bill, H.R. 17, and represents textually my views on the foreign service legislation. Fundamentally, there is no important departure from your original proposals. The revision was made in the Department of State with my full concurrence and approval, and has been submitted to the President, by whom, I understand, it has been transmitted to you with appropriate observations." See *American Consular Bulletin*, IV (November, 1922), 313–14.

[254] See Carr to Phillips, December 21, 1922, in 111/222. The Department decided to exclude the United States Chamber of Commerce from the first hearing. See also Carr to Chauncey Depew Snow, December 15, 1922, in 111/114A; Carr to Ellery C. Stowell, December 15, 1922, in 111/111A. For the second hearing, Rogers requested a career diplomat (Rogers to Carr, September 20, 1923, in 122.1/469). The Department, however, selected the diplomat who was to testify (Wright to Rogers, November 8, 1923, in 111/155A). Hugh Gibson was sent.

[255] Wright to Gibson, November 3, 1923, in 111/155A. Gibson was requested to add no material in the hearings.

[256] See Wright to Rogers, November 8, 1923, in 111/155C. Rogers was contemplating a bill to facilitate further embassy construction. Material for the bill was provided by the Department.

[257] Wright to Rogers, October 13, 1923 in 111/150B. See also Wright to Rogers, November 8, 1923, in 111/155C.

[258] Carr to Phillips, December 21, 1922, in 111/222.

it will be by far the strongest influence that can be exerted in pushing it through Congress with a minimum of delay." [259] The fact that his name was so used had led Hughes's biographers to overestimate his exact role in the legislation.[260] He did not draft the bill, and there is no evidence that he personally changed any of its provisions. The bill's outlines had been fixed before Hughes even became Secretary of State. On the other hand, he contributed to the bill's success through his willingness to exert his influence on its behalf. He made public statements in support of the measure, appeared before the first congressional hearing, and used his personal influence on particular legislators.[261]

He was especially useful in his relationship with the President. As he was the focal point for foreign policy under both Harding and Coolidge, the two Presidents accepted his recommendation on the Rogers' measure. After Hughes convinced Harding, in a letter dated August 22, 1922, of the plan's merits, Harding vigorously supported it.[262] The President corresponded with legislators to gain their approval and was not averse to seeing these statements made public.[263] He aided Hughes in securing an early consideration by Congress of the bill, and he sought to avert personally the stalemate in the Senate through his personal influence with Senator Sterling.[264]

Coolidge relied on Hughes even more greatly than had Harding. On October 8, 1923, Hughes wrote to Coolidge, "Your endorsement would have the effect of retaining the status given it by President Harding as an administrative measure." [265] Coolidge went so far as to recommend action in his first State of the Union address. He informed Congress, "The Foreign Service of our Government needs to be reorganized and improved." [266] He also wrote in support of the bill to key congressmen and was willing to intervene in the event the Connally amendment, imposing percentage restrictions in certain

[259] Carr to Phillips, September 1, 1922, in 111/223.

[260] See Merlo J. Pusey, *Charles Evans Hughes* (New York: Macmillan, 1951), I, 419; Dexter Perkins, *Charles Evans Hughes and American Democratic Statesmanship* (Boston: Little Brown & Co., 1956), pp. 95–96.

[261] E.g., Hughes, *op. cit.*, pp. 250–66 (speech before the United States Chamber of Commerce on May 18, 1922); House Committee on Foreign Affairs, *Foreign Service of the United States*, HR 12543, pp. 1–25; Carr to Hughes, January 20, 1923, in 111/122: "I feel you [Hughes] hold the key to the success of the bill in the Senate, and a few personal words from you to Senator Lodge at your early convenience would have an excellent effect."

[262] Hughes to Harding, August 22, 1922, in 120.1/70A.

[263] Harding to Lodge, August 24, 1922, in 111/106; *New York Times*, December 24, 1922, Sec. 8, p. 6.

[264] Hughes to Harding, January 19, 1923, in 111/253A; Harding to Senator Sterling, March 1, 1923, in 111/129.

[265] Hughes to Coolidge, October 8, 1923, in 111/147A.

[266] *New York Times*, December 7, 1923, p. 4.

classifications, was unwanted by the Secretary.[267] And without delay Coolidge signed the measure into law on May 24, 1924.[268]

Although there were significant exceptions, the members of both services were largely in support of the Rogers' measure too. The exceptions were not in the Consular Service. Its members, by all evidence, were unanimously in favor of the bill. Some of them had personally written to congressmen advocating the bill's passage; others took a great interest in every step in the legislative process.[269] When the bill failed in its first trip through Congress, Carr consoled the consuls, saying, "I have desired to give you these observations by way of indicating that there is no sense of discouragement to be entertained by the service in connection with the failure to put the bill through at the short session." [270] The *American Consular Bulletin* referred favorably to the measure countless times.[271] When Congress's interest in the bill seemed to flag, the *Bulletin* assured its readers, "The President having endorsed the bill . . . the project is considered as an administration measure and therefore is entitled to preferential treatment over others of lesser importance in Congress." [272] The only objection to the bill received by the Department from a consular officer dealt with the possible inadequacy of the retirement provisions.[273]

The exceptions were diplomats. From evidence, it appears that the older officers opposed the measure. Their leader was minister to Czechoslovakia, Lewis D. Einstein. In a letter to Hughes, he complained, "If in every grade and at every stage of promotion there is to be a continuous introduction of other elements and a blending with another organization possessing a different tradition and outlook, the result is unlikely to be good." He informed Hughes that he had taken a poll among a few officers and had found that they agreed with him.[274] Dearing replied, "I am convinced that the slightest pretension to social superiority should be outlawed." [275] While there was no further correspondence between Einstein and the career diplomats in the Department, the latter were still worried about the situation two

---

[267] Hughes to Coolidge, December 10, 1923, in 111/195A. The President wrote Representative Porter and Senator Lodge. Coolidge to Hughes, April 30, 1924, in 111/207. Hughes found the amendments "minor improvements" (Hughes to Coolidge, May 1, 1924, in 111/204C). See *Cong. Rec.*, LXV, 68 Cong., 1 sess. (April 30, 1924), 7577.

[268] *Cong. Rec.*, LXV, 68 Cong., 1 sess. (May 24, 1924), 10068.

[269] Letter to congressmen by D. J. Murphy, January 6, 1923, in 111/136; Hughes to Skinner, February 9, 1923, in 111/124.

[270] Carr to consuls and consuls general, March 7, 1923, in 111/133A.

[271] *American Consular Bulletin*, II–VI (January, 1920–April, 1924), *passim*.

[272] *American Consular Bulletin*, VI (April, 1924), 124.

[273] Edwin N. Gunsaulus to Hughes, April 10, 1923, in 111/116.

[274] Einstein to Hughes, June 20, 1923, in 111/248.

[275] Dearing to Einstein, July 2, 1923, in 111/248.

months later. In a letter to Dearing, Phillips found the sentiment "prejudicial to the Bill." He added, however, that Ulysses Grant Smith, an older career diplomat, had been converted to the measure.[276] Nothing resulted from Einstein's dissatisfaction.

This fact can partly be attributed to the continuation of the Diplomatic Service's strong position. Although there was no rise in the number of applications,[277] the number of inquiries about the service increased by five hundred in 1923.[278] Resignations remained low. The percentage of career men holding upper service posts remained the same, while their number increased.[279] The Undersecretary and two of the three Assistant Secretaries were career diplomats. Another headed the Diplomatic Bureau, and three diplomats administered geographical divisions.[280] When Grew replaced Phillips as Undersecretary in March, 1924, the *American Consular Bulletin* maintained, "The foregoing seems to be an indication of the growing belief that this country should be represented abroad by trained men, and it constitutes a happy augury for the future of the Foreign Service." [281]

In presenting the bill, Representative Rogers assured Congress: "Practically every chamber of commerce and trade organization in the United States and many of the American chambers and trade organizations functioning in other parts of the world have gone on record as favoring this particular reorganization of our foreign service." [282] This statement was no exaggeration. Although the Department did not solicit support, it came nevertheless. On October 17, 1922, the most important commercial organization, the United States Chamber of Commerce, signalized its support. The regional and international chambers and the other trade organizations followed with theirs.[283] Resolutions, letters to congressmen, and editorials ex-

[276] Phillips to Dearing, August 27, 1923, in 111/248.
[277] Minutes (July 9-12, 1923). Forty-five were designated; thirty-six took the examination.
[278] House Committee on Foreign Affairs, *Foreign Services of the United States*, HR 17 and HR 6357, p. 64.
[279] 14/40 in 1922 and 16/47 in 1924. There were vacancies on both dates.
[280] *Biog. Reg.* (1924), *passim*.
[281] *American Consular Bulletin*, VI (April, 1924), 122. See also *New York Times*, February 27, 1924, p. 16.
[282] *Cong. Rec.*, LXIV, 67 Cong., 4 sess. (February 6, 1923), 3143.
[283] Julius H. Barnes to Hughes, October 17, 1922, in 111/110. See also *American Consular Bulletin*, IV (December, 1922), 368; *New York Times*, November 20, 1922, p. 24; Chamber of Commerce of New York to Hughes, December 7, 1922, in 120.1/71; American Chamber of Commerce in Mexico to Hughes, December 28, 1922, in 111/118; Chamber of Commerce of the Levant to Hughes, January 25, 1923, in 111/133; Chicago Chamber of Commerce to Hughes, February 20, 1923, in 111/127; Illinois Manufacturers Association to Hughes, April 28, 1924, in 111/199; National Advertisers Association to Hughes, November 14, 1923, in 111/157.

pressed their approval. An editorial in the *Export and Trade Finance Weekly* insisted, "There is probably no branch of the government in which the exporter has such a great interest." [284] Individual firms also publicly supported the measure.[285] Even the American Federation of Labor joined hands with capital on this issue.[286]

Aid also came from organizations not directly interested in commerce and from newspapers and magazines. The National Civil Service Reform League and its joint committee with business particularly sought to influence opinion in favor of the measure.[287] The near-dormant American Embassy Association recommended the bill's passage.[288] So did the National Republican Club.[289] There was even an unofficial society, the American Diplomatic and Consular Association, established to advance the reorganization. It was, however, squelched when Carr forbade contributions to it "or to any other organization engaged in a propaganda movement or a political lobby." [290] Newspapers and magazines, too, showed their support by editorials.[291] When Hughes wrote to Coolidge, he claimed that "editorial comment was uniformly favorable." [292]

Rogers' measure was fortunate also in that it could draw on a large public interest in foreign affairs. In 1923, Wright wrote to Rogers:

> I am becoming really greatly impressed by the growth of interest . . . which is evidenced by . . . the requests that are received by the Department for suggestions as to persons who may care to speak before such organizations as Polity Clubs at universities, associations of university women, etc., etc., on the foreign relations of the United States.

He also remarked about the "increasing numbers of letters addressed to this Department upon the subject." [293] Memoirs of diplomats,

[284] Derek P. Young, "Reorganizing the Foreign Service," *Export and Trade Finance Weekly*, X (February 23, 1924), 7.

[285] E.g., Leucodescent Co. (2108/146); Chicago and Eastern Illinois Railway (2108/147); Michigan Stove Co. (122.1/150); Northern Assurance Co. (122.1/151); First National Bank of Linden (122.1/153); Clyde Iron Works (122.1/159); Standard Varnish Co. (122.1/177–8).

[286] American Federation of Labor to Hughes, December 10, 1922, in 111/200.

[287] *New York Times*, February 3, 1924, Sec. 1, p. 7.

[288] American Embassy Association to Hughes, December 12, 1922, in 122.1/188.

[289] National Republican Club to Hughes, April 28, 1924, in 111/200.

[290] Carr to R. Gilmore Richardson, November 23, 1923, in 111/228.

[291] E.g., *Outlook*, CXXXVII (January 4, 1924), 180–81; *New York Times*, January 21, 1924, p. 16. The *New York Times* also printed all of Gibson's testimony. See *New York Times*, January 27, 1924, Sec. 8, p. 5.

[292] Hughes to Coolidge, October 8, 1923, in 111/147A.

[293] Wright to Rogers, October 13, 1923, in 111/150B. This growing interest was evidenced in the enrollments for international relations courses. In May, 1922, forty-eight universities reported 3,122 students so enrolled. The following April there were fifty-two

particularly of the war period, frequently made their way to the book lists.[294] The traditional family magazines showed interest as well. *Colliers* ran a long series on professional diplomacy by Maurice Francis Egan.[295] In three successive years, the *Saturday Evening Post* serialized the memoirs of Baron Rosen, Norval Richardson, and Richard Washburn Childs.[296]

The movement for a specific "Foreign Service" training was also picking up strength. The School of Foreign Service was founded in Georgetown in 1919.[297] The previous year New York University initiated a similar program.[298] By 1922, Columbia, Williams, Mount Holyoke, Stanford, Harvard, Ohio State, and the universities of Michigan, Washington, Illinois, and Pittsburgh maintained some form of training program. In December, 1923, a meeting was held in Washington of a National Conference of Foreign Service Training "to discuss problems of mutual interest."[299] Even a Foreign Service fraternity was founded in 1920.[300]

The approval of the measure by the public and by the administration was mirrored in Congress. Although it was indorsed by a Republican administration, the bill's congressional support was by no means partisan. Support came from both sides of the aisle. Representative Linthicum, a Democrat, was as constructively in favor of the bill as was its congressional strategist, Republican Rogers; Senator Underwood as positive as Senator Lodge.[301] The hearings drew from both parties. Hughes and Bacon were counterbalanced by Lansing,

universities and 4,973 students. See *American Consular Bulletin*, VI (January, 1924), 17; Grayson Louis Kirk, *The Study of International Relations* (New York: Council on Foreign Relations, 1947), pp. 2–8.

[294] E.g., T. Jefferson Coolidge, *Autobiography of T. Jefferson Coolidge*, (Boston, 1923); Maurice Francis Egan, *Recollections of a Happy Life* (New York, 1924); Arthur Sherburne Hardy, *Things Remembered* (Boston, 1923); Thomas Skelton Harrison, *Homely Diary of a Diplomat in the East* (Boston, 1917); Burton J. Hendrick, *The Life and Letters of Walter Hines Page*, (3 vols.; Garden City, N.Y., 1922–25); Robert Underwood Johnson, *Remembered Yesterdays* (Boston, 1923); Lew Meriwether, *War Diary of a Diplomat* (Boston, 1919); Ira Nelson Morris, *From an American Legation* (New York, 1923); Oscar H. Straus, *Under Four Administrations* (Boston, 1922).

[295] Maurice Francis Egan, "Flies in the Diplomatic Ointment," *Colliers*, LXV (January 17, 1920), 9–10, *passim*; "Your Move, Mr. Harding," LXVII (February 5, 1921), 11–12, *passim*; "Our Extraordinary Envoys," LXVII (March 26, 1921), 7–8, *passim*; "More Business in Diplomacy," LXIX (February 4, 1922), 9–10, *passim*; "Telling the Diplomatic Truth," LXX (September 9, 1922), 15, *passim*.

[296] *Saturday Evening Post*, CXCIV–VII, *passim*.

[297] Coleman Nevils, *op. cit.*, p. 14.

[298] *New York Times*, December 25, 1916, p. 9.

[299] *American Consular Bulletin*, VI (March, 1924), 77–79.

[300] *Foreign Service Log* (March 3, 1939, Georgetown), I, 5. The fraternity, Delta Phi Epsilon, was founded at Georgetown University. It had seven chapters by 1939.

[301] Carr to Hughes, January 20, 1923, in 111/122: "Confidentially I may say that Senator Underwood will support the bill actively in the Senate, as you are all well aware, is of great importance to its success."

Polk, and former Ambassador John W. Davis.[302] Twice in each chamber the bill was favorably reported out of committee.[303] The support of the chairmen of other committees, particularly from the Appropriations Committee, was sought and received.[304]

At all times the bill received special consideration at the hands of congressional leaders.[305] Opposition to the measure was minimal. Those who dissented did so on rather curious grounds. All accepted the need for reorganization; none doubted the importance of some representation abroad. They did doubt, however, the particular plan and the nation's ability to afford the higher salaries.[306] Even in the absence of significant opposition and with special privileges, the bill failed in its first full-scale introduction to Congress. Although it passed the House by a vote of 203 to 27, it received no attention in the Senate, owing to a last-minute log jam there of important bills.[307] Former Secretary Lansing could still predict its success in the following session, "since it apparently called forth no serious opposition." [308] In the spring of 1924, with virtually no debate, the bill passed both chambers: unanimously in the Senate and by a vote of 134 to 27 in the House.[309]

On May 24, 1924, President Coolidge signed the measure.[310] The movement to provide a new career in foreign affairs had succeeded.

[302] House Committee on Foreign Affairs, *Foreign Service of the United States*, HR 12543, *passim*.

[303] House Rept. 1479, 67 Cong., 4 sess. (January 30, 1923); Senate Rept. 1142, 67 Cong., 4 sess. (February 13, 1923); House Rept. 157, 68 Cong., 1 sess. (February 5, 1924); Senate Rept. 532, 68 Cong., 1 sess. (May 12, 1924). The Committee on Foreign Affairs, according to Albert C. F. Westphal, was particularly disposed to favor the bill "by the loss of power to report appropriations by the Foreign Affairs Committee." See Albert C. F. Westphal, *House Committee on Foreign Affairs* (New York: Columbia University Press, 1942), p. 123. The Senate Committee, which reported the bill unanimously twice, might have been influenced to a degree by the recent experience with the alternative to professional diplomacy — the executive agent. No mention of this, however, appears in debates.

[304] *Cong. Rec.*, LXIV, 67 Cong., 4 sess. (February 6, 1923), 3143.

[305] Carr to Hughes, January 23, 1923, in 111/121: "Mr. Rogers reports the prospects excellent for having his bill considered, under a rule, the latter part of next week." Also Rogers to Hughes, September 20, 1923, in 111/149. On the bill's second trip through Congress, its way was paved by an obliging Representative Porter.

[306] *Cong. Rec.*, LXIV, 67 Cong., 4 sess. (February 6, 1923), 3159–60; *Cong. Rec.*, LXV, 68 Cong., 1 sess. (April 30, 1924), 7566–87.

[307] *Cong. Rec.*, LXIV, 67 Cong., 4 sess. (February 8, 1923), 3285. The measures which prevented action on the Rogers bill were the British debt refunding agreement, the Ship Subsidy bill, the Civil Service reclassification bill, the Alien Property bill, and the President's proposal for the Permanent Court of International Justice at the Hague. The Ship Subsidy bill provoked a filibuster. See *American Consular Bulletin*, V (March, 1923), 78.

[308] Lansing, *op. cit.*, p. 287.

[309] *Cong. Rec.*, LXV, 68 Cong., 1 sess. (April 30, 1924), 7634–35.

[310] *Ibid.* (May 24, 1924), p. 10068.

Many of the movement's supporters took the occasion to estimate the law's effect. Secretary Hughes believed, "Through this salutary legislation young men of ambition are offered a career of almost unparalleled opportunity and attractiveness, and the country receives its best assurance of security and substantial achievement in the future conduct of foreign affairs." [311] Wilbur Carr thought, ". . . a life service has been created in which each member may devote himself with the highest degree of consecration and the greatest assurance of appropriate reward." [312] Finally, the *New York Times* considered its passage as "proof that the country is at last awake to the importance of diplomatic and consular work and that it appreciates the fact that our world position today demands that we strengthen our foreign service in every way possible." [313]

Several questions remain. Why did the experiment in an independent Diplomatic Service fail? It failed because Americans refused to view foreign affairs consistently in realist's terms. This forced the career diplomats to base their defense of the service on the remaining important aspect of American thinking on international affairs — commerce. The compromise with the Consular Service was thus made inevitable. Then, was the concept of professional diplomacy dead too? On the contrary, it was both strengthened and expanded. It was strengthened in that those concomitants of a career which it had lacked it gained through accepting interchangeability. It was also strengthened in that the long-assumed importance of a knowledge of commercial matters for diplomacy was closer to realization through the possibility of service in a consular post. It was expanded in that it now embraced almost all relations, official and otherwise, which America and Americans had with other nations and their citizens.

These two issues seem to pose a paradox. The experiment in an independent Diplomatic Service failed because America did not take political realities sufficiently into consideration; yet the concept of professional diplomacy was both strengthened and expanded. At first sight, the rejection of the League and the Rogers Act appear as mutually contradictory events. This is, however, not true. For most, the Rogers Act was a means of improving America's position in commercial competition. The rejection of the League is irrelevant here. For a man like Hughes, the two events were supplementary. Because America rejected the League, it was doubly important that the nation's remaining machinery for international communication be improved. For men like Rogers and Lodge, the two events were

[311] *American Consular Bulletin*, VI (July, 1924), 241.
[312] *Ibid.*, p. 249.
[313] Editorial, *New York Times*, May 22, 1924, p. 16.

complementary. In rejecting internationalism, the United States asserted its personality as an independent nation-state. Its sovereignty was in no way going to be curtailed by a supranational entity. The traditional expression of this independence was a nation's foreign service. Even persons who rejected the League without subscribing to Lodge's realism, such as Senator William E. Borah, could accept the Rogers Act. His fear of becoming embroiled again in war, particularly as a result of ignorance about the designs of other nations, would dictate his acceptance of trained representation abroad. To insure that this representation did not then betray the people, as Europe's did, he would insist that the service must be filled by representatives of all classes and sections. The Rogers Act aimed at doing both. The fact is, therefore, that the two events, the rejection of the League and the Rogers Act, do not jar or reveal any violent shift of opinion but flow naturally from one to the other.

The First World War triggered the events which led to the abandonment of the experiment in an independent Diplomatic Service and to the strengthening and expanding of the concept of professional diplomacy. It put the commercial, political, and social forces into action, and the Rogers Act was the result of their inevitable collision. But the result was by no means final. What was meant by interchangeability had to be hammered out in practice. All the social implications of the decision to create a single personnel source had not yet appeared. The success which the new career opportunities would have in attracting a steady supply of competent candidates was yet to be determined. Conclusions to these problems would be reached in the period 1924–39.

CHAPTER FIVE

VARIATIONS ON THE THEMES: PROFESSIONALIZATION, DEMOCRATIZATION AND SPECIALIZATION

1924-1939

THE period which fell between the passage of the Rogers Act and the outbreak of war in Europe in 1939 represents a chronological unity in the administrative history of professional diplomacy. Unlike the years preceding 1924 and following 1939, no significant departures occurred. Contrasting economic phases of prosperity and depression, the continued misunderstanding of the intentions of the Rogers Act, and a small scandal, all these had an influence on administration, but they served only to retard temporarily or to accelerate earlier developments. Thinking on foreign policy continued to stress the primacy of economic questions. Isolation was the accepted political position vis-à-vis the world. Even after 1937, when the peace in Europe was rapidly disintegrating, there was no radical reassessment of the needs and scope of the Foreign Service.

In many ways no reassessment was necessary. The professional service, it was generally thought, was capable of handling every eventuality. Thus, the fifteen years between 1924 and 1939 were marked by the continuation of tendencies begun in the First World War period and before. The settlement of 1924 between the two services proved temporary, and a single service was created. The service's professionalization continued. The movement toward democratization, although seriously menaced by the depression years, was sustained. A clearer concept of the specialized nature of the service emerged.

When the career diplomats and consular officers agreed to support the Rogers Act, each group did so without fully accepting or even understanding the other's interpretation of the plan. Because the Departmental personnel remained virtually unchanged after the bill's passage, the fact that this confusion continued is understandable. As noted before, the consular position was one that looked to the fusion of the personnel source and to the frequent interchange of officers between the two branches. It generally recognized the problems involved in the plan, but it anticipated a new service eventually emerging from the Act. Wilbur Carr wrote, "One point to be recognized immediately is that the plan of reorganization is designed primarily in the interest of a future service, and only incidentally in the interest of the present personnel." [1] Sharing this belief, the American Consular Association re-established itself as the American Foreign Service Association and extended its membership to all officers commissioned under the Rogers Act.[2] Other consular officers, however, were less indulgent to the sensibilities of the career diplomats. Consul General Skinner, for instance, believed, "The theory of a unified service is woven inextricably through almost every paragraph of the Act." And he would tolerate no backsliding on this principle.[3]

The diplomats, on the other hand, were equally sure that the new arrangement authorized interchangeability in a two branch service only as the exception and not as the rule. The opinions of Hugh Wilson and J. Butler Wright, presumably, remained unchanged once the bill became law.[4] Undersecretary Grew also claimed, "Interchanges will be carried out with great discrimination and care. There will be no 'weaving back and forth' between the two branches, as the Consuls wish." [5] His attitude toward promotions to the ministerial level was the same. In a letter to Hughes, Grew maintained:

    . . . while the promotion of diplomatic officers to diplo-

---

[1] "Mr. Carr Surveys the Rogers Bill," *American Consular Bulletin*, VI (July, 1924), 249.

[2] *American Consular Bulletin*, VI (August, 1924), 316–17. See also *Good Government*, XLI (October, 1924), 150. A combined journal, the *American Foreign Service Journal*, was also authorized. See *American Foreign Service Journal*, I (October, 1924), 10.

[3] Skinner to Grew, October 8, 1925, in 120.1/151.

[4] E.g. *American Consular Bulletin*, II (March, 1920), 3; *ibid.*, VI (June, 1924), 220; Wright to A. L. P. Dennis, November 23, 1923, in 111/165.

[5] Grew to Thomas S. Perry, January 19, 1924, in Joseph C. Grew, *Turbulent Era*, I, 644. This opinion was shared by the service's closest observer during the period. See Ellery C. Stowell, "The Foreign Service School," *American Journal of International Law*, XIX (October, 1925), 767.

matic missions has for sometime been recognized as a normal and logical step, the promotion of consular officers to diplomatic missions is a new departure under the Rogers Act and that to develop this new principle to the detriment of the diplomatic branch would probably cause discouragement within that branch, a contingency to be avoided if possible.[6]

The Rogers Act accommodated both groups' positions. The wage scale, the promotional hierarchy, and the retirement scheme dealt with "Foreign Service officers," a classification which included members of both branches. On the other hand, the Act did not destroy the two units. An officer might "be assigned to duty in either the diplomatic or consular branch." Officers received separate commissions as diplomatic secretaries or consular officers, and the appointment of a member of one branch to the other required a second commission. Finally, officers abroad were to perform their duties "under their respective commissions as secretaries or consular officers."[7]

The Executive Order of June 7, 1924, which was issued to implement the law, went no further in compromising the two positions. The Order itself was intended "to provide certain rules and regulations for administering the Foreign Service on an interchangeable basis," and the Foreign Service Personnel Board which it created was authorized "to recommend . . . the transfer of such officers from one branch of the service to the other according to the needs of the service." But even with these specific statements the precise position remained obscure. The clause dealing with the functions of the Board assumed the continued existence of separate branches. The membership of the Board included "Foreign Service officers of high rank representing both the diplomatic and consular branches of the Foreign Service." The phrase "according to the needs of the service" implied no quota for the interchanges; it was conceivable that "the needs of the Service" might require no transfers at all. And the clause on promotions did not exclude the maintenance of separate diplomatic and consular efficiency lists.[8] Two departmental orders, both of which were issued on June 9, 1924, also failed to clarify the relationship.[9]

The first three years of the Rogers Act's operation saw the interpretation of the career diplomats prevail. When in 1921 Assistant Secre-

---

[6] Grew to Hughes, December 30, 1924, in Grew, *op. cit.*, I, 644.

[7] 43 Stat. 140 (May 24, 1924).

[8] Executive Order of June 7, 1924. Copy in author's possession. See also *American Consular Bulletin*, VI (July, 1924), 245–53.

[9] Departmental orders of June 9, 1924. Copies in author's possession. See also *American Consular Bulletin*, VI (July, 1924), 245–53.

tary Robert W. Bliss thought that interchangeability was acceptable
if its control were "delegated to the Department," [10] he undoubtedly
had in mind the fact that the career diplomats usually dominated the
most important posts in the Department and could prevent interchangeability from becoming too common. This was certainly true in
1924. Three of the four top positions were held by career diplomats,
the fourth being occupied by Carr.[11] Their position became clear
during the conferences which produced the Executive Order of June
7. One of Carr's major proposals, for instance, was defeated because,
among other reasons, it would tend to bureaucratize the administration and "would take much of the spirit and morale out of the diplomatic branch at least." [12] The three men most instrumental in
determining the Order's final form were career diplomats Grew, Wilson, and Wright. When Carr balked at their plan, he was told to draw
up the Order "as instructed." The Order was later justified on the
grounds that "Hugh Wilson, Butler Wright and I think most of the
diplomatic secretaries in the Department felt that the best possible
plan had been evolved." [13] The vagueness of the Order on interchangeability can probably be attributed to the decisive role played
by the career diplomats.

Their hand, however, can be seen most clearly in the events which
followed the issuing of the Order. On all committees and boards, a
rigid parity between the two branches was achieved. When the membership of the Foreign Service Personnel Board and its Executive
Committee was announced, it included three from each branch. [14]
Grew remarked in a letter to Phillips, "We thus have six members
evenly representing both branches of the service." [15] The Board of
Review had roughly the same arrangements.[16] The position on promotions to the upper service was similar. Accompanying a list submitted to Hughes of the Board's recommendations for promotions,
a letter from Grew stated:

> The list presented to you was therefore arranged in such a
> way that if the President should select any number of offi-
> cers for promotion in the order of their presentation, the
> promotions for the two branches of the Service would either

[10] Bliss to Henry P. Fletcher, April 25, 1921, in 120.1/67.

[11] Joseph Grew was Undersecretary, and Leland Harrison and John V. A. MacMurray
were Assistant Secretaries.

[12] Grew, *op. cit.*, I, 619–20 (entries in diary, May 28 — June 6, 1924). For Carr's plan,
see 111/254, Carr memo, January 14, 1924.

[13] Grew, *op. cit.*, I, 620–21.

[14] Hughes to service personnel, June 21, 1924, in 120.1/80. See also *New York Times*,
June 22, 1924, Sec. 2, p. 2; *American Consular Bulletin*, VI (August, 1924), 317.

[15] Grew to Phillips, June 30, 1924, in Grew, *op. cit.*, I, 626.

[16] Hughes to service personnel, June 21, 1924, in 120.1/80A.

be equal or with the predominance in favor of the diplomatic branch.[17]

By January 1, 1926, two from each branch had been so promoted.[18]

Assignments revealed the bifurcation even more plainly. A departmental circular of July 29, 1924, informed the members of the service that "indiscriminate transfers . . . clearly would not be in the interests of the Government or of the officers themselves." [19] The Register of 1926 listed only nine men as possessing dual commissions. The following year there were sixteen.[20] In a letter to Arthur Lane, Grew admitted, ". . . whenever a vacancy occurred in the diplomatic branch in any class a diplomat was promoted to fill it and the same thing on the consular side."[21] As vacancies occurred more often in the diplomatic branch and as promotions were tied to specific levels of assignment, the number of promotions of diplomats exceeded proportionally those in the consular branch. As of July 1, 1925, 26.5 per cent of all consular officers had had promotions, while 42.8 per cent had had them in the diplomatic branch.[22] A year and a half later the percentages were 37 and 63, respectively.[23] Many of these promotions ignored the fact that consular officers in each class were usually older in years and service than were the diplomats.

There is other evidence that the diplomats' objective of keeping the branches separate was being attained. Separate regulations were issued for the two branches.[24] Separate inspectors were maintained.[25] In the Department's literature the two branches were listed and dealt with separately.[26]

On the other hand, the career diplomats' interpretation of the Act did not diverge in all respects from the consular interpretation. After December, 1924, a single examination was given "irrespective of the branch of the Service to which eventually the successful candidates may be assigned."[27] The first assignment for anyone appointed after

[17] Grew to Hughes, December 30, 1924, in Grew, *op. cit.*, I, 644.

[18] *Biog. Reg.* (1926), pp. 16–56. The two former consular officers were Evan E. Young and Charles C. Eberhardt.

[19] 120.1/74A, Departmental circular of July 29, 1924.

[20] *Biog. Reg.* (1926–27), *passim.*

[21] Grew to Lane, May 3, 1927, in Grew, *op. cit.*, I, 699.

[22] Skinner to Grew, October 8, 1925, in 120.1/151. Percentages calculated by Consul General Skinner. They have not been checked by the author.

[23] Senate Rept. 1069, 70 Cong., 1 sess. (May 3, 1928), p. 3. Percentages have not been checked by the author.

[24] Executive Order 4255, June 18, 1925. Copy of new "Consular Branch" regulations in the possession of the author. See also Executive Order 5642, June 8, 1931. Copy of Order in author's possession.

[25] Skinner to Grew, October 8, 1925, in 120.1/151.

[26] *Biog. Reg.* (1925–27), *passim.*

[27] Kellogg to Porter, June 21, 1927, in 120.31/38.

the Rogers Act was to a vice-consularship. Two officers from the consular branch also were elevated to the ministerial level. The number possessing dual commissions was increasing — nine to sixteen. Furthermore, the career diplomats assumed that the line officers were not dissatisfied with their administration. A letter from Grew in June, 1925, requested criticisms from senior officers in both branches. The replies were described later as "distinctly gratifying." [28] And the diplomat in the lower classes, when comparing his previous rate of promotion, found his post–Rogers Act rate much retarded. Jefferson Patterson lamented this point in his autobiography, claiming that "the consolidation of the diplomatic and consular services in 1924 . . . slowed my advancement." [29]

With the Board evenly split between the two branches, it might be asked why the consular members acquiesced in the diplomats' interpretation? That they did so is obvious from the facts. That they did so willingly is maintained in the possibly biased testimony of Grew and Wilson. On the question of limiting consular promotions to the upper service, Grew claimed that the conclusion was accepted "even by the consular officers." [30] In *Diplomat between the Wars,* Wilson maintained, "I do not remember a single incident in which the decision of the board was taken other than by unanimity." He thought the equal number of consular officers on the Board was "sufficient guaranty that they were adequately protected." [31] The reasons for consular agreement are not too difficult to deduce. Although evenly split between the branches, the Board was certainly dominated by the Undersecretary, who was the chairman, and by Wright, both of whom seemed to have a particularly close relationship with Hughes.[32] Because he would probably be the Board's only permanent member, Carr must have realized that the rapid turnover of career diplomats in the Department would eventually bring a redress. Finally, the three consular representatives probably genuinely believed that the new arrangement should be approached gradually, and this view agreed, at least temporarily, with the diplomats' conviction that "if you try to train a man for both [branches] he will make a success of neither." [33]

[28] Kellogg to Edwards, July 7, 1926, in 120.1/114.

[29] *Diplomatic Duty and Diversion,* p. 8.

[30] Grew to Hughes, December 30, 1924, in Grew, *op. cit.,* I, 643–44.

[31] Hugh Wilson, *Diplomat between the War* (New York: Longmans, Green, 1941), pp. 171–72.

[32] When, for instance, the two plans for reorganization were being discussed, Hughes called in Wright and Grew for consultation. He did not consult with Carr. Furthermore, the career diplomats were successful in securing Hughes's assent to their scheme. See Grew, *op. cit.,* I, 620–21.

[33] Grew to Thomas S. Perry, January 19, 1924, in *ibid.,* I, 644. See also Grew to Skinner, October 25, 1925, in 120.1/151.

Other members of the consular branch lacked the patience displayed by their colleagues on the Board. The first to object was Consul General Skinner. In a letter to Grew, dated October 8, 1925, Skinner complained that a "series of half measures and grudging concessions" had emerged from the administration of the Rogers Act. Claiming that these failed "to reflect the spirit of the act," he then cited the differences in the promotion rates of the two branches, particularly in regard to the members' tenure, and other evidence on the continuing separation. He argued: "The only proper method of procedure is to take the individual standing of every officer, regardless of the character of his previous duty, and with due regard to his length of service, to give him the benefit of his efficiency record." He exhorted the diplomats to forget "their real or imaginary interests" and to realize that "they [the branches] are so interlocked that it is idle to pretend that they can be separated into two groups." [34] In reply, the Board agreed to drop the separate titles in the Department's literature but insisted that "evolutionary" changes in the service were better. [35]

The minor adjustment authorized by the Board, as long as the career diplomats were successful in applying their interpretation, could not have satisfied Skinner, particularly in that the crux of his objection was untouched. Before their objections could be met, either the career diplomats would have to relinquish their control over personnel matters or the Foreign Service Personnel Board and its Executive Committee would have to be forced, by public or service opinion, to accept the consular interpretation of the Rogers Act. And implied in both solutions was the charge that the Board was being used to advance special and not the general interests of the service. To prevent this from recurring, steps would have to be taken to neutralize the Board's personnel. The events which followed Skinner's criticism moved in these three directions.

Service and public opinion began the attack in 1926. Throughout the early months of the year complaints were being registered by officers with the Department that favoritism was being shown to diplomats in assignments at home and abroad. The officers also objected to the relative youth of the diplomats as compared with the consular members of each class. [36] To assuage part of the criticism, the Board suggested to Secretary Frank Kellogg, Hughes's successor, that a departmental order should be issued prohibiting members of the Board from sitting on any board of review. [37] The latter board sat biennially

[34] Skinner to Grew, October 8, 1925, in 120.1/151.

[35] Grew to Skinner, October 25, 1925, in 120.1/151.

[36] Kellogg to Foreign Service personnel, July 21, 1926, in 120.11/1A. Type of criticisms inferred from topics treated in Kellogg's general reply.

[37] Grew to Kellogg, May 27, 1926, in 120.111/2.

to revise efficiency ratings. Before this could be promulgated, however, the Board was attacked from another side. On June 16, 1926, Representative James G. Edwards of Georgia, who had been informed by members of the consular branch that partiality was being shown in appointments to China, inquired of Secretary Kellogg "whether or not these are isolated cases." [38] Kellogg assured him that they were, "that never before in its history has the morale of the Service been so high or its enthusiasm so great," and that a few minor defects in certain administrative provisions "were being adjusted." [39] Shortly thereafter, the Secretary moved to allay members' suspicions by promulgating the order and assuring them that "an officer's advancement is determined by his efficiency record." He then defended his departmental personnel, claiming that the individuals appointed had given "promise of fulfilling their duties most efficiently." [40] Concerning the age disparity of diplomats in each class, Kellogg claimed that the existing situation had arisen owing to the higher rate of resignations and the lower age at which diplomats entered their service before 1924.[41] Within a brief period, these two encounters raised the issue of the career diplomats' "disinterestedness," continued the agitation for some adjustment in promotions for consular officers, and succeeded in neutralizing one aspect of the Board's domain.

Criticism did not abate.[42] The rate of resignations in 1926, which equaled the extraordinary rate attained the previous year, consisted mainly of resigning consular officers.[43] And again some complaints were taken to Congress, for on January 11, 1927, Representative Edwards revived his interest in the question and requested the Department to send him the digest of the replies to Grew's inquiry.[44] On the thirteenth, Grew complied. The criticisms dealt primarily with various aspects of the law, such as annuity contributions, and generally ignored the more serious issues.[45] Nevertheless, presumably on sufficient evidence from members of the service, Edwards introduced on

[38] Edwards to Kellogg, June 16, 1926, in 120.1/114. The particular case involved Edward Cunningham's transfer from China.

[39] Kellogg to Edwards, July 7, 1926, in 120.1/114.

[40] 120.111/2, Departmental Order 378, June 16, 1926; Kellogg to Foreign Service personnel, July 21, 1926, in 120.111/1A.

[41] Kellogg to Foreign Service personnel, July 21, 1926, in 120.111/1A. The average age for consuls in class one was 55.2 years; it was 46.1 years for diplomats. A considerable disparity between the two was maintained throughout the classes. The average age for consuls in the unclassified category was 30.2 years; it was 27.5 years for diplomats in class eight.

[42] 120.1/116, Digest of Foreign Service officers comments, June, 1925 – January, 1927.

[43] The rate was 3.1 per cent annually. Excluding pre-1915 diplomats and post-1924 officers, consular officers made up 73.3 per cent of the resignations.

[44] Edwards to Kellogg, January 11, 1927, in 120.1/114.

[45] Grew to Edwards, January 13, 1927, in 120.1/116.

February 16 a resolution in the House calling on the Secretary of State to provide "certain information concerning the appointments" in the service.[46] His campaign was fortified by the sensational resignation of Lawrence Dennis from the service on March 3. Dennis publicly charged the Personnel Board with showing favoritism to those with "influence" and "possessing wealth" in assignments to "easy berths in over-staffed European missions."[47] This charge unleashed a small flood of press comment. One reporter claimed, "Grew and Wright are accused of being the heads of the inner circle of social diplomats which has set the well-to-do diplomats over the hard-working consul."[48] The *Magazine of Wall Street* referred to the Personnel Board as "the Harvard junta" and to the diplomats as "toast-pushing."[49]

Although Edwards' resolution was not passed, it accomplished much of what the consular officers wished. At a series of meetings of the Personnel Board, the career diplomats led a retreat from their interpretation of the Rogers Act. At first, they were unwilling to abandon the separate lists for promotions. But this decision was made for them by the Department's solicitor, who maintained that the practice was contrary to the Act.[50] On May 2, after re-examining all the records on the basis of relative efficiency, the Board unanimously decided that forty-four "reparation" promotions should be made.[51] Had they based this decision on proportional promotions, rather than relative efficiency, the Board would have had to authorize eighty-eight consular promotions. Fortunately, money existed to make the forty-four promotions and also to include a few diplomatic promotions as a face-saving device.[52] On June 21, 1927, Kellogg made the final expiation of the career diplomats' record by writing to Representative Porter of the Foreign Affairs Committee. He announced that twenty-eight of the promotions were to be made within the month. He then tried to explain the questioned situation on the grounds that the dual lists had been a temporary device until the efficiency records of the diplomats were as comprehensive as the records of the consular officers. This, of course, was an ex post facto rationalization of the events.[53] Finally, the career diplomats' control over the Board ended.

[46] *Cong. Rec.*, LXVIII, 69 Cong., 2 sess. (February 16, 1927), 4012.

[47] *New York Times*, March 3, 1927, p. 14.

[48] *Frederick* [Maryland] *News*, March 18, 1927 (quoted in Grew, *op. cit.*, I, 698–99).

[49] 120.1/140, *Magazine of Wall Street*, April 23, 1927.

[50] Grew to Lane, May 3, 1927, in Grew, *op. cit.*, I, 699.

[51] Kellogg to Porter, June 21, 1927, in 120.31/38.

[52] Grew to Lane, May 3, 1927, in Grew, *op. cit.*, I, 701.

[53] Kellogg to Porter, June 21, 1927, in 120.31/38. Such an explanation does not square with the public and private statements used in my argument. See particularly Grew to Skinner, October 25, 1925, in 120.1/151, and 120.1/74A, Departmental circular, July 29,

Wright, Wilson, and Grew were assigned to the field.[54] Although there were many mitigating considerations, it cannot but be supposed that the scandal over promotions entered into Kellogg's mind when he replaced Grew and Wright with two non-career men — R. E. Olds as Undersecretary and William R. Castle as Assistant Secretary. The Board's composition in the fall of 1927 included two non-career men, two consular officers, Carr, and one career diplomat.[55]

But Congress was not finished. It was as if the consular interpretation wished an "unconditional surrender" from the career diplomats. Grew wrote to Arthur Lane in May, 1927, "Many consuls, and possibly Congress, will feel that we have not gone far enough by way of reparations."[56] He was right. On December 17, 1927, Senator Pat Harrison of Mississippi introduced a resolution "to investigate the administration of the act for the reorganization and improvement of the Foreign Service."[57] In addition to criticisms on the paucity of consular promotions, the resolution was inspired by the elevation of Grew, Wright, and Wilson, all members of the Personnel Board, to the upper service. The three promotions, although no doubt could possibly be raised on their propriety, seemed to symbolize the diplomatic branch's profiting at the expense of the consular branch.[58]

The subcommittee appointed to investigate the service included Senators George H. Moses of New Hampshire, Harrison of Mississippi, and James A. Reed of Pennsylvania. The hearings were held *in camera*, and the testimony, some of which was given through correspondence, was not later printed. Apart from statements from Kellogg and Carr, the subcommittee found it "unavoidable that a considerable share of the testimony taken should be derived from men whose promotion has not been as rapid as they had expected."[59] This fact, when coupled with Grew's assertion that Kellogg's and Carr's statements were "largely ignored,"[60] makes the subcommittee's conclusions, which were printed on May 3, 1928, not at all surprising. In

1924. Nor does it square with Kellogg's own letter to the overseas personnel; see Kellogg to Foreign Service personnel, July 21, 1926, in 120.11/1A.

[54] *Biog. Reg.* (1927), *passim*. All three were elevated to ministerships and ambassadorships.

[55] *Biog. Reg.* (1928), pp. 21–66. The one representative of the career diplomats was G. Howland Shaw.

[56] Grew to Lane, May 3, 1927, in Grew, *op. cit.*, I, 701.

[57] *Cong. Rec.*, LXIX, 70 Cong., 1 sess. (December 17, 1927), 785 (Senate Resolution 76).

[58] Grew had already had an upper service post, while Wright and Wilson were two of the most able men in either service. Whoever served on the Personnel Board would have found it difficult not to appoint the three. Undersecretary Olds publicly exonerated them from any complicity in their appointments, see *New York Times*, January 31, 1928, p. 15.

[59] Senate Rept. 1069, 70 Cong., 1 sess. (May 3, 1928), p. 1–5.

[60] Grew, *op. cit.*, I, 702–3 (diary extract, dated September 7, 1931).

brief, the subcommittee "came early and unanimously to the opinion that the application of the [Rogers Act] had been approached in a manner far at variance from the purpose of the legislation."

The central assumption in the investigation was that "the Act itself did not contemplate the separation of the Foreign Service into branches." From this it was argued that the maintenance of the double list was unjust, and that forty-three diplomats had been consequently "improperly promoted." It was insinuated that the diplomatic officers had used various means to insure their favorable reclassification, that the diplomats had "secured for themselves so great a measure of its [the Act's] benefits," and, referring to the three upper service appointments, that there had been favoritism shown in these.[61] The last charge was made although the Department explicitly denied it.[62] The subcommittee's relevant recommendations, which were also embodied in a bill, included a separation of the handling of personnel matters from Foreign Service officers by establishing a distinct bureau of personnel. It also suggested the reduction of the Personnel Board to three Assistant Secretaries who were to be "wholly disconnected from the Foreign Service." [63]

In the light of evidence on the sincere misunderstanding of the Act by both career diplomats and the consular officers, the subcommittee's conclusions can be accepted as valid only in expressing how one party to the Act looked at its intentions and evaluated its administration. The subcommittee did not seek the diplomatic viewpoint. That the subcommittee knew that confusion was possible was recognized when it admitted a "feeling of settled distinction between those who were engaged in diplomatic functions and those who were engaged in the consular field." That there were difficulties involved in interchangeability was allowed when the report asserted, "complete fluidity cannot be wholly attained at any time."[64] If the subcommittee had followed its central assumption to its logical conclusion, it could not have maintained the impropriety of forty-three diplomatic promotions. Furthermore, the charges of favoritism are, from all evidence, false. Above all, the subcommittee was flogging a virtually dead horse. The previous year had seen, in almost every respect, the abandonment of the career diplomats' position.

Just or unjust, the report inspired a plethora of legislative pro-

[61] Senate Rept. 1069, 70 Cong., 1 sess. (May 3, 1928), pp. 2–4.
[62] *New York Times*, January 31, 1928, p. 15.
[63] Senate Rept. 1069, 70 Cong., 1 sess. (May 3, 1928), p. 5.
[64] *Ibid.*, pp. 3, 6.
[65] *Cong. Rec.*, LXIX, 70 Cong., 1 sess. (April 19, 1928 – May 8, 1928), 1417, 3405, 8163, 9135. The House bills included HR 9187, 11277, 13625, and 13883. The Senate bill was S 4382.

⁄ posals.[65] All of them sought "to take the control of promotions away from those who could be promoted." [66] Many of the bills contained stipulations prohibiting Foreign Service officers from serving on the Personnel Board or from being promoted, if allowed on the Board, to the upper service before three years. Some bills included requirements of a five-year service in consular posts before a promotion to class one. Representative Porter went so far as to limit the number of Foreign Service officers who could be in the Department at one time, hoping to create in their stead a "Home Service." [67] The session's brevity, however, prevented any concentrated effort on legislation.

The Department itself had gone some way toward meeting the criticisms stemming from Congress and the discontented consular officers. Dual commissions increased to forty-four in 1928, to sixty in 1929, and to seventy-nine in 1930. In its major posts, the Department had in 1926 eight career diplomats and four consular officers; in 1928 the representation was equal. From two consular officers in the upper service in 1926, the number rose to four in 1928 and to five in 1929.[68] Undersecretary Olds and Alexander Kirk acted while the hearings were in progress to eliminate the possibility of favoritism by prohibiting members of the Executive Committee of the Foreign Service Personnel Board from voting on assignments and transfers from the branches and "controversies and delinquencies among the service's personnel." The Board was also reconstituted to include the three Assistant Secretaries.[69] In response to the proposals in Congress, Kellogg established on August 8, 1928, an informal committee to make recommendations on legislation to improve the service. Of its nine members, only two were career diplomats.[70] A few days after the appointment of the informal committee the Secretary issued an order abolishing the Board of Review and giving the Personnel Board the job of ascertaining ratings.[71] This eliminated another "interested" group and fulfilled the Moses Report's conclusion that it was wrong to allow line personnel to peruse private personnel records.[72] On November 24, 1928, Kellogg's committee submitted its report, recommending the eradication of the division of the service into branches.[73]

[66] *Ibid.* (May 11, 1928), p. 8306 (speech by Senator Moses).
[67] *New York Times*, April 19, 1928, p. 12.
[68] *Biog. Reg.* (1926–30), *passim.*
[69] Executive Order 4815, February 25, 1928. Copy of Order in author's possession.
[70] "Foreign Service, Congressional, and Presidential Attitudes Toward Personnel Amalgamation After World Wars I and II," (Unpublished article; Historical Division, Department of State, April, 1954), p. 17. G. Howland Shaw and Alexander C. Kirk were the only career diplomats.
[71] Departmental Order 451, August 11, 1928. Copy in author's possession.
[72] Senate Rept. 1069, 70 Cong., 1 sess. (May 3, 1928), pp. 5–6.
[73] "Attitudes Toward Personnel Amalgamation," p. 17.

Finally, President Hoover issued an Executive Order on September 11, 1929, which delegated the power over promotions, assignments, and transfers to a Foreign Service Personnel Board consisting of the three Assistant Secretaries only. A division of Foreign Service Personnel, of whose three members "at least one shall be a Foreign Service officer of high rank," was charged with the routine functions of personnel management. The division's members had no authority in the work delegated to the Board.[74]

Nevertheless, Congress persisted in its attempt to end permanently any possibility of favoritism. Senator Moses' bill, which required a definite tenure in the consular branch and neutralized the Personnel Board, was reintroduced in the Seventy-first Congress. It was passed in the Senate, but failed in the House because of the confusion there over the large number of similar bills.[75] On May 22, 1930, Moses succeeded in attaching his bill as an amendment to Representative Linthicum of Maryland's bill creating a corps of Foreign Service clerical personnel.[76] In all of this the Department had been ignored. Moses justified this procedure on the ground that he did not "deem it to be of prime importance that we should have for a measure the approval of those who have maladministered a previous measure."[77] The Department, however, found some merit in the Moses' provisions and sought only to modify some of their rigid aspects.[78] In this the Department was successful.[79] The bill was passed, with Department support, on February 23, 1931.[80]

Although the Moses-Linthicum Act did not eradicate the provisions of the Rogers Act recognizing the two branches, it sought to prevent these divisions from being used advantageously by their members. To insure the neutrality of those determining transfers, assignments, and promotions, the law put on a statutory basis the Executive Order of September 11, 1929. It also limited personnel in the advisory division to Foreign Service officers of class one. They were further restricted by being prohibited from taking a ministerial or ambassadorial position before three years after their division tenure.[81] With the Act on the books, the process was, thus, nearly complete. The career diplomats'

[74] Executive Order 5189, September 11, 1929. Copy of Order in author's possession.

[75] *Cong. Rec.*, LXXI, 71 Cong., 1 sess. (April 18, 1929), 106; LXXII, 71 Cong., 2 sess. (June 11, 1930), 10483.

[76] *Cong. Rec.*, LXIX, 70 Cong., 1 sess. (May 14, 1928), HR 13745. Copy obtained from the Library of Congress. Subsequent versions did not change.

[77] *Cong. Rec.*, LXIX, 70 Cong., 1 sess. (May 11, 1928), 8306.

[78] J. P. Cotton to Moses, June 20, 1930, in 120/109B.

[79] 120.1/193, Memo to C. B. Hosmer, December 11, 1930. The "revised" bill eliminated Moses' restrictions on the Secretary's control of personnel.

[80] *Cong. Rec.*, LXXII, 71 Cong., 3 sess. (February 23, 1931), 5750.

[81] 46 Stat. 1207 (February 23, 1931).

interpretation of the Rogers Act, though sincerely arrived at and applied, was completely demolished. In its place was accepted the concept of a fused service with free interchangeability. The Personnel Board was neutralized, exposing it to possibly unsympathetic hands, but insuring the service members that improper considerations would not intrude on merit promotions.

From February 23, 1931, to 1939, the remaining barriers to fusion were destroyed. A single set of regulations for the Foreign Service was issued by Hoover on June 8, 1931.[82] Dual commissions only were issued after that same year.[83] For those who entered before 1931, the number of dual commissions steadily increased. By January 1, 1934, 42.3 per cent held commissions as both diplomatic secretaries and consular officers.[84] By 1939, less than 3 per cent did not possess dual commissions. In 1935, President Roosevelt wished that those who had only served in diplomatic capacities would serve a term at a consular post.[85] On April 24, 1935, Jay Pierrepont Moffat and Theodore B. Marriner, among others, received commissions as consuls general.[86] The number of upper service appointments for consuls also increased: six in 1933, ten in 1937, and eleven in 1939.[87] The proportions for the two branches in departmental posts constantly shifted, indicating that this ceased to be an important index.[88] Above all, the common training at the Foreign Service School and in consular posts made the schism a continuously diminishing factor. After 1934, Skinner observed, the only source of appointments for diplomatic posts was from the group which had consular training.[89] In addition, the amalgamation of the agricultural and commercial attachés in 1939, about which more will be said later, brought a large group to be assimilated into the service and obscured the earlier division.[90] Finally, the experience under the pitiless glare of congressional scrutiny would frighten any future administration of the service from pursuing any other approach.

The consular interpretation of the Rogers Act was never ques-

[82] Executive Order 5642, June 8, 1931. Copy of Order in author's possession.

[83] *Biog. Reg.* (1931), *passim.*

[84] Robert P. Skinner, "Ten Years Under the Rogers Act," *American Foreign Service Journal*, XL (July, 1934), 342. Percentage has not been checked by the author.

[85] Nancy Harvison Hooker (ed.), *The Moffat Papers — Selections from the Diplomatic Journal of Jay Pierrepont Moffat* (Harvard University Press, 1956), p. 125.

[86] *Biog. Reg.* (1935), p. 49.

[87] *Ibid.* (1933, 1937, 1939), *passim.*

[88] In 1928, there were six diplomats and six consular officers occupying important departmental posts. In 1931, there were four and five respectively. The ratio in 1933 was 5 to 3. In 1939, on the other hand, the consular officers outnumbered the diplomats seven to four. See *Biog. Reg.* (1928, 1931, 1933, 1939), *passim.*

[89] Skinner, *op. cit.*, p. 342.

[90] There were 105 commercial attachés and nine agricultural attachés.

tioned after 1931. This, however, does not mean that hostility between diplomats and consular officers ceased altogether. There is
subjective evidence aplenty to confirm that it did not.[91] But these
were prejudices that laws or administrative practice could not touch.
Furthermore, there continued to exist the assumptions that "a diplomatic assignment, no matter how low in grade, is more important
than a consular assignment," and that political reporting leads more
rapidly to promotion.[92] But these were judgments based on assignments open to all officers and not ones between watertight branches
of a service. Both situations fail to modify the conclusion that a unified
service had emerged.

No observer of the struggle between the career diplomats and the
consular officers could have failed to notice the *esprit de corps* the two
groups displayed for their respective branches. By recruitment and
promotion in career services, this identification had been nurtured
during the previous two decades. The period 1924–39 saw the same
techniques projected onto the Foreign Service.[93] For the new relationship, regardless of how it was finally resolved, was faced with the same
fundamental problems: how to attract qualified persons to the service
and how to sustain their interest once they were appointed. And
solutions to both depended largely on the service's ability to convince
the public and its own officers that it was a worthwhile lifetime
career.

Success in this project depended partly on the service's maintaining
the principle of controlled entry into its ranks. Exposing officers to
continuous injections of new personnel at any point in the hierarchy
was antithetical to the career concept and harmful to morale. Recognizing this, the Rogers Act formally stipulated that all new officers
would enter the lowest class after passing an examination. The Executive Order of June 7, 1924, established a Board of Foreign Service
Examiners whose job it was "to formulate rules for and hold examinations . . . and to determine from among the persons designated by
the President for examination those who are fitted for appointments."
On the other issues of recruitment, both the Act and the Order were

[91] E.g., Donald Dunham, *Envoy Unextraordinary* (New York: John Day, 1944),
p. 21; G. Howland Shaw, "The American Foreign Service," *Foreign Affairs*, XIV (January, 1936), 328; Robert Buell, "Class of 1925," *American Foreign Service Journal*, XXVII
(December, 1951), 26.

[92] Messersmith to Bundy, November 23, 1932, in 120/144.

[93] There exists no adequate work on the professionalization phase of the development
of the Consular Service for the period 1907–24. Brief references to it will be made in
this study when relevant. For a popular but useful summary of some aspects of the
Consular Service's development, see Tracy Lay, *The Foreign Service of the United
States* (New York, 1925), *passim*.

sketchy. The Order laid down the vague criteria that a candidate was "to be of good character and habits and physically, mentally, and tempermentally qualified for the proper performance of the duties of the Foreign Service." The mental qualifications were bound up with the scope of the examination, and this will be discussed later. Otherwise, aside from a required 80 per cent to pass the combined written and oral examination and the age limits of 21–35 for candidates, the Board of Examiners was free to improvise and develop techniques of recruitment. Fortunately, both parties to the Rogers Act could contribute from their store of experience.[94]

Although often subordinated to larger questions, the premise upon which these improvisations were based was that a greater number of candidates would produce better qualified appointments. To insure a wide public notification of the examinations, the Board immediately agreed to continue the publicity methods used before the Rogers Act.[95] Acting on the same premise, the Board also decided on December 12, 1924, that the examinations should thereafter be held in the thirteen Civil Service centers across the nation.[96] The problems involved in the first two examinations prevented their being administered outside of Washington.[97] After October 3, 1925, however, all written examinations were held in the Civil Service districts.[98]

Two other important factors were the number of examinations held each year and the dates on which they were held. Entering into both were many variables: number of candidates, the schedules of academic institutions, the demands on the Department's personnel, and economy. The Diplomatic Service by 1920 had practically adopted the system of annual examinations, while the Consular Service was moving steadily in the same direction. When it became necessary to set a combined examination, the Board was unsure how frequently to hold them. The number of candidates at the first examination exceeded all expectations. Over three hundred appeared to take the examination.[99] With the second examination's total confirming the first's, the Board agreed in 1926 to hold annual examinations.[100] This system, however, broke down in December, 1928, when the number of competitors fell sharply.[101] The number remained low, forcing the

[94] Executive Order of June 7, 1924. Copy in author's possession.

[95] Minutes (January, 1925). See Ellery C. Stowell, "Examinations for the American Foreign Service," *American Journal of International Law*, XXIV (July, 1930), 579.

[96] Minutes (January, 1925). Memo is dated December 12, 1922. Carr is its author.

[97] Minutes (January, 1925–July, 1925), Memo, March 18, 1925.

[98] 120.11/22, Minutes of the Board of Examiners: Board of Foreign Service Personnel, October 3, 1925.

[99] Carr to Wright, December 12, 1924, in Minutes (January, 1925).

[100] Carr to Wright, March 18, 1925, in Minutes (July, 1925); E. A. Shreve to E. J. Norton, November 16, 1927, in 120.1121/42.

[101] Minutes (January, 1928–December, 1928). The number dropped from 219 to 164.

Board to give examinations whenever "practicable." [102] There was usually an examination offered every six months.[103]

By January, 1931, the decline was effectively over and the number of candidates began increasing: 181 in January; 233 in July, 1931; 277 in January, 1932; and 455 in September, 1932.[104] This steady rise led Joseph C. Green, who then had charge of examinations, to recommend to Carr that annual examinations be restored. He thought "a considerable saving would result in time, energy, and money." [105] While Carr agreed with Green's reasoning, he hesitated to commit himself on the question.[106] Owing to the suspension of examinations on May 12, 1933, for economy reasons, a decision was postponed until after September 26, 1935. When the following May's examination continued the early trend, the Board announced on November 12, 1936, that annual examinations were again to be held.[107]

On the exact timing of the examination similar experimentation took place. The two problems, in fact, were interlocked. A decision to hold a supplementary examination in six months' time determined, willy-nilly, the second examination's date. But the period saw certain considerations made which kept career development in mind. It was early decided that January was the best month in which to hold the examination.[108] This decision was made "because of the desire to hold the Foreign Service School in October, to avoid the heat, and to permit a six months' notice before being ordered to Washington." [109] Although considering the candidates' comfort, January did not easily accommodate itself to the undergraduate seeking to move into the service immediately as a career. Professors Pitman Potter and Ellery C. Stowell criticized the Department on this score, but Carr replied that the candidates were not all recent graduates.[110] Still, the Department was forced to recognize the importance of not conflicting with university examinations. The reason given for the paucity of candidates in the June, 1929, examination was the date's conflict with university examinations.[111] And the 1930 examination, which was originally to be held in June, was rescheduled for July.[112] The return to annual examinations raised the issue a final time. The decision to

[102] Carr to Foreign Service officers, February 24, 1930, in 120.1121/50A.
[103] December, 1928; June, 1929; December, 1929; July, 1930; January, 1931; July, 1931.
[104] Minutes (January, 1931–September, 1932).
[105] Green to Carr, July 19, 1932, in 120.11/22.
[106] Carr to Green, July 23, 1932, in 120.11/22.
[107] 120.1121/114A, R. Walton Moore memo, May 6, 1936. There were 726 candidates. See Minutes (May, 1936). See also *New York Times*, November 13, 1936, p. 3.
[108] E. A. Shreve to E. J. Norton, November 16, 1927, in 120.1121/42.
[109] Carr to Potter, December 1, 1927, in 120.1121/41.
[110] *Ibid.*
[111] Minutes (December, 1929), Memo by Carr, July 25, 1929.
[112] Garland to Carr, February 14, 1930, in Minutes (July, 1930).

hold the 1935 examination in May resulted in several conflicts.[113] Although the examination was held as scheduled, the Board announced that the following examinations would all be held in September.[114] Between this problem and that of annual examinations, two principles were recognized. The career concept required an intake of personnel at specific predictable times, not whenever people were needed. Second, the service had to gear its timing to accommodate the group from which it was increasingly drawing — the recent university graduate.

The type of knowledge needed in the examination, as opposed to its subject content, was another area of experimentation. In addition to the two-day examination schedule of seven hours each day, the service inherited from its predecessors a heavy emphasis on short-answer questions. For these memory, far more than understanding, was required. Consequently, the problem of the "cram-school" was also inherited. Between 1925 and 1931, the problem became increasingly obvious. Of the successful candidates in that period 51.6 per cent had attended Agnus Crawford's school alone.[115] And it has been estimated that Crawford had had about 90 per cent success with his pupils.[116]

Members of the Department and the service's friends deplored the situation. Ellery Stowell claimed, "It now remains to improve the nature of the written examination." [117] Undersecretary Cotton thought the cramming system "neither necessary nor desirable and is unjust." [118] On January 8, 1931, Secretary Stimson retained Joseph C. Green of the Division of Western European Affairs and charged him, along with his Committee of Revision, with investigating the the examination system in "an attempt to demand knowledge . . . rather than useless statistics obtained by cramming." Stimson added that it would be desirable to "develop a type of examination suitable for a recent university graduate rather than for a commercial expert." [119]

The Committee compared the systems used by other nations and

[113] Green to Carr, March 17, 1936, in 120.1121/30. The date made it particularly difficult to obtain examiners.

[114] *New York Times*, November 13, 1936, p. 3.

[115] 120.11/22, Data for Committee on Revision of the Foreign Service Examination, June 2, 1931.

[116] Interview with the Honorable Donald W. Richardson of the Board of Foreign Service Examiners, July 28, 1957.

[117] Ellery C. Stowell, "The Moses-Linthicum Act and the Foreign Service," *American Journal of International Law*, XXV (July, 1931), 517.

[118] Cotton to Carr, November 20, 1930, in 120.11/22.

[119] Stimson to Green, January 8, 1931, in 120.11/22. See also Green to Stimson, March 2, 1931, in 120.112/15. Green's committee included: John V. A. MacMurray, George Grafton Wilson, Edward L. Thorndike, and L. L. Thurstone.

by commercial organizations and sought testimony from successful recent candidates. On May 11, 1931, the Committee submitted its report to Stimson. Their suggested modifications "would result, we believe, in a more careful measurement of the educational background and intellectual capacity of the candidates." The examination period was extended to three days to facilitate, among other things, "the introduction of certain types of questions which require a longer period in which to write a satisfactory answer." [120] The examination was designed to test the intelligence of the candidates, not their memories.

The report was accepted on August 6, 1931.[121] The Committee was then charged with compiling an examination that embodied the recommendations.[122] In January, 1932, the new examination was given to 181 candidates.[123] A rough analysis of the examination was made the following September, after which Green recommended that four more examinations be held before an exhaustive evaluation should be undertaken.[124] In the interim, however, the Committee on Revision continued to offer suggestions, and these were supplemented by comments from members of various faculties and "distinguished citizens." [125] On September 20, 1937, the Board of Foreign Service Personnel agreed that an exhaustive analysis of the system undertaken by an "expert" was in order.[126] This was completed and accepted in February, 1939. The basic format of the 1931 revision, however, was untouched. An increased emphasis was placed on mathematical reasoning and understanding a foreign language. The examination was also extended to a fourth day, and a revised procedure for orals was established.[127]

Both revisions failed to eliminate the "cram-schools." But the schools did have to change their methods to fit the new examinations. Instead of drilling facts, the schools concentrated on teaching "with a view to filling in the gaps in the knowledge of particular candi-

[120] 120.1121/83, Report of the Committee to Study the System of Examinations, May 11, 1931, pp. 1–3.

[121] Castle to George Grafton Wilson, August 6, 1931, in 120.112/26A.

[122] Board of Examiners to Committee on Revision, July 27, 1932, in 120.11/22.

[123] Minutes (January, 1932).

[124] Green to Carr, September 12, 1932, *ibid.*

[125] Green to Nathaniel B. Davis, May 3, 1945 in 120.1121/5–345; Green to members of various faculties and "distinguished citizens," September 14, 1937, in 120.11/22.

[126] Messersmith to Green, September 20, 1937, in 120.1121/139. Carl Bingham of Princeton was appointed, Green insisting that he was "the best man in the country to undertake the analysis."

[127] Green to members of the Committee on Revision, February 21, 1939, in 120.11/22; 120.1121/152, Report of the Committee on Revision, February 6, 1939; 120.1121/158, Bingham's analysis, April 6, 1939.

dates."[128] Between 1932 and 1937, the Turner Diplomatic School claimed that 38 per cent of the successful candidates had had its instruction.[129] A second school was operating simultaneously in Washington, and it has been estimated that 50 per cent of the successful candidates had attended one of the two.[130] The institutions were known to the Board of Examiners, and there was a measure of contact between them and the Department.[131]

After the Rogers Act, the oral examination continued in importance. Although no attempt was made, because of cost and time, to make it geographically more convenient for candidates to take it, the oral was nevertheless the object of continued experimentation. On the assumption that the written examination, owing to its stress on memory, eliminated many competent candidates, the Board decided in 1925 to invite to the oral all those who had received between 60 and 75 per cent on their written parts.[132] This made a substantial difference in terms of numbers. A memo of April 28, 1927, claimed, "88 candidates have already notified the Department that they intend to present themselves for orals . . . it is possible that we may have over a hundred." Only 201 took the written examination.[133] Once the new examination system was installed, however, the minimum grade for an oral interview was raised to sixty-five.[134] As confidence grew on the new examination, the passing average was raised to seventy.[135]

There were also experiments made on its timing and conduct. For the first few examinations, the oral was held between three and four months after the written part and during a single period. When the annual examination was abandoned, the Board began holding the orals at fixed times every other month.[136] This often resulted in the cancellation of individual sessions and much confusion.[137] In 1936, when annual examinations were restored, the orals followed them at four- to five-month intervals and during concentrated periods.[138] With regard to their conduct, the orals' criteria and procedure were all

[128] Hon. Joseph C. Green to the author, October 30, 1957.

[129] 120.11/22, Brochure from Turner's Diplomatic School, 1938.

[130] The second school was operated by Franklin Roudybush (see Franklin Roudybush, "Foreign Service Training" [Unpublished monograph; Washington: George Washington University, 1945]). Estimate by Hon. Donald W. Richardson of the Board of Foreign Service Examiners in interview with author, July 28, 1957.

[131] Colonel Cambell Turner to Board of Examiners, September 23, 1939, in 120.1121/164.

[132] Board of Examiners to Board of Foreign Service Personnel, October 3, 1925, in 120.11/22.

[133] Minutes (February, 1927), Memo from Shreve to Grew, April 28, 1927.

[134] Green to Carr, May 18, 1932, in 120.1121/79.

[135] Green to Carr, April 14, 1933, in 120.1121/105.

[136] 120.1121/62, Examination Regulations of 1931, December 8, 1930.

[137] E.g., Carr to press, April 7, 1932, in 120.1121/78.

[138] Minutes (May, 1936–September, 1939).

inherited from previous practice. By 1929, however, the system of panel interviews had given way to one in which each candidate was individually interviewed by an examiner.[139] The criteria also changed. In 1939, the revision of the examination system resulted in the redefining of the personality categories.[140]

The vast majority of Foreign Service officers entered the career after passing an examination. The solicitude which the service showed every detail of the examination underlines its importance throughout the period.[141] There were, however, two major exceptions to the principle of entry by examination. A third exception, which permitted transfers from the Department "after five years of continuous service," was immediately so rigidly circumscribed by orders and departmental circulars that it was used only seldom.[142] Qualifications must even be made about one of the major exceptions. Although used frequently, it never completely departed from the examination principle. Part of the Moses-Linthicum Act of 1931 created a corps of Foreign Service clerks. To provide an incentive for them, the law allowed clerks with five years' continuous service to be exempt from taking the written part of the Foreign Service examination. The law also extended the Foreign Service age limits to forty-five for this group.[143] The service had not opposed the Act, and the Department had always made it convenient for clerks to take the examination.[144] Besides, the career was protected by a clause in the Act which required an individual review of each clerk-candidate by the Board of Foreign Service Personnel.[145] And in its operation the exception did not mean that preferential treatment was shown to clerks on the oral as well. Carr complained in a memo:

> The members of the Examining Board have been astonished at the lack of preparation displayed by these candi-

[139] *American Foreign Service Journal*, XVI (April, 1939), 230.

[140] 120.1121/158, Professor Bingham's analysis, April 6, 1939. The four areas for judgment were: appearance, manner, and adaptability; diction, readiness, clarity, and precision in oral expression; forcefulness, earnestness, effectiveness of personality; initiative, imagination, elasticity, and resourcefulness.

[141] E.g., Messersmith to Shaw, July 7, 1938, in 120.11/22: "As you know, it is my very real conviction that we must give this matter of the examination . . . our very careful thought to the end that the examination may give us the very best material we can get in this country for the Foreign Service."

[142] 43 Stat. 104, Executive Order 4022, June 7, 1924 (copy in author's possession). See also 120.1/74A, Departmental circular, July 29, 1924. The former made transfer dependent upon the recommendation of the Board of Foreign Service Personnel, while the latter stated, as a general policy, that "indiscriminate transfers . . . clearly would not be in the interests of the Government or of the officers themselves."

[143] 46 Stat. 1207 (February 23, 1931).

[144] E.g., Carr to overseas clerical personnel, September 24, 1927, in 120.1121/52.

[145] 46 Stat. 1207 (February 23, 1931).

dates as a group and consider it advisable to explain that in waiving the written examination it does not follow that requirements as to education, general knowledge and breadth, personality and suitability for the Service are also waived.

The particular occasion in question saw thirty-two out of forty clerks fail to pass the oral examination. Thereafter, clerks had to accompany their applications with a statement of preparation.[146] Furthermore, only two or three entered the service annually in this fashion, and they entered the unclassified grade. Not only was the career principle unviolated by this exception, but it must also be stated that some observers believed "many of the best officers in the career entered in this way. . . ." [147]

The second major exception to the principle of entry by examination occurred in 1939. Through the Reorganization Act of that year, 105 overseas officers from the Department of Commerce and nine from the Department of Agriculture were co-opted into the Foreign Service at all levels.[148] This move appears on the surface to betray the career concept. Many qualifications, however, must again be made. The movement was initiated by Foreign Service officers, not by the Department of Commerce. The co-optation was aimed at ending an administrative anomaly, which had had a bad effect on the service's morale, and establishing a unity of command overseas. Furthermore, both groups had been organized along career lines, and their members had entered by examinations. The positions they occupied were also incorporated, and it was assumed that they would continue holding them. While some officers objected to introducing specialists into the service, the evidence also indicates that the new arrangement was one desired by most career officers.[149] Thus, even the two major exceptions to the examination principle did not operate in a way to harm the career concept.

In addition to entrance by examination, the principle of rewarding merit, usually through promotions, was important to the service's continued professionalization. The period 1924–39 saw distinct progress in the direction of improving categories of evaluation, of developing means of acknowledging merit, and of purging the service of its less efficient members. Of central importance in these were the

[146] Carr to Foreign Service personnel, March 13, 1937, in 120.1121/131A.
[147] *American Foreign Service Journal*, XIV (December, 1937), 719.
[148] 53 Stat. 1431 (April 24, 1939).
[149] American Assembly, *The Representation of the United States Abroad* (Harriman, New York: Arden House, 1956), p. 16; interviews conducted by author between July 28, 1957, and September 2, 1957.

efficiency records of all officers. Initially, these records were based on comments by superior officers, but these comments were later translated into individual ratings, at two-year intervals, by a board of review and later by the Division of Foreign Service Personnel.[150] The Executive Order of June 7, 1924, went into no detail about the ratings, assuming as it did that the two sets of efficiency records were not reducible to a single standard. Promotions were governed by the clause which directed the Personnel Board "to submit lists of those Foreign Service officers whose records of efficiency entitle them to advancement in the service. . . ."[151] After the misunderstanding over the Rogers Act, the Executive Order of June 8, 1931, elaborated a single standard for the entire service. Thereafter men who were appraised as "excellent," "very good," "satisfactory" or above, were eligible for promotion.[152] These new categories were strengthened by hinging merit rewards to them. By the Moses-Linthicum Act, an annual increment of $100 for classes five through eight and $200 for classes one through four was authorized for those rated "satisfactory" or above. "Extraordinary or conspicuously meritorious service" could, in addition, be rewarded by the Secretary.[153]

An incentive of a reverse sort was the possibility of being involuntarily separated from the service for a low efficiency rating. This was first recognized in the reclassification clause of the Rogers Act. By it the Secretary of State could recommend a reduction in rank for the officer or even dismissal from the service.[154] On June 30, 1924, Grew wrote to Phillips:

> A good many dead boughs have been separated from the Service through age retirement and the abolition of the unassigned list, while other men have been demoted and have been clearly given to understand that their cases will be further dealt with in the near future.[155]

Under the Rogers Act stipulation, eight diplomatic secretaries and thirteen consular officers were demoted.[156] The entire process was viewed by the *New York Times* as proving that "the Foreign Service constitutes a profession in the same sense as the army and navy." [157]

---

[150] Executive Order 4022, June 7, 1924; Executive Order 5189, September 11, 1929. Copies in author's possession.

[151] Executive Order 4022, June 7, 1924, p. 1.

[152] Executive Order 5642, June 8, 1931. Copy in author's possession.

[153] 46 Stat. 1207 (February 23, 1931).

[154] 43 Stat. 140 (May 24, 1924).

[155] Grew to Phillips, June 30, 1924, in Grew, *op. cit.*, I, 626.

[156] *Good Government*, LI (October, 1924), 145.

[157] Editorial, *New York Times*, July 3, 1924, p. 20.

Further eliminations were authorized by the Executive Order of June 7, 1924. The Order allowed the "separation from the service" of any officer whose efficiency rating was "below the required standard for the Service." A probationary period was also provided.[158] An officer so separated from the service was given only 75 per cent of his annuity payments.[159] The Moses-Linthicum Act stiffened the standard and sought to modify some of its hardships. A continued rating of unsatisfactory, after a notice and a hearing, made a man liable for separation. Depending on the officer's tenure, various financial adjustments were also authorized. These adjustments mitigated much of the hardship surrounding this action and permitted the service to judge its members more critically.[160] A final safeguard was included in the Executive Order for June 8, 1931. It required that an opportunity for reply be given any officer who had received an adverse rating.[161]

How often these provisions were used cannot be known. Personnel records are closed, and the possibility of voluntary resignation before being involuntarily separated was probably used in many instances. Thus, no accurate evidence can be shown. It can probably be assumed that a large number of below standard officers were dropped during Stimson's economy drive. It has also been claimed that Secretary Hull between 1936 and 1939 eliminated "forty or fifty persons from the lower ranks of the Service" for inefficiency.[162] However, if only for their existence, the clauses dealing with involuntary separation served as a spur to efficiency.

The chief incentive for efficiency, and certainly the most encouraging factor for potential candidates, was the number of career appointments made to the upper service and to important posts in the Department. The Rogers Act and all subsequent Orders directed the Secretary of State to submit to the President the names of those who "have demonstrated special capacity for promotion to the grade of Minister." [163] The period did not see the upper service entirely in the hands of career men, but it did see an increasing reliance upon them.

[158] Executive Order 4022, June 7, 1924, p. 2. The period, however, was not a specific length of time.

[159] 43 Stat. 140 (May 24, 1924).

[160] 46 Stat. 1207 (February 23, 1931). If the officer were over forty-five and had ten years of service, he received a pension equivalent to 25 per cent of his salary. If under forty-five, and with less than ten years of service, he was returned his annuity payments and was given a year's salary.

[161] Executive Order 5642, June 8, 1931, p. 6.

[162] August C. Miller, Jr., "The New State Department," *American Journal of International Law*, XXXIII (July, 1939), 505.

[163] 43 Stat. 140 (May 24, 1924); Executive Order 4022, June 7, 1924, p. 1; Executive Order 5189, September 11, 1929.

The continuance of the mixed system inspired Grew to say in 1927, "For the present we must rely upon the application of Napoleon's principle that every private carried a field marshal's baton in his knapsack. . . ." [164] The career appointments to the upper service served this purpose.

Every administration and its Secretary of State in the period advanced the cause of professional diplomacy. Hughes's record has already been discussed. When he resigned in 1925, nearly 40 per cent of all upper service posts, including a third of the ambassadorships, and the major offices in the Department were held by career men. [165] Hughes had always been sympathetic to the interests of the service and sought, when the time was appropriate, to advance them. Before leaving his office, Hughes wrote to Coolidge: "I assume . . . you will wish to give appropriate recognition to the officers of the Foreign Service, as it is only by offering reasonable opportunity for promotions . . . that the esprit de corps can be maintained." [166]

In President Coolidge, the Foreign Service had neither friend nor foe. Fortunately, Coolidge's provincialism led him to rely completely for foreign affairs on his Secretaries of State. Officers complained that the President had not "a clear comprehension of what we are trying to accomplish with the Foreign Service," but their fortunes rested mainly with Hughes and later with Secretary Kellogg. [167] In the latter's hands, the service was safe. When Hughes resigned, he reassured Grew that Kellogg, who was called to his position from the ambassadorship to Britain, was "in close touch with foreign affairs and also with the Foreign Service." [168] This fact Kellogg publicly affirmed on April 25, 1925. [169]

Throughout his first year, Kellogg retained the position under Hughes. Grew warned him in 1926 that the morale of the service would suffer unless the number and desirability of posts for career men increased. He added that an increase would provide an "incentive to the best young men of the country." [170] Kellogg heeded Grew's advice and began rewarding career men with upper service posts. Of the twenty-five appointments made under Coolidge, fifteen were career men. In 1927, 45.1 per cent of the posts were held by pro-

[164] Joseph C. Grew, "Letter to the American Foreign Service Journal," *American Foreign Service Journal*, IV (March, 1927), 94.
[165] "Hughes' Record in the Foreign Service," *ibid.*, II (March, 1925), 100; *Biog. Reg.* (1926), pp. 16–56.
[166] Hughes to Coolidge, February 18, 1925, in 120.31/14A.
[167] Grew to Kellogg, November 29, 1926, in Grew, *Turbulent Era*, I, 688.
[168] *Ibid.*, p. 645 (diary extract, January 10, 1925).
[169] "Kellogg's Pledge," *American Foreign Service Journal*, II (April, 1925), 110.
[170] Grew to Kellogg, November 29, 1926, in Grew, *Turbulent Era*, I, 687.

fessionals. Over a third of the ambassadorships were in career hands. The ratio between career and non-career appointments reached fifty-fifty by 1928. Similarly, the important posts in the Department were retained by Foreign Service officers. Even after the schism over the Rogers Act's intentions, two of the three Assistant Secretaries were career men. Between eight and nine career officers continuously manned the more important divisions within the Department.[171]

Coolidge's successor, Herbert Hoover, and his Secretary of State, Henry Stimson, sustained the career's progress. Before his inauguration, Hoover was convinced that, particularly in Latin America, career men were preferable to political appointments. Part of his program for improving Latin American relations included appointing career men to this area.[172] Before Hoover left office, eighteen out of the nineteen Latin American posts were filled by career men.[173] And with this Stimson was in agreement. He was even interested enough in the morale of the service to visit many of the missions.[174] The *New York Herald Tribune* thought that the Secretary was particularly praiseworthy for "the attention he has given to the problems of attracting and rewarding career men." [175] In 1932, 51 per cent of the upper service posts, including nearly half of the ambassadorships, were held by professionals. The Department had one career man as Assistant Secretary and eight professionals in other important posts.[176]

The career position did not change greatly under Roosevelt and Hull. Much has been made about the President's distrust of the Foreign Service. Yet, even the authority for this belief, Langer and Gleason's *Challenge to Isolation*, specifically qualified it by insisting, "It would in fact be a mistake to underline the President's suspicion." [177] In any event, the President's preoccupation with domestic affairs, at least until 1937, left Secretary Hull in charge of foreign policy and gave him a strong voice in the appointment of ambassadors and ministers.[178] Although Assistant Secretary Raymond Moley briefly menaced the career officers, the new administration had early decided upon a rough balance between career and non-career appointments.[179]

---

[171] *Biog. Reg.* (1925–29) *passim*. Francis White and Nelson T. Johnson were Assistant Secretaries of State.

[172] Herbert Hoover, *Memoirs of Herbert Hoover* (London: Hollis & Carter, 1952), II, 332.

[173] *Biog. Reg.* (1931), pp. 20–59.

[174] 120.1/202, transcript of press conference, September 12, 1931. For line reaction to Stimson, see Culbertson to Stimson, April 15, 1931, in 120.1/94.

[175] Editorial, *New York Herald Tribune*, June 13, 1931.

[176] *Biog. Reg.* (1932), pp. 20–59. Francis White was the career officer as Assistant Secretary of State.

[177] William L. Langer and S. Everett Gleason, *Challenge to Isolation* (New York: Harper's, 1952), pp. 8–9.

This was decided because of "the terribly complicated international situation" and was sustained by the diplomatic side of economic recovery.[180] The first set of appointments gave a slight edge to political appointees, but career men figured prominently among departmental personnel. William Phillips was Undersecretary; Carr and Jefferson Caffery were Assistant Secretaries; and five career men headed divisions in the Department.[181]

In the second term, the career position was advanced. The Undersecretary and two of the Assistant Secretaries in 1937 were career men.[182] Sumner Welles, the Undersecretary, was particularly close to Roosevelt and encouraged him to appoint professionals.[183] Career men occupied nearly 52 per cent of the upper service posts in 1937. Two years later the proportion had increased to 54 per cent. Over 60 per cent of the ambassadorships in 1939 were in career hands. Furthermore, these appointments were to some of the most important missions. Although Paris, London, and Moscow were manned by non-career men, Tokyo, Rome, and Berlin in 1939 had professionals in charge.[184]

Of greater importance than increasing numbers was the fact that career men were retained from administration to administration, irrespective of the party in power. A career man commissioned under Hoover was retained, without being recommissioned, by Roosevelt. Only one career man in the period was dropped, and his case involved personal, not political, animosities.[185] Nevertheless, it must not be assumed that politics played no role in career promotions. Senator Jesse Metcalf, for instance, intervened on behalf of Peter A. Jay's appointment.[186]

A final point must be raised in this regard. If it was assumed that the Foreign Service was non-partisan, was it necessary for career officers in the upper service to submit, along with the political appointees, their resignations to each new President? No concrete answer can be given. In this, as in much administrative practice, considerable

[178] *Ibid.*, p. 2; Cordell Hull, *The Memoirs of Cordell Hull* (London: Hodder & Stoughton, 1948), I, 194.

[179] Hooker, *op. cit.*, p. 90; Hull, *op. cit.*, I, 181.

[180] Hull, *op. cit.*, p. 161; "Roosevelt's Foreign Policy," *American Foreign Service Journal*, XIII (January, 1936), 19.

[181] *Biog. Reg.* (1933), pp. 24–63. Twenty-seven were non-career; twenty-six were career.

[182] *Ibid.* (1937), pp. 26–67. Sumner Welles was Undersecretary, and Hugh Wilson and George S. Messersmith were Assistant Secretaries.

[183] "Career Diplomats Boosted," *New York Times*, July 18, 1937, Sec. 4, p. 7.

[184] *Biog. Reg.* (1937–39), *passim*. Grew was in charge of Tokyo; Phillips, Rome; and Wilson, Berlin.

[185] Hull, *op. cit.*, I, 183. Hugh Gibson was forced to resign. The main reason was his intimate relationship with Hoover.

[186] Grew, *Turbulent Era*, I, 655 (diary extract, March 15, 1925).

confusion reigned. The Harding episode by no means settled the question. When Coolidge was elected in his own right, he sought the opinion of Hughes. The Secretary replied: "It is the practice of dip-lomatic officers, *other than men of career*, to submit their resignations at the close of an administration and, aside from this, the resigna-tions of all diplomatic officers are always at your command." [187] This would appear to settle it. No career man was recommissioned in 1925 for the same post; all retained their earlier commissions.[188] On the other hand, if this had become settled practice, there would not have been the controversy in the press which arose on this issue at the begin-ning of Hoover's tenure. In the *New York Times* on October 7, 1928, a statement appeared to the effect that twenty-two career ministers were contemplating withholding their resignations.[189] The press then accorded the topic wide coverage, implying throughout that this was a new departure in administration.[190] Nevertheless, external evidence indicates that no resignations were submitted, for the commission dates were unchanged from the 1928 *Register*.[191] Again, under Roose-velt, the same controversy arose. J. V. A. MacMurray, former career minister to China, complained about the custom of proffering resig-nations whenever there was a change of President.[192] This complaint, however, even when coupled with evidence of Grew's resignation, is contradicted by the fact that the commissions were not changed in 1933.[193] Although evidence supports both sides, it can probably be concluded, in the absence of access to the personnel files, that it was common for career ministers and ambassadors both to submit and withhold their resignations. In either case, a formal resignation was supererogatory. To replace an appointment, the President needed only to appoint a successor. No President in the period was inclined to do this.

It was also important to the career concept that the service was kept free from favoritism and partisanship. As has been seen, confi-dence was badly shaken over the question of interchangeability. It was, however, restored with the various reparation appointments and adjustments in the Personnel Board. Generally, the Department was very solicitous about allaying fears on these issues. An early fear that

[187] Hughes to Coolidge, February 18, 1925, in 120.31/14A (emphasis by author).

[188] *Biog. Reg.* (1926), pp. 16–56.

[189] *New York Times*, October 7, 1928, p. 3.

[190] See *Literary Digest*, XCIX (November 3, 1928), 14; *Good Government*, XLVI (Jan-uary, 1929), 7.

[191] *Biog. Reg.* (1928), pp. 21–66; (1929), pp. 21–69.

[192] *American Foreign Service Journal*, X (February, 1933), 79–80.

[193] Joseph C. Grew, *Ten Years in Japan* (London: Hammond, 1944), p. 80; *Biog. Reg.* (1933), pp. 24–63. See also *Washington Post*, July 13, 1933 (quoted in *American Foreign Service Journal*, X [August, 1933], 265).

"designation after application" would facilitate partisan considerations proved unfounded. In 1931, Wilbur Carr publicly stated, ". . . the permission is granted as a matter of course to candidates who appear to have had the necessary educational training." [194] No assertion could have been made about the written examinations. They were marked partly by the Civil Service Commission and partly by independent examiners. The candidates were known by numbers, and the Board took fantastic security precautions to prevent any early leakage.[195] To a charge that partisan considerations entered into the oral evaluation, Grew replied that all judgments were made "without respect to the candidate's social or political affiliations." [196] When economy measures prevented the appointment of forty-one certified candidates, a major reason for issuing an Executive Order extending their eligibility was that dropping them might imply that "the action had been prompted by partisan motives." [197] And charges of nepotism were easily countered in 1933 by the fact that there were in the service only five sons of Foreign Service officers, three cousins, and two brothers. Another eleven had acquired kinship through marriage — usually after entrance to the service.[198] Finally, all available evidence suggests that the individual members honored their neutrality. Grew, for instance, refused to aid in drafting the Republican party's foreign policy plank in 1924 because of his "Service status." When a member of the service was found contributing money to a political campaign, the Undersecretary rebuked him, claiming;

> Such a step as you are reported to have taken therefore not only may impair your own future usefulness but it leaves the whole Service open to the charge that while enjoying the advantages of civil service principles, its members are nevertheless unwilling to undertake civil service obligations.[199]

Despite these many advances in professionalization, there existed many facets of administration that were sources of discouragement to career men. Because most of them dealt with less publicized or unpublicized parts of administration, they tended to discourage the appointed and not the aspirant. It is true that both could perhaps

[194] "University Training for the Foreign Service," in *Report of the Conference on University Training for the National Service* (Minnesota, 1932), pp. 150–51.
[195] 120.1121/26–33, Memoranda surrounding annulled examination of January 10, 1927. Thereafter, a minute by minute record was kept of the whereabouts of the examination.
[196] Grew to correspondent to Department, January 11, 1926, in 120.11/22.
[197] 120.1121/114A, Wilson memo, September 23, 1935.
[198] Committee on Appropriations, *Hearings on Foreign Service Appropriations for 1935*, 73 Cong., 2 sess. (December 5, 1933), p. 84.
[199] Grew, *Turbulent Era*, I, 618, 683–84.

despair over the policy of appointing non-career men to many upper service posts, but only the impatient could not welcome the continuously improving position of the service in this regard. A chief source of internal discouragement, however, was the chronic understaffing of missions.[200] Another was the unoffical exile some officers had to endure. Owing to a lack of funds, the promised three-year sabbatical in the United States often went unhonored. In 1937, Hull reported that sixteen officers had been continuously abroad for nearly seven years.[201]

Discouragement was particularly great over the rate of promotion. Secretary Stimson testified in 1929, ". . . one of the chief causes for discouragement among Foreign Service officers is the slowness of promotion." This slowness was the product of many forces, none of which were part of deliberate service policy. Congress was particularly at fault. Appropriations were invariably such that only the higher classes could be advanced.[202] The various economy measures constricted promotions even further. Promotions in 1935 for 280 officers above class five were their first in four years.[203] Another cause of the slow rate was in the organization of the Foreign Service itself. The average age difference in 1937 between the members of class one and class five was 5.2 years. Members of class two were even two years junior to the members of class three. There were also only negligible differences in lengths of service. The average service in class one was 24.7 years; in class three it was 22.4 years.[204] Inequities naturally flowed from these situations. Both had arisen through the Rogers Act reclassification, but they were sustained by the niggardliness af appropriations and by the percentages imposed upon the classes. The limited number of annual promotions resulted in the promotion of those with "excellent" or "very good" ratings almost exclusively, overlooking in the process the large number with "satisfactory" ratings. It would, however, be a mistake to suggest that this led a great many to abandon the career. When the inequities were most rife, the nation was in the depression. Few officers would leave the service's relative security.

The period 1924–39 saw large advances and a few reverses in the

[200] Subcommittee on Appropriations, *Hearings on State Department Appropriations*, 70 Cong., 2 sess. (November 20, 1928), p. 17. See also editorial, *New York Times*, March 16, 1929, p. 18; Bullitt to Hull, August 19, 1936, in 112/1275½. By implication, Bullitt's report underlined the understaffing of most posts.

[201] Cordell Hull, "A Better Deal for our State Department," *American Foreign Service Journal*, XIV (August, 1937), 512.

[202] Committee on Appropriations, *Hearings on State Department Appropriations, for 1930*, 71 Cong., 2 sess. (November 25, 1929), p. 23.

[203] *New York Times*, September 17, 1935, p. 7.

[204] *American Foreign Service Journal*, XIV (December, 1938), 719. Average has not been checked by author.

professionalization of the service. How successful were these advances in attracting and retaining qualified personnel? How effective were the reverses in discouraging qualified applicants and officers? Answers to both are partly dependent on the success which the service had in convincing the public that it was a genuine profession. In this it was eminently successful. The public widely accepted the service as a profession. The public administrator Leonard D. White, using the Foreign Service as a model in his *Government Careers for College Graduates*, insisted, "There can be no doubt that the invention of a career service in the State Department has already proved a marked success." [205] The *Washington Post* believed, "The pity of it is that this instance of the triumph of the merit system is so unique as to deserve attention." [206] Similar statements appeared in papers as widely spread geographically as Fargo, North Dakota, and Newport, Rhode Island. [207] The report of a congressional subcommittee held, "There is a steady improvement in the type and calibre of officer personnel that is being taken into the Service." [208] On the other hand, the service did not wholly escape criticism. One congressman complained, "He [the officer] does everything in his power to look and act and talk like a Britisher." [209] But even its detractors admitted that a profession existed and that it was moving ahead. A *Nation* editorial agrued, "We are one with General Dawes in dreading the going over of the diplomatic service to career men." [210]

The success of the career in attracting candidates can be shown both relatively and absolutely. Except for the December, 1928, examination, the number taking the Foreign Service examination after 1924 exceeded any figure attained at a Diplomatic Service examination — including the one held in Paris in 1919. Even at the December, 1928, examination, there were four times as many candidates as appeared for any normal Diplomatic Service examination.[211] A comparison with the number taking the Consular Service examination substantiates the same point. The highest figure reached in a Consular examination was in June, 1921, when 164 appeared.[212] The low-

---

[205] *Government Careers for College Graduates* (Chicago: Civil Service Assembly, 1937), p. 7.

[206] Editorial, *Washington Post*, May 10, 1936.

[207] *American Foreign Service Journal*, XIV (September, 1937), 529, 566–67. Editorials from the *Newport News, Fort Wayne Journal Gazette*, and the *Fargo Morning Forum*.

[208] 120.1/571B, Report of a Subcommittee of the Committee on Appropriations, December 4, 1941, p. 7.

[209] *Cong. Rec.*, LXXVIII, 73 Cong., 2 sess. (February 2, 1934), 1871 (speech by Representative Britten of Illinois).

[210] "American Diplomats," *Nation*, CXXV (July 6, 1927), 5.

[211] Minutes (December, 1928). There were 164 at that examination. The Diplomatic Service could barely approach forty.

[212] 120.11/22, Minutes of the Board of Examiners of the Consular Service, 1906–23.

est point for the Foreign Service was December, 1928, when 168 took the examination.[213] The 1936 examination had 4.3 times as many candidates as did the most popular consular examination.[214] Thus, in terms of comparative examination statistics, the Foreign Service was more successful in attracting candidates than either of its predecessors.

When compared with each other, the totals of attendance at the various examinations show an increasing popularity of the Foreign Service as a career. In January, 1925, 317 took the examination; the examination of September, 1939, attracted 512. This represented an increase of 61.5 per cent in fifteen years. The increase, however, was not steady. The appeal of the career was marked by two phases: a decline through 1928 and an increase of interest beginning in 1929. Using the first examination in 1925 as a base, the subsequent four years' examinations show an almost steady decline: July, 1925–26, had 91.1 per cent; 1927 had 63.4 per cent; January, 1928, had 69 per cent; and December, 1928, had 51.7 per cent. At this point, the Board began biannual examinations. The 1929 examinations showed 73.5 per cent; 1930–31 had 105 per cent; July, 1931–32, had 160.8 per cent; and September, 1932, had 143.5 per cent. According to Green, "The number has increased in an astounding manner." After an interval of three and a half years without examinations, a high point was reached in 1936, when the figure stood at 229.3 per cent. Thereafter, the figure fell to 143.8 per cent and then gradually rose to 161.5 per cent.[215]

What factors explain this pattern? Did the offering of examinations at Civil Service centers affect their attendance? In terms of numbers, the answer is no. The examinations were held first at Civil Service centers at the beginning of the decline and were held there throughout the "depressed" period. This may have been a factor in the rise in the 1930's, but no important case can be made out for it. Did increasing the number of examinations held annually account for the pattern? It is true that the number of candidates began increasing when biannual examinations were introduced, but this, it is felt, was coincidental. This factor fails to explain the increases from 1936 onward. Did the change in the examination system in 1931 affect the pattern? By this interpretation, candidates would apply knowing that the necessity for "cram" instruction was over. This, however, fails as an explanation on the ground that the upswing began before the introduction of the new examination.

[213] Minutes (December, 1928).
[214] Minutes (May, 1936). There were 727 in the 1936 examination.
[215] Minutes (January, 1925–September, 1939); Green to Carr, August 23, 1932, in Minutes (September, 1932).

Two major explanations, however, are possible. The less important one relates the pattern to the internal administration of the service. The publicity during the interchangeability episode reached its height at the low point of the decline. The decline began after the first Edwards' controversy; the rise coincided with the improving fortunes of the career and the ending of the schism. The more important explanation relates the developments to the external economic situation. The business boom in the 1920's tempted men who might otherwise join the service to enter business. 1927–29 were the high points in economic development, and low points in recruitment. After the crash, however, the percentage mounted rapidly. The canceling of the 1933 examination was vigorously opposed.[216] Business never proved a threat after 1930. Inspired by President Roosevelt, many young people turned to the federal government for employment. Alan Steyne claimed, "The dismal era of the early thirties, with business jobs scarce and often unattractive, for the first time presented governmental careers in an organization like the Foreign Service in an attractive garb to young college graduates." [217]

But the service's success in obtaining candidates can be seen by other indices. Competition was becoming more fully nationwide. A comparison of geographical origins of the candidates for the service with those for the Diplomatic Service is useful. Although similar information is not available for the Consular Service, it can be assumed that its pattern did not vary greatly from the post–Rogers Act patterns. Comparing the 1920–22 Diplomatic Service examinations with the Foreign Service examinations held in 1925–26, 1931, and 1937–38, the following facts appear. The concentration in the Middle Atlantic and East North Central regions steadily decreased: 58.8 per cent for the Diplomatic Service; 50.2 per cent for the 1925–26 examination; 48.9 per cent for the July, 1931, examination; and 44.3 per cent in the 1937–38 group.[218] The percentages from the three southern regions steadily increased: 10.9 per cent in the Diplomatic Service examinations; 14.9 per cent in 1925–26; 18.2 per cent in 1931; and 20.1 per cent in 1937–38. An increasing percentage was also registered in the Pacific and Mountain regions: 7.5 per cent in the Diplomatic Service examinations; 11.4 per cent in 1925–26; 17.8 per cent in July, 1931; and 13.9 per cent in 1937–38.[219]

---

[216] Minutes (September, 1933); editorial, *Washington Post*, April 23, 1933. Many of the letters asked that the examination, if not appointments, would be conducted as scheduled. The Department refused.

[217] 120.1/1–145, Guide Book to the Foreign Service, 1944.

[218] New England had 11.8 per cent in the Diplomatic Service, 15.9 per cent in 1925–26, 5.3 per cent in 1931, and 13.5 per cent in 1937–38.

[219] The West North Central had 10.9 per cent in the Diplomatic Service, 6.6 per cent in 1925–26, 9.3 per cent in 1931, and 7.8 per cent in 1937–38.

The first probable explanation of this pattern, although it is beyond documentation, is that as the service became more widely known as a profession its geographical representation broadened. A second, more mechanistic, explanation is useful. Administering the examinations at Civil Service centers, which were at thirteen various parts of the nation, facilitated the candidacies of many who would not otherwise travel to Washington. This explanation can be argued on the basis of the diminishing number who took the examination in Washington.[220] But it can be more graphically seen by comparing the percentages from the most distant states from Washington before and after the innovation. The percentage from the East South Central, Mountain, and Pacific regions, at the 1920–22 Diplomatic Service examinations was 11.7. The last examination administered only in Washington had 10.2 per cent. The first examination under the new system saw 20.9 per cent; the July, 1931, examination had 25.8 per cent; and the 1937–38 examination had 19.5 per cent.

A further index of the career's success can be seen in the changing ages of those applying to take the examination. In 1927, Carr wrote, ". . . the experience of the Department shows that relatively few men apply immediately following a college course. . . ."[221] And in the examinations held between 1927 and January, 1931, the age group showing the greatest preponderance was the 25–29 category, from which 39.8 per cent of all candidates came. The 20–24 group had 34.6 per cent, while those thirty and older represented 25.5 per cent. By the September, 1932, examination the percentages had shifted. The 25–29 age category declined slightly to 38.7 per cent. The percentage in the 20–24 group increased to 47.2, while those thirty and over sank to 14 per cent. The 1937 percentages changed only slightly: 47.8 per cent for the 20–24 group; 38.2 per cent for the 25–29 group, and 14 per cent for the final group. Although the median entering age of successful candidates in the period dropped only from twenty-seven to twenty-six, the statistics on the ages of those applying show that younger men were increasingly becoming candidates in the expectation of making the service a life career, and fewer candidates over thirty, having tried other vocations, turned to the Foreign Service in later life.[222]

The number of applications and the age and geographical origin of the candidates substantiate the assertion that the Foreign Service

[220] Minutes (December, 1929, and September, 1939). Nearly 63 per cent took the examination in Washington in 1929. In 1939, less than a third took it there.

[221] Carr to Potter, December 1, 1927, in 120.1121/41.

[222] Medians determined by author from data found in official records. 1920–25: twenty-seven years; 1926–30: twenty-five years; 1931–35: twenty-six years; 1936–40: twenty-six years.

by 1939 had increased in popularity and was making a successful appeal as a lifetime career. A more important question to ask is whether, from these applicants, qualified personnel was recruited? But recruiting qualified personnel depended, first of all, on attracting qualified candidates. In terms of formal academic qualifications, the candidates for the examinations between 1925 and 1939 steadily improved. Of the group applying between 1927 and 1931, 7.9 per cent had never been to a university; 31 per cent had been but had not taken a degree; and 61 per cent had degrees. A further 11 per cent of the last category had experience on the postgraduate level. By 1932, a shift was apparent. Those without university experience fell to 5.4 per cent, those without degrees to 16.8 per cent, and those with degrees rose to 77.6 per cent. Of the last category 28 per cent had experience on the postgraduate level. This trend was continued in the 1936–39 group. Only 2.8 per cent were without university experience; 14.3 per cent were without degrees; and 82.8 per cent had degrees. Those with postgraduate experience increased to 43.7 per cent.

This conclusion makes an investigation of the quality of personnel more meaningful. As compared with the group applying, the group appointed had higher formal academic qualifications. While 61 per cent of the candidates in 1927–31 had degrees, 84.6 per cent of those appointed had them. While 31 per cent were without degrees, this was true of only 11.8 per cent of the successful. And 3.5 per cent, compared with 7.9 per cent of those applying, succeeded without having had a university experience. The most startling difference, however, is between those with postgraduate experience in the two groups. While only 11 per cent of the candidates had experience on the postgraduate level, 67.4 per cent of the successful did. This same pattern was reproduced with the 1932 examination group and the 1935 appointments, and with the two groups between 1936 and 1939.[223] Furthermore, the percentage of the successful with higher qualifications increased. Those without a university experience fell from 3.5 per cent in the 1925–32 group to 2.5 per cent in 1935, to .9 per cent in 1936–39. The percentage with degrees increased: 84.6 per cent in

[223] Percentages for those appointed:

	1935
No experience	2.5
No degree	10.2
Degree	87.1
Graduate	76.4

	1936–39
No experience	0.9
No degree	7.6
Degree	91.3
Graduate	74.7

1925–32; 87.1 per cent in 1935; and 91.3 per cent in 1936–39. Finally, there was an increase in those with postgraduate experience: 67.4 per cent in 1925–32; 76.4 per cent in 1935; and 74.7 per cent in 1936–39.

This record, when compared with the percentages under the Diplomatic and Consular Services, is equally convincing. A comparison with the Consular Service at the time of the Rogers Act shows the 1925–32 Foreign Service to have a higher concentration of members with university degrees and postgraduate experience: 68.7 per cent to 84.6 per cent, and 44.4 per cent to 67.4 per cent, respectively. Comparisons with later Foreign Service groups are even more convincing.[224] Even when compared with the "better educated" Diplomatic Service, the new organization holds up well. In virtually every category, the qualifications of those in the Diplomatic Service were similar to those in the 1925–32 group.[225] Comparisons with later Foreign Service groups are favorable to the latter.[226]

This argument can also be substantiated by reference to comparative statistical performance on the examinations. An average of 15.4 per cent of the candidates for the Consular Service passed the examinations given between June, 1921, and January, 1923. The figure for the Foreign Service from 1925 to July, 1931, is 19.4 per cent. This increase, coinciding with the increasing qualifications and the maintenance of the same type of examination, is understandable. After Green's new examination system was instituted, the percentage fell sharply. An average of 5.5 per cent of the candidates passed each examination. With the percentage falling and the qualifications increasing, there can be no other conclusion but that the caliber of the successful candidate also increased.

But statistical evidence alone is insufficient. Did those administering the service feel that qualified personnel were being appointed? An answer to this, first of all, would require an approximation of what each administrator thought was the ideal Foreign Service type. This, of course, is impossible.[227] On the other hand, it is not difficult to deduce from the decision in 1931 to change the examination system

[224] See n. 223, above.

[225] Percentages for the Diplomatic Service. No experience: 3.5 per cent; experience: 11.6 per cent; degree: 84.8 per cent, and postgraduate: 50.9 per cent.

[226] Cf. n. 223 with n. 225, above.

[227] 120.11/22, General memo from Messersmith, January 19, 1938 – February 2, 1938. An evaluation of the 1937 examination by Moffat, Shaw, and Messersmith graphically demonstrates this point. Shaw, a liberal idealist, felt that the service was getting a "disproportionate representation" of the "go-getting American business type." The more socially oriented Moffat thought that the service was appointing "too many men who had the brains and the academical learning but who were completely devoid of background and ability to make successful contacts with their fellow men."

that the previous system had failed to get the service qualified personnel. Although the academic qualifications possessed by candidates were increasing, this increase did not necessarily mean that there was a higher quality officer appointed. With dissension raging within and better opportunities in business without, the service found it "difficult . . . to attract for the . . . entrance examinations the desired number of candidates of outstanding caliber." [228]

The depression's effect on job opportunities, the turn in internal fortunes, and Green's examination system, virtually coincided. The period 1932–39 has been recognized as one of great success in attracting highly qualified men. [229] This can be evidenced, for instance, in the Department's anxiety to retain the forty-one men stranded on the eligibility list by the economy measures. [230] However, it should not be implied that there was no dissatisfaction with specific groups. The 1937 group particularly came under strong attack, leading Green to recommend that "the Department ought to be establishing liaison with faculty members and administrations to encourage applicants." [231] Nevertheless, this period saw the central recruitment assumption of the Rogers Act confirmed.

The difficulty of evaluating the service's success in sustaining the interest of its members is even greater. One index which can be used is the resignation rate, but it only expresses the complete failure to sustain interest. Although other qualifications can be raised against using the resignation rate, it does confirm two points. When internal dissensions and external opportunities were high, the resignation rate was high. The period 1925–29 had an annual resignation rate of 3.8 per cent. Its highest point was in 1929, when it reached over 6 per cent. This was nearly twice as high as the British rate of the same year. [232] On the other hand, when internal fortunes were high and external opportunities low, as they were from 1930 onward, the resignation rate was low. Excluding the number ejected by the economy legislation, the average rate during the period 1930–39 was 1.3 per cent. This was maintained even in the face of the great deprivation during 1933–35.

Another index is found in the statements made by officers about their service and by observers. Officers, first of all, considered the

---

[228] 120.1/1–145, Guide Book to the Foreign Service, 1944.
[229] *Ibid.* See also Selden Chapin, "Training for the Foreign Service," *The Public Service and University Education*, ed. Joseph E. McLean (Princeton University Press, 1949), p. 111.
[230] 120.1121/114A, Wilson memo, September 23, 1935.
[231] Green to Messersmith, February 2, 1938, in 120.11/22.
[232] *Foreign Office List* (London, 1929), p. v. The 1929 rate for Great Britain was 3.7 per cent.

career a disciplined organization. Assistant Secretary George S. Messersmith, referring to the Department of Commerce's overseas service, wrote, "There was no discipline in Commerce, unfortunately, and some of these men . . . will find it difficult to adjust themselves to the new state of affairs." [233]

They, above all, identified their own interests with it. In 1926, Grew asserted: "There is an indefinable spirit throughout our ranks . . . which seems to me to bring us closer together in the work that we are doing, even than the bonds of school or college, fraternity or club." [234] Thirty years later a Foreign Service officer maintained, "It seemed to me then, it seems to me now, that there is no more interesting, vital, challenging job in the world." [235] An observer of the immediate post–Second World War period recognized this spirit, when he wrote: "The sense of dedication, of shared privilege and experience, was so strong, the feelings of participation in a profession set aside from the laity was so real, that the question of justification was frequently deemed unworthy of reply." [236]

By 1939, the Foreign Service was successful both in attracting qualified candidates and in sustaining the interest of those appointed. This statement does not mean that all drawbacks to the career were eliminated. Nor does it mean that every Foreign Service officer felt that the public sufficiently appreciated his career. Is there a profession in existence that does not have drawbacks? Do professional men ever feel that their careers are sufficiently appreciated?

Creating an "aristocracy of talent" for foreign affairs required more than an improved examination system and certain rewards for merit. An improved examination system would insure that the most qualified personnel would be selected from among the available candidates. Rewarding merit would not only sustain the interest of those appointed but would also encourage many persons, knowing that their labors would be recognized, to compete for the career. But, even with both, recruitment for the Foreign Service could not have progressed past the point reached by the pre-1924 Diplomatic Service had the Rogers Act not also assumed that successful recruitment for the career depended on freeing it from the existing financial limitations. The only method of testing the major recruitment assumption of the Rogers Act was to permit anyone, regardless of financial means,

[233] Messersmith to White, June 9, 1939, in 120.1/409A.

[234] *American Foreign Service Journal*, III (June, 1926), 183.

[235] Edwin F. Stanton, *Brief Authority: Excursions of a Common Man in an Uncommon World* (New York: Harper's, 1956), p. 2.

[236] Harold Stein, "The Foreign Service Act of 1946," in *Public Administration and Policy Development*, ed. Harold Stein (New York: Harcourt, Brace, 1952), p. 274.

to apply and, if physically and mentally qualified, to be appointed. This was not only sound administrative policy but it was also the only approach acceptable in a liberal democracy. The administration after the Rogers Act succeeded in democratizing as well as further professionalizing the service. "Democratization," of course, is not meant in the sense that the service accurately represented every group in American society. It is meant in the sense that the career had a wide recruitment base, that the barriers had been removed from almost every aspect of the service, and that its social character changed markedly from that of its Diplomatic Service progenitor.

The Foreign Service inherited the wage policy of the Consular Service, and, in many minds, the social reputation of the Diplomatic Service. Although the composition of the new unit on July 1, 1924, bore little relation to that of the Diplomatic Service, the Foreign Service nevertheless was labeled with all the familiar epithets. Drew Pearson obliquely referred to it as "a social club whose members are selected from bluestocking Bostonians, wield thin forks with their left hands, and are no more representative of American life than the Redskins whom their ancestors pushed west." [237] Robert Bendiner thought that the officers' backgrounds "tend in the main to reduce democracy to an abstraction." [238] At the same time, however, there were many who sought to convince the public of the opposite case. A writer, for instance, in the *Washington Star* insisted, "The majority of Foreign Service officers have no other income than their salaries and post allowances." [239]

For the prospective candidate, this public image was a vital consideration. Doubtless, many were dissuaded from applying because of the service's reputation. On the other hand, evidence shows that the candidates took the Rogers Act's intentions about democratization at face value.[240] Although at the time complaining about the salary, one officer asserted, "Many of the officers who have since [1924] entered the Service believe they were brought into it under false pretences." [241] Proof that the candidates considered the career open to all may also be seen by examining the backgrounds of those applying. In the September examinations of 1932, 1936, and 1937, between 20.2 and 24.9 per cent of the candidates who listed their father's occupation listed it as "worker." A decreasing percentage listed the occupation as

---

[237] *Washington Merry-Go-Round* (New York, 1931), p. 134.
[238] *The Riddle of the Department of State* (New York: Farrar and Rinehart, 1942), p. 111.
[239] Joseph H. Baird, "Professionalized Diplomacy," *Washington Star*, August 6, 1939.
[240] Grummon to Carr, November 20, 1929 in 120.1/176; *American Foreign Service Journal*, XXII (November, 1945), 55; Shaw, *op. cit.*, p. 329.
[241] *American Foreign Service Journal*, XXII (November, 1945), 55.

"executive" and "professional": 54.1 per cent, 49.2 per cent, and 48.1 per cent. An increasing percentage listed "white collar worker": 25.5 per cent, 25.7 per cent, and 28.7 per cent. Secondary school preparation, although not corresponding exactly to the national percentages,[242] was overwhelmingly in favor of those educated at state-supported schools. In 1936–37, for instance, 74.9 per cent came from public high schools and 17.8 per cent from private schools. The number of universities and colleges represented among the candidates further substantiates the assertion that a wide recruitment base existed. The examinations in 1932–39 saw candidates from an average of 182.4 institutions. The 1936 examination alone had representatives from 242 universities and colleges.[243] It is true that Harvard supplied 5.4 per cent of all the candidates in the same period, but it is also true that the City College of New York, Georgetown, George Washington, and Stanford universities were annually well represented.[244] Finally, between 1925 and 1939, nearly five thousand candidates took the examination.[245] When coupled with the statistics on the candidates' backgrounds, this figure should refute any allegation that the service failed to draw from a wide democratic base.

To argue that candidates without private means applied is not to argue that they, if successful, were able to enter fully into the career. Here again, however, the contention is that the Rogers Act and its subsequent administration broke down nearly every financial barrier and permitted, with a single exception, anyone who could physically and mentally qualify to enter the service. The administration of the examination, for instance, moved consciously in this direction. The decision in 1925 to hold examinations in Civil Service centers was made partly "to reduce to a minimum the financial outlay required of candidates."[246] On this point, it could be argued that the continuation of the oral examination in Washington would militate against the impecunious. But the odds were not overwhelmingly against the successful candidate in the written examination. There

---

[242] Using the private school figures for 1935–36 and the public secondary school figures for 1938, the following percentages result: 94.3 per cent attended public secondary schools and 5.7 per cent attended all types of private secondary schools. See Joseph Whitaker, *An Almanack* (London, 1939), p. 644.

[243] Minutes (May, 1936).

[244] In the September, 1938, examination, City College had fifteen candidates, Georgetown, fourteen, and Stanford, thirteen. Princeton had nine, Yale, twenty-two, and Harvard, thirty-five. See Minutes (September, 1938).

[245] Minutes (1925–39).

[246] Carr to Potter, December 1, 1927, in 120.1121/410.

[247] From January, 1932, onward, the candidate would have a 31.2 per cent chance of succeeding. Before 1932, his chances were even better.

was nearly one chance in three that he would be successful in Washington.[247] Nor was the policy of holding the examinations there designed to discourage certain types of candidates. Appropriations being what they were, any other system was unthinkable.

Implicit in the decision to revise the examination in 1931 in order to eliminate "cramming" was the desire to end an unofficial financial limitation.[248] Attending a "cram-school" required not only a protracted residence in Washington but also an expenditure of money for tuition. One course cost $300 for four months' instruction.[249] Although the schools were not eliminated after 1931, their importance was much reduced. Furthermore, many entered between 1924 and 1939 without having had this instruction. And it cannot be said that service policy required such training, and the Board often discouraged it for applicants.[250]

In the substance of the examination itself, the same democratic presupposition was maintained. It cannot be shown, assuming that categories of education have social implications, that the examination showed deliberate favor to one group over another — with one possible exception. It became steadily more difficult for a candidate without a college education to pass the written examination. But, for a profession legitimately requiring for admission a kind of knowledge best acquired at a university this shrinking figure is understandable.[251] On the other hand, the Board of Examiners rigorously avoided any charge of favoritism. Before 1931, the examinations were devised and graded by the Civil Service Commission and could hardly be said to show a bias toward any type of educational institution.[252] After 1931, a committee, representing several universities, compiled the examinations.[253] The examinations were later critically reviewed by many other academics.[254] A separate group, representing an even greater variety of institutions, marked the examinations.[255]

[248] Cotton to Carr, November 20, 1930, in 120.11/22.

[249] 120.11/22, Brochure from Turner's Diplomatic School, 1938.

[250] Interview with the Hon. Donald W. Richardson of the Board of Foreign Service Examiners, July 28, 1957.

[251] Green to Carr, September 12, 1932, in Minutes (June, 1932). At the time of the first administration of the revised examination, Green maintained that the increasing number of college graduates caused the shift toward the university-educated Foreign Service officer. He thought it was not caused by "any considerations arising from the type of examination." Subsequent information has proved this false.

[252] Grew to Stowell, December 15, 1924, in 120.1121/18.

[253] 120.1121/83, Report of the Committee on Revision, May 11, 1931. MacMurray was from Johns Hopkins, Wilson from Harvard, Thorndike from Columbia, and Thurstone from Chicago. The institutions which provided the critique of each examination were geographically spread and otherwise diverse.

[254] Green to faculties, September 14, 1937, in 120.11/22.

[255] E.g., Green to Carr, June 24, 1937, in 120.112/34. The examiners in 1937 came from Wisconsin, Harvard, Nebraska, California, Princeton, and West Virginia universities.

In 1936, when there was a concentration in the hands of a few eastern universities, there was criticism from the Board.[256] The following year the job was spread, and Joseph Green, in a memo to Carr, emphasized, "You will note the wide geographical distribution of universities represented."[257] Above all, the examinations were successfully taken "by candidates educated in all parts of the country and all classes of institutions of higher learning."[258] An average of 48.6 universities and colleges were represented successfully at each examination between 1932 and 1939. This does not mean that certain institutions did not do better generally than did others. Although candidates educated at state-supported secondary schools were in the majority in the applicants, they usually dwindled to 50 per cent of those successful in the written examination. Harvard, Yale and Princeton, although representing only 12 per cent of the candidates, provided 27.4 per cent of those successful in the 1932–39 examinations. But this, it is contended, was absolutely divorced from any conscious policy, and such an occurrence is bound to happen in competitive examinations. It should also be noted that other institutions had a higher percentage of their candidates succeed. For instance, Stanford University in 1936 had a 42.8 per cent success, while Harvard registered 35 per cent.

The oral, more than the written examination, has been the target of those charging the service with undemocratic practices.[259] But here again evidence argues the contrary. The members of the examining panels represented as diverse backgrounds as did the candidates themselves.[260] These boards, furthermore, were constantly changing, permitting no prejudice to last for long. There was also a service aversion to any allegation of favoritism. Assistant Secretary Castle thought examiners were more critical of Harvard applicants "because they are sensitive over accusations as to the 'Harvard clique' in the Department of State."[261] Commenting on the 1939 examination, the *American Foreign Service Journal* expressed this aversion:

> The results of the last examination for the Service should go a long way to demolish this convenient theory . . . it will be seen that only one of the thirty-five who finally passed was stained with the incriminating crimson dye.[262]

[256] Board of Examiners to Green, March 23, 1936, in 120.112/32.
[257] Green to Carr, June 24, 1937, in 120.112/34.
[258] Minutes (January, 1932–September, 1939).
[259] E.g., Bendiner, *op. cit.*, p. 121.
[260] Letter from the Hon. Joseph C. Green to the author, October 30, 1957.
[261] *American Foreign Service Journal*, VII (November, 1930), 12.
[262] Editorial, *ibid.*, XVII (June, 1940), 318.

The fact that no improper considerations were made can also be seen in statistics. A slightly higher percentage of those from state-supported secondary schools passed the oral than passed the written. Exactly 50 per cent passed the written in 1939–41, while 54.3 per cent were appointed between 1936 and 1939. Harvard, Yale, and Princeton represented 27.4 per cent of the successful candidates in the written examination in 1936–39; they represented 28 per cent of the appointments in the same period.

But it would have been folly to open recruitment to all who could qualify if the career, once a person without private means was appointed to it, proved too expensive for him. The assumption made in 1924 was that any officer, on the basis of his salary alone, could occupy any post in the Foreign Service. And to facilitate career promotions to the upper service, the Rogers Act further authorized representational allowances. The next six years saw a continuous improvement on this position. An expanded program of building was begun in 1926.[263] On June 26, 1930, allowances were granted for rent, light, heat, and fuel.[264] The following February representational allowances were given to upper service and Foreign Service personnel.[265] In the Moses-Linthicum Act, the salary scale was increased by $1,000 for the higher grades and $500 for the lower.[266] Security benefits were also increased. An early amendment to the Rogers Act safeguarded the pension provisions for officers promoted to the upper service,[267] and the Moses-Linthicum Act provided sick leaves and improved the disability features of the pension scheme.[268]

It was not long after the granting of representational allowances that the process was temporarily reversed. The worsening of the depression led the Hoover administration to propose economies in public expenditures. Stimson's first economy was to leave vacancies when they arose and to freeze promotions.[269] Both avoided any alteration in the compensation structure of the service. On this policy, the *New York Times* claimed: "Although some foreign diplomatic missions here are feeling the pinch of stringent government finances, no such prospect is in sight for American diplomats resident abroad." [270] The following year, however, this too was reversed. The appropriations

[263] 44 Stat. 404 (May 7, 1926). The main feature of the Foreign Service Buildings Act was its authorization of a ten million dollar fund for construction. No longer did the Department have to request money for each structure.

[264] 46 Stat. 173 (June 26, 1930).

[265] 46 Stat. 1207 (February 23, 1931).

[266] *Ibid.*

[267] 44 Stat. 902 (July 3, 1926).

[268] 46 Stat. 1207 (February 23, 1931).

[269] *New York Times*, August 30, 1931, p. 2.

[270] *Ibid.*

for 1932 cut back the merit raises provided by the Moses-Linthicum Act, forbade paid leaves, and substantially reduced all allowances. The representational allowance alone fell from \$125,000 to \$25,000.[271] There were also some eliminations of personnel. In the 1933 appropriation, post and representational allowances were completely stopped, and the rental allowance was reduced by half.[272]

Roosevelt's first administration only brought an intensification of the problem. Not only were the allowances not restored but the salary itself was sizably reduced. By the Economy Act of March 20, 1933, the salary of every officer was reduced 15 per cent.[273] There was another unofficial reduction of 30 per cent through devaluation when America went off the gold standard.[274] The next February an Executive Order reduced salaries another 10 per cent, and a further 5 per cent was cut on July 1, 1934.[275] The housing allowance was also reduced.[276]

The effect on the service of these cuts was nearly disastrous. Carr described the months after the Economy Act as the "most trying period through which the Foreign Service has ever passed.[277] Secretary Hull maintained, ". . . much of the Foreign Service is now more or less in a state of demoralization so far as any actual efficiency is concerned." [278] There were public reports of families being separated, the acceptance of charity, the negotiating for large loans, "mental breakdowns and even suicide." [279]

Fortunately, the plight of the officers won the sympathy of citizens, the press, and Congress. The secretary of the Merchants' Association of New York and other public spirited citizens wrote the Department in protest about the situation.[280] A resolution of the Womens' Patriotic Conference on National Defense deplored the cuts.[281] Articles appeared in periodicals and newspapers.[282] And in Congress, Mrs.

[271] 47 Stat. 475 (July 1, 1932).

[272] 47 Stat. 1371 (March 1, 1933).

[273] 48 Stat. 8 (March 20, 1933).

[274] Committee on Appropriations, *Hearings on the Department of State Appropriations for 1935*, 73 Cong., 2 sess. (December 5, 1933), p. 121.

[275] Carr to "interested party," April 18, 1935, in 102/191.

[276] 47 Stat. 1371 (March 1, 1933); 48 Stat. 529 (April 7, 1934). The total reduction was 67 per cent of the 1932 amount.

[277] *American Foreign Service Journal*, XI (February, 1934), 62.

[278] *Ibid.* (April, 1934), p. 168.

[279] *Ibid.*, p. 107; *Cong. Rec.*, LXXVII, 73 Cong., 2 sess. (February 2, 1934), 1867 (speech by Congresswoman Rogers).

[280] *American Foreign Service Journal*, XI (February, 1934), 65.

[281] *Ibid.*, XII (March, 1935), 143.

[282] E.g., Ellery C. Stowell, "Cramping Our Foreign Service," *American Journal of International Law*, XXIX (April, 1935), 314–17; editorials, *New York Times*, November 19, 1933; February 1, 1934; editorial, *Elizabeth Daily Journal*, January 19, 1935, p. 8; Nicholas Roosevelt, "Diplomacy in Rags," *Christian Science Monitor*, February 14–23, 1934.

Edith N. Rogers and Representative John A. Reagan criticized the administration for its policy.[283]

The administration, however, was not unaware of the situation. After failing to get a fund from Congress to protect salaries from excessive devaluation, Roosevelt shipped gold abroad to pay the checks of officers.[284] Carr believed, "This saved the Service in some twenty-three countries from disintegrating." [285] Later losses were eased by a congressional fund.[286] An appropriation in 1934 restored 10 per cent of the salary and permitted the merit raises to begin again. [287] By the Act of February 13, 1935, the entire salary was restored, and an earlier law granted restitution for losses through devaluation.[288] Cost of living allowances were again authorized in 1934, and the 1935 housing allowance was increased.[289] By 1936, the representational allowances were restored.[290] Thereafter the allowances increased until 1939.[291] A better annuity system was added that same year.[292]

Was the assumption of the Rogers Act correct? Was the salary, except during the depression interlude, large enough to open the career to the man without private means? Answering this requires recognizing a host of variables. The costs at different posts varied greatly, and, above all, the question "How much salary is enough?" admits of an answer for every officer. However, certain conclusions can be drawn. Evidence indicates that the salary was large enough to permit a man without private means to remain in the service and to occupy almost every post. There were, of course, frequent complaints about the salary.[293] One officer wrote to the Department that he had taken the examination under the misapprehension that the salary "would permit me to serve therein without the prerequisite of an outside income." [294] Against this there is strong evidence to support this study's contention. If the salary were too small, the Board of Examiners, as its Diplomatic Service predecessor had, would have surely made a statement to this effect. It could not afford to attract men who would immediately have to resign. Furthermore, there were public and private statements that a man could enter without having private

[283] *Cong. Rec.*, LXXVI, 72 Cong., 2 sess. (January 25, 1933), 2544–45.
[284] *New York Times*, June 3, 1934, Sec. 4, p. 4.
[285] *American Foreign Service Journal*, XI (February, 1934), 66.
[286] *New York Times*, June 3, 1934, Sec. 4, p. 4.
[287] 48 Stat. 529 (April 7, 1934).
[288] 49 Stat. 6 (February 2, 1935); *ibid.*, 1138 (February 13, 1935).
[289] 48 Stat. 529 (April 7, 1934); 49 Stat. 67 (March 22, 1935).
[290] 49 Stat. 1309 (May 15, 1936).
[291] 50 Stat. 261 (June 16, 1937); 52 Stat. 248 (April 27, 1938). See *New York Times*, March 25, 1937, p. 29.
[292] 53 Stat. 583 (April 20, 1939).
[293] E.g., *American Foreign Service Journal*, XIV (September, 1937), 568.
[294] Grummon to Carr, November 20, 1929, in 120.1/176.

means. Assuring the Chaplain of Princeton that this was the case, Carr in 1928 added, "The Foreign Service, I fear, has suffered to some extent from a false glamour which is supposed to surround certain of its work." [295] Career officer Messersmith, who was not independently wealthy, believed the service to be "unquestionably as democratic a one as could be devised." [296] Another officer wrote in the *American Foreign Service Journal*, "The vast majority of Foreign Service officers are satisfied with the present scale of salaries as such. . . ." [297]

But, if this were so, why was it necessary to petition Congress for an improvement in compensation? In the first place, all but one of these petitions involved allowances, not salary. The intention here was to make the government pay for those expenses incurred through official duty. The improvements were also requested during a period of intense competition with business for service personnel. It was never intended that official salaries should compete with private ones, but the exodus from the service in 1927–29 made some move in this direction imperative. And some adjustments had to be made for salaries fixed by law in the midst of changing economic circumstances. Finally, if the salaries were too small, the percentage of resignations from those who were probably without private means, such as graduates of state-supported secondary schools and state universities, would have been greater than those for graduates of boarding schools and Harvard, Yale, and Princeton. But this was not the case. In the period 1924–46, the percentage of resignations for those appointed between 1924 and 1929 from state-supported secondary schools was 30.5. It was 45.3 for those who had attended boarding schools. Those appointed from the same categories in 1930–35 registered a resignation percentage of 19.3 and 26.9, respectively. On the university level, those appointed from state universities had a resignation percentage of 26.4 in 1924–29 and 17.3 in 1930–35, while Harvard, Yale and Princeton registered 45.3 per cent in 1924–29 and 25.7 per cent in 1930–35. The depression pattern was substantially the same. [298] And

[295] Carr to Chaplain of Princeton, November 21, 1928, in 120.1/174.

[296] 120.11/22, Messersmith memo, February 2, 1938.

[297] *American Foreign Service Journal*, XIV (December, 1937), 718 (statement by Selden Chapin).

[298]

	Appointments (per cent)	Resignations (per cent)
Secondary schools (1924–32):		
Public schools	51.4	40.7
Boarding schools	27.8	33.3
Country day schools	13.9	11.1
Other	6.8	14.8
Universities (1924–32):		
Harvard	15.4	22.2
Yale, Princeton	19.5	25.9

in average tenures registered by all groups, there is no evidence to suggest that officers without private means were forced to cut short their careers.[299]

If officers without private means remained in the service, then, a fortiori, they served in a variety of posts and were promoted to all grades. But here a qualification to the democratization thesis must be raised. Certain posts in class one and many upper service positions were beyond the reach of the officer who lived on his salary alone. The great bulk of complaints made about the salary referred to this bar. When Allen W. Dulles resigned, because of financial reasons, from the counselorship at Peking, the *New York Times* maintained, ". . . the higher ranks are, in practice, open to rich men." [300] About the upper service posts, Hugh Gibson remarked: "But can a $10,000-a-year class one man accept an ambassadorship, if it is offered? Not unless he has a private income. It is impossible." [301]

This was admitted privately by an officer who thought that many of the men who were admitted "would soon be 'strangled' and who would be of no use to the Department because they were not men of independent means." [302] Nevertheless, men without private incomes were appointed to counselorships and to the upper service. The various allowances and mission construction were designed to aid these appointments. Of the promotions to class one in 1929 only two of the nine men had independent means. And three of the ten ministerial appointments had only their salaries.[303] If it can be assumed that the vast majority of consular officers had only their salaries, then upper service posts were increasingly occupied by such men. There were seven ministerial appointments of former consular officers in 1931. In 1937 there were eight ministerial and two ambas-

	Appointments (per cent)	Resignations (per cent)
Other Ivy League	8.9	25.9
Eastern Private	17.8	7.4
State universities	20.8	3.7
Other	18.7	14.8

[299] For example, the tenures for 1929 by university backgrounds reveal (in years):

Harvard	13.8
Yale, Princeton	12.8
Other Ivy League	12.2
Eastern Private	12.2
State universities	14.6

The terminal date used for these figures is 1946.

[300] *New York Times*, September 28, 1926, p. 26; editorial, October 3, 1926, Sec. 9, p. 5.

[301] Hugh Gibson, "Diplomats Pay to Work," *Saturday Evening Post*, CCIX (May 8, 1937), 25.

[302] Green to Shaw, February 15, 1939, in 120.11/22. Green is repeating part of a conversation with an unnamed member of the Board.

[303] Carr to Brady, May 11, 1929, in 120.31/57.

sadorial appointments. A third ambassadorial appointment was made in 1938.[304] Still, some posts remained closed, but this fact, while qualifying the democratization thesis, does not refute it.

A further qualification, however, is in respect to the appointment of women to the service. There was one woman in the service at the time of the Rogers Act. A second entered in 1925.[305] This second appointment, when coupled with the fact that eight took the examination, sparked a discussion about future appointments. One officer suggested that a separate branch be established for women.[306] Hugh Gibson inquired of Assistant Secretary Castle, "Don't you think it would be a wise thing to refrain from taking in any more women until we can form idea of their usefulness from observation of those we have already taken in?"[307] The Foreign Service Personnel Board disapproved of both suggestions, although it tacitly accepted a policy of moderation.[308]

In the meantime the service was being thought of as an increasingly promising career for women. In 1928, a pamphlet entitled "Opportunities for Women as Officers in the Foreign Service of the United States" was issued by the Federation of Women's Clubs.[309] Between 1926 and 1931, 7.3 per cent of all candidates were women, an average of seventeen applying annually. A third woman was appointed in 1927, two in 1929, and one in 1930.[310] On the occasion of the last appointment, the *New York Times* remarked, "The appointment of women to the Foreign Service, which was a novelty a few years ago, is no longer unusual."[311]

But the Board could hardly feel satisfied with the appointments. Although six women had entered by 1930, only two remained in 1931.[312] An average tenure of 3.5 years was served by the four who resigned. In addition to the problem of resignations, it was found that women could not be assigned to many posts.[313] Although an average of seventeen continued to apply annually in the period

---

[304] *Biog. Reg.* (1933, 1937, 1939), *passim.*

[305] Minutes (January, 1925).

[306] Grew to Hugh Wilson, January 19, 1925, in Grew, *Turbulent Era*, I, 646–47. Wilson made the suggestion. Grew opposed it.

[307] Gibson to Castle, July 15, 1925, in 120.1/125.

[308] Grew to Gibson, July 15, 1925, in 120.1/125; Carr to Wright, August 14, 1925, in 120.1/125; E. J. Norton to Mrs. Edward Dexter Knight, November 1, 1926, in 120.1/117.

[309] 120.1/175, "Opportunities for Women as Officers in the Foreign Service of the United States," 1928.

[310] Minutes (1927–30).

[311] *New York Times*, March 26, 1930, p. 16.

[312] *Biog. Reg.* (1931), pp. 20–59.

[313] Herbert Wright, "Can a Woman Be a Diplomat," *American Foreign Service Journal*, XVII (August, 1940), 454.

1931–39, no woman was successful.[314] In private correspondence, one member claimed that "it is the opinion in the Department that the Foreign Service is not a suitable place for women. No one says this publicly, but it is a fact." [315] It was not until the Reorganization Act of 1939 that women were again permitted into the service. By this Act, six women from the foreign service of the Department of Commerce became Foreign Service officers.[316]

On racial minorities little evidence exists. Few Negroes applied and few were appointed.[317] There were two in the service in 1935, and their number had increased to eight by 1942.[318] Like women, however, the use of Negroes in the service was limited. It was not uncommon for states to object to Negro representation. Haiti, a Negro republic, objected because "Haitians looked down upon the American negro." They were, however, appointed to Liberia, the Azores, and France.[319] There were no Asians in the service during the period, and no evidence exists on the religious question.

What type of service, socially speaking, flowed from wide recruitment and open ranks? Upon entering the Foreign Service's common personnel source in 1924, the Diplomatic Service's character was changed radically. While 72.3 per cent of the career diplomats had attended boarding schools, only 24.3 per cent of the new service had. While 16 per cent of the career diplomats attended state-supported secondary schools, 63 per cent of the new service had. University representation was similarly affected. While 63.8 per cent of the career diplomats had attended Harvard, Yale, and Princeton, only 24.3 per cent of the new service had. While 9.2 per cent had attended state universities, the new service could boast of 27.7 per cent. As this change was wrought primarily through the differences in size of these categories in the Consular Service, the latter's percentages, while altered, were not similarly affected.[320] Although it can be argued that the continued existence of separate branches

---

[314] Minutes (January, 1931–September, 1939).
[315] Albert Halstead to H. Hall Hall, June 3, 1932, in 120.1/214.
[316] 53 Stat. 1431 (April 24, 1939); *Biog. Reg.* (1929), pp. 27–64.
[317] Letter from the Hon. Joseph C. Green to the author, October 30, 1957.
[318] Stowell, "Cramping Our Foreign Service," p. 315; Ludlow Werner, "Negroes in the Foreign Service," *New York Age*, October 10, 1942.
[319] President Borno to Stimson, December 25, 1929, in 124.38/28.
[320] Educational background of consular officers:

Universities (per cent)		Secondary Schools (per cent)	
Harvard	5.4	Public school	73.2
Yale, Princeton	9.3	Boarding school	13.9
Other Ivy League	9.5	Country day school	9.1
Eastern private	26.0	Other	7.1
State universities	32.2		

prevented this social change from becoming immediately effective, it can also be argued that it was effective by 1930.

At no point, using the same categories, did subsequent recruitment into the Foreign Service even approach the composition under the Diplomatic Service, while at most points it neared the level established by the Foreign Service in 1924. The percentage of appointments from state-supported secondary schools never dipped below 50 per cent: 56.2 in 1924–25; 52.7 in 1926–30; 51.7 in 1931–35; and 54.3 in 1936–39. The percentage of the 1924–39 total for state-supported secondary schools was 60.5. Although higher than the 1924 standard, the percentages for boarding schools never reached half the concentration that existed under the Diplomatic Service: 26.5 in 1924–25; 27.5 in 1926–30; 33.6 in 1931–35; and 32 per cent in 1936–39. Harvard, Yale, and Princeton, while playing an important role, found this role considerably reduced from the Diplomatic Service position: 32.7 per cent in 1924–25; 36.1 per cent in 1926–30; 40.5 per cent in 1931–35; and 28 per cent in 1936–39. State universities registered 20.6 per cent in 1924–25; 19.2 per cent in 1926–30; 28.8 per cent in 1931–35; and 25.2 per cent in 1936–39. Finally, this sustained social diffusion of personnel was further aided by the Reorganization Act of 1939. The 113 members co-opted that year had a representation from state-supported secondary schools of 69.6 per cent and from boarding schools of 9 per cent. The representation from Harvard, Yale, and Princeton, was 15 per cent, while the state universities provided 26.7 per cent.[321]

Does not the continued importance of Harvard, Yale, and Princeton also modify the democratization thesis? The answer would have to be in the affirmative if many other factors were not present. It has already been pointed out that the largest group to apply came from these three institutions. A host of nearly self-evident reasons explain the continuing interest of their alumni.[322] Furthermore, al-

[321] Background of co-opted personnel:

	Secondary schools (per cent)
Public schools	69.6
Boarding schools	9.0
Country day schools	9.8

	Universities (per cent)
Harvard	8.0
Yale, Princeton	7.0
Other Ivy League	3.5
Eastern Private	29.4
State universities	26.7

[322] E.g., *American Foreign Service Journal*, VII (January, 1930), 11; XVI (February, 1939), 106. The second reference is a reprinted article from the *Princeton Alumni Weekly*

though they were relatively more successful on the written examination than other groups, it has been shown that roughly the same percentage which passed the written examination were ultimately appointed. And any attempt to restrict their entry into the service would be contrary to democratic presuppositions. Finally, it should be pointed out that, in the group 1930–35 for instance, 19 per cent of the officers from Harvard and 26.6 per cent of the officers from Yale and Princeton had attended state-supported secondary schools.[323]

Even considering the possible qualifications, it can be asserted that the professional service for foreign affairs had been democratized in the period 1924–39. Can a profession of eight hundred, demanding as it does high intellectual qualifications, ever accurately reflect its society? Did the existence of minor barriers to merit make the entire establishment undemocratic?

The scope of the professional service for foreign affairs was widened by the Rogers Act. With its original function as the representative of the American government to other governments, it was absorbed into a unit which served nearly every transaction that America and Americans had abroad. Another aspect of the Foreign Service's development in the period of 1924–39 was the further delineation of the skills which officers needed to conduct these transactions. When Joseph Grew asserted, ". . . certainly the Foreign Service is just exactly as much a profession as law or medicine or the ministry," he was referring to more than competitive examinations and promotions by merit. He was also referring to the growing specialization of the Foreign Service.[324]

What skills was it desirable for an officer to possess? Here a linguistic problem arises. It was widely held that an officer should be a "generalist," that is, a man who could handle any conceivable problem. From this it was argued that "the best education — the only really valuable education for that career, is general education."[325] But the concepts of "generalist" and "general education" assumed different connotations when applied to the service. They did not refer to the classical training preferred by the British service. Nor

which stressed the fact that nine members of the "Class of 1930" were Foreign Service officers. It asked, "Will any other class of any University accept the challenge?"

[323] The scholarship percentages for Princeton and Yale in 1937–38 were 22.8 and 19.2, respectively. Harvard in 1936–37 had 17.9 per cent on scholarship. Percentages calculated from data sent to author by Financial Aid officers of the three universities.

[324] Joseph C. Grew, "Address to the Class of 1926," *American Foreign Service Journal*, III (June, 1926), 181.

[325] DeWitt Clinton Poole, "University Training for the Foreign Service," *University Training for the National Service*, p. 162; see also Carr, *op. cit.*, pp. 146–59.

did they exactly coincide with the Diplomatic Service's cultivated agent. The problems that confronted the American Foreign Service officers were overwhelmingly economic. A 1937 *Register* in a list of the service's functions, said that it:

> analyzes and reports on particular economic conditions and trends of significance to the United States, deals with market conditions, statistics of trade, finance, production and labor, crops, forest, fishing, and mineral resources, shipping in all its ramifications, legislation, tariffs, and vital statistics.[326]

If this were the work of the "generalist" and required a "general education," then these phrases had lost their traditional meaning. "Specialization" had come to refer to "cultural relations" and "military and naval matters." Ellery Stowell, catching the essence of the service's orientation, wrote, "The day of the old social type of diplomat is passing, to give place to officers who are familiar with commercial and other data upon which international intercourse is based." [327]

The written examination assumed this type of knowledge as a minimum standard for appointment. Carr wrote, ". . . the possession to a proper degree of the qualities revealed by the written test is essential to the usefulness to the Government and the success, from a professional standpoint, of each candidate." [328] The "qualities" desired on the examination were summed up in a Board of Examiner's directive of December 15, 1924. In addition to modern languages, American history, and facility with English, the candidate had to have command over the elements of international, commercial, and maritime law; political and commercial geography; the natural, industrial, and commercial resources and commerce of the United States "with especial relation to the possibilities of trade expansion and protection"; world history since 1850, with particular attention to political and economic tendencies; the elements of political economy; and arithmetic "as used in commercial statistics, tariff calculations, exchange, and simple accounting." And the weight given the commercial aspects of the examination was over 80 per cent of the total.[329] One observer pointed out, ". . . the examinations are almost vocational in character. There is none of the effort made

[326] Pp. 355–56.

[327] Stowell, "Cramping Our Foreign Service," p. 317.

[328] Carr to Board of Foreign Service Personnel, October 21, 1925, in 120.11/22.

[329] 120.1121/4, Department directive on examinations, December 15, 1924. See also Minutes (January, 1927).

by the British examination to draw out the general educational quali-fications of the applicant. . . ."[330]

Although the Committee on Revision in 1931 was charged with providing an "examination for a recent university graduate rather than for a commercial expert," the new examination did not com-pletely depart from its predecessor's objectives.[331] It is true that the papers dealing directly with economic topics were reduced in weight to less than 50 per cent of the total. But the third General Examina-tion and the history papers often demanded economic knowledge.[332] The main difference between the new and the old systems was that the former was a "test of the candidates general knowledge of funda-mental economic principles, and his ability to analyze economic prob-lems with logical consistency."[333] Any attempt to change this orienta-tion was frowned upon. Green, who advocated questions "relating to philosophy, literature, and art," hesitated to include them because it "might be considered by the Board of Examiners as involving an unjustifiable departure from the requirements laid down by the Board."[334] The second revision of the examination in 1938–39, while moving steadily toward measuring intelligence, did not neglect these requirements.[335]

The officers who passed through this alembic showed certain defi-nite intellectual characteristics. In the first place, they were probably trained in the social sciences. As candidates from this category in 1932–37 comprised over 50 per cent of all candidates and had the highest examination averages, it cannot be doubted that they made up the largest group of those appointed.[336] Furthermore, an increas-ing number of officers entered with a specific training in Foreign Service subjects. In 1924–31, 6.1 per cent of all officers had been so trained. The 1932–39 group showed an increase to 17.2 per cent, Georgetown University providing 9.5 per cent and the Fletcher School, 7.1 per cent. A further 17.8 per cent entered with this train-

[330] Henry K. Norton, *Foreign Office Organization* (Philadelphia, 1929), p. 38.

[331] Stimson to Green, January 8, 1931, in 120.11/22.

[332] Minutes (September, 1932). The third General Examination included questions of fact to test "with accuracy and extent of the candidate's information in regard to history; government; geography, law, and economics; natural, industrial, and commer-cial resources and commerce of the United States." See 120.1121/83, Report of the Com-mittee for Review of the Foreign Service Examination, May 11, 1931.

[333] Green to T. M. Wilson, February 18, 1936, in Minutes (May, 1936).

[334] Green to T. M. Wilson, June 4, 1936, in 120.11/22.

[335] 120.1121/152, Second Report of the Committee for the Revision of the Foreign Service Examination, February 6, 1939. Explicitly economics papers constituted 35 per cent of the new examination.

[336] 120.11/22, Bingham's report, November 22, 1938. The average percentage for those trained in the social sciences was 57.4, 56.6 for the humanities, and 48.0 for the natural sciences.

ing under the Reorganization Act. It should not, however, be assumed that this training was a *sine qua non* for appointment. Of the 105 candidates from Georgetown University between September, 1932, and 1939, only sixteen were successful.[337] Finally, a point which was made before in a different context, a large percentage of each group entered after some sort of postgraduate instruction.[338]

One of the more important moves toward developing the skills for the career was the creation of the Foreign Service School. There were, of course, "schools" in both the Diplomatic and Consular Services. But the Diplomatic Service's was never really developed and many officers still went to the field without a term of instruction. By the Executive Order of June 7, 1924, a Foreign Service School was formally established, and a year's instruction, which was also to count as a probationary period, was prescribed for the appointees.[339] The demands on personnel, however, made a full year's training unfeasible, and the Executive Order of September 11, 1929, reduced the requirements to an unspecified length of time.[340] The school normally held lectures for two hours each day on political and economic problems and the workings of the various departments of the government. A special series dealt with aspects of Foreign Service work, such as political and commercial reporting and introductions to visa, immigration, and extradition procedures. The remainder of each day was spent in practical work in the Department's divisions.[341]

There were other in-service methods of developing particular skills. Continuing the system of language students the early Foreign Service appropriations authorized tuition payments for officers learning Turkish, Chinese, and Japanese.[342] The appropriation of 1927 extended this to include eastern European languages.[343] A further extension was granted in 1937, when officers were allowed to be stationed abroad or in American universities for language instruction.[344] A few officers were also being sent to the Harvard Business School to do advanced work in economics and finance.[345] Finally, the nature

[337] Minutes (September, 1932–September, 1939).

[338] 1925–32: 67.4 per cent; 1935: 76.4 per cent; 1936–39: 74.7 per cent.

[339] James B. Stewart, "Foreign Service Officers Training School," *American Foreign Service Journal*, X (June, 1933), 225. Executive Order 4022, June 7, 1924 (copy of Order in author's possession).

[340] Executive Order 5189, September 11, 1929. Copy of Order in author's possession.

[341] See Stowell, "The Foreign Service School," *American Journal of International Law*, XIX (October, 1925), 764–65.

[342] 43 Stat. 1014 (February 27, 1925).

[343] 44 Stat. 1178 (February 24, 1927).

[344] 50 Stat. 261 (June 16, 1937).

of the service lent itself to specialization. In 1938, Assistant Secretary Messersmith remarked, "The Service is so large, the work at different posts so varied and the demands upon the Service so wide that that there is ample opportunity for an officer to specialize."[346]

It was this growing specialization that partly led to the Reorganization Act of 1939. The development of differentiated skills, such as financial and commercial reporting, made superfluous the existence of other official units abroad.[347] Their continuance was marked by great social tensions and, above all, by senseless duplication of work.[348] By the Reorganization Act, 105 officers from the Department of Commerce's overseas branch and nine officers from the Department of Agriculture were absorbed into the Foreign Service at appropriate levels. Although no specific means were created for perpetuating this type of specialization, the Act did authorize a change in the service's administrative boards to include representatives from the departments of Commerce and Agriculture. It also permitted training and service for officers in the other departments.[349]

But the Reorganization Act was primarily in response to a need to determine the service's exact jurisdiction in relation to other overseas agencies. This was the most important development of specialization in the period. Although most of the events, such as the behind-the-scenes maneuvering and congressional procedure, leading to its enactment are irrelevant here, the policy considerations which underlay it are relevant. It should, however, not be thought that this problem had its origins between 1924 and 1939. The jurisdictions of the various overseas services had long been a point of controversy. It had been particularly so between the Department of State's consular officers and the Department of Commerce's attachés.[350] But other groups were involved as well. The Bureau of Efficiency's investigation in 1920 of official foreign trade promotion revealed that fourteen departments and commissions maintained offices abroad. The Bureau's chief rec-

---

[345] Committee on Appropriations, *Hearings on the Department of State Appropriations for 1938*, 75 Cong., 1 sess. (January 26, 1937), p. 162.

[346] 120.1/374, Messersmith memo, November 18, 1938, p. 16.

[347] James B. Stewart to Carr, May 12, 1937, in 120.1/203; 120.1/374, Messersmith memo, November 18, 1938.

[348] Brett to Department, May 18, 1932, in 121.1/144; 120.1/222, Messersmith memo, December 20, 1932. Messersmith believed that "the commercial attachés had complicated our relations with foreign powers by undertaking matters which lie solely within the Department of State." The social tensions stemmed primarily from the fact that commercial attachés were able to avoid the social stigma abroad of being a consul.

[349] 53 Stat. 1431 (April 24, 1939).

[350] See Maurice Francis Egan, "More Business in Diplomacy," 30; Chauncey Depew Snow, "Governmental Foreign Trade Promotion," 112; Samuel McClintock, "A Unified Foreign Service," *American Political Science Review*, XVI (November, 1922), 600.

ommendation, which was widely supported by publicists, was "that all resident foreign trade agents of the United States Government stationed abroad shall be assigned to the State Department." [351]

Although the Bureau's recommendation was not adopted, certain rudimentary steps were taken to define the various jurisdictions. As early as March, 1919, an Economic Liaison Committee was created to facilitate consultation between the departments of State, Commerce, Agriculture, and Treasury, and the Shipping Board. [352] An Executive Order of April 8, 1924, attempted to define the duties of commercial and agricultural attachés in relation to the Consular Service. [353] When the Rogers Act created the Foreign Service, the new unit acquired this problem. It was, however, in the process of worsening. The Department of Commerce, especially under Hoover, was increasingly adopting the professional characteristics of the Foreign Service and intrenching itself in the trade promotion field, arguing that the Foreign Service could not offer sufficiently specialized information. [354] On June 5, 1930, a similarly organized foreign service for the Department of Agriculture was created. [355]

These developments were opposed by members of the service. [356] Three events, however, temporarily scotched opposition. On May 2, 1932, the departments of Commerce and Agriculture agreed to limit their agents to capitals of countries. [357] A second agreement the following year, between the departments of State and Commerce only, provided that all instructions and reports would go through the Department of State and instituted weekly co-ordination meetings. [358] Finally, the depression's economy measures greatly damaged the Department of Commerce's service. Its appropriation was cut in half, twenty-five of its fifty-seven offices were closed, and more than half of its personnel dismissed. [359] Nevertheless, the Department of Commerce service began competing again with the Foreign Service. When the Commerce service tried to secure in 1937 an improved pension scheme, the Department of State decided the time was ripe to co-opt the group into the Foreign Service. [360] Later the Department of Agri-

[351] House Exec. Doc. 650, 66 Cong., 2 Sess. (January 26, 1920), p. 37. See also McClintock, *op. cit.*, p. 611; Wilbur J. Carr, "To Bring our Foreign Service Up-to-Date," *Independent*, CV (February 26, 1921), 220.

[352] Carr, *ibid.*, p. 207.

[353] *New York Times*, April 9, 1924, p. 23.

[354] 44 Stat. 394 (March 3, 1927).

[355] 46 Stat. 497 (June 5, 1930).

[356] *American Consular Bulletin*, VI (April, 1924), 150.

[357] 120.1/224, Carr memo, May 2, 1932.

[358] Carr to Welles, July 26, 1937, in 120.1/304.

[359] 120.1/349½, Dunn memo, October 6, 1938.

[360] Carr to Bullitt, March 27, 1937, in 120.1/301; Carr to Welles, July 27, 1937, in 120.1/305; *Cong. Rec.*, LXXXI, 75 Cong., 1 sess. (January 26, 1937), 411.

culture's service was included in the plan.[361] After long negotiations and against considerable opposition from business, both services were absorbed by the Foreign Service on June 7, 1939.[362]

The assumptions which underlay the new arrangement also expressed the jurisdiction of the Foreign Service. One assumption was the product of the changing economic milieu. With the depression world-wide, tariff walls were everywhere being erected. All effective trade promotion, therefore, dealt with governments as much as with merchants.[363] The only agency competent to deal with other governments was the Foreign Service. It was also only logical "to have the entire question handled by officers who would ultimately be called upon to decide the nature and character of the protest that was to be made." [364] And the Foreign Service was the only service capable of serving "our business and financial interests as a whole and not any special groups or individuals." [365] Above all, America's foreign relations were to be expressed by a single voice. As all American interests abroad impinged on foreign relations, that single voice was to be the Foreign Service. The previous arrangement had caused untold confusion and worked to the detriment of general American interests.[366] In the words of Assistant Secretary Messersmith, who was the most important figure in the Reorganization Act's success, "When heading into such heavy seas, we must have the best possible Foreign Service and this can only be brought about by getting a single representation abroad, under the Department of State, which is the instrument of the President in the conduct of our foreign relations." [367] In 1944, Assistant Secretary Shaw could state, "The Foreign Service . . . was the only regularly organized and administered Foreign Service of any branch of the United States Government." [368]

[361] J. B. Hickerson to Messersmith, September 30, 1937, in 120.1/308.

[362] 53 Stat. 1431 (April 24, 1939); Executive Order 8185, June 29, 1939 (copy of Order in author's possession).

[363] Messersmith to Samuel D. McReynolds, December 5, 1938, in 120.1/383A.

[364] Carr to Lane and Pasvolsky, March 26, 1937, in 120.1/300.

[365] Messersmith to Lockett, May 17, 1938, in 120.1/323½.

[366] 120.1/346, Messersmith memo, October 5, 1938.

[367] *Ibid.*

[368] Shaw to S. Rosenthal, April 11, 1944, p. 5, in 120.1/4–1144.

BIBLIOGRAPHICAL ESSAY

STATISTICAL SOURCES

Unless otherwise indicated, all percentages used in this study have been calculated by the author and are based on both official and unofficial sources. There are no partial samplings. The percentages refer to all members who have entered the service since 1779. Names were obtained from official sources, in particular from the *Register of the Department of State* and the *Journal of the Executive Proceedings of the Senate of the United States*. Each entrant was then checked in various biographical registers (e.g., *Historical Register of Yale University* [New Haven: Yale University Press, 1939]; *Quinquennial Catalogue of the Officers and Graduates of Harvard University — 1636–1925* [Cambridge, Mass.: Harvard University Press, 1925]) in an attempt to ascertain the age at entrance to the service, state of origin, secondary school training, university and postgraduate experience, occupation prior to entering the service, and promotional record. It should be noted that most of the percentages reflect the fact that the same man may be accounted in more than one category, e.g., an officer who attended both a public secondary school and a private boarding school. In most categories it was possible to find complete information for each officer.

Area demarcations are the same as those used by the Bureau of the Census (see United States Department of Commerce, Bureau of the Census, *Statistical Abstract of the United States: 1940* [Washington, 1940]): *New England*: Maine, New Hampshire, Vermont, Massachusetts, Rhode Island, and Connecticut. *Middle Atlantic*: New York, Pennsylvania, New Jersey, Delaware, Maryland, and the District of Columbia. *East North Central*: Ohio, Indiana, Illinois, Wisconsin, and Michigan. *West North Central*: Iowa, Kansas, Nebraska, South Dakota, North Dakota, Minnesota, and Missouri. *South Atlantic*: Virginia, North Carolina, South Carolina, Georgia, and Florida. *East South Central*: Tennessee, Alabama, Mississippi, Kentucky, and West Virginia. *West South Central*: Louisiana, Texas, Arkansas, and Oklahoma. *Mountain*: Montana, Wyoming, Utah, New Mexico, Arizona, and Colorado. *Pacific*: California, Nevada, Oregon, Washington, and Idaho.

The following table of appointments will give the reader a close idea of the number of officers being considered in the percentages:

1779–1888	216
1889–1905	118
1906–1923	210
Rogers Act	511 [*]
1924–1939	472
Reorganization Act of 1939	114 [*]

[*] Historical Division Figures.

Excluding vacancies, the following table of total upper service posts (ambassadors and ministers) will assist the reader in appreciating the growing career-orientation of these appointments:

	Ambassadors	Ministers
1905	9	27
1910	10	28
1915	12	28
1921 [*]	9	28
1925	13	32
1930	14	31
1935	17	35
1940	18	34

[*] Diplomatic relations were nearer to "normal" in 1921 than in 1920.

MANUSCRIPT SOURCES

The National Archives, the Record Center and the Historical Division of the Department of State are the chief sources of official correspondence and memoranda used in this study. The categories of documents which have been inspected include "functions," "organization," and "examinations" for the Diplomatic Service, the Consular Service, the Foreign Service, and the Department of State. As of 1957, the material in the National Archives included all the main correspondence through 1931. Correspondence of subsequent years is found in the Record Center. A few speeches and some personal diaries are to be found in the Advisory and Review Branch of the Historical Division. Of greatest value are the Minutes of the various boards of examiners, which, along with copies of all the examinations, are in the Record Center. The author was not allowed to examine the personal files (classification: 123). Nor was he able to examine the private papers of Wilbur J. Carr, which were then in the possession of Dr. Katharine E. Crane. It is unlikely, however, that the conclusions would be altered by material in Carr's private papers, since the events in the development of the Foreign Service are already thoroughly documented. Questionnaires, interviews, and letters to the author, cited in the footnotes, are in the author's possession.

PRINTED SOURCES

Much of the data for this study has been drawn from official publications.[1] The *American State Papers,* the *Papers Relating to the Foreign Relations of the United States* and the House and Senate *Documents, Executive Documents, Miscellaneous Documents,* and *Reports* are indispensable sources for information regarding the size of the service prior to 1869, the amounts of annual appropriations, the attitudes of many interest groups, and the internal administration of the service. Correspondence, too, is often appended to reports, and these letters supplemented very well the material found in the National Archives and the Record Center. The chief source of executive data is the *Register of the Department of State.* It contains the information needed to analyze the organization and growing career-orientation of the service. It also provided most of the biographical information. In particular, the 1874 *Register,* although not wholly accurate, is the chief source of names for the earliest members of the service. Also, the *Annual Reports* of the Civil Service Commission provide useful information for comparing the rates of professionalization in various parts of the government.

Almost every major figure in the development of the Foreign Service has published his letters, memoirs, or autobiography, or has been the subject of biography in which susbtantial excerpts from his private correspondence are printed. This is true of Joseph C. Grew, Jay P. Moffat, William Phillips, W. W. Rockhill, Henry White, F. M. Huntington Wilson, Hugh R. Wilson, and, of course, the significant presidents and secretaries of state. Other works by and about diplo-

---

[1] A complete listing of all the sources used in this study can be found in the University Library, University of Cambridge. See Warren Frederick Ilchman, *The Development of a Professional Service for Foreign Affairs in the United States* (Ph.D. diss., University of Cambridge, August, 1959).

mats are cited in the footnotes. They help document the course of public interest in the service and service attitudes toward the development of the career. Of great value are the books by or on Larz Anderson, Willard L. Beaulac, T. Jefferson Coolidge, Donald Dunham, Lloyd C. Griscom, Herbert J. Hagerman, John Hay, Ben Moran, John Lothrop Motley, Jefferson Patterson, William Franklin Sands, Post Wheeler, and Andrew D. White.

Contemporary opinion is documented from four sources: congressional publications, newspapers, periodicals, and "timely" books. Congressional opinion was here given priority and receives, therefore, the most thorough analysis. The volumes of the *Congressional Globe, Congressional Record, Debates and Proceedings in the Congress of the United States,* and *Register of Debates in Congress* are the most important sources for determining congressional attitudes toward foreign affairs, professional diplomacy, and the needs of America's overseas commerce.

Newspaper editorial opinion is heavily relied upon as well. The *New York Times* has been checked for the period 1890–1940. Other citations of newspapers are based on clippings found in the National Archives or the Record Center or from excerpts included in the *American Foreign Service Journal, Congressional Record,* or House and Senate *Reports.*

Opinion from both specialized and general periodicals is important to the study's argument. One of the best continuous sources of information and attitudes is the *American Foreign Service Journal* (formerly the *American Consular Bulletin*). This has been checked for the period 1919–57. It should be added that the *Journal* is considerably guarded in much of its criticism. *Good Government,* for the period 1890–1930, provides the evidence for the attitudes of the professional civil service reformers. The *Annual Reports* and the special studies of the National Civil Service Reform League are also very useful. Of greatest value for business opinion on professional diplomacy is the *Bankers' Magazine.* No religious journal gives much space to the subject, but the *Catholic World, Methodist Review,* and the annual reports of the overseas missions of various denominations do occasionally consider it.

General periodicals vary in their importance. For the period 1865–1900, the two best journals for pro-service sentiment are the *Nation* and the *North American Review.* The *Atlantic Monthly* and *Scribner's Magazine* deal occasionally with the subject. The *Outlook* and *Harper's Monthly* are the most useful periodicals for the years 1900–1914. During the general World War I period, the *New Republic, Nation, Dial,* and *Forum* were particularly alive to the implications for professional diplomacy of America's changing role in foreign affairs. After 1918, articles and editorials on the service or on the needs of foreign commerce are commonplace in most major periodicals.

"Timely" books on foreign affairs, commerce, civil service reform, and travels in other lands constitute a less important source of contemporary opinion. In this, the author was greatly assisted by the bibliographical information found in Robert E. Osgood's *Ideals and Self-Interest in America's Foreign Relations* (University of Chicago Press, 1953).

INDEX

249

Williams, John S., 120
Wilson, F. M. Huntington, 52, 63, 78–79, 92, 94, 97–98, 101–2, 104, 111, 114 n., 126–7, 130, 246
Wilson, George G., 204 n., 227 n.
Wilson, Hugh, 75, 76, 113–14, 116 n., 137, 165, 188, 190, 192, 196, 213 n.
Wilson, James, 19
Wilson, Woodrow, 119, 124–26, 129, 133, 143, 158

Wolcott, Oliver, 22
Women, and Service, 63, 169, 234–35
Wright, J. Butler, 137, 142, 145, 152, 155, 161, 165, 166, 168, 178, 182, 188, 190, 192, 196

X Y Z Affair, 21

Yeamans, George H., 27, 42
Young, Evan E., 191 n.